Intergroup Dialogue

Intergroup dialogue is a form of democratic engagement that fosters communication, critical reflection, and collaborative action across social and cultural divides. Engaging social identities is central to this approach. In recent years, intergroup dialogue has emerged as a promising social justice education practice that addresses pressing issues in higher education, school and community settings. This edited volume provides a thoughtful and comprehensive overview of intergroup dialogue spanning conceptual frameworks for practice, and most notably a diverse set of research studies which examine in detail the processes and learning that take place through dialogue.

This book addresses questions from the fields of education, social psychology, sociology, and social work, offering specific recommendations and examples related to curriculum and pedagogy. Furthermore, it contributes to an understanding of how to constructively engage students and others in education about difference, identities, and social justice.

This book was originally published as a special issue of *Equity & Excellence in Education.*

Ximena Zúñiga is Associate Professor in Social Justice Education in the Department of Student Development, part of the School of Education at the University of Massachusetts at Amherst, USA. Her scholarly, research, and practice interests include theorizing intergroup dialogues using qualitative and action research methodologies, critical dialogic theory, and social justice education in higher education.

Gretchen E. Lopez is Director of the Intergroup Dialogue Program and Assistant Professor of Cultural Foundations of Education in the School of Education at Syracuse University, USA. The research she conducts focuses on issues of race and gender in higher education and intergroup dialogue as an expression of social justice education in college, university, and high school settings.

Kristie A. Ford is Director of the Intergroup Relations Program and Associate Professor of Sociology at Skidmore College, USA. Her research explores the connections between race, gender, and intersecting social identities in relationship to body management practices, and social justice focused pedagogical practices in higher education.

Intergroup Dialogue

Engaging Difference, Social Identities and Social Justice

Edited by
Ximena Zúñiga, Gretchen E. Lopez and Kristie A. Ford

Routledge
Taylor & Francis Group

LONDON AND NEW YORK

First published 2014
by Routledge
2 Park Square, Milton Park, Abingdon, Oxfordshire OX14 4RN

and by Routledge
711 Third Avenue, New York, NY 10017, USA

First issued in paperback 2015

Routledge is an imprint of the Taylor & Francis Group, an informa business

British Library Cataloguing in Publication Data
A catalogue record for this book is available from the British Library

ISBN 13: 978-1-138-94953-9 (pbk)
ISBN 13: 978-0-415-81970-1 (hbk)

Typeset in Times New Roman
by Taylor & Francis Books

Publisher's Note
The publisher accepts responsibility for any inconsistencies that may have arisen during the conversion of this book from journal articles to book chapters, namely the possible inclusion of journal terminology.

Disclaimer
Every effort has been made to contact copyright holders for their permission to reprint material in this book. The publishers would be grateful to hear from any copyright holder who is not here acknowledged and will undertake to rectify any errors or omissions in future editions of this book.

Contents

CONTENTS

Citation Information

The following chapters were originally published in *Equity & Excellence in Education*, volume 45, issue 1 (February 2012). When citing this material, please use the original page numbering for each article, as follows:

Chapter 2
"I now harbor more pride in my race": The Educational Benefits of
Inter- and Intraracial Dialogues on the Experiences of Students of
Color and Multiracial Students
Kristie A. Ford and Victoria K. Malaney
Equity & Excellence in Education, volume 45, issue 1 (February 2012)
pp. 14–35

Chapter 3
From Dialogue to Action: The Impact of Cross-Race Intergroup Dialogue on
the Development of White College Students as Racial Allies
Craig John Alimo
Equity & Excellence in Education, volume 45, issue 1 (February 2012)
pp. 36–59

Chapter 4
Fostering a Commitment to Social Action: How Talking, Thinking, and
Feeling Make a Difference in Intergroup Dialogue
Chloé Gurin-Sands, Patricia Gurin, Biren (Ratnesh) A. Nagda and Shardae Osuna
Equity & Excellence in Education, volume 45, issue 1 (February 2012)
pp. 60–79

Chapter 5
Engaged Listening in Race/Ethnicity and Gender Intergroup Dialogue Courses
Ximena Zúñiga, Jane Mildred, Rani Varghese, Keri DeJong and Molly Keehn
Equity & Excellence in Education, volume 45, issue 1 (February 2012)
pp. 80–99

Chapter 6
White Educators Facilitating Discussions About Racial Realities
Stephen John Quaye
Equity & Excellence in Education, volume 45, issue 1 (February 2012)
pp. 100–119

Please direct any queries you may have about the citations to
clsuk.permissions@cengage.com

Notes on Contributors

Adriana Aldana is a joint PhD student in Social Work and Developmental Psychology at the University of Michigan, USA.

Craig John Alimo is a Multicultural Education Specialist in the Multicultural Education Program-Staff Diversity Initiatives in the Office of the Vice Chancellor for Equity & Inclusion at the University of California, Berkeley, USA. His research interests revolve around design, facilitation, and evaluation of social justice education; intergroup dialogue; agent identities; and social justice ally development.

Mikel Brown is a coordinator and facilitator of the Intergroup Social Change Agents. He presently facilitates the Better Choices Domestic Violence Program and does relapse prevention counseling.

Barry Checkoway is Professor of Social Work and Urban Planning at the University of Michigan, USA.

Kristen L. Davidson is a doctoral candidate in the Educational Foundations, Policy and Practice program at the University of Colorado Boulder, USA. She pursues philosophically grounded qualitative research on educational policies that affect equal opportunity, especially school choice.

Keri DeJong is a doctoral candidate in Social Justice Education, Department of Student Development, School of Education at the University of Massachusetts Amherst, USA. She is an experienced intergroup dialogue facilitator, trainer, and consultant. Her primary research interests are youth oppression/adultism, postcolonial perspectives on childhoods, and intergroup dialogues.

Kristie A. Ford is Director of the Intergroup Relations Program and Associate Professor of Sociology at Skidmore College, USA. Her research explores the connections between race, gender, and intersecting social identities in relationship to body management practices, and social justice focused pedagogical practices in higher education.

Shayla R. Griffin is a coordinator and facilitator of the Intergroup Social Change Agents. She is a doctoral candidate in the joint program in social work and social science (anthropology) at the University of Michigan, USA.

Patricia Gurin is the Nancy Cantor Distinguished University Professor of Psychology and Women's Studies, Emeritus, and Director of Research with the Program on

Intergroup Relations, University of Michigan, USA. Her research interests have focused on political mobilization of low power groups and on intergroup relations among low and high power groups.

Chloé Gurin-Sands recently received her BA in Spanish with minors in Latino/a Studies and Women's Studies from the University of Michigan, USA. During her time at the University, she served as a peer facilitator and research assistant with the Program on Intergroup Relations.

Louise B. Jennings is an Associate Professor in the School of Education at Colorado State University, USA. Her scholarship examines the cultural and discursive work of critical educational practice around issues of equity, diversity, community engagement, and social justice.

Pamela Jewett is an Associate Professor in the Department of Instruction and Teacher Education at the University of South Carolina, USA. Her research focuses on children's literature, critical literacy, and content-area literacies.

Molly Keehn is a doctoral candidate in Social Justice Education, Department of Student Development, School of Education at the University of Massachusetts Amherst, USA. Her research interests include the role of storytelling in intergroup dialogues and white identity development.

Rita Kohli is a Postdoctoral Fellow in the Urban Education and Pre-teaching pathway of the Liberal Studies Program at Santa Clara University, USA. She researches urban education, teacher education, racial justice, race relations in schools, critical race theory, and internalized racism.

Tasha Tropp Laman is an Associate Professor in the Department of Instruction and Teacher Education at the University of South Carolina, USA. Dr. Laman studies multilingual classrooms, writing instruction, and field-based teacher education.

Gretchen E. Lopez is Director of the Intergroup Dialogue Program and Assistant Professor of Cultural Foundations of Education in the School of Education at Syracuse University, USA. The research she conducts focuses on issues of race and gender in higher education and intergroup dialogue as an expression of social justice education in college, university, and high school settings.

Victoria K. Malaney is a graduate of Skidmore College, USA. She is currently pursuing a master's in Higher Education Administration at the University of Massachusetts Amherst, USA focusing on social justice and multiracial college student identity development.

Jane Mildred is a Professor of Social Work at Westfield State University, USA. Her scholarly interests include comparative child welfare, dialogues across differences, teaching social justice issues, and teaching about children and childhood from a critical/social justice perspective.

Michele S. Moses is Professor of Educational Foundations, Policy and Practice at the University of Colorado Boulder, USA. She specializes in philosophy and education policy studies, with particular expertise in higher education policy issues related to race, class, and gender, such as affirmative action and equal opportunity policies.

Biren (Ratnesh) A. Nagda is Associate Professor of Social Work and Director of the Intergroup Dialogue, Education, and Action (IDEA) Center at the University of Washington, USA. His research and teaching interests focus on education and social work practices that promote social justice.

A. Wendy Nastasi is a doctoral student in Cultural Foundations of Education in the School of Education at Syracuse University, USA, the Central NY Regional PAGE Director with Imagining America, and a current member of the Intergroup Dialogue facilitation team. Her research positions philosophy as praxis, focusing on youth action as a vehicle for democracy in education.

Shardae Osuna is a recent graduate of the University of Michigan-Ann Arbor, USA, where she received her BA in Honors Psychology and Sociology with minors in Japanese and Community Action and Social Change. She is currently pursuing social entrepreneurship as a means of combining her passions for social justice and film production.

Stephen John Quaye is an Assistant Professor in the Student Affairs Program at the University of Maryland, USA. His research concentrates on the influence of race relations on college and university campuses, specifically the gains and outcomes associated with inclusive racial climates, crossracial interactions, and racially-conscious pedagogical approaches.

Katie Richards-Schuster is an Assistant Research Scientist with the Michigan Youth and Community Program and directs the Community Action and Social Change Undergraduate Minor in the University of Michigan, School of Social Work, USA.

Stephanie Rowley is Professor of Psychology and Education at the University of Michigan, USA.

Mariana Souto-Manning is an Associate Professor of Education in the Department of Curriculum and Teaching at Teachers College, Columbia University, USA. From a critical perspective, her research examines the sociocultural and historical foundations of early schooling, language development, and literacy practices in pluralistic settings.

Rani Varghese is a doctoral candidate in Social Justice Education, Department of Student Development, School of Education, and a graduate certificate student in the Women, Gender & Sexuality Studies Program at the University of Massachusetts Amherst, USA. Her research interests include engaging issues of social justice in social work education and the use of intergroup dialogue in higher education.

naomi m. warren is a coordinator and facilitator of the Intergroup Social Change Agents. She currently works as an immigration attorney in St. Louis, Missouri, USA.

Jennifer L. Wilson was an Associate Professor in the Department of Instruction and Teacher Education at the University of South Carolina, Columbia, USA. She studied talk, critical literacy, and adolescent literacy. She was the university liaison for the first middle level professional development school at Hand Middle School located in Columbia, SC.

NOTES ON CONTRIBUTORS

Ximena Zúñiga is Associate Professor in Social Justice Education in the Department of Student Development, part of the School of Education at the University of Massachusetts at Amherst, USA. Her scholarly, research, and practice interests include theorizing intergroup dialogues using qualitative and action research methodologies, critical dialogic theory, and social justice education in higher education.

Intergroup Dialogue: Critical Conversations about Difference and Social Justice

Ximena Zúñiga
University of Massachusetts
Amherst

Gretchen E. Lopez
Syracuse University

Kristie A. Ford
Skidmore College

Dialogue is a moment where humans meet to reflect on their reality as they make it and remake it ... through dialogue, reflecting together on what we know and don't know, we can then act critically to transform reality. (Freire, cited in Shor & Freire, 1987, p. 13).

To engage in dialogue is one of the simplest ways we can begin as teachers, scholars, and critical thinkers to cross boundaries, the barriers that may or may not be erected by race, gender, class, professional standing, and a host of other differences. (hooks, 1994, p. 130).

... for dialogue to be possible, people—particularly those who enjoy relative privilege—must take responsibility for identifying and reducing socially determined asymmetries that dictate who gets to speak, what forums and forms of speech are deemed legitimate, whose speech counts and to whom it counts. It is difficult to imagine what might motivate such efforts on the part of those who are comfortable within current social structures, but precisely this kind of imagining is needed. (Wood, 2004, p. xx).

Intergroup dialogue, the primary focus of this book, is a form of democratic engagement that fosters critical understanding, communication, and collaborative action across race and other social group boundaries about contentious issues in educational and community settings. In education, intergroup dialogue has emerged as a promising social justice education practice that fosters meaningful and thoughtful conversations and learning about social justice issues such as racism, sexism, heterosexism, and ethno-religious oppression (Adams, 2007; Dessel & Rogge, 2008; Maxwell, Fisher, Thompson, & Behling, 2011; Mayhew & Fernandez, 2007; Zúñiga, Nagda, Chesler, & Cytron-Walker, 2007). An alternative to more formal "top down" instruction, intergroup dialogue engages multiple voices and experiences in the creation of shared meaning and new ways of thinking, relating, and acting, both inside and outside of the classroom. Intergroup dialogue may be broadly described as a democratic practice that fosters communication, critical self-reflection, analysis of social structures and conditions that contribute to social inequality; it also encourages collaborative social action across cultural and social divides. The goals of intergroup dialogue include critical co-inquiry, consciousness-raising about the causes and effects of social group inequalities, conflict transformation, and civic engagement in activities that foster learning and social change.

Challenged by increasingly polarized public debates about a number of pressing issues impacting public life in the United States (e.g., health care, school re-segregation, immigration, reproductive rights, gay marriage, and environmental pollution), more and more people from diverse backgrounds are engaging in dialogues across differences within local and regional communities, K-12 schools, colleges and universities, and workplaces. The call for dialogue as a way of addressing polarized issues is not new, but the growing number of institutional and grassroots efforts to establish and support dialogic practices in school cafeterias and libraries, college residence halls, houses of worship, and community centers represents widespread interest in this practice (Judkins, 2012; Schoem & Hurtado, 2001; Thomas, 2010).

In the United States, intergroup dialogue practices gained national attention in the late 1990s as a result of President Clinton's call for a national conversation on race and reconciliation across racial and ethnic boundaries (Schoem, Hurtado, Sevig, Chesler, & Sumida, 2001). The practice of intergroup dialogue, particularly in higher education, has been influenced by IGD,[3] the critical-dialogic educational model pioneered by the Program on Intergroup Relations at the University of Michigan, Ann Arbor, during a time of intense racial strife. The IGD approach to intergroup dialogue has been applied and extended in numerous settings and has been the focus of considerable empirical research (e.g., Gurin, Nagda, & Zúñiga, 2013; Lopez & Zúñiga, 2010; Schoem & Hurtado, 2001; Zúñiga et al., 2007; Zúñiga, Nagda & Sevig, 2002). IGD and other approaches to intergroup dialogue have also gained recognition through various national and regional efforts, including the Ford Foundation's "difficult dialogues" initiative, launched in 2005, and the work of other national organizations such as the American Association of Colleges and Universities (AACU), the Democracy Imperative, and the Deliberative Democracy Consortium (Thomas, 2010). Intergroup dialogues based on other practice models have also been initiated in K-12 schools and communities with the support of organizations such as Everyday Democracy (formerly called Study Circles), National Conference on Community and Justice, Public Conversation Project, and the Southern Poverty Law Center, among others (Dessel & Rogge, 2008; Schoem & Hurtado, 2001; Walsh, 2007; Wayne, 2008). Despite this widespread interest in intergroup dialogues, these efforts are often underfunded and reflect the work of a small number of organizers and leaders, as well as the political and institutional will of a handful of school principals or superintendents, college presidents or provosts, or community leaders (Chesler, Lewis, Crowfoot, & 2005; Thomas, 2010).

This book responds to the increased interest in intergroup dialogue by providing educators, practitioners, and researchers with a collection of empirically-based studies about the application and individual and collective impacts of a range of intergroup dialogue practices in formal and non-formal educational settings. These studies address various social justice issues, involve diverse populations, and reflect different and overlapping foundational and pedagogical frameworks. While the main focus of this volume is on intergroup dialogue practices in higher education and K-12 educational settings, we also include additional approaches to dialogue that have influenced the discourse and practice of intergroup dialogue across numerous cultural and institutional contexts. As a whole, the chapters in this book provide substantial support for the continuation and expansion of intergroup dialogue practices in multiple settings. In the following sections of this introduction, we examine the conceptual foundations of intergroup dialogue and situate intergroup dialogue as a social education between justice and pedagogy. Next we introduce approaches to intergroup dialogue reflected in this volume. After a brief review of prior research, we conclude with a discussion of contributions that the 11 chapters in this volume make to our understanding of intergroup dialogue.

CONCEPTUAL FOUNDATIONS OF INTERGROUP DIALOGUE

The dialogic practices that we refer to as intergroup dialogue are grounded in a variety of intellectual, cultural, and practice traditions (Dessel, 2011; Ellinor & Gerard, 1998; Schoem & Hurtado, 2001; Zúñiga & Nagda, 2001; Zúñiga et al., 2007). Broadly speaking, intergroup dialogue practices are rooted in the dialogic and transformative learning traditions in education that were originally stimulated by the progressive education movement of 1930s, 1940s, and 1950s and inspired by the work of John Dewey (Diaz, 2009; Shapiro, Wasserman, & Gallegos, 2012). Intergroup dialogue practices have also been influenced by Martin Buber's (1970) "I-Thou dialogic principle," the intellectual and practical contributions of the intergroup education movement of the 1940 and 1950s, and Gordon Allport's (1954) "intergroup contact hypothesis." More recently, dialogic practices have been shaped by the writings of the postcolonial Brazilian educator Paulo Freire (1970, 1974), who is known globally for his alternative theory of dialogue as "praxis," and by critical, anti-racist, and feminist theorists and educators such as Patricia Hill Collins (1993, 2012), bell hooks (1994), and Iris Marion Young (1990). While there are important distinctions across these various intellectual legacies, all of these traditions underscore core humanist philosophical premises: the importance of subjectivity, the role of lived experience in the construction of meaning and generation of new knowledge, and the emancipatory potential of relational communication and learning.

Early Influences on Intergroup Dialogue

Dewey (1916, 1938), a pragmatist philosopher who was deeply concerned about the relationship between education and democracy, underscored the centrality of experience and experimentation as ways to counter the negative impact of traditional rote learning practices on student engagement in public schools. He urged educators to encourage democratic practices in their classrooms to help students develop the values, skills, and dispositions needed to engage in generative discussions and experimentation, and to prepare learners for democratic citizenship (Burbules, 2000; Preskill & Brookfield, 2009). Dewey believed that democratic educators needed to provide students with opportunities to work together and to build on their own experiences and on real life situations and problems to reflect critically about their experiences (Brockbank & McGill, 2000). Even though questions related to issues of identity, difference, and power were not addressed in Dewey's work, a set of dialogic and transformative education practices from citizenship education, learner-centered pedagogies, experiential learning, and constructivist approaches to teaching and learning are considered legacies of Dewey and the "progressive movement" in education (Adams, 1997; Banks, 2004; Cho, 2013).

In contrast, Buber's (1970) humanistic and existential philosophy of dialogue highlights the centrality of responsive communication to help actualize our ontological relational existence. In Buber's view, the "I-Thou" relationship allows for authentic and reciprocal responses that help break away from the tendency to manipulate or objectify relationships and to see them as a means to an end. While Buber stressed the importance of listening and being fully present and emphasized the idea of embracing the other as critical dimensions of dialogic communication and learning, he did not inquire into how social asymmetries might influence why some learners are more disposed to listen or the kind of personal work that is needed to be able be open to do so. Regardless, Buber's work underscored the role of face-to-face interaction and self-awareness, in actualizing transformative learning.

Allport (1954), a social psychologist, became deeply interested in the cognitive nature of prejudice and how it shaped perceptions within majority-minority relations. Allport posited that internalized prejudices about social groups different from one's own could only be challenged through a form of relational learning structured under specific sociological conditions. The core premise was that if individuals from dominant ("majority") social identity groups were able to interact with members of non-dominant ("minority") social identity groups in an environment able to equalize asymmetrical relations under the right conditions, prejudice would be reduced. Allport proposed the following four conditions for this type of face-to-face encounter, commonly known as the "contact hypothesis": a) equal status (e.g., equal numbers of participants from participating groups); b) learning activities that actively engage participants in the development of a sense of common interest and shared humanity between the groups; c) shared goals; and, d) the support of institutional authorities (e.g., school principal, teacher, college president, city mayor). Allport's theory had a strong influence on the intergroup education movement of the 1950s and 1960s, which grew out of the social unrest following the Great Migration of large numbers of African Americans from the South to the industrial cities in the North (Banks, 2005). His theory also influenced contemporary pedagogical practices aimed at prejudice reduction, anti-racist, multi-cultural, or social justice education (Adams, 1997; Banks, 2005).

Contemporary Influences on Intergroup Dialogue

While many earlier philosophers and educators largely ignored the role of power and status in cross-group encounters, they laid the groundwork for the contributions of critical, post-colonial, anti-racist, and feminist theorists and educators. One of the most powerful influences on contemporary intergroup dialogue practice, Paulo Freire (1970), made dialogue the center of his educational philosophy and in *Pedagogy of the Oppressed* argued for a sociopolitical and constructivist view of knowledge and dialogical ways of teaching and learning. Freire viewed dialogue as inextricably linked to processes of *conscientization* (consciousness-raising) and education for freedom (see also Freire, 1974). In contrast to Dewey, Buber, and Allport, Freire offers a strong cultural and social critique of hierarchical and oppressive relations in education and society. He calls for a mutual learning process that allows teachers to learn from students as much as students learn from teachers. Members of oppressed and oppressor groups can learn from each other as well and become "critical co-investigators" of social realities to liberate themselves from hegemonic practices, an acceptance of oppressive scripts, and the belief that oppressor-oppressed relations cannot be changed (see also Cho, 2013).

Intergroup dialogue theory and practice have also been strongly influenced by national and international anti-colonial, civil, human rights, and feminist movements, and by feminist and anti-racist theorists and educators in the United States. These movements have highlighted how socially constructed identities, such as race and gender, influence a person's access to resources and political power, as well as their ability to speak and shape public and private relationships and discourses. Feminist theorists and educators, in particular, have examined how structural, hierarchical "relations of rule" (Smith, 1990) are reflected and reproduced in the classroom, how certain types of knowledge are valued and others devalued (Belenky, Clinchy, Goldberger, & Tarule, 1986; Collins, 1990, 1993; Haraway, 1988) and how the concept of "knowledge" itself has been constructed as objective, rational, and detached from relationships and emotions (Miller, 1986). Anti-racist educators and critical race theorists have also examined the relationship between social constructions of race and multiple forms of oppression, including cultural as well as physical colonization and emotional as well as physical exploitation, and have addressed the implications of these oppressive relationships for educational practices (Delgado & Stefancic, 2001; Ladson-Billings & Tate, 1995).

Common to all of these perspectives is the idea that all discourse and all relationships, including educational discourse and relationships, reflect the relative power, beliefs, and perspectives of those involved and where they are situated in relationship with one another in social hierarchies (Kincheloe, 2008). Some writers in cultural studies argue that these differences are so great that genuine dialogue and understanding across differences are limited or impossible because we live in a world where each voice does not carry equal weight (Boler, 2004; Burbules, 2000; Ellsworth, 1989). Patricia Hill Collins (1993, 2012), a Black feminist standpoint theorist, offers a different perspective. She argues that our ability to dialogue and connect with one another may be constrained by our differences, but we must begin to challenge dominant-subordination relations in educational settings anyway. One way we can do this is by trying to equalize the use of power in these settings so that "people of different levels of power can use race, class, and gender as categories of analysis to generate meaningful dialogue" (Collins, 2012, p. 224). Another way is to equalize racial or gender balances in classrooms so that members of marginalized groups who may normally feel silenced, invisible, or misrepresented can more easily share their own counter-hegemonic stories. Educators can also encourage everyone to identify ways of reducing social asymmetries that dictate who gets to speak and listen, and when, how, and why (Collins, 2012;

Wood, 2004). Through intentional processes such as these, Collins (2012) argues, relationships across differences are forged as people struggle to hear one another and to develop empathy for each other's perspectives. In a similar vein, building on Freire's work, hooks (1994) contends that dialogues between members of oppressed and oppressor groups require the development of authentic relations in which "all who are involved help each other mutually, growing together in a common effort to understand the reality which they seek to transform" (Freire, 1978, cited in hooks, 1994, p. 54). Through this intentional and collaborative praxis, participants may begin to develop agency for transforming their subjective and material social realities. In other words, critical dialogues across differences create spaces for intervening in and transforming the relationships between agency, power, and struggle.

INTERGROUP DIALOGUE AS SOCIAL JUSTICE PEDAGOGY

Numerous efforts have been made in formal and non-formal educational settings to address issues of diversity, inequality, and social justice. While some of these efforts have focused on reducing prejudice or enhancing multicultural understanding, others have emphasized the study of social oppression and its many manifestations, particularly differences in power, status, and access to resources within and across social identity groups. Intergroup dialogue practices in educational settings reflect the third approach, social justice education, which addresses both difference and inequality while seeking to foster the dispositions and skills that may be needed to work together to address social injustices (Adams, Bell, & Griffin, 2007; Adams et al., 2011; Goodman, 2001; Hackman, 2005). In this section, we situate intergroup dialogue as social justice education pedagogy and provide an overview of intergroup dialogue principles and practices. Next, we look at several approaches to intergroup dialogue practice that fit within this broader umbrella.

Intergroup Dialogue and Social Justice Education

Social justice education may be described as an interdisciplinary approach for examining social justice issues and addressing them through education. This approach to transformative education examines and addresses "the enduring and ever-changing aspects of social oppression" that perpetuate social exclusion and social inequities in particular historical periods and social contexts by examining "how 'common sense' knowledge and assumptions make it difficult to see oppression clearly" (Bell, 2007, p. 1). Social justice education relies on the development of critical consciousness and transformative pedagogical practices to foster educational change in classrooms, schools, and organizations. As such, it examines the sociopolitical and ideological dimensions of systems of privilege and oppression (e.g., adultism, ableism, sexism, and racism) while accounting for their "historical roots, intergenerational legacies, within-group differences, and local as well as global manifestations" (Adams et al., 2013, p. xxvi).

Social justice educators understand social identity group differences, both within and across groups, as socially and politically constructed; that is, as subjective rather than objective, as fluid rather than static, as specific rather than abstract, and as rooted in particular historical, geographic, and cultural contexts. Because differences are often used to justify inequality on the basis of hegemonic beliefs and explanations, especially when these differences legitimize access to privilege for social groups associated with what is considered "normal," social justice education explicitly links conversations related to group differences to questions related to equity and social justice (Adams, 2011; Adams et al., 2013; Young, 1990). Social justice education is important because dominant cultural norms about how people should think, feel, live, or behave are assumed to be universal, when, in reality, people from marginalized or disadvantaged groups may not have the same means, experiences, or values as members of dominant or privileged groups and may not conform or subscribe to these beliefs and norms.

In classrooms, social justice educators integrate content knowledge about single and intersecting forms of oppression with a pedagogy that gives careful epistemological and relational considerations to how participants learn/unlearn about issues of oppression and how they consider taking action for individual and collective empowerment, equity, inclusion, and social justice (Adams, 2007; Bell & Griffin, 2007). Such pedagogical considerations are crucial because learners do not live or learn in a vacuum; they are historically, politically, culturally, and subjectively situated as members of social groups (knowingly or unknowingly) that have different social positions and may have a history of conflict with one another. For this reason, social justice education theory and practice strives for a "conscious and reflexive blend of content and process, intended to enhance equity across multiple social identity groups (e.g., race, class, gender, social orientation, and ability) to encourage critical perspectives and social action" (Carlisle, Jackson, & George, 2006, p. 57).

As a form of social justice education, intergroup dialogue seeks to engage difference, social identity, and social justice through an intentional process that attempts to enhance equity across two or more social identity groups with distinct subject positions and statuses in asymmetrical power relations. It does so by addressing some of the intergroup contact conditions outlined by Allport (1954). For example, most intergroup dialogues try to include fairly equal numbers of participants and facilitators from each of the groups participating in the dialogue. In addition, intergroup dialogue, like other forms of social justice education, gives particular attention to the experiences of marginalized groups and makes an effort to enhance equity by amplifying the voices of those who have had to struggle to be heard. Intergroup dialogue also challenges *all* participants to grapple with the interconnected histories and circumstances of their singular or intersecting privileged and disadvantaged social group identities within micro and macro sociopolitical contexts in order to engage and sustain a process in which multiple points of view can be explored and held as valid. Collins (2012) argues that honoring multiple perspectives is vital because in dialogue across differences participants bring a partial point of view that stems from their own experience and understanding of that experience; therefore, they need to hear other's partial perspectives to make sense of their own perspective and develop empathy for individuals from different social identity groups. Furthermore, in intergroup dialogue, it is just as important that members of privileged groups understand how they and others have been privileged by systems of advantage and domination as it is for members of less-advantaged groups to understand how they have been affected by systems of disadvantage and subordination (Zúñiga et al., 2007). Meaningful dialogue also requires that all participants gain a nuanced and complex understanding of how oppression becomes established and reproduced and how it can be challenged and transformed at the individual, group, community, institutional, and cultural levels. According to Collins (2012), this kind of learning requires developing a critical consciousness—"coming to see how our individual biographies are shaped by and act on our specific historical and social contexts" (p. 130)—that can help participants understand how their distinctive group histories reflect power differences, privilege, and oppression. Educators hope that this critical consciousness will help participants develop a clearer understanding of socially constructed social group differences and begin to situate their lived experiences as social actors who have agency and can transform, as hooks (1994) states, "the barriers erected by race, gender, class, professional standing, and a host of other differences" (p. 130).

While intergroup dialogues often focus on a single issue (e.g., racial/ethnic relations or gender relations) or forms of oppression (e.g., racism or sexism), the range of possible issues and questions that emerge will vary from group to group. Issues of multiple and intersecting social identities and varied positions of power will inevitably arise in dialogues across differences. Hence, seldom are there "fixed boundaries" to a single social category (e.g., race or gender) or relationship (e.g., white people and people of color or men and women). Regardless of the primary focus of the dialogue, the diversity of ideas and experiences brought by the participants will ultimately shape the conversation and the extent to which participants grapple with singular or intersecting privileged and targeted social identities within a particular dialogue.

Intergroup Dialogue as Critical Dialogic Praxis

The practice of intergroup dialogue underscores Freire's (1970, 1974) definition of education as a practice for freedom by seeking to coordinate the processes of unlearning oppression with learning liberation. Toward this goal, intergroup dialogue seeks to embody the examination and transformation of oppressive social realities (critical praxis) with a socially-situated critical communicative and consciousness raising practice (dialogic praxis). Thus, intergroup dialogue can be conceived of as a critical-dialogic praxis that simultaneously supports *criticality* (the capacity to critically examine social hierarchies and dominant beliefs or explanations) and *liberation* (the capacity to free oneself and help support others to free themselves from oppressive scripts and habits through authentic dialogue, problem-posing, and reciprocal and empowered relations). Ultimately, intergroup dialogue may enable the development of a sense of individual and collective agency for creating social change and more equitable and just relationships across differences in power and perspective (Freire, 1970; Fassett & Warren, 2007; Shor & Freire, 1987).

In considering intergroup dialogue a critical dialogic praxis, it is important to keep in mind Freire's (1970) and Collins' (2012) recognition that multiple perspectives and unequal power relations are always present among participants and facilitators, learners and teachers, and members of oppressed and oppressor groups. This recognition frames how dialogue processes are conceived, theorized, and structured when diverse groups meet inside and outside of the classroom (Zúñiga et al., 2007). In such settings, multiple voices are valued, but not unquestioned. Participants' stories are encouraged as entry points for critical social inquiry to understand why people experience both common and different social realities and why they act in the ways that they do (Nieto, 2005). This level of engagement is not easy. Participants must be willing to engage in difficult conversations that critically examine how differences in perspective, values, and access to cultural and material resources impact social identities and relationships between groups within as well as outside of the group, and facilitators must have the knowledge and skills to help them do this. Moreover, dialogue across status differences may only be possible when people from more advantaged social identity groups are challenged to take responsibility for identifying and reducing "socially determined asymmetries that dictate who gets to speak, what forums and forms of speech are deemed legitimate, whose speech counts and to whom it counts" (Wood, 2004, p. xx). This challenge requires a structured and intentional process and is addressed somewhat differently in different models of intergroup dialogue practice.

Regardless of the form it takes, however, intergroup dialogue addresses some of the challenges inherent in bringing members of different social groups together by promoting dialogue rather than debate or discussion. Debate aims to convince and to establish the superiority of one point of view over another, while discussion emphasizes "breaking things apart, seeing its elements" rather than "unfolding meaning that comes from the many parts" (Ellinor & Gerard, 1998, p. 20). The goal of dialogue is not to convince, but to critically analyze prevailing ideas and expand what is known in a space where listening, respect, appreciation, and inquiry build relationships and understanding. It is a process that engages the heart and the capacity to act, as well as the intellect (Huang-Nissen, 1999; Romney, 2003). Also different from "mere talk" or casual conversation, dialogue is an intentional practice that has a focus and a purpose (Romney, 2003; Shor & Freire, 1987). Intergroup dialogue challenges participants to be mindful, involved, responsive, and willing to explore contentious issues in collaborative way.

APPROACHES TO INTERGROUP DIALOGUE PRACTICE

In this section we briefly review four approaches to intergroup dialogue practice. These approaches share overlapping and distinct pedagogical features and specific goals as they strive to engage participants in a critical examination of social realities using dialogic and transformative pedagogical methods: (1) the critical-dialogic approach known as IGD; (2) "Cultural Circles" programs; (3) the Study Circles practice approach; and (4) the conflict transformation model. We situate individual chapters within each of these approaches to demonstrate the differing approaches to intergroup dialogue, but we recognize that our categorization may not fully capture the nuances of the pedagogies and practices described by the various authors and that the categories might not be mutually exclusive.

One of the most commonly used and most researched intergroup practice approaches, particularly in higher education, is the critical dialogic practice approach known as IGD (or Intergroup Dialogue) that developed out of the program on Intergroup Relations at the University of Michigan (Gurin et al., 2013; Sorensen, Nagda, Gurin, & Maxwell, 2009; Zúñiga et al., 2002). This critical dialogic approach embodies many of the premises discussed in the previous sections and it extends the focus of traditional intergroup education efforts by explicitly attending to, examining, and addressing misperceptions and intergroup tensions rooted in issues of difference, social identity, and social inequality through structured, facilitated, and sustained conversations across race and other social group boundaries. Prior to the development of the IGD approach, most intergroup education efforts emphasized group similarities and cooperation without fully considering the pervasive effects of systemic power and privilege on intergroup relations, including whose voices are heard and whose worldviews are valued and understood in conversations across differences. IGD, however, explicitly recognizes and works with similarities and differences in values, ideologies, and social statuses that result from historical and contemporary social inequalities (Zúñiga et al., 2002, 2007).

The IGD approach relies on four design features to structure facilitated conversations across differences: (1) intimate engagement in small groups that is sustained over a period of weeks or months; (2) explicit attention to process (How are we talking about this issue?) and content (What are we talking about?); (3) an intentional design that scaffolds learning through structured activities and dialogic methods that encourage critical examination of social justice issues; and (4) the sequencing of four phases of dialogue. These phases build on each other and support participants to: a) build relationships and guidelines for dialogue; b) clarify expectations, share stories, and gain insight into the dynamics of privilege and oppression; c) explore controversial issues at the interpersonal, institutional, and cultural level; and d) end the experience with action planning and alliance building. Together these design considerations lend coherence to a very layered and recursive group experience (Zúñiga et al., 2007).

While each IGD program is tailored to the specific goals and needs of the campus (or school or community) that it serves, these programs generally share certain characteristics. For instance, IGD groups or courses involving undergraduate college students often meet for a sustained period of time over 8 to 14 weeks. In higher education settings, IGD programs may be structured as undergraduate courses or co-curricular activities and typically include 12 to 18 dialogue participants, with both or all of the social identity groups participating in the dialogue represented in fairly equal numbers. Examples of IGD groups that have been held on college campuses include men and women; white people, multiracial people and people of color; Latinos(as) and Blacks; lesbians, gay men, bisexual and heterosexual people; and Christians, Muslims and Jews. IGD groups are co-led by two trained facilitators who share salient social identities with participants in the dialogue (for instance, a race/ethnicity dialogue involving white participants and students of color would be co-facilitated by a white person and person of color with different gender identities). More recently, there have been efforts to implement IGD groups involving members of a single social identity group to encourage dialogue and actions about specific intragroup issues (e.g., men and masculinity, white racial identity and allyship, multiraciality, and pan-ethnic people of color dialogues) (Ford, 2012). While facilitators typically use a structured curriculum to guide the dialogue group, training models used to prepare and support IGD facilitators vary across programs and institutions (e.g., Maxwell, Nagda, & Thompson, 2011).

Seven chapters in this volume examine activities based on this critical dialogic approach (IGD). In Chapter 2, the authors investigate students' experiences in race/ ethnicity dialogue and multiracial identity dialogue courses in a small, private, predominantly white, liberal arts college. Chapters, 3, 4, and 5 draw from data from a multi-institution study—the Multiversity Intergroup Dialogue Research Project (MIGR), a field experiment conducted in nine colleges and universities with a design that included random assignment of student applicants to undergraduate IGD courses or a waitlist control group (Gurin et al., 2013). Chapter 3 focuses on the development of white students as racial allies and social change agents through race/ethnicity intergroup dialogue courses. In Chapter 4, the authors explain the connection between pedagogy, communication process, and psychological processes in race/ethnicity and gender intergroup dialogue courses for individual participants' commitment to action. In Chapter 5, the authors study aspects of the dialogic processes, and underscore the role of listening in influencing the type of outcomes in gender and race/ethnicity dialogue courses. Lastly, Chapters 7, 8 and 9 provide illustrative examples of extensions of the IGD model outside higher education. Chapter 7 describes and reports on the ethnic identity and racism awareness outcomes of participants in a sustained youth dialogue program. Chapter 8 examines the learning experiences of a group of high school students in urban and suburban contexts, who come together during a one-day institute that was designed using IGD pedagogical principles to address the racial divide that impacts their high school experiences. In Chapter 9, the authors discuss the development and outcomes of co-curricular intergroup dialogue activities within public high schools.

The second approach to intergroup dialogue draws on Freire's (1970) "problem posing" method, commonly known as critical pedagogy (Kincheloe, 2008), which brings together diverse groups of people in "cultural circles" or "dialogue circles" to investigate cultural power relations and dominant ideologies and how they shape classrooms and communities (Fassett & Warren, 2007; Preskill & Brookfield, 2009; Souto-Manning, 2010). This approach to intergroup dialogue strives to foster a dialogic praxis through *conscientização*, the capacity to become aware of injustices and to act to change them (Freire, 1970). Freire and Myles Horton, for instance, used dialogue circle methods in the countryside of Brazil and Chile, and in the Appalachia region of the U.S., to facilitate the empowerment of these marginalized groups (Horton, Freire, Bell, Gaventa & Peters, 1990). In these two examples "circles of learners" or "cultural circles" of adult learners and community leaders came together to interrogate how particular social, cultural, and linguistic contexts impact the social realities in which they live and how these realities could be transformed (Arnold, Burke, James, Martin, & Thomas, 1991; Pheterson, 1990; Souto-Manning, 2010).

The Cultural Circles approach does not always make an explicit effort to address Allport's (1954) conditions of intergroup contact by bringing diverse groups together, though it does acknowledge the need to balance power and voice and to target social identities within the dialogue process and discourse. Transformation takes place through "dialogue and problem solving in a cyclical and recursive process which leads to transformative action" (Souto-Manning, 2010, p. 19). This dialogue model has been used in schools and communities across the globe in different educational settings (Preskill & Broofield, 2009; Jennings, Jewett, Laman, Souto-Manning, 2010; Vella, 2008; Souto-Manning, & Wilson, 2010), and increasingly with urban youth through popular education and participatory action research efforts (Camerotta & Fine, 2008; Checkoway & Gutierrez, 2011).

Variations of this approach to dialogue may be found in Chapters 6, 10, and 11. In these three chapters, authors examine specific dialogic practices used in formal and non-formal educational context that rely on Freire's problem posing pedagogy. Chapter 6 analyzes the role of white faculty in facilitating critical discussions about race in the diverse college classrooms. While this case study does not describe classrooms that fully illustrate the "circle" approach to dialogue, the focus of this chapter is on democratic discussion practices that strive to mirror some of the tenets of Freire's problem posing pedagogy. Chapter 10 examines critical interracial dialogue involving teachers of color about their experiences as racial minority teachers. Lastly, Chapter 11 reviews five empirical studies to analyze the discursive practices used in critical dialogues across educational settings with diverse populations.

A third approach to intergroup dialogue, Study Circles, seeks to foster dialogue and deliberation about public issues in collaborative ways, to explore issues of difference, and to analyze the ways in which socially constructed difference may be used to reproduce inequality and social hierarchies in schools and community policies and practices (Schoem & Hurtado, 2001; Walsh, 2007; Zúñiga & Nagda, 2001). Similar to the IGD approach, practitioners working from this model often intentionally address Allport's (1954) conditions for intergroup contact when convening diverse groups of people to talk about race related issues, including stakeholders and authorities, based on the need to equalize the representation from participating groups. One successful application of this approach is the Everyday Democracy Study Circles practice approach (Flavin-McDonald & Barrett, 1999; McCoy & Scully, 2002), also known as deliberative civic dialogues, which aids communities in making progress on tough issues through community building, dialogue, deliberation, and action. Drawing from principles of deliberative democracy and intergroup education (equal representation, inclusion, diversity, and sharing of knowledge and decision-making), Study Circles bring diverse groups of people in schools and local communities together in small groups to build relationships, dialogue, and deliberate about issues, and explore actions for change (Fanselow, 2007; Pincock, 2008; Wade, 2007; Walsh, 2007) In some regions in the US, the Study Circle approach has been applied to dialogue about race and immigration among youth, within and across schools, with teachers and with community leaders. A variation of this deliberative approach to intergroup dialogue is described and examined in Chapter 12. The authors focus on public dialogue about affirmative action policies.

A final approach to intergroup dialogue focuses on conflict transformation in schools and communities. Dessel and Rogge (2008) define this approach as "a facilitated group experience that may occur once or may be sustained over time and is designed to give individuals and groups a safe and structured opportunity to explore attitudes about polarized issues" (p. 201). One application that illustrates this orientation toward intergroup dialogue is known as Sustained Dialogue (Parker, 2006; Saunders, 2003), which uses a multi-stage conflict resolution process that draws from work in international conflict resolution and peace building. In Sustained Dialogue, students and community members of diverse backgrounds meet over time to build mutual respect, identify issues of conflict, dialogue about conflicting issues, and, in some instances, generate action plans (Diaz, 2009). Another application that has had a strong impact in civic dialogues is the one developed by The Public Conversations Project (Chasin et al., 1996). This application actively seeks to prevent and transform conflicts driven by differences in identity, beliefs, or values. Examples of this application have been used in communities (Romney, 2003) and in colleges and universities (Buie & Wright, 2010; Thomas, 2010). While none of the chapters in this volume reflect the main tenets of this approach to intergroup dialogue, several of the practices described and empirically studied in this volume strive to build participants' capacity to address intergroup conflicts, particularly intergroup dialogue practices involving youth. For instance, three of the chapters described earlier, Chapters 7, 8 and 9, describe IGD efforts in schools that seek to raise racial awareness while addressing social identity based differences and conflicts between social identity groups. Furthermore, addressing intergroup conflicts in a constructive way is also a major concern for the IGD approach in higher education.

RESEARCH ON INTERGROUP DIALOGUE

Parallel to the growth of interest in intergroup dialogue, is a growing body of empirical research within the social sciences and applied fields that offers empirical evidence of the educational benefits of intergroup dialogue for college students in higher education (Dessel & Rogge, 2008; Ford, 2012; Gurin, 1999; Hurtado, 2005; Zúñiga et al., 2007), K-12 schools (Dessel, 2010; Spencer, Brown, Griffin & Abdullah, 2008; Wade, 2007), and with youth and communities (Dessel & Rogge, 2008; Walsh, 2007; Wayne, 2008). For the most part, this research focuses on the IGD approach. Participation in IGD in college has been shown to have positive effects on students' beliefs about group inequalities and behavioral intentions to create change (Lopez, Gurin, & Nagda, 1998; Nagda, Gurin, & Lopez, 2003), communication and understanding of intergroup conflicts (Díaz, 2009; Gurin, 1999; Gurin, Nagda & Lopez, 2004; Lopez, Gurin & Nagda, 1998; Nagda & Zúñiga, 2003), ability to bridge differences across groups (Nagda & Zúñiga, 2003), and commitment to fostering self-directed and other directed actions for social justice (Nagda, Kim, & Truelove, 2004; Zúñiga, Williams,& Berger, 2005). More recent studies conducted as part of a national, multi-institutional longitudinal study of IGD, some of which are reported in this volume, also offer strong evidence of the positive effects of undergraduate dialogue courses for college students involved in race/ethnicity and gender IGD (Gurin, Nagda, & Sorensen, 2011; Gurin et al.,2013; Nagda, Gurin, Sorensen, & Zúñiga, 2009). Research on intergroup dialogues with young people in schools and youth organizations has also demonstrated positive effects in the areas of social identity awareness, reduction of prejudice and stereotyping, understanding of institutional racism and other forms of discrimination, and an increased capacity for addressing conflicts constructively and social action (e.g., Fanselow, 2007; Griffin, 2012; Nagda, McCoy, & Barnett, 2006; Spencer et al., 2008; Wade, 2007). Similarly positive outcomes have been reported from studies in community settings, particularly regarding alliance building across racial groups and civic action, such as organizing around immigration, achievement gaps in schools, and racial profiling (e.g., Dessel, Rogge, & Garlington, 2006; DeTurk, 2006; Pincock, 2008; Wheatley, Christman, & Nicolas, 2012). While this body of research has provided a clearer understanding of the educational and social outcomes associated with intergroup dialogue, particularly IGD, gaps in knowledge remain within the literature. There are a number of empirical questions that need to be asked about intergroup dialogue processes and outcomes across social identity groups and settings. There is also a need for more theoretical understanding and empirical research in response to program growth and increased offerings across K-12 and community, as well as higher education settings (Bowman, 2011; Dessel & Rogge, 2008; Stephan & Stephan, 2001).

As stated earlier, the main purpose of this volume is to present empirically-based studies about intergroup dialogue in formal and non-formal educational settings that address various social justice issues, involve different populations, and reflect different and overlapping foundational and pedagogical frameworks. We provide an overview of these chapters here, focusing first on higher education settings and next on dialogue efforts in schools and communities. This collection of chapters provides conceptual, empirical, and practice-based knowledge about a wide range of dialogue practices by a multi-disciplinary group of researchers and educators in the fields of education, sociology, psychology, and social work. Together, these chapters extend rigorous analyses and applications of intergroup dialogue to postsecondary, K-12, and education-community initiatives. The authors examine the processes and the effects of intergroup dialogue using quantitative, qualitative, descriptive, and mixed methods research. They also discuss pedagogical and facilitation considerations and pose questions about the limits and challenges of intergroup dialogue education.

Part II of the book focuses on intergroup dialogue in higher education. The five studies conducted in higher education contexts cover the potential effects of intergroup dialogue courses; capture student experiences, reflections, and applications; and consider faculty challenges in facilitating democratic discussions in college classrooms. Part III focuses on six dialogue efforts in schools and communities. These studies provide a broader perspective on critical dialogues across differences in education and communities. They include implementation across differing institutional or social contexts and are inclusive of a wider set of communities and participants.

Part II: Intergroup Dialogue in Higher Education

The first four chapters in this section focus on the IGD approach in higher education. The first chapter in this section, "I Now Harbor More Pride in my Race: The Educational Benefits of Inter- and Intra-Racial Curricular Dialogues on the Experiences of Students of Color and Multiracial Students," by Kristie A. Ford and Victoria K. Malaney, investigates students' experiences in race/ethnicity dialogue and multiracial identity dialogues within a small, private, predominantly white, liberal arts college located in the northeast U.S.. Importantly, this work focuses much needed attention on the experiences of students of color and multiracial students in both intergroup and intragroup dialogue courses. The authors examine how these students "make sense of their own racial group membership and how they navigate raced interactions in college" before and after the class. Applying a theoretical and research framework based in critical race theory (Delgado & Stefancic, 2001) and Freire's *Pedagogy of the Oppressed* (1970), as well as earlier work on intergroup dialogue and students of color in higher education, Ford and Malaney summarize results from a qualitative analysis of students' writing (n=31) at the beginning and end of each course. They identify a range of student learning outcomes and provide examples of students' shifts or "script changes" during the semester with respect to the following inductively-derived themes: the salience and complexity of racial/ethnic identities, self-esteem, individual biases, analysis of power and privilege, and sense of personal responsibility to create change. In doing so, they are able to uncover some of the educational benefits of engaging students of color and multiracial students in race-focused dialogue courses.

In "From Dialogue to Action: The Impact of Cross-Race Intergroup Dialogue on the Development of White College Students as Racial Allies," Craig Alimo focuses attention on what white college students learn through intergroup dialogue. More specifically, Alimo underscores the role of intergroup dialogue courses focused on race and ethnicity in the development of white students as racial allies and social change agents. This quantitative study analyzes pre- and post-test survey data from a multi-institution study—the Multiversity Intergroup Dialogue Research Project (MIGR). This project implemented intergroup dialogue courses at nine colleges and universities in varied geographic areas and the design included random assignment of student applicants to dialogue courses or a waitlist control group (see also Gurin et al., 2013). Alimo assesses the development of confidence and frequency in white students' commitment to actions that are aligned with allying behavior. The chapter reports that dialogue students (n=181) more frequently participated in allying behavior than students in a waitlist control group (n=174) but did not necessarily feel more confident about how to appropriately do so. The conceptualization framework used by this study, as well as the quantitative results forward discussions both about the impact of learning through intergroup dialogue for white students and the possible processes by which this may shape students' future actions. Similar to the next chapter, this study is significant in its emphasis and findings related to the relationship between dialogue and action.

Chloé Gurin-Sands, Patricia Gurin, Biren (Ratnesh) A. Nagda, and Shardae Osuna closely examine the question of intergroup dialogue processes that are critical for fostering student action in "Fostering a Commitment to Social Action: How Talking, Thinking, and Feeling Make a Difference in Intergroup Dialogue." The authors apply a multi-method approach to explaining the connection between student participation in race/ethnicity and gender intergroup dialogue courses and their commitment to action. They conducted a quantitative analysis of qualitatively coded categories/variables from students final papers (n=739) collected as part of the multi-institution (MIGR) study mentioned above. They tested and found support for a theoretical model connecting dialogue pedagogy, communication and psychological processes, and students' actions, including educating and collaborating with others. Gurin-Sands and colleagues report that students in race dialogues wrote more about educating others as compared to students in the gender dialogue courses. This pattern mirrors some of the trends reported in the next chapter by Zúñiga and colleagues, where distinct patterns were found for intergroup dialogues that focused on race in contrast to those focused on gender in the MIGR.

In "Engaged Listening in Race/Ethnicity and Gender Intergroup Dialogue Courses," Ximena Zúñiga, Jane Mildred, Rani Varghese, Keri DeJong, and Molly Keehn also study dialogue processes and underscore the role of listening in these courses. Drawing from the MIGR data set, these authors focus on engaged listening in intergroup dialogue and present findings from a two-phase qualitative grounded theory analysis of a sample of interviews (n=248/40) conducted with students who completed a race/ethnicity or gender dialogue. By examining moments of engaged listening, the study explores when and why participants in intergroup dialogue listen and what they gain from engaged listening. The authors also identify a number of differences in the patterns of findings for engaged listening in race/ethnicity and gender dialogues. Findings suggest that participants in race/ethnicity dialogue courses recall more moments of engaged listening and may have gained a more complex understanding of structural inequality from engaged listening than participants in the gender intergroup dialogue courses did.

The final chapter in this section examines white instructors' experiences facilitating democratic discussions about race in undergraduate classrooms, particularly when teaching white students. Specifically, in "White Educators Facilitating Discussions About Racial Realities," Stephen Quaye asks, "How do educators engage students in constructive discussions about racial realities in postsecondary classroom settings?" Using a white faculty development framework for facilitating classrooms discussions that blend dialogue and discussion as democratic forms of discourse in postsecondary classrooms (Brookfield & Preskill, 2005), Quaye presents a qualitative analysis of two instructors' narratives to provide an understanding of the challenges and successes some white educators face when facilitating difficult conversations about race and racism in their courses. This study illustrates ways that white instructors might use specific pedagogical tools, including self-disclosure and storytelling about their own racial identity development, to engage white students in constructive conversation.

Part III: Intergroup Dialogue in Schools and Community Settings

The focus of Part III is on intergroup dialogue in school and community settings. Authors apply a range of methodologies as well as approaches to dialogue. In some ways, the results described provide further support for arguments and findings highlighted in the studies that focus on higher education settings. In other ways, this second set of studies identifies key issues for specific populations (e.g., K-12 students and teachers) that are deserving of further attention and that may diverge from research and practice in higher education settings with college students and faculty.

In "Raising Ethnic-Racial Consciousness: The Relation Between Intergroup Dialogues and Adolescents' Ethnic-Racial Identity and Racism Awareness," Adriana Aldana, Stephanie J. Rowley, Barry Checkoway, and Katie Richards-Schuster present results from research conducted through the Youth Dialogues on Race and Ethnicity in Metropolitan Detroit. Drawing from racial identity development frameworks, this quantitative study examines student (13–19 years old, n=147) change in racial consciousness while participating in cross-racial dialogue. Survey measures included a range of learning outcomes, drawing from established measures and earlier research, including ethnic-racial identity and racism awareness among youth. These researchers report pre- and post-increases in racial consciousness. They further tested ethnic-racial group differences among students and report significant differences for ethnic-racial identity but not for racism awareness. This study, considered together with research from higher education settings, begins to provide a more detailed picture of the shared and distinct effects of intergroup dialogue for students of color and white students.

The next chapter continues to focus attention on diverse adolescent youth and centers student voices in doing so. In "Writing the Divide: High School Students Crossing Urban-Suburban Contexts," Gretchen E. Lopez and A. Wendy Nastasi apply a qualitative-based program evaluation to understand and analyze student perspectives (n=88) on participation in a cross-school, urban-suburban, dialogue that reflect several dimensions of the IGD approach. While the Aldana et al. chapter presents a youth dialogue initiative that is sustained over time outside of school contexts, Lopez and Nastasi describe a university-community collaboration that brings together two public schools with the Syracuse University Intergroup Dialogue Program. The university program hosts a one-day institute for local high school students taking English courses focused on race, rhetoric, and voice. The institute dynamically engages students in dialogue and writing as activism; it involves meaningful small group work, including drafting letters advocating an issue of shared concern across students and schools. The study provides examples of students' writing, including responses to open-ended evaluation surveys. Through inductively guided research, three themes emerged. Students wrote about growing awareness of inequalities, reflections on agency, and interest in further engagement. These findings connect to the conclusions established in the research based in higher education described above that details the impact of intergroup dialogue for students' awareness of inequalities, understanding of social responsibility, and the significance of alliances.

The next chapter, "Critical Education in High Schools: The Promise and Challenges of Intergroup Dialogue," also addresses IGD practices with high school students and identifies both the promise and challenges of such work. Shayla R. Griffin, Mikel Brown, and naomi m. warren discuss building intergroup dialogue programs and/or offerings within public high schools. With an emphasis on practical applications, this chapter features the Intergroup Social Change Agents (I-SCA) project between the University of Michigan Ann Arbor's School of Social Work and four public high schools in the surrounding area. Applying a critical multicultural (Banks & Banks, 2009) and critical pedagogy (Freire, 1970) framework, the authors provide a model for what a high school intergroup dialogue structure might look like and outline the potential impact it can have on students, including challenging stereotypic attitudes, enhancing communication skills, decreasing discriminatory and/or bullying behaviors, and furthering intergroup relationships.

In "Racial Pedagogy of the Oppressed: Critical Interracial Dialogue for Teachers of Color," Rita Kohli shifts attention to the experiences and reflections of teachers of color in school settings. Kohli qualitatively analyzes dialogues involving teachers of color from diverse backgrounds enrolled in a social justice-based teacher education program. The analysis presented in this suggests that this group of Black, Latina, and Asian American women teachers benefited immensely from participation in critical race dialogues premised on Freire's (1970) work on the significance of consciousness-raising. Kohli found the teachers broadened their understanding of racial oppression and applied this to critical self-reflection as well as pedagogy in their current class-rooms. Kohli addresses the need for more initiatives like this for teachers of color, given the role(s) they play in public schools in contemporary U.S. context. Like Quaye's chapter, Kohli's work is important in providing examples of reflections from educators on the difficulties of negotiating race in the classroom and the various strategies that are adopted and adapted in turn.

"Supporting Critical Dialogue Across Educational Contexts" further develops questions of facilitation and extends the analysis of critical dialogue across varied education, community, and international settings. Tasha Tropp Laman, Pamela Jewett, Louise B. Jennings, Jennifer L. Wilson, and Mariana Souto-Manning draw from five empirical studies to analyze discursive practices used across educational settings. The data considered include middle school students discussing immigration picture books, a teacher study group exploring text on homelessness, a teacher education class studying critical literacy, working-class adults in a culture circle in Brazil discussing poverty, and teens in youth organizations discussing their photo essays that challenge negative stereotypes toward youth. The authors stress that "genuine dialogue is often imperfect and unfinished" and suggest specific practices for facilitating dialogic communication across varied educational spaces/populations from the collective findings. Their analysis articulates the importance of time as a necessary condition for critical dialogue, space as dynamic and co-constructed, and the significance of using authentic texts.

The last chapter in this section focuses on a single public dialogue event about affirmative action policy. In "Speaking Across Difference in Community Dialogues on Affirmative Action Policy," Kristen L. Davidson and Michele S. Moses raise interesting questions about what forms of discourse carry more weight in civic dialogues across group-based differences. The authors conducted civic dialogue groups and research in the months preceding the 2008 election to ban affirmative action in Colorado. They frame this research study within Young's (2000) discussion of multiple legitimizing forms of discourse in deliberative efforts across social group differences, bringing another literature to bear on intergroup dialogue and its effects with a focus on the raced and classed impact of who is able to shape the discourse in cross-race civic dialogues. This study uses a qualitative research methodology to explore the communicative processes exhibited in the dialogue groups to examine the significance of participants' social group memberships, including race, gender, and professional status. While a range of communicative strategies were identified and used in these groups, the findings suggest that participants' professional status appears to influence both the amount of participants' contributions and the extent to which ideas were considered most persuasive; participants' race and gender was also identified as potential contributing factors. These findings suggest the need for more in-depth research on public dialogues, especially regarding current local, state, and national level debates and group-based policy discourse. The study also highlights the need to study professional status and related constructs of socio-economic status and their potential role in group-based public discourse, persuasion, and ultimately policy and social change.

This collection of empirical studies extends our knowledge about intergroup dialogue and the ways it may be engaged in a number of different settings to further social justice education inquiry and practice. Importantly, these studies also suggest new directions and questions for research. These studies support earlier research that suggests that intergroup dialogue has a number of positive effects for both students of color and white students. They also suggest that intergroup dialogue may have positive effects for college and university and K-12 teachers as well. This might be an important and interesting area for future research. Furthermore, these studies provide evidence of the need for, and significance of, critical dialogic practice and research with community participants, which is also an area that is under-researched. This collection of studies clearly captures how intergroup dialogue is not simply about "talk"; it strengthens listening and communication skills and fosters the development of critical consciousness. Further research on which aspects of intergroup dialogue help build these skills and consciousness, and illustrate how and why they may be useful in the context of growing inequality across educational, social, and community lines, is also needed. Finally, the studies in this book offer considerable insight on how critical processes in intergroup dialogue lead to action and/or cognitive and affective orientations important for collective organizing and social change and suggest areas of future inquiry that may help to build on this important outcome. Taken together, these studies further our knowledge of intergroup dialogue as a transformative social justice education pedagogy and its implications for practitioners and participants in schools, higher education, and communities.

SUMMARY

The studies in this book make a number of important contributions to the intergroup dialogue literature. Both the practices and research methodologies used by the authors and their colleagues, as well as the extension of intergroup dialogue approaches to new contexts, suggest new ways for engaging with issues of difference, identity, and social justice through formal educational and community-based initiatives. While the approaches to intergroup dialogue represented by these studies may differ in regard to design, structure, time, facilitation, focus, and setting, they share a common sense of purpose and a commitment to critical dialogic theory and pedagogical practice. All build from an understanding that structural forms of group inequality are socially unjust and must be addressed. All attempt, in some way, to reconcile rifts, particularly across race/ethnicity and class lines, and to work proactively with aspects of the conflicts caused by these inequities at the local level. Significantly, all maintain a belief in the transformative power of sustained critical dialogue as a way to begin bridging current social, cultural, political, and economic divides. While several of the studies offer evidence for the positive effects of intergroup dialogue for particular groups, populations, or communities, others generate specific methods and strategies for implementing and facilitating intergroup dialogue in the face of challenges experienced by communities and organizations. We believe that by bringing these various approaches together in one volume, new insights about intergroup dialogue will be generated.

NOTES

1 This chapter builds on our Guest Editor Introduction to the special issue of Equity and Excellence in Education, 45(1), published in February 2012, entitled "Intergroup dialogue: Engaging difference, social identity and social justice."
2 We would like to thank Javier Campos, Molly Keehn and Cassie Sanchez, Dave Neely, Jane Mildred, and Cassie Sanchez for their valuable input and feedback in the completion of this chapter.
3 Consistent with the current literature, we will use "intergroup dialogue" when referring to intergroup dialogue more broadly and "IGD" when referring to the specific dialogue approach developed at the University of Michigan in the late 1980s and then developed further at numerous institutions of higher education across the US.

REFERENCES

Adams, M. (1997). Pedagogical frameworks for social justice education. In M. Adams, L. A. Bell, & P. Griffin (Eds.), *Teaching for diversity and social justice: A sourcebook* (pp. 30–43). New York, NY: Routledge.

Adams, M. (2007). Pedagogical frameworks for social justice education. In M. Adams, L. A. Bell, & P. Griffin (Eds.), *Teaching for diversity and social justice* (2nd ed., pp. 15–33). New York, NY: Routledge.

Adams, M. (2012). Social justice education. In D. Christie (Ed.), *The encyclopedia of peace psychology* (Vol. III, pp. 333–336). New York, NY: Wiley-Blackwell.

Adams, M., Bell, L. A., & Griffin, P. (Eds.). (2007). *Teaching for diversity and social justice* (2nd ed.). New York, NY: Routledge.

Adams, M., Blumenfeld, W., Castañeda, R., Hackman, H., Peters M., & Zúñiga, X. (2013). Readings for diversity and social justice: A general introduction. In M. Adams, W. Blumenfeld, R. Castañeda, H. Hackman, M. Peters, & X. Zúñiga (Eds.), *Readings for diversity and social justice* (3rd ed., pp xvi–xxxii). New York, NY: Routledge.

Allport, G. W. (1954). *The nature of prejudice*. Reading, MA: Addison.

Arnold, R., Burke, B., James, C., Martin, D., & Thomas, B. (1991). *Educating for a change*. Toronto, Canada: Between the Lines Press.

Banks McGee, C. (2005). *Improving multicultural education: Lessons from the intergroup education movement*. New York, NY: Teachers College Press.

Banks, J. A. (2004). Democratic citizenship education in multicultural societies. In J. A. Banks (Ed.), *Diversity and citizenship education: Global perspectives* (pp. 3–16). San Francisco, CA: Jossey-Bass.

Banks, J. A., & Banks, C. A. M. (2009). *Multicultural education: Issues and perspectives* (7th ed.). Hoboken, NJ: Wiley.

Belenky, M., Clinchy, B., Goldberger, N., & Tarule, J. (1986). *Women's ways of knowing: The development of self, voice, and mind.* New York, NY: Basic Books.

Bell, L. A. (2007). Theoretical foundations for social justice education. In M. Adams, L. A. Bell, & P. Griffin (Eds.), *Teaching for diversity and social justice* (2nd ed., pp. 1–14). New York, NY: Routledge.

Bell, L. A., & Griffin, P. (2007). Designing social justice education courses. In M. Adams, L. A. Bell, & P. Griffin (Eds.), *Teaching for diversity and social justice* (2nd ed., pp. 67–87). New York, NY: Routledge.

Boler, M. (2004). *Democratic dialogue in education: Troubling speech, disturbing silence.* New York, NY: Peter Lang.

Bowman, N. A. (2011). Promoting participation in a diverse democracy: A meta-analysis of college diversity experiences and civic engagement. *Review of Educational Research, 81*(1), 29–68.

Brockbank, A., & McGill, I. (2000). *Facilitating reflective learning in higher education.* Buckingham, United Kingdom: Society for Research into Higher Education and Open University Press.

Buber, M. (1970). *I and thou.* New York, NY: Simon & Schuster.

Buie, S., & Wright, W. (2010). The difficult dialogues initiative at Clark University: A case study. *New Directions for Higher Education: Educating for Deliberative Democracy, 152,* 27–34.

Burbules, N. (2000). The limits of dialogue as a critical pedagogy. In P. Trifonas (Ed.), *Revolutionary pedagogies: Cultural politics, instituting education, and the discourse of theory* (pp. 251–273). New York, NY: Routledge Falmer.

Cammarota, J., & Fine, M. (Eds.). (2008). *Revolutionizing education: Youth participatory action research in motion (Critical youth studies).* New York, NY: Routledge.

Carlisle, L., Jackson, B., & George, A. (2006). Principles of social justice education: The social justice education in schools project. *Equity & Excellence in Education, 39*(1), 55–64.

Chasin, R., Herzig, M., Roth, S., Chasin, L., Becker, C., & Stains, R. (1996). From diatribe to dialogue on divisive public issues: Approaches drawn from family therapy. *Mediation Quaterly, 13*(4), 323–344.

Checkoway, B., & Gutierrez, L. (Eds.). (2011). *Youth participation and community change.* New York, NY: Routledge.

Chesler, M., Lewis, A., & Crowfoot, J. (2005). *Challenging racism in higher education: Promoting justice.* Lanham, MD: Rowman & Littlefield.

Cho, S. (2013). *Critical pedagogy and social change: Critical analysis on the language of possibility.* New York, NY: Routlege.

Collins, P. H. (1990). *Black feminist thought: Knowledge, consciousness and the politics of empowerment.* London, United Kingdom: Harper Collins.

Collins, P. H. (1993). Toward a new vision: Race, class, and gender as categories of analysis and connection. *Race, Gender and Class 1*(1), 36–45.

Collins, P. H. (2012). *On intellectual activism.* Philadelphia, PA: Temple University Press.

Cox, C. (2002). 911 one year later: People of faith gather for understanding. The Boston Hearld, 8 September 2002.

Delgado, R., & Stefancic, J. (2001). *Critical race theory: An introduction.* New York: New York University Press.

Dessel, A. (2010). Effects of intergroup dialogue: Public school teachers and sexual orientation prejudice. *Small Group Research, 41*(5), 556–592.

Dessel, A. (2011) Dialogue and social change: An interdisciplinary and transformative history. *Smith College Studies in Social Work, 81*(2–3), 167–183.

Dessel, A., & Rogge, M. E. (2008). Evaluation of intergroup dialogue: A review of the empirical literature. *Conflict Resolution Quarterly, 26*(2), 199–238.

Dessel, A., Rogge, M. E., & Garlington, S. B. (2006). Using intergroup dialogue to promote social justice and change. *Social Work, 51*(4), 303–315.

DeTurk, S. (2006). The power of dialogue: Consequences of intergroup dialogue and their implications for agency and alliance building. *Communication Quarterly, 54*(1), 33–51.

Dewey, J. (1916). *Democracy and education: An introduction to the philosophy of education.* New York, NY: Macmillan.

Dewey, J. (1938). *Experience and education* (2nd Ed.). New York, NY: Macmillan.

Díaz, A. (2009). *Composing a civic life: Influences of sustained dialogue on post-graduate civic engagement and civic life* (Unpublished doctoral dissertation). Santa Barbara, CA: Fielding Graduate University.

Ellinor, L., & Gerard, G. (1998). *Dialogue: Rediscover the transforming power of conversation.* New York, NY: Wiley.

Ellsworth, E. (1989). Why doesn't this feel empowering? Working through the repressive myths of critical pedagogy. *Harvard Educational Review, 59,* 291–324.

Fanselow, J. (2007). Making schools work for everyone: Study circles in Montgomery County, Maryland. *National Civic Review, 96*(1), 49–54.

Fassett, D. L., & Warren, J. T. (2007). *Critical communication pedagogy.* Thousand Oaks, CA: Sage.

Flavin-McDonald, C., & Barret, M. H. (1999). The Topsfield Foundation: Fostering democratic community building through face-to-face dialogue. In P. J. Edelson & P. L. Malone (Eds.), *Enhancing creativity in adult and continuing education: innovative approaches, methods, and ideas.* San Francisco, CA: Jossey-Bass.

Ford, K. (2012). Shifting white ideological scripts: The educational benefits of inter- and intra-racial curricular dialogues on the experiences of white college students. *Journal of Diversity in Higher Education, 5*(3), 138–158.

Freire, P. (1970). *Pedagogy of the oppressed.* New York, NY: Continuum.

Freire, P. (1974). *Education for critical consciousness.* New York, NY: Continuum.

Goodman, D. (2001). *Promoting diversity and social justice: Educating people from privileged groups.* Thousand Oaks, CA: Sage.

Griffin, S. (2012). *When the black kids moved in: Racial reproduction and the promise of intergroup dialogue in an exurban high school.* (Unpublished doctoral dissertation). Ann Arbor, MI: University of Michigan.

Gurin, P. (1999). Selections from *The Compelling Need for Diversity in Higher Education, expert reports in defense of the University of Michigan: Expert report of Patricia Gurin. Equity and Excellence in Education, 32*(2), 37–62.

Gurin, P., Nagda, B. A., & Lopez, G. E. (2004). The benefits of diversity in education for democratic citizenship. *Journal of Social Issues, 60*(1), 17–34.

Gurin, P., Nagda, B. A., & Sorensen, N. (2011). Intergroup dialogue: Education for a broad conception of civic engagement. *Liberal Education, 97*(2), 46–51.

Gurin, P., Nagda, B. A., & Zúñiga, X. (2013). *Dialogue across differences: Practice, theory, and research on intergroup dialogue.* New York, NY: Russell Sage.

Hackman, H. W. (2005). Five essential components for social justice education. *Equity & Excellence in Education, 38*(2), 103–109.

Haraway, D. (1988). Situated knowledges: The science question in feminism and the privilege of partial perspective. *Feminist Studies, 14*(3), pp. 575–599.

hooks, b. (1994). *Teaching to transgress: Education as the practice of freedom.* New York, NY: Routledge.

Huang-Nissen, S. (1999). *Dialogue groups: A practical guide to facilitate diversity conversations.* Blue Hill, ME: Medicine Bear.

Horton, M., Freire, P., Bell, B., Gaventa, J., & Peters, J. M. (1990). *We make the road by walking: Conversations on Education and Social Change.* Philadelphia, PA: Temple University Press.

Hurtado, S. (2005). The next generation of diversity and intergroup relations research. *Journal of College Development, 44,* 320–334.

Jennings, L., Jewett, P., Laman, T., Souto-Manning, M., & Wilson, J. (Eds.). (2010). *Sites of possibility: Critical dialogue across educational settings.* Cresskill, NJ: Hampton Press.

Judkins, B. M. (2012). Intergroup dialogues: Building community and relational justice. *Catalyst: A Social Justice Forum, 2*(1), 27–36.

Kincheloe, J. L. (2008). *Critical pedagogy* (2nd Ed.). New York, NY: Peter Lang Primer.

Ladson-Billings, G., & Tate, W. (1995). Toward a Critical Race Theory of Education. *Teachers College Record, 97*(1), 47–68.

Lopez, G. E., Gurin, P., & Nagda, B. A. (1998). Education and understanding structural causes for group inequalities. *Journal of Political Psychology, 19*(2), 305–329.

Lopez, G. E., & Zúñiga, X. (2010). Intergroup dialogue and democratic practice in higher education. *New Directions for Higher Education, 152,* 35–42.

Maxwell, K. E., Fisher, B. R., Thompson, M., & Behling, C. (2011). Training peer facilitators as social justice educators. In K. E. Maxwell, B. A. Nagda, & M. C. Thompson (Eds.), *Facilitating intergroup dialogues: Bridging differences, catalyzing change* (pp. 41–54). Sterling, VA: Stylus.

Maxwell, K. Nagda, B., & Thompson, M. (Eds.). (2011). *Facilitating intergroup dialogue.* Sterling, VA: Stylus.

Mayhew, M., & Fernández, S. (2007). Pedagogical practices that contribute to social justice outcomes. *The Review of Higher Education, 31*(1), 55–80.

McCoy, M. L., & Scully, P. L. (2002). Deliberative dialogue to expand civic engagement: What kind of talk does democracy need? *National Civic Review, 91*(2), 117–135.

Miller, J. B. (1986). *Toward a new psychology of women* (2nd Edition). Boston, MA: Beacon Press.

Nagda, B. A., & Gurin, P. (2007). Intergroup dialogue: A critical-dialogic approach to learning about difference, inequality, and social justice. *New Directions for Teaching and Learning, 111,* 35–45.

Nagda, B. A., Gurin, P., & Lopez, G. E. (2003). Transformative pedagogy for democracy and social justice. *Race, Ethnicity and Education, 6*(2), 165–191.

Nagda, B. A., Gurin, P., Sorensen, N., & Zúñiga, X. (2009). Evaluating intergroup dialogue: Engaging diversity for personal and social responsibility. *Diversity and Democracy, 12*(1), 4–6.

Nagda, B. A., Kim, C. W., & Truelove, Y. (2004). Learning about difference, learning with others, learning to transgress. *Journal of Social Issues, 60*(1), 195–214.

Nagda, B., McCoy, M. L., & Barnett, M. H. (2006). *Mix it up: Crossing social boundaries as a pathway to youth civic engagement.* Retrieved from http://www.tolerance.org/mix-it-up/map

Nagda, B. A., & Zúñiga, X. (2003). Fostering meaningful racial engagement through intergroup dialogues. *Group Processes and Intergroup Relations, 6*(1), 111–128.

Nieto, S. (2005). *Why we teach.* New York, NY: Teachers College Press.

Parker, P. N. (2006). Sustained dialogue: How students are changing their own racial climate. *About Campus, 11*(1), 17–23.

Pheterson, G. (1990). Alliances between women: Overcoming internalized oppression and internalized domination. In L. Albrecht & R. Brewer (Eds.), *Bridges of power: Women's multicultural alliances* (pp. 34–48). Philadelphia, PA: New Society.

Pincock, H. (2008). Teaching through talk? The impact of intergroup dialogue on conceptualizations of racism. *Research in Social Movements, Conflicts and Change, 29,* 21–53.

Preskill, S., & Brookfield, S. D. (2009). *Learning as a way of leading: Lessons from the struggle for social justice.* San Francisco, CA: Jossey-Bass.

Romney, P. (2003). *The art of dialogue. Animating democracy.* Retrieved from http://www.americansforthearts.org/animatingdemocracy/resource_center/resources_content.asp?id=215

Saunders, H. H. (2003). Sustained dialogue in managing intractable conflict. *Negotiation Journal, 19*(1), 85–95.

Schoem D., & Hurtado, S. (2001). *Intergroup dialogues. Deliberative democracy in school, college, community and workplace.* Ann Arbor, MI: The University of Michigan Press.

Schoem, D. L., Hurtado, S., Sevig, T., Chesler, M., & Sumida, S. (2001). Intergroup dialogue: Democracy at work in theory and practice. In D. L. Schoem & S. Hurtado (Eds.), *Intergroup dialogue: Deliberative democracy in school, college, community and workplace* (pp.1–36). Ann Arbor, MI: The University of Michigan Press.

Shapiro, S., Wasserman, I. L, & Gallegos, P. (2012). Group work and dialogue: Spaces and processes for transformative learning in relationships. In E. W. Taylor & P. Cranton (Eds.), *The handbook of transformative learning: Theory, research and practice* (pp. 355-372). San Francisco, CA: Jossey-Bass.

Shor, I., & Freire, P. (1987). What is the "dialogical method" of teaching? *Journal of Education, 169*(3), 11–31.

Smith, D. E. (1990). *Texts, facts and femininity: Exploring the relations of ruling.* London, United Kingdom: Routledge.

Sorenson, N., Nagda, B. A., Gurin, P., & Maxwell, K. E. (2009). Taking a "hands on" approach to diversity in higher education: A critical-dialogic model for effective intergroup interaction. *Analysis of Social Issues & Public Policy, 9*(1), 3–35.

Souto-Manning, M. (2010). *Freire, teaching, and learning: Cultural circles across cultural contexts.* New York, NY: Peter Lang.

Spencer, M., Brown, M., Griffin, S., & Abdullah, S. (2008). Outcome evaluation of the intergroup project. *Small Group Research, 39*(1), 82–103.

Stephan, W. G., & Stephan, C. W. (2001). *Improving intergroup relations.* Thousand Oaks, CA: Sage.

Thomas, N. L. (Ed.). (2010). Educating for deliberative democracy [Editor's notes]. *New Directions for Higher Education, 152,* 1–9.

Vella, J. K. (2008). *On teaching and learning: Putting the principles and practices of dialogue education into action.* San Francisco, CA: Jossey-Bass.

Wade, J. (2007). *Evaluation of the Montgomery County Public Schools study circles program.* Report of the Department of Shared Accountability. Retrieved from: http://www.montgomeryschoolsmd.org/uploadedFiles/departments/studycircles/aboutus/Study_-Circles_Final_Eval_Mar10.pdf

Walsh, K. C. (2007). *Talking about race: Community dialogues and the politics of difference.* Chicago, IL: University of Chicago Press.

Wayne, E. K. (2008). Is it just talk? Understanding and evaluating intergroup dialogue. *Conflict Resolution Quarterly, 25*(4), 451–478.

Wheatley, A., Christman, S., & Nicolas, G. (2012). Walking the talk: Empowering communities through dialogue. *Journal for Social Action in Counseling and Psychology, 4*(1), 1–17.

Wood, J. T. (2004). Foreword. Entering into Dialogue. In R. Anderson, L. Baxter & K. Cissna, (Eds.), *Dialogue: Theorizing Difference in Communication Studies* (pp. xv–xxiii). Thousand Oaks, CA: Sage.

Young. I. M. (1990). *Justice and the politics of difference.* Princeton, NJ: Princeton University Press.

Young, I. M. (2000). *Inclusion and democracy.* New York, NY: Oxford University Press.

Zúñiga X., Lopez, G., & Ford, K. (2012). Intergroup dialogue: Critical conversations about difference, social identity and social justice. Guest Editors Introduction: *Equity and Excellence in Education, 45*(1), 1–13.

Zúñiga, X., & Nagda, B. A. (2001). Design considerations for intergroup dialogue. In D. L. Schoem & S. Hurtado (Eds.), *Intergroup dialogue: Deliberative democracy in school, college, community and workplace* (pp. 306–327). Ann Arbor, MI: University of Michigan Press.

Zúñiga, X., Nagda, B. A., Chesler, M., & Cytron-Walker, A. (2007). *Intergroup dialogue in higher education: Meaningful learning about social justice.* ASHE-ERIC Higher Education Report Volume 32, Number 4. San Francisco, CA: Jossey-Bass.

Zúñiga, X., Nagda, B., & Sevig, T. D. (2002). Intergroup dialogue: An educational model for cultivating engagement across differences. *Equity & Excellence in Education, 35*(1), 7–17.

Zúñiga, X., Williams, E., & Berger, J. (2005). Action-oriented democratic outcomes: The impact of student involvement with campus diversity. *Journal of College Student Development, 46*(6), 660–678.

"I now harbor more pride in my race": The Educational Benefits of Inter- and Intraracial Dialogues on the Experiences of Students of Color and Multiracial Students

Kristie A. Ford and Victoria K. Malaney

Skidmore College

How do students of color and multiracial students learn to make sense of and navigate race within historically white institutions (HWIs)? And, what pedagogies and inter-/intragroup dynamics facilitate increased understanding of issues of race, racial identity development, and racism in the U.S.? This project examines students' of color (SOC) and multiracial students' learning in the Intergroup People of Color–White People Dialogues and Intragroup Multiracial Identity Dialogues at a small private liberal arts college in the Northeast. Through qualitative, inductively-derived analyses of student papers, this study advances understanding of how SOC/multiracial students make sense of their own racial group membership and how they navigate raced interactions in college. It also continues and extends national efforts to conduct and disseminate research on both the substantive nature and process of the Inter-/Intragroup Dialogues and their impact on students.

I admit, it's been a roller coaster semester for me, but the People of Color–White People Dialogues helped me keep my feet on the ground while allowing my brain to go to new places, far and beyond from where it ever was before . . . You know how people say, "You will always remember a specific class from college that changed your life," well that class is Dialogue. I continue on this journey next semester, ready to learn, grow and take on the world. —Rob, Latino man

It has been a challenging journey, but Multiracial Identity Dialogue has opened my perspectives and forced me to recognize that there are differences in society because I am usually blinded by the notion that I have not been triggered by references to my identity. —Makayla, multiracial woman

Racial diversity is the "buzz-word," or prevailing theme, in institutions of higher education; given that, many colleges and universities are looking for ways to become more racially and ethnically diverse (Chito Childs & Matthews-Armstead, 2006; Humphreys, 2002). Less attention, however, has been paid to the positive classroom-based pedagogical interventions that help students of color (SOCs) and bi/multiracial[1] students thrive in historically white institutions (HWIs).

Critical race theory (CRT) seeks to critically understand the experiences of people of color through an analysis of race, racism, and power (Delgado & Stefancic, 2001). Two CRT principles relevant to the framing of this study include recognizing that: (1) racism is normalized within U.S. society and impacts the everyday lived experiences of people of color; and, (2) people of color have their own "voice of color" or unique experiences with oppression (Delgado & Stefancic, 2001, pp. 7–9). With a somewhat different focus, Freire (1970) examines oppression through a pedagogical lens—focusing on dialogic modes of engagement that liberate, rather than oppress, groups. To that end, Freire argues: "We can legitimately say that in the process of oppression someone oppresses someone else; we cannot say that in the process of revolution someone liberates someone else, nor yet that someone liberates himself, but rather that human beings in communion liberate each other" (p. 133). Applying these theoretical frameworks to understand the racial experiences of SOC/multiracial students within HWIs we explore the following research questions: How do SOC/multiracial students learn to make sense of and navigate race in HWIs? And what pedagogies and inter-/intragroup dynamics facilitate increased understanding of issues of race, racial identity development, and racism in the U.S.?

In order to better prepare all students for an increasingly diverse society, it is crucial that colleges/universities find innovative ways of integrating race into the curriculum. To address these concerns, many institutions of higher education have developed Intergroup Relations Programs to help students navigate diverse learning environments, particularly in the first two years of college (Hurtado, 2005). This study explores the effect of two undergraduate courses on race, Inter- and Intragroup Dialogues, offered by an Intergroup Relations Program at a small, private, liberal arts college in the Northeast. These courses use inter- and intraracial dialogue modalities in an effort to assess the educational benefits of this pedagogy and its impact on student outcomes (generally) and the experiences of SOC/multiracial students (specifically). The former (interracial dialogue) brings students across racial identities together; the latter (intraracial dialogue) engages students from one shared racial identity category (Adams, Bell, & Griffin, 2007; Tatum, 2003). More concretely, in this article, we examine SOC/multiracial student learning in the Intergroup People of Color–White People Dialogues (POC-W) and Intragroup Multiracial Identity Dialogues (MRID).

Extrapolating from Freire's (1970) work, we use the term "oppressive raced scripts" to signify students' reinforcement of internalized, often negative, messages or shared storylines about race, racism, and power. In contrast, we use the term "liberatory raced scripts" to signify the modified narratives that SOC/multiracial students embrace as they progress in their understanding of their racial identity in inter- and intraracial settings (Delgado & Stefancic, 2001; Freire, 1970; Lewis, Chesler, & Forman, 2000; Root, 1990, 1992, 1996; Tatum, 2003). In particular, we are interested in exploring how the Inter-/Intragroup Dialogues may affect SOC/multiracial students' understanding of race, hopefully resulting in script changes that reflect a more empowered "voice of color" (Delgado & Stefancic, 2001, p. 9) or affirmative sense of self (Root, 1990, 1992, 1996; Tatum, 2003).

INTER- AND INTRAGROUP DIALOGUE PEDAGOGY

Social justice education courses are one way to support the development of SOC/multiracial students within HWIs. By social justice education, we mean the study of structural and institutional inequities experienced by members of different social identity groups (e.g., race, gender, and sexuality) due to varying levels of power and privilege. This approach not only focuses on cognitive learning, but also seeks to apply these principles to create a more equitable and just world (Adams et al., 2007).

Intergroup dialogue is one of the most common social justice education practices being used to foster student engagement across differences in diverse college settings (Adams et al., 2007).

Zúñiga et al. (2007) defines intergroup dialogue as a facilitated, face-to-face encounter that aims to cultivate meaningful engagement between members of two or more social identity groups that have a history of conflict. Intergroup dialogue's objective is to provide a safe space for students to explore commonalities and differences, examine structures of power and privilege, and work toward equality and social justice. A race dialogue, for instance, would bring together students of color and white students; a gender dialogue might unite men, women, and transgendered students. The pedagogical components that distinguish intergroup dialogue from more traditional courses include establishing: (1) structured interaction (e.g., small group of students, equal representation of two or more social identity groups);[2] (2) active and engaged learning that balances both content (e.g., sociological and psychological readings) and process knowledge (e.g., critical self-reflection, experiential activities); and, (3) facilitated learning environment led by two trained peer-leaders (Nagda, Gurin, Sorensen, & Zúñiga, 2009; Zúñiga et al., 2007).

In addition to intergroup dialogue, increasingly dialogue practitioners are structuring intra-group dialogue courses to support the exploration of a single target or agent group identity. Target group refers to social identities that are subordinated within the societal power structure; agent group, in contrast, refers to social identities that hold societal power or privilege (Adams et al., 2007; Tatum, 2003). For example, the University of Michigan's Intergroup Relations Program recently implemented intragroup dialogues on multiracial identity (target group) and white racial identity (agent group).[3] Structurally and pedagogically similar to intergroup dialogue, in intra-group dialogue, students meet together to explore common experiences, issues of privilege and oppression, and the meaning of their racial group membership.

Students in the MRID, for instance, are able to explore feelings of ambiguity and confusion that often surface as multiracial individuals learn to navigate the complexity of their racial/ethnic identities within a monoracial-focused society. While the curricula may differ slightly, depending upon the focus of the dialogue, both courses follow a four-stage pedagogical model (forming relationships; exploring differences and commonalities of experience; discussing controversial topics; building alliances),[4] incorporate engaged learning activities and assignments (e.g., testi-monials; social identity profile; cycle of socialization; privilege walk/cross the line; collaborative project; social justice box),[5] and contain foundational readings on key concepts (e.g., dialogue, debate, and discussion; socialization processes; socio-historical context of race relations in the U.S.; race and racial identity development; social identities and their intersections; discrimination and oppression; differing manifestations of racism; alliances and social change).

To explore the outcomes related to Inter-/Intragroup Dialogue, we begin by providing an overview of literature relevant to the development and experiences of SOC/multiracial students within predominately white college settings. Next, we explain our research methodology and present seven central themes that highlight students' pre- and post-dialogue learnings. Finally, we end with a discussion of the diversity-related implications of incorporating social justice education courses into the curricular offerings at HWIs.

LITERATURE REVIEW

Research on the Racial Identity Development of People of Color/Multiracial People

Race is a characteristic that is "ascribed, symbolically mediated as status or stigma, socially con-structed, and consciously manipulated or performed" (Willie, 2003, p. 9). For this article, we are interested in the raced experiences of people of color. We use the term "people of color" to refer to racial groups that have been historically marginalized or oppressed within the U.S. context, including people who identify as African American/black, Latino/Hispanic/Chicano(a), Asian/Pacific Islander/Asian American, American Indian/Native American, or multiracial (Tatum, 2003). While the racial/ethnic groups represented under the people of color category are heterogeneous and are defined by differing socio-historical contexts, immigration statuses, languages, ethnicities, cultures, and skin tones—the experiences of this socially constructed group often differs from the white hegemonic norm (Tatum, 2003).

Racial identity development, according to Tatum (2003), refers to the "process of defining for oneself the personal significance and social meaning of belonging to a particular racial group" (p. 16). For people of color, this process is certainly not monolithic. Cross (1991), for instance, developed a five-stage black racial identity development model: (1) pre-encounter: racial assimilation; (2) encounter: racial awareness and anger; (3) immersion/emersion: racial re-education and pride; (4) internalization: racial redefinition; and, (5) internalization-commitment: racial integration and change. More recent models also outline similar stages specific to the identity development of Latino/a (Ferdman & Gallegos, 2001) and Asian Americans (J. Kim, 2001). In addition, comparable to Cross (1991), Helms (1990, 1995) created a parallel people of color profile for racial/ethnic groups more broadly: (1) conformity; (2) dissonance; (3) immersion/emersion; (4) internalization; and (5) integrative awareness.

Finally, the developmental process of multiracial individuals can be especially complicated due to a number of factors, including: racial ancestry, socialization patterns, and the socio-historical context; the relationship between the one-drop rule and internal and external perceptions of self; underlying tensions between embracing or denying aspects of one's identity; colorism and ethnic options; white skin privilege and passing; physical appearance and exoticism; racial/cultural attachment, sense of belongingness, and identity confusion; and intersecting social identities and political consciousness (Root, 1990, 1992, 1996; Spickard, 1992; Tatum, 2003; Wijeyesinghe, 2001; Xie & Goyette, 1998). In an effort to better understand the multiracial experience, recent research (e.g., Renn, 2003; Root, 1990, 1992, 1996; Wallace, 2001) has focused on the development of a multiracial identity model. Root (1996), for instance, articulates four possible interrelated themes or trajectories relevant to constructing a multiracial identity: (1) "having *both* feet in *both* groups," (p. xxi) in other words acknowledging and identifying with two (or more) racial groups; (2) shifting ethnicity or race depending on the situation or setting; (3) self-identifying exclusively as multiracial, without a clear reference to specific racial identities; and/or, (4) identifying primarily with one dominant race, while also appreciating the other races/ethnicities that also shape identity. Elaborating point two, Hyman (2010) argues that multiracial individuals can choose to code-switch—or change their behaviors, style, or language—based on their surroundings. This gives them the flexibility to use their multiple racial identities to their advantage in different social and academic settings (Hyman, 2010). Moreover, Wallace (2001) contends that multiracial people can acquire a healthy sense of self by identifying with any individual ethnicity or a combination of ethnicities. Finally, Renn (2003) expands upon Root's (1996) framework by adding another component to her model: (5) multiracial individuals can choose to "opt out of racial identities altogether by deconstructing them" (p. 385).

While these conceptual models cannot fully capture the complex, enduring, and non-linear nature of racial identity formation, they do provide general frameworks for understanding how

SOC/multiracial students can theoretically transition from an identity that lacks salience to an identity that reflects a positive racialized sense of self (Tatum, 2003; Wijeyesinghe, 2001).

Research on the Experiences of SOC/Multiracial Students at HWIs

Researchers continue to examine what factors determine a positive climate for racial diversity (Gurin, 1999; Henderson-King & Kaleta, 2000; Hurtado, Milem, Clayton-Pedersen, & Allen, 1998; Mayhew, Grunwald, & Dey, 2005). In particular, Hurtado et al. identify four dimensions of campus life that impact perceptions of diversity on a campus: the (1) "campus' historical legacy of inclusion or exclusion of various racial or ethnic groups; (2) its structural diversity (i.e., the numerical and proportional representation of diverse groups on campus); (3) its psychological climate (i.e., perceptions, attitudes, and beliefs about diversity); and, (4) its behavioral climate (i.e., how different racial and ethnic groups interact on campus" (p. 391). If these four dimensions are not proactively addressed by colleges/universities, SOC/multiracial students often end up navigating difficult race-related climate issues.

The higher education literature has documented that SOCs, particularly SOCs within predominately white academic settings, experience the classroom in racially inscribed ways that subsequently affect their academic experiences and social lives on campus (Lewis, Chesler, & Forman, 2000; Massey, Charles, Lundy, & Fisher, 2003; Suarez-Balcaza et al., 2003). Through focus groups, Lewis et al. report that SOCs (black, Latino/a, Asian, and American Indian) experience racial and behavioral stereotyping by white students; pressures to assimilate; exclusion and marginality; white ignorance and interpersonal awkwardness; and white resentment and hostility around affirmative action. Moreover, discriminatory attitudes, behaviors, and biased incidents (Pewewardy & Frey, 2002; Suarez-Balcaza et al., 2003), racial "micro-aggressions" or "unconscious and subtle forms of racism" (Solórzano, Ceja, & Yosso, 2000, p. 60), academic performance-related stereotype threat or anticipatory discrimination (Steele & Aronson, 1995), the hegemonic college curriculum (Lewis et al., 2000), the lack of faculty of color role models (Neville, Heppner, Ji, & Thye, 2004), and the role of white faculty in reinforcing tokenism within the classroom (Gonsalves, 2002; Lewis et al., 2000) present other challenges for this group of students.

Gonsalves (2002), for instance, finds that black male students are affected by the quality of white faculty interactions both in and outside of the classroom. Specifically, culturally insensitive remarks made by white professors can negatively influence SOCs' academic coursework; in contrast, SOCs are more apt to interact with white professors who demonstrate some cultural sensitivity and awareness to issues of race and identity. Similarly, Neville et al. (2004) document the race-related stressors (e.g., faculty insensitivity, low academic expectations, lack of role models, racial isolation, interpersonal and institutional racism) that affect black college students' academic, personal, and social adjustment. Finally, Cureton's (2003) research suggests that black students' academic success is affected by interpersonal factors, perceptions of the campus climate, and the social and cultural opportunities at the college or university.

While there is a growing body of literature on SOCs, particularly black students, more work needs to be done on the educational experiences of multiracial students at HWIs. Developing a sense of belonging on campus is crucial to all students' academic and social success; within the literature on multiracial student development (O'Connor, Lewis, & Mueller, 2007; Renn,

2003; Root, 1990, 1992, 1996), social connectedness is highlighted as an especially salient theme (Johnson et al., 2007; Rockquemore & Brunsma, 2001; Root, 1992). Unlike their monoracial peers, multiracial students tend to be internally divided because their intersecting racial/ethnic identities challenge monolithic racial categories (Root, 1996). Consequently, to be accepted by others, many find it easier to embrace a single racial identity (Renn, 2003; Root, 1996). For example, Williams, Nakashima, Kich, and Daniel (1996) argue that a "multiracial person disappears into a monoracial projection fostered by teachers, fellow students, or both. Unless interracial themes, histories, and concepts are presented as part of the course, either the credibility of the multiracial individual as a person of color is questioned or resisted" (p. 364). Moreover, as Williams et al. (1996) explain, in HWIs this complexity is never fully addressed; multiracial students are thus forced inside (e.g., token representative for a particular racial group) and outside (e.g., selection of which racial affinity group/club to join) of the classroom, to choose which monoracial background to publicly embrace and adhere to (Johnson et al., 2007; Williams et al., 1996).

Intergroup Dialogue

In part, Inter-/Intragroup Dialogue, and the conceptual and pedagogical assumptions underlying it, was created to help address the historical exclusion of SOC/multiracial students and the related campus climate issues within HWIs; it was also designed to increase students' level of positivity toward interactional diversity (Gurin, 1999; Zúñiga et al., 2007). Applying contact theory, social identity theory, and intergroup contact theory (Allport, 1954; Engberg, 2004; Pettigrew, 1998; Tropp & Pettigrew, 2005), social psychologists have documented the positive outcomes associated with intergroup interaction, including mutual appreciation and understanding, constructive engagement with conflict, and collective action (Fiske, 2002; Huddy, 2001; Pettigrew, 1998; Schoepflin, 2006). Pettigrew also suggests that when the intergroup contact has equal status within the setting (e.g., equal racial representation of students), shared goals (e.g., community norms), cooperation in pursuit of those goals (e.g., group dynamics), and support from authorities (e.g., peer-facilitators), it allows for closeness and/or intergroup friendships to develop.

Likewise, emergent scholarship on intergroup dialogue has confirmed that dialoging across different social identity groups fosters positive effects in communication and personal growth within students, while furthering the prospects for social change (e.g., Gurin & Nagda, 2006; Lopez, Gurin, & Nagda, 1998; Nagda & Zúñiga, 2003; Sorensen, Nagda, Gurin, & Maxwell, 2009). As a result, Sorenson et al. and Hurtado et al. (1998) conclude that there are great benefits associated with having diversity in institutions of higher education, if utilized appropriately. Some of the benefits include students overcoming fears related to intergroup interactions, working together cross-racially, and becoming more likely to make integrated lifestyle choices post-college (Sorenson et al., 2009). Although these outcomes, to differing degrees, are evident for both students of color and white students, less is qualitatively understood about the dialogic educational benefits and identity development processes of marginalized social identity groups (generally)[6] and SOC/multiracial students (specifically). Consequently, in addition to understanding white student experiences (Ford, 2011), we need to focus on the positive classroom-based pedagogical interventions that help SOC/multiracial students thrive within HWIs.

This project extends research on Inter-/Intragroup Dialogues by assessing SOC/multiracial students' learning across inter- and intraracial dialogue settings. Specifically, it focuses on: (1) how SOC/multiracial students make sense of race, racism, and racial identity; (2) how their understanding of these concepts is affected by participation in an Inter- or Intragroup Dialogue on race; and, (3) the pedagogies and group dynamics that promote this understanding.

METHODOLOGY

This Institutional Review Board approved research takes place at a small private liberal arts college in the Northeast. In accordance with national trends within higher education, women out-number men on campus, 60% and 40% respectively. Approximately 20% of students self-identify as people of color and 80% identify as white. While the College continues to recruit and enroll increasingly diverse cohorts of first-year students, significant diversity-related challenges are still present at this HWI. Like many comparable institutions, this College faces a range of ongoing is-sues, including: (1) SOC/multiracial students are generally the sole representatives of their racial group(s) within a classroom; (2) SOCs, particularly black and Latino/a students, are often pre-sumed to come from low income backgrounds and receive scholarships, an assumption that results in internal and external stereotypes regarding academic qualifications; and (3) biased incidents regarding race, social class, gender, and sexuality remain prevalent occurrences on campus.

Despite these identified campus climate issues, the College recognizes the importance of social justice education and recently included a provision in the revised 2010 Strategic Plan that focuses on developing the diversity-related knowledge and skills of faculty, staff, and students in hopes of building a more inclusive community. The plan also acknowledges the importance of Inter-/Intragroup Dialogue in achieving its overall mission (College website).

Within this context, a comparative approach was used in this pre-dialogue/post-dialogue design to qualitatively explore SOC/multiracial students' learning in the Inter-/Intragroup Dialogues held in 2009–2010. SOC/multiracial students interested in participating in a semester-long race dialogue were either enrolled in an Intergroup POC-W dialogue with white students or an intragroup experience (the MRID).[7] In total, the sample contained five sections of POC-W ($n = 21$) and one section of the MRID ($n = 10$) that enrolled an aggregate of 31 students. The group consisted of 10 men and 21 women representing the following racial identities: Hispanic/Latino/a ($n = 11$), Asian/Asian American ($n = 9$), multiracial ($n = 7$), and African American/black ($n = 4$). In addition, participants represented a range of other group and social identities, including differing class years (first-year students through seniors), nationalities (e.g., dual citizens, U.S. citizens); religious affiliations (e.g., Buddhist, Christian, agnostic, spiritual, non-religious); sexualities (e.g., gay, bisexual, heterosexual); and social classes (e.g., working, middle, upper).

An inductively-derived qualitative analysis of two written, graded assignments,[8] a four-page preliminary paper, and an eight-page final paper, allowed for a nuanced exploration of SOC/multiracial students' articulation of race, racial identity, and racism. Both papers required students to critically reflect on their experiences with and understandings of race, by addressing three topical areas: (1) social identities; (2) social structures; and (3) dialogue experiences. The final papers also required students to integrate course readings into their analysis. Specifically, the papers explored questions such as:

1. **Social Identities**: "What are some experiences that have made your race/ethnicity visible to you? What and how were you taught, explicitly or implicitly, about what it means to be a person of color/multiracial person, in terms of attitudes, behaviors, your future, the nature of the society, etc.? Broadly speaking, what does it mean to you to be a person of color/multiracial person? What do you know about your ethnic/cultural heritage (i.e., the culture, country or region of the world from which your ancestors came)? And how might this affect your feelings about being considered part of your racial group?"

2. **Social Structures**: "Throughout your life, have most of your friends and other people close to you been of the same racial/ethnic background? If so, why do you think this was the case? If not, what do you think led you to cross racial/ethnic lines in these relationships? Have you been subject to discrimination based on your race/ethnicity? If so, what type of discrimination (be specific with examples)? Has your racial/ethnic identity brought you any privileges or benefits? If so, what types of privileges or benefits (be specific with examples)? How do you think demographic changes that are currently underway in the U.S. and the world will affect your experiences with and attitudes relating to race/ethnicity and racism?"

3. **Dialogue Experiences:**
   o Preliminary Paper: "What are some of your hopes, or learning objectives, for this dialogue? What are some of your fears or concerns about participating in this dialogue?"
   o Final Paper: "What has been the impact of this semester's dialogue on your knowledge and views about being a person of color/multiracial person in U.S. society? What has been the impact of this semester's dialogue on your knowledge and views about race/ethnicity and racism? What, if any, are your goals for personal next steps concerning the topic of this dialogue? How, if at all, do you expect to use what you have learned in the future (both at the College and beyond)?"

Student grades were not contingent on participating in this research project. Upon completion of the dialogue, the 59 papers (28 preliminary/31 final)[9] of consenting students were assigned a number and cleaned of any personally identifiable information. To ensure consistency in the coding process, the papers were hand-coded by us and two trained research assistants of differing racial identities. Specifically, this inductive process included reading each paper several times, identifying core themes through open and focused coding, creating a coding scheme, and then entering the data into the Qualitative N-Vivo software program for further analysis (Emerson, Fretz, & Shaw, 1995). Finally, by examining relevant excerpts and developing conceptual memos, themes from the preliminary and final papers were compared to discern common patterns across the students' narratives over time. While we also documented student-specific shifts in perspective, for this article, we were primarily interested in presenting themes that reflect group, rather than individual-level, pre- to post-dialogue differences. To protect confidentiality, participant names were changed in the analysis of the data.

Potential Limitations

It is important to acknowledge that the results from this small, non-random sample, which includes an unequal number of POC-W and MRID participants, is not necessarily generalizable across various institutional contexts or representative of larger student populations. In particular, because

Inter-/Intragroup Dialogue courses are voluntary, this self-selected group of students may have been more attuned to or interested in exploring issues of race than the average student. Finally, it is unclear, without additional longitudinal data, if these results are sustainable over an extended period of time.

RESULTS

In both the Inter- and Intragroup Dialogues, SOC/multiracial[10] student papers demonstrated self-reported growth—in content learning and dialogue processes—over the course of the semester. Reflecting on this experience, all 31 of the students noted the ways in which they have been positively transformed. For example:

> I definitely went into the racial dialogues feeling that I would know a lot ... Perhaps I did have a lot of diverse experiences with race but that doesn't qualify me as some type of race expert, and coming to race dialogues definitely showed me that I had so much to learn from my peers and from myself as well. —Sergio, Latino man

> The POC-W dialogue course forced me to confront my insecurities and develop emotionally while coming to recognize the make-up of society in ways I never had before, bringing me one step closer to self-actualization and teaching me how to be more of the person I want to be in society ... The most important thing a student could take away from the [POC-W] dialogue course is the importance of knowing yourself before you can know others. It is impossible for one to fathom understanding, let alone appreciating and critically considering another opinion until they are on relatively solid ground with who they feel they are, what they believe, and how their identity places them in their larger world. —Nadia, biracial Latina

> Looking back on this experience, I can see how much of a journey we have all embarked on. It has been a long one, but one that is never finished. It's sort of like going hiking—you have to acquire the tools (and learn to use them) before you can actually begin the climb. We have tools and use them, and we're climbing; we have all climbed a great deal. However, with everything, we will take on more complicated tools and learn how to use them as our journey continues. —Rose, Asian American woman

The SOC/multiracial students have clearly expressed benefiting from their experiences in the POC-W and MRID. This finding aligns with Denson and Chang's (2008) research, which suggests that undergraduate education is positively impacted by diversity-related courses on college campuses. Inter-/Intragroup Dialogue courses, in particular, provide unique opportunities for students to gain a background in social justice that can help prepare them for their futures as, in Rose's words, their "journey continues." What follows is an overview of some of the pre- and post-dialogue themes and representative examples each. In particular, notable changes from pre- to post-dialogue included understanding the: (1) saliency and meaning of racial identity; (2) complexity of racial identity development; (3) relationship between skin color and self-esteem; (4) individual biases and prejudices; (5) structures of power and privilege/agent and target identities; (6) experience of race at the College; and, (7) importance of personal accountability and responsibility in creating change. More concretely, Table 1 outlines six primary themes, and the related raced scripts, that changed from pre- to post-dialogue; it also lists one major theme

TABLE 1
Student of Color/Multiracial Learning Outcomes

	POC-W	MRID
(a) Pre-Dialogue Themes, (b)Post-Dialogue Themes, (c) New Scripts, Post-Dialogue		
1. Saliency and Meaning of Racial Identity	√	√
a. "Race is central to my identity." OR "I do not identify with a race."		
b. "I now understand the meaning, complexity, and importance of my racial identity."		
2. Complexity of Racial Identity Development		√
a. "I do not know where I fit in . . . I feel torn between two different cultures."		
b. "I no longer feel divided . . . I am whole."		
3. Relationship Between Skin Color and Self-Esteem	√	√
a. "I am not comfortable in my skin; I wish that I was lighter."		
b. "I am comfortable in my skin; I now feel proud to be brown."		
4. Individual Biases and Prejudices	√	√
c. "I now recognize that I also hold stereotypes and biases against other groups."		
5. Structures of Power and Privilege/Agent and Target Identities	√	√
a. "The system is unfair and limits opportunities."/"I am oppressed because of racism."		
b. "I better understand how racism is embedded in our social structures."/"Although I may be oppressed as a SOC/multiracial person, I am still privileged in other ways."		
6. Experience of Race at the College	√	√
a. "Coming to this College was a culture shock."		
b. "Coming to this College is still a culture shock, but now I have a community of support."		
7. Personal Accountability and Responsibility	√	√
a. "I want to create change."		
b. "It is my responsibility to take action, develop allies, and create change."		

√ = theme present in the corresponding dialogue section.

that only emerged in the final papers, and delineates the intergroup (POC-W) and intragroup (MRID) differences.

The Saliency and Meaning of Racial Identity

Most of the SOC/multiracial students in the sample began with a nuanced understanding of race and racism when they entered the race dialogues. In her preliminary paper (i.e., pre-dialogue), Leigh, a black woman, for instance, stated:

> My identity is one of the important aspects of my life and I always questioned, who am I? Who do I want to be? I feel as if I always have to be aware of my race because of all the negative things that have happened in the past to Blacks and things even now. I do not believe that the "majority" is out to get us, but I have to be aware, proud, and even pay respects to my race because we have struggled and still are struggling to make a place for us in America and also the world.

This type of statement is not surprising given the socio-historical context of race relations in the U.S.; generally, targeted (or non-privileged) racial identity groups are more aware of systematic dis/advantage based on power structures than their privileged counterparts (Tatum, 2003). Most

SOC/multiracial students emphasized the centrality of race in their lives (pre-dialogue), and were able to re-define race and further embrace its significance by the end of the semester (post-dialogue). This pattern did not hold true for all participants. In an attempt to challenge the social construction of race, an Asian American woman, early in the MRID process, preferred to identify as "raceless":

> I view myself as raceless, and though it sounds isolating, it has been liberating as an idea. On paperwork, there is no box under Race/Ethnicity to be checked off for "None." When asked, "Where are you from?" I answer that I am from New York. I know that isn't what is being asked of me, and [I] am always urged on with a remark like, "No, originally . . .?" I want to understand what others feel when they answer questions about race and ethnicity, if only to understand what it means to be proud of one's heritage . . . I know that by claiming racelessness I am denying myself the opportunity to feel a part of a community. —Sarai, Asian American woman, pre-dialogue

Throughout the course of the dialogue, however, an interesting shift in consciousness occurred. This student refined her position on "racelessness" as she began to understand both the individual and societal implications of race:

> I used to feel raceless. I used to think that to admit a racial identity was an individual choice, and I, personally, chose to ignore race as a presence in my life . . . Race is not an individual choice, but a system that exists to establish power dynamics. I can no longer choose to ignore my race, because I am now aware that it has been imposed on me by society. —Sarai, Asian American woman, post-dialogue

Identifying as raceless is a well-documented strategy and identity stage within the literature; by disconnecting from a marginalized racial identifier, it allows SOCs to better assimilate into dominant cultural values and norms (J. Kim, 2001; Tatum, 2003; Tuan, 1998). In doing so, however, Tuan argues that Asian Americans, like Sarai, often ignore institutionalized racism and its effects on their lived experiences.

The Complexity of Racial Identity Development

In other ways, the complexity of racial identity constructions emerged in many of the initial student papers. More concretely, in the MRID, many of the multiracial students articulated identity confusion (and, in a few cases, internalized oppression/self-hatred) around a lack of belongingness or feeling unsure about where they "fit in" (Johnson et al., 2007; Rockquemore & Brunsma, 2001; Root, 1990, 1992, 1996). The notion of racial authenticity becomes relevant here. As Jackson (2001) explains, while representations of racial authenticity are arbitrary and contextually determined, they nonetheless have social implications. Moreover, situational identities and negotiations over self-image are often dependent on group recognition and monitoring of authenticity (Howard, 2000). Feeling racially inauthentic—due to mode of dress, complexion, mannerisms, or others' opinions—resonates with a number of the multiracial student experiences.

Sarai, for instance, discussed the impact of 9/11 on Muslims and individuals who are assumed to be Muslim based on dress or language use: "I remember after 9/11 how my race seemed to flare out, obvious to others, and I feared I would be linked to the terrorists . . . Many Muslims altered their customs so that they would not attract much attention. I didn't have to do this because I was already 'one of them,' I was more American than any other culture. I think this was when I started to really feel unsettled by racial issues. Because I wore jeans and tank tops I did not endure the discrimination that others did." Likewise, Nadia, a biracial Latina, wrote about visibly "passing" as white and feeling disconnected from communities of color. Other students clearly expressed a sense of double-consciousness (DuBois, 1989), or feeling torn between two different cultures or identities:

> I was accused of being "the least black, black kid," an insult I would come to hear regularly . . . They told me I wasn't black because I was raised by white people. Thus, I began to hang out with my white friends more frequently. However, the ridiculing continued, only now I became the token black kid . . . I slowly began to lose my biracial identity, convinced that I had to choose between black or white. —Aaron, biracial man, pre-dialogue

> My parents expect me to excel in school, obey their every wish, and more importantly not lose my cultural identity . . . But my parents failed to realize that by bringing me to the United States at such a young age I would lose my cultural identity indefinitely. They brought me into a culture that stresses individuality rather than loyalty to tradition. To solve this dilemma I formed a double identity one that I wanted and another superficial one that my parents wanted. —Stanley, Asian American man, pre-dialogue

> I feel paradoxically too American to be [Asian], and too "brown" to be American . . . But I hope I can make sense of what it means to be this racial hybrid. —Sarai, Asian American woman, pre-dialogue

In contrast, by the end of the semester, these same students were not only able to make sense of what it means to be a "racial hybrid," they were also able to develop a fluid sense of identity that embraced this complexity. Sydney, a biracial woman, noted: "instead of attempting to label myself as one ethnicity or the other, I have found it suits my chameleon nature to just be both." The recurrent theme—"I no longer feel divided; I am whole"—is also evident in the subsequent quotations:

> I found reason to identify as mixed only, without having to explain my exotic racial make-up to everyone I meet. I'm not divided within myself but rather united with all those around me who identify as multiracial as well, regardless of their race percentiles. These realizations inspired a satisfaction with and growth of my character, and I now harbor more pride in my race than I had ever before. —Aaron, biracial man, post-dialogue

> Really, I am handed three cultures—the one based on my upbringing, one given by birth, and the one society gave me. However, difficult at times it is, I can appreciate my complexity . . . [This course] personally played into my multiple social identities through validating my feelings. My understanding of my own social legitimacy was definitely something I did not have before MRID. Multiracial individuals are constantly re-defining their identity and struggling with straddling two or more identities they will never fully fit into . . . I might be a walking contradiction, but I am a legitimate one, and if society has a problem with it, they only have themselves to blame for shaping my identity in this way. —Rose, Asian American woman, post-dialogue

> Before I entered this course, I tried very hard to fit in a category and that usually meant identifying as Hispanic/Latina, but now I realize that although society makes it this way, it shouldn't be like this . . . I am also Biracial. From now on, I will use my fractioned identity to challenge society's social binaries and embrace difference. —Marianna, Latina woman, post-dialogue

In sum, this experience provided a safe space for many SOCs, especially multiracial students, to develop a sense of empowerment and pride in their multiple and intersecting social identities, and to use these identities to challenge racial binaries.

Skin Color and Self-Esteem

Porter and Washington (1993) define two different types of self-esteem: "group self-esteem" refers to how the individual feels about racial or ethnic group membership, and "personal self-esteem" refers to how the individual feels about the self in a comprehensive manner. For SOC/multiracial students, developing both a positive group and personal self-esteem can be challenging as they strive to fit into U.S. racial and cultural constructs (Porter & Washington, 1993). Specifically, since SOC/multiracial students are in the racial minority at HWIs, race often becomes a prominent, visible marker of difference (Johnson et al., 2007; Root, 1992; Tatum, 2003). Julian, a Latino male, believes that "being a person of color in America means that one must give in to 'white culture.' By giving in I mean having to compromise some of our own ethnic ties or traditions in order to assimilate." Root (1992) acknowledges that the development of healthy self-esteem is even more complicated for multiracial people due to a number of factors, including lack of social acceptance and sense of belonging, social stress, and challenging family dynamics.

In contrast to their preliminary papers, which reflected SOC/multiracial students' struggles to develop a positive racial sense of self, their final paper reflected a better understanding of themselves, and a more positive outlook on their futures. To that end, Lacey contended:

> Through the POC-W dialogue, I became aware of how my racial and ethnic identity has shifted; I am more aware of my minority status, but I am also not afraid to identify as a person of color. I think I am more confident in my identity as a biracial individual. Furthermore, through this class I realized how comfortable I am in my brown skin, and how proud I am to be brown. —Lacey, biracial woman, post-dialogue

Inter-/Intragroup Dialogues helped others to realize the implications of internalized oppression and resist tendencies to hide or downplay their cultural background:

> Us minorities who have come from different backgrounds felt that we had to hide ourselves when we arrived at [the College], to be more Americanized and behave less Asian, Hispanic, or black. We felt this way because the majority of the campus is white . . . In order to be accepted we have to abandon our backgrounds, to be more "white," to be civilized, to be a normal American. But what did that all mean? Was abandoning who we are helping or hurting ourselves? At least in one point of our lives we wished we were not who we are, either to have straight hair instead of curly, or to have whiter skin than dark. We dislike ourselves all because of what society tells us is perfect, what is beautiful, and what is acceptable. —Mai, Asian American woman, post-dialogue

In the above examples, students grappled with the societal implications of having a darker skin tone; other SOC/multiracial students, however, dealt with a divergent issue: visibly looking white. In contrast to students who viewed their complexion as a liability, these students had to reconcile the privileges associated with unintentionally passing for white. Within the context of this article, "passing" refers to social situations in which a person of color or multiracial person knowingly or unknowingly identifies (or is identified by others) as white (Root, 1992).

> I believe that because I welcome this biracial background, and truthfully, [I] look more white than I do Hispanic, I have many privileges laid at my feet. This advantage is something I was completely unaware of before I took this POC-W dialogue class. The dialogue was in some ways very hard for me, because it forced me to see aspects of my identity that I do not necessarily relate with or care for. I was challenged to confront my own whiteness . . . I acknowledge this privilege and rather than remaining oblivious, rejecting, or misusing it, I feel more capable of actively putting these benefits to good use. —Sydney, biracial woman, post-dialogue

This quotation suggests that the POC-W dialogue helped empower Sydney to take ownership of the relationship between her skin tone, racial identity, and self-esteem. Most notably, Sydney was able to articulate the societal implications of phenotypically passing (Root, 1992) and explore proactive ways to use her white skin privilege to create change.

Individual Biases and Prejudices

Through this dialogue experience, SOC/multiracial students were also able to dissect their previously held biases and preconceptions. To that end, Liane, a black woman noted: "One of the main things that I learned about myself is that while I may not be quick to publically judge others based on stereotypes that I am aware of, I do still sit by some stereotypes and they arise sometimes . . . I have learned to question myself more now than I have ever about my actions, others' actions, and my own perceptions and viewpoints." Likewise, a multiracial and black woman more specifically relate their realizations regarding unrecognized raced stereotypes and/or prejudices of other racial/ethnic groups:

> MRID has also helped me to better recognize my actions towards others regarding race. For example, I asked my classmate to take a "super Asian" photo of several of our friends. I soon realized that this foolish comment set a stereotype of Asians . . . it is essential for me to recognize and correct racial terminologies when they fit the stereotypes of particular races. —Makayla, multiracial woman, post-dialogue

> I believe that my resentment [of white people] stems from the fact that the majority of those with privilege are oblivious to the fact that they have such privilege. The more I was forced to read, listen, and discuss various aspects of race and identity, the closer I came to confronting my feelings with honesty and clarity. I resent those with agency because of my lack thereof . . . I guess I resent white people because it is *I* who ultimately finds it hard to connect with them. Like all problems, the first step is to acknowledge that it is there. Now that I can identify my problem and one of the basis of my feelings I am more equipped to challenge myself and attempt to pivot my center of view . . . I can now look back on situations like that and analyze my own biases and prejudices. If anything, this course has reminded me that I am not free from the stains of racial prejudice and biases. Not only do I have biases against other races, but I've learned that I have several against my own race as well. —Danielle, black woman, post-dialogue

These quotations demonstrate the value of engaged pedagogies and how the co-learning process can promote change in students. Without comparable opportunities to meaningfully grapple with issues of race, as Henderson-King and Kaleta's (2000) research reminds us, a student will often "become less positive in her or his feelings toward people of color, as well as some other groups, over the course of a semester" (p. 145). In this study, it is quite the opposite; these data demonstrate how student assumptions and biases can be realized and, hopefully, reconsidered.

Structures of Power and Privilege/Agent and Target Identities

Although many SOC/multiracial students generally begin the course with a more sophisticated understanding of race, power, and privilege than their white counterparts (Ford, 2011), they nonetheless develop a deeper appreciation for these issues over time. Delgado and Stefancic (2001), using CRT, argue that "racism is ordinary, not aberrational" —it is "the usual way society does business, the common, everyday experience of most people of color"' (p. 7). As a result of the Inter-/Intragroup Dialogues, SOC/multiracial students began to more fully recognize the complicated structures of power and privilege in the U.S. as well as its relationship to racial hegemony.

A common pedagogical exercise used to demonstrate the implications of privilege is the "privilege walk." The privilege walk is an interactive activity designed to visually highlight the interpersonal and structural implications of privilege based on race, gender, social class, or sexuality (Adams et al., 2007). Through this exercise, Camille, an Asian American woman, came to the following realization about structures of power and privilege:

> I remember I knew that [name], who was a Caucasian male, was going to end up in the very front while the rest of the Caucasian girls in the class were going to trail behind him. I ended up in the middle while my friends were at the back. Half of me was like, "Oh wow, this is a bit brutal," but the other half thought well this is the harsh truth or reality. This is what the real world is like out there.

This quotation demonstrates the process in which Camille and her classmates started to come to terms with the hegemonic nature of whiteness and white privilege in the U.S.

In addition, many of the SOC/multiracial students began to recognize their multiple, intersecting identities—some of which are denied power (target identities), and others of which receive societal privileges (agent identities). Highlighting this point, Sydney notes: "Something that I am incredibly grateful to this class and its members for is helping me own my identity and the power it brings me," and Marianna, who identifies as Latina, recognizes: "Although I have been oppressed because of my ethnicity and socioeconomic class, I have realized that I am both dominant and subordinate." Elaborating this point, Sarai and Makayla discussed how their various social identities intersect in complicated ways:

> I have begun to become really sensitive and aware of my heterosexual privilege. An experience with a friend revealed how paralyzing his status as a homosexual has been in his life. Being heterosexual, I often talk about my partner without any qualms and can even joke or dream about my future husband or wedding day. For my friend, there is no such luxury . . . Knowing what it feels like to be privileged passively, that is, without actively seeking that privilege or using it to oppress others, was really alarming . . . This course has really challenged me to examine the effect of these systems on my social self, and until now I had never noticed much of their impact. —Sarai, Asian American woman, post-dialogue

I don't feel that I belong to an oppressed category because I usually fall in the advantaged group of the identity wheel. I can pass as white (race), am Christian (religion), am straight (sexual orientation), financially secure (class), am able-bodied (ability), am over 21 years of age (age), and am a female (gender/sex) who has not encountered any problems with this latter point . . . However, I felt mortified to be at the front of the "privilege walk" during one of our class discussions. As I am one of the few students in the multiracial class who can afford college without financial assistance, I can also pass as white . . . Therefore, my ashamed reaction was expected because it implied that even though I challenge the status quo, I am linked to the "oppressor" compared to an individual of color as the "oppressed." —Makayla, multiracial woman, post-dialogue

The Experience of Race at the College

Despite this newly developed appreciation for the complexities underlying their multiple inter-secting social identities, for most SOC/multiracial students, the experience of race at the College remains challenging. For instance, many students, particularly those from racially diverse home-towns, expressed how unprepared they were to deal with the "shock" of coming to such a racially homogenous environment:

Arriving here to [the College] I was hit with a severe cultural shock. I was taken by surprise by the amount of Caucasian students on campus and how small the minority community is . . . It became very apparent the first day of school at [the College], while sitting in my first course of the day and realizing that I was the only female of color in the room . . . I was hit very hard by reality which made me feel as though I do not belong here sometimes. —Bryanna, Latina woman, pre-dialogue

Moreover, this sense of isolation was often amplified for students who experienced overt (e.g., racist remarks; discriminatory treatment) or covert (e.g., tokenism; stereotypical assumptions) forms of racism when interacting with some white faculty, staff, and students in various curricular and co-curricular venues on campus (Gonsalves, 2002; Lewis et al., 2000; Neville et al., 2004; Pewewardy & Frey, 2002). According to Lewis et al. (2000), SOCs, particularly black students, encounter raced and gendered insults from their white peers. These disparaging comments serve as a constant reminder to black students that they are the outsiders within HWIs. Lacey confirmed this sentiment: "Being at a predominately white campus has made me feel more of a minority and more black than I have ever felt before."

In spite of these challenges, the College sites that were perceived to be the most welcoming/ nurturing include offices that support SOCs' achievement; individual faculty members, most commonly faculty of color or white faculty sensitive to issues of race, and spaces that support non-traditional curricular endeavors (e.g., Inter-/Intragroup Dialogue). Elaborating the final point, an Asian American man notes that his experience at the College was positively changed by having the opportunity to engage with race in a space designed for SOC/multiracial students:

My experience at [the College] can be defined by a constant challenge to establish a unique personal identity that is true to my own background and heritage in the face of the dominant cultures represented on campus . . . MRID has helped me get in touch with a variety of diverse voices and experiences that I had previously been distracted from proactively seeking out . . . Virtually all of my friends are white, and I knew that even if they sympathized with me, they could never truly understand or relate. When I entered the Dialogue, I realized that for the first time ever at [the College], I was in a room of only people of color. When I found that I was not alone, that was when I was ready to become less defensive and listen. I realized that I did not have to speak at great lengths about the problem of racial injustice at [the College], because everyone in the room was already aware of it. —Trent, Asian American man, post-dialogue

Through this experience, Trent recognized that he is not alone in the struggle for racial justice.

Personal Accountability and Responsibility in Creating Social Change

Lastly, the SOC/multiracial students acknowledge that a change in mindset is an important first step on the path to creating a more racially diverse and inclusive environment at the College and beyond. Accordingly, Kylie, an Asian American woman, revealed: "I also found through this class, how to empower my target status, to de-victimize myself, as I had realized that while it was the responsibility of those that perpetuate discrimination to end the cycle, I could do my part to not let these institutionalized forms of discrimination inhibit my own personal progress." The next step is taking action. Rob, a Latino man, assumes responsibility for helping to transform campus climate by affirming: "Gone are the days where I would not speak up when someone uses a derogatory comment. I will not conform and accept the privileges that come with it. I will use my knowledge to challenge the status quo." Finally, Gabriela and Taylor articulated their vision for social change in the following manner:

> It takes one person at a time to make a difference. The domino effect will begin with me and the other students in my class. We can all talk to our friends and show them the importance of becoming allies and therefore help fight whatever cause it may be. —Gabriela, Latina woman, post-dialogue

> I do not have all the answers but once we stop trying to point fingers and focus on problems facing humanity, I believe race relations will improve greatly. I'm not asking people to forget who they are, rather I am asking them to bring this to the proverbial table and listen with the same amount of vigor in which they speak. Without openness and understanding nothing can change. —Taylor, biracial man, post-dialogue

In the end, through this process of personal growth and transformation, SOC/multiracial students understand that it is their responsibility to create positive social change for their well-being and the well-being of those around them.

The SOC/multiracial students in the inter- (POC-W) and intragroup (MRID) dialogues underwent an important journey, a journey that has helped them to discover and re-connect with the meaning and importance of race in their lives. By revising their oppressive, raced scripts (e.g., "I do not know where I fit in," "I am not comfortable in my skin," "I am oppressed because of racism"), they were more willing to embrace the complexities underlying their intersecting racial identities (e.g., "I no longer feel divided . . . I am whole"), to grapple with internalized oppression (e.g., "I now feel proud to be brown"), to explore preconceptions (e.g., "I now recognize that I also hold stereotypes and biases against other groups"), and to recognize structures of power and privilege (e.g., "Although I may be racially oppressed, I am still privileged in other ways"). Finally, they wanted to use this newly acquired knowledge to create change in their lives and the lives of others. Accordingly, Rob noted:

I am leaving for home this summer an educated soldier, fighting for truth and justice, my weapons being the knowledge I gained from class. I can fight racism and prejudice with the theory of color-blind racism, my skills as a facilitator and my increasing passion and dedication towards social justice work around the world. —Rob, Latino man, post-dialogue

Through this process, Rob—and the other SOC/multiracial students—have indeed been transformed; the noted change in racial scripts from pre- to post-dialogue are one indicator of the progress they have made in understanding their racial identity (Cross, 1991; Ferdman & Gallegos, 2001; J. Kim, 2001; Renn 2003; Root, 1990, 1992, 1996; Tatum, 2003).

IMPLICATIONS AND CONCLUSION

This class provided a voice for individuals to talk about their own social identity groups. As a result, one of the things I learned in this course is the aspects of my social identity that I am comfortable with, and the aspects I am still struggling to understand. —Lacey, Biracial woman

POC-W was a pleasant surprise that allowed me to have the perfect balance of reading views from scholars, hearing views from my classmates, and sharing my own views in a comfortable environment . . . I believe this kind of [co-learning] environment really helped us learn from each other as well as learn about ourselves. —Riley, Asian American woman

According to H. Kim and Markus (1993) "talking is an important part of peoples' social lives. Talking is also affected by the 'relationship' because talking also functions as a tool of connecting and maintaining connectedness among people" (p. 183). As Riley and Lacey's comment suggest, SOC/multiracial students have their own unique raced stories that need to be told (Delgado & Stefancic, 2001); in order to effectively do so, establishing a safe, co-learning environment is fundamental to Inter-/Intragroup Dialogue pedagogy and its related outcomes (Gurin & Nagda, 2006; Lopez, Gurin, & Nagda, 1998; Nagda & Zúñiga, 2003; Sorensen et al., 2009). While SOC/multiracial students began this process at different places in their racial identity development (Cross, 1991; Ferdman & Gallegos, 2001; J. Kim, 2001; Renn, 2003; Root, 1990, 1992, 1996; Tatum, 2003), by merging content (e.g., sociological and psychological concepts) and process knowledge (e.g., affective engagement), students were able to grow, both personally and intellectually, from this unique dialogic experience (Nagda et al., 2009; Zúñiga et al., 2007). In sum, as these data suggest, being able to learn with and from each other, through Inter-/Intragroup Dialogue pedagogies, often facilitated notable transformations in students.

Tatum (2003) argues: "For many people of color, learning to break the silence is a survival issue. To remain silent would be to disconnect from her own experience, to swallow and internalize her own oppression. The cost of silence is too high" (p. 198). Through this experience, many SOC/multiracial students have been able to break the silence and identify their own unique "voice of color;" they have also developed a new understanding of how the normalization of racism affects people of color in the U.S. (Delgado & Stefancic, 2001). More concretely, through liberatory raced scripts, the SOC/multiracial students in this sample have grown to better understand the saliency and meaning of racial identity, as well as its complexity; they also recognize that true social change requires a concerted effort from both target (SOC) and agent (white) groups in intra- and interracial settings. Although the racial climate at this HWI proves challenging at times, they are eager to engage with race issues within a supportive and affirming classroom or institutional context. Establishing a positive climate for diversity, however, is not easy (Gurin, 1999; Hurtado et al., 1998); it requires HWIs to be sensitive to a range of identity issues that SOC/multiracial students commonly encounter—including social and academic marginalization, tokenism and exoticization, and racial discrimination (Lewis et al., 2000; Tatum, 2003)—so that these students can establish and maintain a positive racialized sense of self (Porter & Washington, 1993; Tatum, 2003; Wallace, 2001; Wijeyesinghe, 2001).

More broadly, the implications of this study suggest that the identity-specific challenges that SOC/multiracial students encounter in HWIs can be partially combated if colleges and universities provide more opportunities for meaningful interaction within and across social identity groups (Hurtado, 2005). This will not only help to better support SOC/multiracial students while in college; it will also prepare them to enter an increasingly diverse and global world. Hurtado (2005) argues, "We can no longer leave intergroup relations to chance, because they play a central role in ensuring that students can function in a diverse workforce and pluralistic society" (p. 607). Inter-/Intragroup Dialogue courses are crucial to these efforts as they promote affirmative race-related learning outcomes in white students (Ford, 2011) and SOC/multiracial students. As a result of this type of dialogue-focused pedagogical intervention, students, like Aaron, are able to confidently state: "I now harbor more pride in my race than ever before." Future research can build on these promising results by further exploring the nuances of SOC/multiracial student development across pedagogical approaches and demographic settings; it should also integrate a post-post-dialogue component to assess the sustainability of these outcomes over time.

Hurtado's (2005) study concludes that the "quality of student interactions with diverse peers is key (positive and meaningful interaction) in producing a host of important outcomes" (p. 606). This study confirms Hurtado's fundamental premise: In order to foster meaningful racial climate change on college campuses, and encourage amendments to prevailing racial scripts, HWIs need to make a real commitment, through courses like Inter-/Intragroup Dialogue, to social justice education.

NOTES

1. In the remainder of this article, we use the term "multiracial" to be inclusive of individuals who identify as bi- or multiracial.
2. Depending upon the institutional context, colleges and universities might have to approach the balancing of social identities differently. At the private college represented in this study, this is achieved through reserved seating and an application process.
3. For more, see: www.igr.umich.edu.
4. For more explanation of the four stages, see Zúñiga et al., 2007, pp. 27–28.
5. Zúñiga et al. (2007) and Adams et al. (2010) provide an overview of some of these activities.
6. For more discussion on raced differences in dialogue experiences, see: Ervin (2001), Hyers and Swim (1998), and Miller and Donner (2000).
7. Due to the complexity of racial identity constructions, the POC-W and MRID sections were not necessarily mutually exclusive. Accordingly, some students of multiracial background, identified more closely with the SOC experience and were placed in the POC-W dialogue; and, some monoracial SOCs more closely identified with the multiracial experience for a variety of reasons (e.g., Asian adoptees, Latino/a identity, multi-ethnic/national blended family situation, etc.) and were placed in the MRID.
8. The grading criteria for the papers included assessment of: (1) writing clarity and organization; (2) critical engagement with the assignment prompt; and (3) integration of the readings (for the final paper).

9. The discrepancy in numbers is due to the fact that three students only submitted their final papers for analysis.

10. Broad racial categories are used, instead of more specific racial identifiers, to protect student identities. For example, students from the African Diaspora (e.g., African American, Caribbean, African) are identified as "black;" students from various regions in Asia (e.g., India, Korea, Japan) are identified as "Asian" or "Asian American;" and "Latino/a" is inclusive of people from Latin America or of Spanish-speaking decent (e.g., Puerto Rico, Dominican Republic, Spain). Although the experiences of SOCs from various racial/ethnic backgrounds are certainly not monolithic, the data presented here reflect trends found across these racial groups.

REFERENCES

Adams, M., Bell, L. A., & Griffin, P. (Eds.). (2010). *Teaching for diversity and social justice* (2nd ed.). New York, NY: Routledge.

Allport, G. W. (1954). *The nature of prejudice*. Reading, MA: Addison-Wesley.

Chito Childs, E., & Matthews-Armstead, E. (2006). Racial divides on a diverse campus: An exploration of social distance at a state liberal arts university. In R. M. Moore, III (Ed.), *African Americans and Whites: Changing relationships on college campuses* (pp. 103–115). Lanham, MD: University Press of America.

Cross, W. (1991). *Shades of black: Diversity in African-American identity*. Philadelphia, PA: Temple University Press.

Cureton, S. (2003). Race-specific college student experiences on a predominantly white college campus. *Journal of Black Studies, 33*(3), 295–311.

Delgado, R., & Stefancic, J. (2001). *Critical race theory: An introduction*. New York, NY: New York University Press.

Denson, N., & Chang, M. J. (2008). Racial diversity matters: The impact of diversity-related student engagement and institutional context. *American Educational Research Journal, 46*(2), 322–353.

Du Bois, W. E. B. (1989). *The souls of black folk*. New York, NY: Bantam.

Emerson, R. M., Fretz, R. I., & Shaw, L. L. (1995). *Writing ethnographic fieldnotes*. Chicago, IL: University of Chicago Press.

Engberg, M. E. (2004). Improving intergroup relations in higher education: A critical examination of the influence educational interventions on racial bias. *Review of Educational Research, 74*(4), 473–524.

Ervin, K. S. (2001). Multiculturalism, diversity, and African American students: Receptive, yet skeptical? *Journal of Black Studies, 31*(6), 764–776.

Ferdman, B. M., & Gallegos, P. I. (2001). Racial identity development and Latinos in the United States. In B. Jackson & C. Wijeyesinghe (Eds.), *New perspectives on racial identity development: A theoretical and practical anthology* (pp. 32–66). New York, NY: New York University Press.

Fiske, S. T. (2002). What we know now about bias and intergroup conflict, the problem of the century. *Current Directions in Psychological Science, 11*(4), 123–128.

Ford, K. (2011). *"What can I learn from other white people?" The educational benefits of inter- and intra-racial curricular dialogues on white students' racial identity development*. Unpublished manuscript.

Freire, P. (1970). *Pedagogy of the oppressed*. New York, NY: Seabury.

Gonsalves, L. M. (2002). Making connections: Addressing the pitfalls of white faculty/black male student communication. *College Composition and Communication, 53*(3), 435–465.

Gurin, P. (1999). Selections from the compelling need for diversity in higher education, expert reports in defense of the University of Michigan. *Equity & Excellence in Education, 32*(2), 36–62.

Gurin, P., & Nagda, B. A. (2006). Getting to the what, how, and why of diversity on campus. *Educational Researcher, 35*(1), 20–24.

Helms, J. E. (1990). *Black and white racial identity: Theory, research, and practice*. Westport, CT: Greenwood.

Helms, J. E. (1995). An update of Helm's white and people of color racial identity models. In J. G. Ponterotto, J. M. Casas, L. A. Suzuka, & C. M. Alexander (Eds.), *Handbook of multicultural counseling* (pp. 181–198), Thousand Oaks, CA: Sage.

Henderson-King, D., & Kaleta, A. (2000). Learning about social diversity: The undergraduate experience and intergroup tolerance. *The Journal of Higher Education, 71*(2), 142–164.

Howard, J. A. (2000). Social psychology of identities. *Annual Review of Sociology, 26*(1), 367–393.

Huddy, L. (2001). From social to political identity: A critical examination of social identity theory. *Political Psychology, 22*(1), 127–156.

Hurtado, S. (2005). The next generation of diversity and intergroup relations research. *Journal of Social Issues, 61*(3), 595–610.

Hurtado, S., Milem, J., Clayton-Pedersen, A., & Allen, W. (1998). *Enacting diverse learning environments: Improving the climate for racial/ethnic diversity in higher education.* ASHE-ERIC Higher Education Report, Vol. 26, No. 8. Washington DC: ERIC Clearinghouse on Higher Education.

Hyers, L. L., & Swim, J. K. (1998). A comparison of the experiences of dominant and minority group members during an intergroup encounter. *Group Processes & Intergroup Relations, 1*(2), 143–163.

Hyman, J. (2010). The new multiracial student: Where do we start? *The Vermont Connection, 31*, 128–135.

Jackson, J. L., Jr. (2001). *Harlem world: Doing race and class in contemporary black America.* Chicago, IL: University of Chicago Press.

Johnson, D. R., Soldner, M., Leonard, J. B., Alvarez, P., Kurotsuchi Inkelas, K., Rowen-Kenyon, H., & Longerbeam, S. (2007). Examining sense of belonging among first-year undergraduates from different racial/ethnic groups. *Journal of College Student Development, 48*(5), 525–542.

Kim, H. S., & Markus, H. R. (1993). Speech and silence: An analysis of the cultural practice of talking. In M. Fine & L. Weis (Eds.), *Beyond silenced voices: Class, race, and gender in United States schools* (pp. 181–196). Albany, NY: State University of New York Press.

Kim, J. (2001). Asian American identity development theory. In B. Jackson & C. Wijeyesinghe (Eds.), *New perspectives on racial identity development: A theoretical and practical anthology* (pp. 67–90). New York, NY: New York University Press.

Lewis, A. E., Chesler, M., & Forman, T. A. (2000). The impact of "colorblind" ideologies on students of color: Intergroup relations at a predominantly white university. *The Journal of Negro Education, 69*(1/2), 74–91.

Lopez, G., Gurin, P., & Nagada, R. (1998). Education and understanding structural causes for group inequlities. *Journal of Political Psychology, 62*(3), 553–576.

Massey, D. S., Charles, C. Z., Lundy, G. F., & Fisher, M. J. (2003). *The source of the river: The social origins of freshman at America's selective colleges and universities.* Princeton, NJ: Princeton University Press.

Mayhew, M. J., Grunwald, H. E., & Dey, E. L. (2005). Curriculum matters: Creating a positive climate for diversity from the student perspective. *Research in Higher Education, 46*(4), 389–412.

Miller, J., & Donner, S. (2000). More than just talk: The use of racial dialogues to combat racism. *Social Work with Groups, 23*(1), 31–53.

Nagda, B. A., Gurin, P., Sorensen, N., & Zúñiga, X. (2009). Evaluating intergroup dialogue: Engaging diversity for personal and social responsibility. *Diversity & Democracy, 12*(1), 4–6.

Nagda, R., & Zúñiga, X. (2003). Fostering meaningful racial engagement through intergroup dialogues. *Group Processes and Intergroup Relations, 6*(1), 111–128.

Neville, H. A., Heppner, P. P., Ji, P., & Thye, R. (2004). The relations among general and race-related stressors and psychoeducational adjustment in black students attending predominately white institutions. *Journal of Black Studies, 34*(4), 599–618.

O'Connor, C., Lewis, A., & Mueller, J. (2007). Researching "black" educational experiences and outcomes: Theoretical and methodological considerations. *Educational Researcher, 36*(9), 541–552.

Pettigrew, T. F. (1998). Intergroup contact theory. *Annual Review of Psychology, 49*, 65–85.

Pewewardy, C., & Frey, B. (2002). Surveying the landscape: Perceptions of multicultural support services and racial climate at a predominately white university. *Journal of Negro Education, 71*(1/2), 77–95.

Porter, J. R., & Washington, R. E. (1993). Minority identity and self-esteem. *Annual Review of Sociology, 19*, 139–161.

Renn, K. A. (2003). Understanding the identities of mixed-race college students through a developmental ecology lens. *Journal of College Student Development, 44*(3), 383–403.

Rockquemore, K. A., & Brunsma, D. L. (2001). *Beyond black: Biracial identity in America.* Thousand Oaks, CA: Sage.

Root, M. (1990). Resolving "other" status: Identity development of biracial individuals. *Women & Therapy, 9*(1–2), 185–205.

Root, M. P. P. (1992). *Racially mixed people in America.* Newbury Park, CA: Sage.

Root, M. P. P. (1996). *The multiracial experience: Racial borders as the new frontier.* Thousand Oaks, CA: Sage.

Schoepflin, T. (2006). Let's talk about *The Simpsons* or something: Interracial interaction at a predominantly white university. In R. M. Moore, III (Ed.), *African Americans and Whites: Changing relationships on college campuses* (pp. 129–140). Lanham, MD: University Press of America.

Solórzano, D., Ceja, M., & Yosso, T. (2000). Critical race theory, racial microaggressions, and campus racial climate: The experiences of African American college students. *The Journal of Negro Education, 69*(1/2), 60–73.

Sorensen, N., Nagda, B. A., Gurin, P., & Maxwell, K. E. (2009). Taking a "hands on" approach to diversity in higher education: A critical-dialogic model for effective intergroup interaction. *Analyses of Social Issues and Public Policy, 9*(1), 3–35.

Spickard, P. (1992). The illogic of American racial categories. In M. P. P. Root (Ed.), *Racially mixed people in America* (pp. 12–23). Newbury Park, CA: Sage.

Steele, C. M., & Aronson, J. (1995). Stereotype threat and the intellectual test performance of African Americans. *Journal of Personality and Social Psychology, 69*(5), 797–811.

Suarez-Balcazar, Y., Orellana-Damacela, L., Portillo, N., Rowan, J. M., & Andrews-Guillen, C. (2003). Experiences of differential treatment among college students of color. *The Journal of Higher Education, 74*(4), 428–444.

Tatum, B. D. (2003). *"Why are all the black kids sitting together in the cafeteria?" and other conversations about race.* New York, NY: Basic.

Tropp, L. R., & Pettigrew, T. F. (2005). Relationships between intergroup contact and prejudice among minority and majority status groups. *Psychological Science, 16*(12), 951–957.

Tuan, M. (1998). *Forever foreigner or honorary Whites? The Asian ethnic experience today.* New Brunswick, NJ: Rutgers University Press.

Wallace, K. R. (2001). *Relative/outsider: The art and politics of identity among mixed heritage students.* Westport, CT: Ablex.

Wijeyesinghe, C. L. (2001). Racial identity in multiracial people: An alternative paradigm. In B. Jackson & C. Wijeyesinghe (Eds.), *New perspectives on racial identity development: A theoretical and practical anthology* (pp. 129–152). New York, NY: New York University Press.

Williams, T. K., Nakashima, C. K., Kich, G. K., & Daniel, G. R. (1996). Being different together in the classroom: Multiracial identity as transgressive education. In M. P. P. Root (Ed.), *The multiracial experience: Racial borders as the new frontier* (pp. 359–379). Thousand Oaks, CA: Sage.

Willie, S. S. (2003). *Acting black: College, identity, and the performance of race.* New York, NY: Routledge.

Xie, Y., & Goyette, K. (1998). The racial identification of biracial children with one Asian parent: Evidence from the 1990 census. *Social Forces, 76*(2), 547–570.

Zúñiga, X., Nagda, B. A., Chesler, M., & Cytron, A. (2007). *Intergroup dialogue in higher education: Meaningful learning about social justice.* ASHE Higher Education Report, Vol. 32, No. 4. Hoboken, NJ: Wiley.

From Dialogue to Action: The Impact of Cross-Race Intergroup Dialogue on the Development of White College Students as Racial Allies

Craig John Alimo

University of California, Berkeley

Institutions of postsecondary education are poised to leverage the presence of racial diversity to educate for social change. The purpose of this study was to examine how a race/ethnicity intergroup dialogue facilitates the development of confidence and frequency of white college students' engagement in actions that are congruent with the development of white racial allies. Participants were part of the Multiversity Intergroup Dialogue Research (MIGR) project that included nine college and universities. Using an experimental design with stratified random assignment, MANCOVA analyses were used to determine the differences in outcomes of confidence and frequency of taking actions between experimental dialogue participants and paired waitlist control groups. Covariates included pretest responses, repeated survey measures, and college involvement variables. Multivariate analyses revealed that dialogue participants reported higher levels of confidence and frequency of engagement, whereas univariate analyses revealed higher levels of frequency for engagement of dialogue participants when compared to waitlist control groups.

Diverse learning environments present in institutions of postsecondary education can be used to engage and educate students on social issues and foster development of leadership for social change (Alimo & Komives, 2009). Social justice educational interventions and programmatic efforts like intergroup dialogue in higher education purposefully leverage the educational benefits offered by the presence of diversity to help shape student behaviors to enact this change (Zúñiga, Nagda, Chesler, & Cytron-Walker, 2007).

Intergroup dialogue in higher education includes programs that invite college students from different social identity groups that have a history or potential for conflict to meet face to face (Zúñiga, 1998; Zúñiga, Nagda, & Sevig, 2002; Zúñiga, Nagda, Sevig, Thompson, & Dey, 1995; Zúñiga & Sevig, 1997). The social identity groups invited for dialogues vary, however, the groups in a given dialogue share a role in a given manifestation of social oppression, for example the dialogues that were the focus of this study focused on racism; as such, college students of color and white college students were the focus of these race/ethnicity intergroup dialogues. Students engaged in conversations about issues such as interracial relations, community, diversity, conflict, and societal change. This type of program provides an opportunity to address issues of interracial relations in ways that are more sustained than informal discussions, formal classroom discussions, or one-time programs. Like a traditional class, these intergroup dialogues take place over 6 to 15 weeks with two to three hours of face-to-face contact per week. They are different from traditional courses in that the students are largely the source of the knowledge and are led by trained facilitators who represent the social groups present in the dialogues.

In addition to improving interracial relations, race/ethnicity intergroup dialogues may specifically encourage white students to develop confidence and skills to begin to personally consider and confront their relationship with individualized forms of racism, racism and racist behaviors they may experience with others, and to collaborate with others in advocacy groups that work towards social change. The process of white college students developing confidence to advocate regularly against racism is a quality scholars associate with becoming white allies for racial justice (Reason, Roosa Millar, & Scales, 2005).

Prior research has begun to address the notion of individuals taking action-oriented behaviors (Gurin, Dey, Hurtado, & Gurin, 2002; Nagda, Kim, & Truelove, 2004; Nelson Laird, Engberg, & Hurtado, 2005) and ally development (Broido, 1997, 2000; Zúñiga, Williams, & Berger, 2005). However, there have been few empirical studies that have examined the impact of a social justice educational program, like intergroup dialogue, on the development of white racial ally development for college students (Reason, Roosa Millar et al., 2005).

This study investigated the impact of a race/ethnicity intergroup dialogue on outcomes that are congruent with the development of white racial allies. Specifically, this study examined how racism-themed intergroup dialogue increased white college students' confidence and frequency of taking three types of action: (a) self-directed, (b) other-directed, and (c) intergroup collaborative. Self-directed actions are behaviors that stem from a desire to take steps to address social inequality. These include checking one's biases, avoiding the use of language that reinforces negative stereotyping, making efforts to educate oneself about other groups, and making efforts to get to know people from diverse backgrounds (Bishop, 2002; Helfand & Lippin, 2001; Nagda et al., 2004). Other-directed actions are how individuals address or respond to witnessing social inequalities exhibited by other people. Such actions include challenging derogatory comments and reinforcing others for behaviors that support diversity or racial justice (Nagda, Gurin, & Lopez, 2003; Nagda et al., 2004). Intergroup collaborative actions are behaviors in which individuals engage with their community in some form to work toward the betterment of society. An example of this type of action is joining advocacy groups that address racism.

As colleges and universities create various educational and leadership programs to prepare graduates for active engagement in a diverse democratic society, it is necessary to measure the efficacy of these programs (Alimo & Komives, 2009; Gurin et al., 2002). This study seeks to expand this research by examining the action that students take to address forms of social injustice from a white anti-racist standpoint (Halewood, 1997; Mahoney, 1997). This study also furthers a transformative paradigm by examining the impact of intergroup dialogue on white college students' confidence and frequency of taking action as agents of change (Mertens, 2010; Reason, Scales, & Roosa Millar, 2005). Given that these actions are framed in the context of working toward confronting racism and that the focus population is white college students, the conceptual frameworks for this study include bias reduction and contact theory; whiteness; Critical Whiteness Studies and transformative research; and social justice ally development.

CONCEPTUAL FRAMEWORKS

Bias Reduction and Contact Theory

Dovidio, Gaertner, Stewart, Esses, ten Vergert, and Hodson (2004) developed a framework for evaluating intergroup programs and interventions that maps the integral processes of intergroup relations interventions that work toward the goal of bias reduction. Dovidio et al. based this framework on findings from the 50 years of research on the intergroup contact hypothesis (Allport, 1979; Nagda, 2006; Pettigrew, 1998), which posits that a variety of conditions in intergroup programs are necessary for bias reduction (such as intergroup cooperation in activities, equal status within the group, supportive norms for the group, friendship potential, and communication). Intergroup dialogue programs draw upon this theory to create these conditions in race/ethnicity dialogues. The present study focuses on white college students' standards of behavior, as highlighted by Dovidio et al., as it reveals how white college students make judgments about the kinds of behavior they believe they should do. White college students who enroll in the race/ethnicity intergroup dialogues engage with students of color, learn about themselves, and learn about concepts and theory that may produce changes in racial attitudes and behaviors. Learning about race, racism, and systems of whiteness may provide the necessary information to be able to influence the behavioral choices in the future that contribute to racial justice in society.

Whiteness

The concept of whiteness links to the social construction of race, the particular sets of expectations of what is known as socially normative in society, and the systems of unearned privilege and social power of white people, particularly in a United States historical context (Burchell, 2006). Frankenberg (1993) defined whiteness as an associated set of social dynamics and a "location of structural advantage" (p. 1), where white people actively contrast themselves to other races in society and take steps to keep this advantage in place. Kivel (1996) and Frankenberg (1993) note active and subtle methods that keep systems of whiteness in place by creating a set of unnoticed cultural expectations. These societal norms buttress the construction of a racial hierarchy and white supremacy (Herbert, 2000).

Critical Whiteness Studies and Transformative Research

Mertens (2005) categorizes research that addresses politics and social oppression under the larger rubric of a transformative paradigm. Mahoney (1997) states that "transformative work against segregation and racial oppression must directly confront racism and the social construction of race . . . while seeking points of potential change in the social construction of Whiteness" (p. 654). It is important to generate knowledge about the racial socialization process of white people in the United States as well as how to most effectively eliminate conscious and unconscious racist attitudes and behaviors. Doing so helps inform educators and activists to create programs that may encourage an evolution in the racial identity development of white people from one that is less complex and informed of white supremacy to one that includes a higher awareness of the impact of race and racism in society, as well as one that is associated with positive and anti-racist behaviors (Hardiman, 2001; Helms, 1995; Hitchcock, 2002; McLaren, 1999).

Social Justice Ally Development

Social justice allies are "members of dominant social groups (e.g., men, Whites, heterosexuals) who are working to end the system of oppression that gives them greater privilege and power based upon their social group membership" (Broido, 2000, p. 3). Social justice ally development is the process by which agents evolve into advocates for social justice. A number of studies have explored different aspects of individual college students' engagement in social justice ally behaviors. For example, Broido (1997; 2000) and Broido and Reason (2005) have addressed aspects of confidence as it relates to a broader category of allies for social justice. This research includes the value that college students place on actions that promote social justice (Hurtado, Engberg, Ponjuan, & Landreman, 2002; Nagda et al., 2004; Nelson Laird et al., 2005), an examination of anticipated actions they might take (K. Maxwell, 1997), commitments to address societal institutions to enact change (Gurin et al., 2002; Nagda, Gurin, & Lopez, 2003), and intentions to join organizations or work for social change after college (Gurin, 1999; Gurin, Nagda, & Lopez, 2004; Vasques Scalera, 1999).

WHITE RACIAL ALLY DEVELOPMENT AND INTERGROUP DIALOGUE

White Racial Ally Development

Prior research has identified confidence and frequency of taking ally actions as indicators of social justice allies (Broido, 1997, 2000; Reason, Broido, Davis, & Evans, 2005) and, more specifically, white racial allies (Reason, Roosa Millar et al., 2005). Reason, Scales et al. (2005) associated white students' engagement with whiteness as a function of a white racial identity developmental process. They note three essential developmental tasks: (a) acquiring both an intellectual and affective understanding of racism and privilege; (b) recognizing systems of whiteness; and (c) engaging in action(s). Reason, Roosa Millar et al. (2005) found that the white students' range of their sense of whiteness was an emergent theme in the development of white racial allies. Further, they found that pre-college experiences and college experiences both in coursework and in their co-curricular activities served as influences in the development of white racial allies. These studies cited the importance of engagement with content or whiteness as a contributing factor for white college students to gain information and to begin to understand their socio-political or white privilege. Understanding these concepts helped build confidence to take actions and to engage in them (Reason, Roosa Millar et al., 2005).

Relevant Studies on Intergroup Dialogue

Research studies on intergroup dialogue have addressed behaviors and actions related to social change and ally development (Gurin et al., 2004; Nagda et al., 2003; Nagda et al., 2004;

Sorensen, Nagda, Gurin, & K. Maxwell, 2009). These studies also have documented negative or neutral gains in behavioral outcomes of white college students (Alimo, Kelly, & Clark, 2002; Geranios, 1997), positive behavioral action outcomes (Vasques Scalera, 1999), and higher rates of confidence in one's ability to take action as a result of contact with other college students of color (Nagda & Gurin, 2007; Nagda, Gurin, Sorenson, & Zúñiga, 2009; Nagda et al., 2004; Zúñiga et al., 2002; Zúñiga et al., 2005). Zúñiga et al. (2005) investigated students' motivation to reduce their own prejudices and to promote inclusion and social justice as a result of the impact of the campus climate and their participation in a diversity-focused, living-learning program. Results from multiple regression analysis found that interaction with diverse others, enrollment in diversity-related courses, and attendance at programs associated with a diversity-related residence hall living-learning helped predict both outcomes. Related to the current study, Nagda et al. (2004) investigated students' motivations and confidence in taking actions that reduce their own prejudices (self-directed actions) and that promote diversity (other-related actions) by comparing one lecture-focused section of a diversity course with a another section that included an intergroup dialogue. From multivariate analyses comparing the intergroup dialogue section to the lecture section, an overall impact in a positive direction was found for the dialogue section between pretest and posttest repeated measures. Additionally, from univariate analyses, intergroup dialogue yielded higher rates of confidence in taking other-related actions.

RESEARCH METHODS

Research Questions

This study used multivariate analysis of covariance (MANCOVA) to examine the research question: Does participation in a race/ethnicity intergroup dialogue facilitate the development of confidence and frequency of white college students taking three types of action when compared to a control group, when taking into account prior confidence and frequency of action? Confidence, in this study, is analogous to concepts of self-efficacy (Bandura, 1997). Beliefs of personal efficacy influence one's choice of activities as well as one's motivation to engage in those actions. Further, self-efficacy makes "an important contribution to the acquisition of the knowledge structures on which skills are founded" (Bandura, 1997, p. 35). Frequency refers to an individuals' perception of the relative number of occurrences they engage in various behaviors that are congruent with white racial ally actions (Sorensen et al., 2009). Investigating confidence and frequency of taking action calls to question the impacts of intergroup contact (Allport, 1954) on white college students' beliefs about standards of behavior (Dovidio et al., 2004) such that they are motivated to make choices to engage in anti-racist behaviors or take actions that are indicative of a more complex and anti-racist white identity (Giroux, 1999; Hardiman, 2001; Helms, 1995; Tatum, 1999) and white racial allies (Broido & Reason, 2005; Reason & Davis, 2005; Reason, Roosa Millar et al., 2005; Reason, Scales et al., 2005). As white students engage in developing relationships with students of color and learning about racism, whiteness, and white privilege, white students' confidence in taking actions against racism may increase. As such, two hypotheses emerge from the question so as to investigate confidence and frequency separately.

Hypothesis One

When controlling for prior self-reported rates of self-directed, other-directed, and intergroup collaborative actions, white college students who participated in a race/ethnicity intergroup dialogue will report higher rates of engaging in self-directed, other-directed, and intergroup collaborative actions than a similar control group of white college students who did not participate in the intergroup dialogue.

Hypothesis Two

When controlling for prior self-reported rates of self-directed, other-directed, and intergroup collaborative actions, white college students who participated in a race/ethnicity intergroup dialogue will report higher rates of confidence of taking self-directed, other-directed, and intergroup collaborative actions than a similar control group of white college students who did not participate in the intergroup dialogue.

Design of the Study

Experimental Design with Stratified Random Assignment

The sample for this study was white undergraduate students from nine different colleges and universities in the U.S. who applied to participate in dialogue courses offered through the MIGR Project. All students who expressed a desire to be enrolled in the race/ethnicity dialogue completed an application. As each campus representative received applications they were randomly assigned into one of two groups: an experimental group and a wait-list control group (Nagda, Gurin, Sorensen, & Zúñiga, 2009; Nagda, Sorensen, Gurin-Sands, & Osuna, 2009). The experimental group was comprised of students who were then enrolled in the race/ethnicity dialogues, and the control group consisted of students placed on a waitlist that offered enrollment in a dialogue the following semester. All students who applied to enroll in the dialogues on the campuses presumably had the same level of motivation for being in the dialogues by virtue of filling out an application, thus creating a form of control for student self-selectivity.

Sample: Multi-University Intergroup Dialogue Research Project (MIGR)

The MIGR project was chosen because of its focus on investigating the impacts of intergroup dialogues; The MIGR is a specific program that capitalizes on the presence of racial diversity on college and university campuses as an application of the arguments made by Gurin's research (1999) in defense of the University of Michigan's admissions policies in the *Gratz v. Bollinger* (2003) and *Grutter v. Bollinger* (2003) Supreme Court cases. The MIGR team consisted of representatives and practitioners from eight Carnegie Comprehensive Doctoral Universities and one Postbaccalaureate College (The Carnegie Foundation for the Advancement of Teaching, 2010). The MIGR team agreed to make the elements of the individual intergroup dialogue programs as identical as possible across campuses in order to address threats to external validity. Such agreements included the use of similar publicity and campus communications strategies for the study, a student selection process that included a review of applications, and stratified random assignment procedures. Further MIGR project agreements included a common set of goals for training dialogue facilitators, project curricula, activities, readings, and syllabi in efforts to make the program as similar as possible.

Given the structure of intergroup dialogue, which features two groups that have current or historical conflict, it was necessary for the randomly assigned participants in both conditions to be further stratified into sub-populations (Cochran, 1977). Leaders of the MIGR Project agreed that the optimal size of the experimental and control groups was 16 students with stratified sub-populations of approximately four women of color, four men of color, four white women, and four white men.

Pretest-Postest Design

Students in both the experimental and control groups were administered a pretest (T_1) and posttest (T_2). The pretest was administered prior to the race/ethnicity intergroup dialogue treatment with the experimental group, and the posttest was administered at the end of the semester. The variables of interest for this study, confidence and frequency of engagement in ally behaviors, were assessed on both the pre- and posttests. Responses to these questions on the posttest were the dependent variables, and responses to the same questions on the pretest were the covariates, in order to control for the ally behaviors prior to the treatment. These pretest responses were used to measure students' initial predispositions regarding the dependent measures before the treatment was administered to the experimental group. Figure 1 depicts the design of this study.

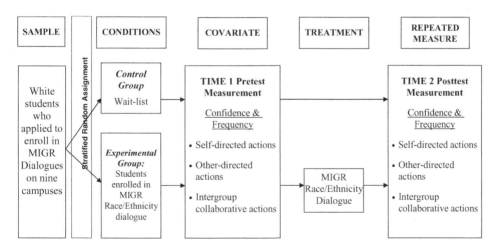

FIGURE 1   Research Design.

Demographics

A portion of the 1,463 students in the entire MIGR encompassed the sample for this study. This portion was composed of only the white students who were enrolled in a race/ethnicity intergroup dialogue or matched control waitlist group ($n = 385$). Of the 385 participants, 20 did not complete a posttest, yielding 365 participants for this study. There were 192 women (experimental group $n = 94$, control $n = 98$) and 173 men (experimental group $n = 85$, control $n = 88$) in the group. The mean age of the students in the study was 20.5 with a median age of 20. There were 65 students in their first year of school (experimental $n = 38$, control $n = 27$); 97 students in their second year (experimental $n = 48$, control $n = 49$); 104 students in their third year (experimental $n = 48$, control $n = 56$); and 88 students in their fourth year (experimental $n = 46$, control $n = 42$). Students in the study come from families that are well educated: 67.1% have a mother and 76.2% have a father with a baccalaureate degree or higher and grew up in mostly, nearly, or all-white neighborhoods. There were no statistical differences in the proportion of the demographics between the experimental and control groups with the exception of two categories: prior enrollment in race or ethnic studies courses and participation in internships. Because of this possible threat to internal validity (specifically selection bias), these differences were addressed in the analyses. Additional demographics are available in Table 1.

TABLE 1
Sample Demographics, Academic Majors and Courses, and Campus Involvements

	Condition		
	Control	Dialogue	Total
Demographics			
Women	94	98	192
Men	85	88	173
First-Year Students	27	38	65
Second-Year Students	49	48	97
Third-Year Students	56	48	104
Fourth-Year Students	42	46	88
Academic Majors			
Social Sciences	70	80	150
Math, Science, Engineering, or Architecture	25	22	47
Arts or Humanities	38	42	80
Business	24	33	57
Nursing, Social Work, Education, or Public Health	16	7	23
Classes			
Prior enrollment in race or ethnic studies department/program courses*	81	62	143
Enrollment in a course in other departments that addressed topics of race/ethnicity	99	94	193
Campus Involvements			
Participation in internships*	175	184	359
Participation in intergroup dialogue	13	21	34

Note: *$p \leq .05$ between control and dialogue groups at pretest.

Procedures

Pretest

Data were collected from the Fall term of 2005 through the Winter term of 2007. At the beginning of each semester, representatives from each of the nine institutions distributed a paper version of the "Group Attitudes and Experience on Campus—Survey I" to the experimental groups at the first meeting of each of the race/ethnicity dialogues. Control groups were given the same survey in a similar time period in a different location. All students were informed of their right to exit the study at any time and signed informed consent waivers. All student participants in the control groups received $15 for completing the pretest and were notified during this administration that they would receive $20 for completing the posttest.

Treatment

The race/ethnicity intergroup dialogue on each of the nine participating campuses in this study served as the treatment for the experimental group. The treatment was offered each semester for two years (Fall 2005–Spring 2007) and featured approximately 24 contact hours as a credit-bearing course. The treatment consisted of shared reading assignments (with the exception of one week for purposes of customization and relevance for each campus), classroom exercises, classroom discussion processes, and other assignments. There was variance in who delivered the treatment on each of the nine campuses, but all facilitators were subject to a common training. Undergraduate students, graduate students, faculty, and professional staff served as facilitators.

Posttest

Students in the dialogues as well as the wait-list control groups completed the "Group Attitudes and Experience on Campus—Survey II" posttest immediately after the intergroup dialogue, which was just prior to the commencement of final exams on all of the campuses. Students from the control group were administered the same posttest during the same day (or week) as the experimental group in a different room on campus. Campuses followed the same procedures for administration of the posttest to both experimental and waitlist control groups. In order to attract and remind wait-list control group members to be in attendance during the administration of the posttest, control group members were emailed and telephoned by their host institution. All student participants in the study received $20 for completing the posttest.

Survey Measures

The Group Attitudes and Experiences on Campus Surveys I & II represent a combination of measures that have been used in education, psychology, and sociology, some of which were adapted for the MIGR project (Multi-University Intergroup Dialogue Research Project, 2008). The original items were developed by Nagda et al. (2004). Construct validity of the scales was assessed using factor analysis and analyses of internal consistency. Using principal component analysis with orthogonal (varimax) rotation, Nagda et al. (2004) produced a two component solution conforming to the Kaiser rule of retaining factors with eigenvalues larger than 1 (Meyers, Gamst, & Guarino, 2006; Tacq, 1997). All of the measures were pretested and analyzed for psychometric properties (in 2004) and during the dialogue experiments for pretest and posttest data (Multi-University Intergroup Dialogue Research Project, 2008). After pretest and posttest in the current study, the items were subject to another principal components analysis with varimax rotation and Cronbach alpha tests of internal consistency. Internal consistency values ranged from $\alpha = .681$ to $\alpha = .890$. Survey I contains 215 questions and Survey II contains 213 questions encompassing 44 measures. The variables from the surveys that have been selected for this study are the questions that measure the constructs of confidence and frequency of taking self-directed, other-directed, and intergroup collaborative action.

Reliability

The constructs representing the dependent variables for this study feature the use of scales rather than single items. The scales were first used in Nagda et al.'s (2004) study (Table 2). These items were developed to measure an individual's confidence in engaging in a variety of actions as

TABLE 2
Reliability of Dependent Variable Clusters

Variable Clusters and Items	Confidence			Frequency		
	Pilot α	$T_1 \alpha$	$T_2 \alpha$	Pilot α	$T_1 \alpha$	$T_2 \alpha$
Self-Directed Actions	.807	.713	.755	.762	.704	.755
Recognize and challenge the biases that may affect my own thinking						
Avoid using language that reinforces negative stereotypes						
Make efforts to educate myself about other groups						
Make efforts to get to know people from diverse backgrounds						
Other-Directed Actions	.794	.692	.707	.842	.681	.700
Challenge others on derogatory comments						
Reinforce others for behaviors that support cultural diversity						
Intergroup Collaborative Actions	.825	.880	.890	.766	.861	.887
Join a community group/organization that promotes diversity						
Get together with others to challenge discrimination						
Participate in a coalition of different groups to address some social issues						

Note. Pilot = 2005 Pilot administration of the instrument; T1 = pretest; T2 = posttest.

well as the frequency at which he or she has done so. The items for the confidence and frequency of taking action scale that Nagda et al. (2004) developed is based on an integration of Dovidio et al.'s (2004) main concerns in the reduction of bias and Gurin et al.'s (2002) behavioral-based, democratic outcomes. Although these measures do not directly measure constructs of white racial ally development, measures of confidence and frequency of taking actions do align with prior theory development and research documenting the development of social justice allies (Broido, 1997, 2000; Broido & Reason, 2005; Reason & Broido, 2005) as well as white racial allies (Reason, Roosa Millar et al., 2005; Reason, Scales et al., 2005) with eigenvalues larger than 1 (Meyers, Gamst, & Guarino, 2006; Tacq, 1997).

The six composite scales that comprise the questions regarding confidence and frequency of self-focused actions, other-focused actions, and intergroup collaborative actions in this study are individual items that use a seven point Likert interval scale: 1 = Not at all; 2 = Not very much; 3 = A little; 4 = Somewhat; 5 = Quite a bit; 6 = A fair amount; and 7 = Very much. Responses to these items on the pretest are used as the covariates for the study. Responses to these items on the posttest represent the dependent variables. The independent variable in this study was condition (experimental group or control group) resulting from random assignment.

RESULTS

An attrition analysis was performed. Of the original students in the MIGR data, 20 students did not complete a posttest, representing a 95% retention rate in the study (Barry, 2005). Preliminary descriptive analyses (i.e., chi-square distributions and t-tests) were conducted to inspect for similarity between experimental and control groups. Chi-square distribution and t-test analyses indicated statistically significant differences ($p \leq .05$) between the experimental and control group on some demographic variables, which are noted in Table 1 with an asterisk. The control group reported statistically significant higher mean scores on courses taken in Race/Ethnic studies programs or departments and participation in internships since coming to college. The initial application process asked students to respond to their prior involvement in intergroup dialogues. All students who had identified prior involvement in intergroup dialogues (in their applications) were eliminated from the pool of students to be randomly assigned to a treatment group. Despite this process, there still were students who responded on the pretest as having participated in an intergroup dialogue. Perhaps the question assessing prior involvement was not worded clearly and student participants assumed that their involvement in the MIGR study was understood as prior involvement. Further cross-tabulation analysis revealed that 21 students in the experimental group (11.5% of the 365 participants in the data set for this study) and 13 in the control group (7.5%) reported prior involvement. This was a problem because the presence of students who had experienced an intergroup dialogue prior to their participation in this study would present a confounding variable that could provide an alternative explanation to the impact of the dialogues on white racial ally development. Because of this, two strategies were employed: an adjustment to the critical value of the analyses and the use of multiple MANCOVA analyses with variance in the participants.

Because of the potential for individuals in each nested dialogue group on each campus to influence the responses of one another on the administration of the posttest, it was necessary to ensure independence in responses and to control possible inflated Type I error by applying

TABLE 3
Dependent Variable Correlations

		T_2 Confidence Self	T_2 Confidence Other	T_2 Confidence Intergroup	T_2 Frequency Self	T_2 Frequency Other	T_2 Frequency Intergroup
T_2	r	1					
Confidence	p						
Self	N	340					
T_2	r	.747	1				
Confidence	p	<.001					
Other	N	333	338				
T_2	r	.636	.614	1			
Confidence	p	<.001	<.001				
Intergroup	N	335	333	340			
T_2	r	.609	.472	.371	1		
Frequency	p	<.001	<.001	<.001			
Self	N	336	332	333	338		
T_2	r	.501	.657	.433	.701	1	
Frequency	p	<.001	<.001	<.001	<.001		
Other	N	334	334	334	332	338	
T_2	r	.301	.345	.566	.435	.513	1
Frequency	p	<.001	<.001	<.001	<.001	<.001	
Intergroup	N	333	332	333	332	332	338

Note: T_2 = posttest; r = Pearson correlation; p-value is two-tailed.

a Bonferroni adjustment to the critical value of the analyses (S. Maxwell & Delaney, 1999; Weinfurt, 1995). Although a more conservative approach than other adjustment schemes (such as Holm), S. Maxwell and Delaney (1999) as well as Tabachnick and Fidell (2007) suggest calculating the Bonferroni adjustment by dividing an assigned error rate, such as the traditional $p \le .05$, by the number of tests to be performed. In the case of this study, there were nine tests. Therefore, $p \le .05/9 = .0055$.

Multiple analysis of covariance (MANCOVA) was conducted to answer the research questions. MANCOVA procedures account for conceptual overlap or redundancies of the multiple measures and reduce the risk of increasing Type I error (Meyers et al., 2006; Tabachnick & Fidell, 2007; Weinfurt, 1995). Because of these differences in the experimental and control groups noted above, MANCOVA procedures were performed three times (Analyses A, B, & C) to test the sum of the differences in how the sample is contributing to differences in the dependent variables.

Correlations

An analysis of the dependent variables indicated that they were all significantly correlated at $p \le .05$, ranging from $r = .217$ to .747 (Table 3). These results were consistent with analyses performed by Zúñiga et al. (2005) on the same dependent variables. Mahalanobis distance was calculated for detection of the presence of outliers ($\chi^2 = 33.97$, $df = 6$, $p < .001$). The critical value distance was greater than the critical value ($\chi^2 \leq 22.46$); therefore, ten outliers were removed from the overall sample, reducing the number of cases for analysis from 365 to 355 (experimental group: $n = 181$; control group: $n = 174$). Recalculated distances were within acceptable parameters ($\chi^2 = 18.29$, $df = 6$, $p < .001$) as were tests for linearity. Tests for homogeneity of regression slopes revealed that all covariates were significant at $p = .05$ or greater. Box's M tests were performed with all three MANCOVA analyses, and yielded significance values larger than .001, indicating the variance-covariance matrixes were within acceptable parameters (Pallant, 2007) with the exception of Analysis A.

MANCOVA Analysis A—Initial Design

MANCOVA was performed in keeping with Figure 1. This analysis included comparing the control and experimental group responses on the dependent variables (confidence and frequency of self-directed, other-directed, and intergroup collaborative actions), in which the responses from the pretest on the same items are used as a covariate. Levene's tests for each of the dependent variables indicated scores above .05, except for one dependent variable: T_2 frequency of intergroup collaborative action ($p = .020$). Due to this one violation, Tabachnick and Fidell (2007) suggest altering the significance level for the analysis to a more stringent level. However, the significance level was adjusted prior to the analyses (to $p < .0055$), rendering the recommendation moot. MANCOVA analysis indicated statistically significant differences between the dialogue and control groups on the combined dependent variables, $F(6, 271) = 5.600$, $p = .000$; Wilks' $\lambda = .890$; $\eta^2 = .110$. Univariate analyses are recommended if multivariate differences are found (Pallant, 2007; Tabachnick & Fidell, 2007) to further investigate which dependent variables may be contributing group differences. Differences in individual dependent variables may reveal implications for theory or further research. Univariate analyses revealed statistically significant group differences between the experimental and control groups: T_2 frequency of self-directed actions, $F(1, 276) = 26.833$, $p < .001$, $\eta^2 = .089$; T_2 frequency of other-directed actions, $F(1, 276) = 12.018$, $p = .001$, $\eta^2 = .042$; and T_2 frequency of intergroup collaborative actions, $F(1, 276) = 15.259$, $p < .001$, $\eta^2 = .052$ (Table 4). However, effect sizes (identified by eta squared or η^2) of between .01 and .090 are considered to be small or marginal (Pallant, 2007; Tabachnick & Fidell, 2007). Mean scores revealed dialogue participants reported slightly higher levels of frequency of taking actions at the posttest than the control group on all three levels: individually-directed ($M = 22.341$, $SD = 4.291$) compared to the control ($M = 19.984$, $SD = 4.775$), other-directed ($M = 9.595$, $SD = 2.682$) compared to the control group ($M = 8.617$, $SD = 2.916$), and intergroup collaborative ($M = 10.620$, $SD = 5.203$) compared to the control group ($M = 8.678$, $SD = 4.833$) (see Table 4). The variance accounted for by the covariates is noted in Table 5.

MANCOVA Analysis B—Additional Covariates

Analysis B was similar to analysis A, with the addition of two covariates. The analysis: Prior courses taken in Race/Ethnic studies programs or departments and prior participation in internships since coming to college account for the differences in the experimental and control group

TABLE 4

Multivariate and Univariate Analysis of Covariance of Confidence and Frequency of Self-Directed, Other-Directed, and Intergroup Collaborative Actions as a function of Confidence and Frequency of Self-Directed, Other-Directed, and Intergroup Collaborative Actions as Covariates

	Multivariate	η^2	Univariate										
			T_2 Confidence						T_2 Frequency				
			Self-Directed Actions	η^2	Other-Directed Actions	η^2	Intrgrp Collab. Actions	η^2	Self-Directed Actions	η^2	Other-Directed Actions	η^2	Intrgrp Collab. Actions	η^2
						Analysis A								
Source Condition	$F_{(6, 271)}$ 5.600**	.110	$F_{(1, 276)}$ 7.053	.025	$F_{(1, 276)}$ 3.671	.013	$F_{(1, 276)}$ 3.290	.012	$F_{(1, 276)}$ 26.83**	.089	$F_{(1, 276)}$ 12.018**	.042	$F_{(1, 276)}$ 15.259**	.052
						Analysis B								
Source Condition	$F_{(6, 259)}$ 5.643**	.116	$F_{(1, 264)}$ 6.439	.024	$F_{(1, 264)}$ 4.223	.016	$F_{(1, 264)}$ 1.647	.006	$F_{(1, 264)}$ 26.019**	.090	$F_{(1, 264)}$ 13.193**	.048	$F_{(1, 264)}$ 14.822**	.053
						Analysis C								
Source Condition	$F_{(6, 235)}$ 5.824**	.129	$F_{(1, 240)}$ 7.390	.030	$F_{(1, 240)}$ 3.554	.015	$F_{(1, 240)}$ 1.093	.005	$F_{(1, 240)}$ 26.185**	.098	$F_{(1, 240)}$ 8.296**	.033	$F_{(1, 240)}$ 13.124**	.052

Note. T_2 = posttest; F ratios generated from Wilks' λ statistic; Analyses B & C include additional covariates of enrollment in race/ethnic studies courses and internship experiences during college; Analysis C includes cases removed that indicated prior involvement in intergroup dialogue.

**$p > .0055$.

TABLE 5

Estimated Marginal Mean Scores and Standard Errors as a Function of Treatment Condition

	T₂ Confidence						T₂ Frequency					
	Self-Directed Actions		Other-Directed Actions		Intergroup Collab. Actions		Self-Directed Actions		Other-Directed Actions		Intergroup Collab. Actions	
	M	SE	M	SE	M	SE	M	SE	M	SE	M	SE
Analysis A												
Control	21.933	.260	10.272	.168	13.948	.324	19.984	.323	8.617	.200	8.678	.353
Dialogue	22.906	.251	10.726	.162	14.776	.313	22.341	.311	9.595	.193	10.620	.340
Analysis B												
Control	22.009	.266	10.266	.174	14.028	.335	19.917	.335	8.564	.206	8.673	.360
Dialogue	22.978	.260	10.781	.170	14.645	.327	22.372	.327	9.639	.201	10.663	.351
Analysis C												
Control	22.00	.271	10.319	.179	14.047	.349	19.800	.347	8.597	.215	8.564	.361
Dialogue	23.072	.271	10.809	.179	14.577	.349	22.384	.347	9.499	.215	10.468	.361

Note. T₂ = posttest.

differences noted above. There was a statistically significant difference between the experimental and control groups on the combined dependent variables, $F(6, 259) = 5.64$, $p = .000$; Wilks' $\lambda = .884$; $\eta^2 = .116$. Univariate results revealed statistically significant differences between the experimental and control groups on frequency measures: T_2 frequency of self-directed actions, $F(1, 264) = 26.019$, $p < .001$, $\eta^2 = .090$; T_2 frequency of other-directed actions, $F(1, 264) = 13.193$, $p < .001$, $\eta^2 = .048$; and T_2 frequency of intergroup collaborative actions, $F(1, 264) = 14.822$, $p < .001$, $\eta^2 = .053$ (Table 4). The effect sizes of the univariate analyses, like in analysis A, are considered marginal (Pallant, 2007; Tabachnick & Fidell, 2007). Mean scores indicated that dialogue participants reported slightly higher levels of frequency of taking actions on the posttest than the control group on all three levels: individually-directed ($M = 22.372$, $SD = 4.324$) compared to the control ($M = 19.917$, $SD = 4.774$), other-directed ($M = 9.639$, $SD = 2.655$) compared to the control group ($M = 8.564$, $SD = 2.910$), and intergroup collaborative ($M = 10.663$, $SD = 5.173$) compared to the control group ($M = 8.673$, $SD = 4.763$) (Table 4). The variance accounted for by the covariates is noted in Table 5.

MANCOVA Analysis C—Cases Removed

Analysis C was similar to Analysis B (additional covariates to account for group differences between pretest differences on courses in Race/Ethnic studies and participation in internships), except the participants who identified prior participation in an intergroup dialogue (experimental $n = 21$, control $n = 13$) were removed from the sample, leaving 321 cases in the dataset (experimental $n = 161$, control group $n = 160$). Multivariate analyses revealed a statistically significant difference between the dialogue and control groups on the combined dependent variables, $F(6, 235) = 5.824$, $p < .001$; Wilks' $\lambda = .884$; $\eta^2 = .129$. Univariate results revealed statistically significant group differences on the frequency measures: T_2 frequency of self-directed actions, $F(1, 240) = 26.185$, $p < .001$, $\eta^2 = .098$; T_2 frequency of other-directed actions, $F(1, 240) = 8.296$, $p = .004$, $\eta^2 = .033$; and T_2 frequency of intergroup collaborative actions, $F(1, 240) = 13.124$, $p < .001$, $\eta^2 = .052$ (Table 4). The effect sizes of the univariate analyses for frequency of other-directed and frequency of intergroup collaborative actions are considered marginal. Involvement in the dialogues has a medium effect on the frequency of self-directed actions measure (Pallant, 2007; Tabachnick & Fidell, 2007). Mean scores indicated that dialogue participants reported slightly higher levels of frequency of taking actions on the posttest than the control group on all three levels: individually-directed ($M = 22.384$, $SD = 4.284$) compared to the control ($M = 19.800$, $SD = 4.757$), other-directed ($M = 9.499$, $SD = 2.687$) compared to the control group ($M = 8.597$, $SD = 2.917$), and intergroup collaborative ($M = 10.468$, $SD = 4.995$) compared to the control group ($M = 8.564$, $SD = 4.749$). The variance accounted for by the covariates is noted in Table 5.

Hypothesis One

All three of the MANCOVA analyses (i.e., Analyses A, B, and C) confirmed differences between the experimental and control groups with small effect sizes.

Hypothesis Two

It was hypothesized that white college students who participated in the MIGR race/ethnicity intergroup dialogue would report higher rates of confidence of engagement in the three types of actions than the control group. As with the first hypothesis statement, all three of the MANCOVA analyses consistently support this hypothesis. The results were consistent for all three analyses. However, when observing the univariate differences for confidence, all three of the group differences were not statistically significantly different.

DISCUSSION

This study was framed in the context of a transformative research paradigm that Mertens (2005) describes as research that addresses social oppression and those affected by it. Investigating the impact of the race/ethnicity intergroup dialogue on white college students is one of many studies that seeks to work to eliminate racism vis-à-vis developing agents of change in a population that is traditionally know as agents of racism (Hardiman & Jackson, 1992, 1994). Should research that addresses racism via white people also be considered a part of an emerging transformative paradigm? Currently, the philosophical position of research that examines the role of white people in addressing racial oppression lies in a paradigmatic intersection between critical race theory, critical inquiry/theory, and the emerging field of critical whiteness studies. Lincoln and Guba (2000) note that paradigmatic categories "are fluid, indeed what should be a category keeps altering [and] enlarging. Even as [we] write, the boundaries between the paradigms are shifting" (p. 167). This study aligns with other literature in that the standpoint of white people is one standpoint that is necessary to address racism and might be considered an additional criterion in Mertens' categorization of a transformative research paradigm.

This study builds upon prior research on intergroup contact (Allport, 1954; Nagda, 2006; Pettigrew, 1998) and how engagement in race/ethnicity intergroup dialogue shapes the choices and behaviors of white college students (Dovidio et al., 2004). Like the Nagda et al. (2004) study, dialogue participants more frequently engaged in ally behaviors indicative of the development of white racial allies. The study also applied theory developed by prior studies on the development of social justice ally and white racial ally developmental to ground the investigation (Broido, 1997, 2000; Reason, Roosa Millar et al., 2005; Reason, Scales et al., 2005). Heretofore, research addressing the topic has been limited to qualitative studies with smaller sample sizes. This study begins to address issues of generalizability by drawing from a larger population from nine different college and university campuses.

Hypothesis One: Frequency in Taking Action

The first hypothesis was accepted; intergroup dialogue did have an impact on frequency of engaging in behaviors that align with white racial ally development, albeit that the effect sizes for all three analyses were small. A practical question may lie in how a university administrator may value an experimental study using random assignment versus much smaller completed qualitative studies on the same topic when making policy decisions. As the sample size of a study increases, researchers can achieve greater statistical power but can also find limited effect sizes (Meyers et al., 2006; Pascarella & Terenzini, 2005). Pascarella and Terenzini note that "even in the studies with the best research designs and strongest statistical controls for important individual student characteristics ... effects tend to be quite small and inconsistent" (p. 634).

The small effect sizes of frequency of taking actions (with the range of partial $\eta^2 = .033-.098$, see Table 4) may be due to a hidden similarity of the control and experimental groups, such as levels of student motivation or to an unanticipated overrepresentation of students in social science majors throughout the applicant pool. Milem and Umbach (2003) found that students "in social and artistic majors are more likely than other majors to report that they plan to engage in activities that break the cycle of segregation in our society" (p. 623). The dynamic described in Milem and Umback may also be present in the current study since participants self-selected to be in it. Over 64% of the students in the sample that reported their major at pretest were either majoring in the social sciences ($n = 150$, 42.0%) or arts or humanities ($n = 80$, 22.4%). STEM (Science, Technology, Engineering and Math) majors accounted for only 13.1% ($n = 47$). If the students in the study had different motivations to enroll in the race/ethnicity intergroup dialogue as opposed to the current study where all the participants assumedly had the same desire to enroll in the dialogues, there may have been greater variance in their responses.

By measuring the effects of the race/ethnicity intergroup dialogue on equivalent groups and addressing confounding variables, this study furthers research on the concept of white racial ally development and reinforces studies that address the importance of providing such programs to develop leaders for a diverse democracy (Alimo, 2010; Alimo & Komives, 2009; Gurin et al., 2002; Hurtado, 2005; Hurtado, Milem, Clayton-Pedersen, & Allen, 1998; Zúñiga et al., 2005). Few studies make causal claims for the impact of social justice educational programs like intergroup dialogue does (Nagda, Gurin, Sorensen, & Zúñiga, 2009; Sorensen et al., 2009).

Hypothesis Two: Confidence in Taking Action

The rejection of the second hypothesis was somewhat surprising given prior research that indicates increases in confidence as a result of participation in similar intergroup dialogues (Nagda et al., 2004; Nagda, Gurin, Sorensen, & Zúñiga, 2009; Sorensen et al., 2009; Zúñiga et al., 2005). Confidence was found to be a critical element of Broido's (1997, 2000) phenomenological account of the development of the more generalized category of social justice allies in college. These contrasting findings may be attributable to the previous studies' use of different research designs and to researchers not restricting their analyses to only white students. Previous studies did not compare conditions, such as participation in an intergroup dialogue to a control group.

This raises an interesting question regarding a possible temporal sequencing of how frequency of action may precede confidence. Nagda et al. (2004) found that confidence mediated frequency in students engaging in actions as a result of enrollment in a class with an intergroup dialogue component. Additionally, developing confidence has been linked to the development of white ally development in both research and theoretical literature (Kivel, 2002; Reason, Roosa Millar et al., 2005; Reason, Scales et al., 2005; Vasques Scalera, 1999). Kivel notes that one must have courage and confidence to be able to engage in actions that work toward ending racism. Similarly, Reason, Scales et al. (2005) suggest that an understanding of whiteness builds confidence to take actions.

These findings and suggestions may be in contrast to research on motivation. Bandura (1982), for instance, suggests that the acquisition of new information may actually decrease confidence. One might surmise that if white students are not aware of the impacts of race and racism prior to their experiences in the race/ethnicity intergroup dialogue, they may be steeped in white privilege. Although these white students may aspire to work against racism by virtue of enrollment in the dialogue (Edwards, 2006), they may be largely unaware of the complexity of whiteness surrounding them (K. Maxwell, 2004). If white students are learning new information and addressing issues of whiteness, it may be understandable that the dialogue would increase awareness but lower levels of confidence. An implication for student development or social justice educators may be to alter expectations of educational outcomes of these types of programs for white college students from increased to decreased levels of confidence, if there is an expectation of increased self-awareness. Similarly, such expectations might need to shift for other types of ally development or education that is focused on dominant identities (Miller, 1994; Reason, Broido et al., 2005) to comingle expectations of increased self-awareness with decreased confidence in taking actions. An additional implication for educators would be to include education units to increase confidence in the design of such interventions but to do so in a particular temporal sequence. Social justice educators may need to consider adding such elements into the facilitative environment of continuity as described by Bell and Griffin (1997).

This issue of temporal sequencing where action precedes confidence may also align with the work of Reason, Roosa Millar et al. (2005), which suggests that taking actions builds confidence. If aspiring white racial allies are engaging in various forms of taking actions, perhaps some at lower risk levels (such as focusing on self-related actions or other-related actions with friends) they are building confidence to engage in intergroup collaborative actions (Edwards, 2006). A third administration of the survey might reveal a statistically significant difference on the dependent variables when comparing responses on the pretest to a post-posttest. Such a study may confirm a temporal sequencing as to when confidence develops, unlike the sequencing suggested by theorists like Kivel (2002) and research like Broido's (1997, 2000).

LIMITATIONS

There were limitations to this study. First, despite employing stratified random assignment sampling techniques, there were statistical differences between the control and dialogue groups on some characteristics, as well as between students who reported being in an intergroup dialogue prior to the experiment. Second, there was variability in who facilitated the dialogues. Despite the use of "facilitator fidelity forms" that were employed to avert egregious differences in the delivery of the treatment to the experimental groups throughout the project, it is impossible for each person on each campus to administer the same exact treatment moment-to-moment, week-to-week. This is particularly true when considering that each dialogue group had its own dynamic fueled by different individuals on different campuses. These limitations illustrate the challenges of working with nested data. Computer programs and statistical modeling that allow researchers to engage in hierarchical linear modeling may be better suited for such analyses (Shadish & Cook, 2009). Despite this limitation, there were differences between the experimental and wait-list control groups at the posttest, suggesting that these limits may have been managed by the research design and analyses. On the other hand, inquiries into the development of white racial allies incorporate notions of the social construction of identity, emotions, hope, development, and change among other concepts that are difficult to quantify. Earlier research in this area has evolved from qualitative methodological approaches, and theory capturing the concept of white racial ally development may need further development. Finally, the notion of taking anti-racist actions may be fueled by social desirability (Crowne & Marlowe, 1960). Although some research on social justice education suggests that social desirability may not be a factor in anti-racist attitudes (Hogan & Mallott, 2005), more complex studies have indicated the lack of the influence of social desirability on dependent measures could be attributable to covert or unknown racial bias (Cobb, 2002; Paquette, 2006).

Finally, the scales used for the dependent variables in this study indicate a good degree of internal consistency with values ranging from $\alpha = .698$ to $\alpha = .905$ (Table 2), yet there were still low effect sizes. This may indicate adequate internal consistency, but poor construct validity. Perhaps these survey items are not ideal for measuring white racial ally development. The current study attempts to build upon the work of previous, inductive studies and is an initial attempt at measuring a larger sample. Further study may be necessary to better measure white racial ally development.

CONCLUSION

Intergroup dialogue in higher education has been recognized by a number of professional organizations as an innovative practice (American Association for Higher Education, National Association for Student Personnel Administrators, & American College Personnel Association, 1998; Hurtado, Milem, Clayton-Pedersen, & Allen, 1999; Tatum, 1992). As researchers call for the creation of interventions to take advantage of the presence of diversity on campus (Gurin et al., 2002; Hurtado, 2005; Pascarella & Terenzini, 2005), the current study shows how intergroup dialogue may contribute to the development of behaviors congruent with white racial ally development.

Interventions like the MIGR race/ethnicity intergroup dialogues can be the types of programs that can begin to help build a citizenry of white people who take action "so that white youth can understand the struggle against the long legacy of white racism while using . . . their own culture as a source for resistance, reflection and empowerment" (Giroux, 1999, p. 250). If institutions of postsecondary education espouse interest in developing citizens and leaders for social change, implementing programs like intergroup dialogue in higher education may encourage increases in democratic outcomes, specifically in developing white racial allies—students who engage in self-directed, other-directed, and intergroup collaborative actions.

REFERENCES

Alimo, C. J. (2010). *From dialogue to action: The development of white racial allies*. Doctoral dissertation, University of Maryland, College Park, MD.

Alimo, C., Kelly, R. D., & Clark; C. (2002). Intergroup dialogue program student outcomes and implications for campus racial climate: A case study. *Multicultural Education, 10,* 49–53.

Alimo, C., & Komives, S. R. (2009). Leveraging diversity with dialogue for leadership: Research and scholarship updates. *Concepts & Connections, 16*(1), 7–10.

Allport, G. W. (1954). *The nature of prejudice.* Cambridge, MA: Addison-Wesley.

Allport, G. W. (1979). *The nature of prejudice* (Unabridged, 25th anniversary ed.). Reading, MA: Addison-Wesley.

American Association for Higher Education, National Association for Student Personnel Administrators, & American College Personnel Association. (1998). *Powerful partnerships: A shared responsibility for learning.* Retrieved from http://www.aahe.org/teaching/tsk_frce.htm

Bandura, A. (1982). Self-efficacy mechanism in human agency. *American Psychologist, 37*(2), 122–147.

Bandura, A. (1997). *Self-efficacy: The exercise of control.* New York, NY: Freeman.

Barry, A. E. (2005). How attrition impacts the internal and external validity of longitudinal research. *Journal of School Health, 75*(7), 267–270.

Bell, L. A., & Griffin, P. (1997). Designing social justice education courses. In M. Adams, L. A. Bell, & P. Griffin (Eds.), *Teaching for diversity and social justice: A sourcebook* (pp. 44–58). New York, NY: Routledge.

Bishop, A. (2002). *Becoming an ally: Breaking the cycle of oppression in people* (2nd ed.). New York, NY: Zed Books.

Broido, E. M. (1997). *The development of social justice allies during college: A phenomenological investigation.* Doctoral dissertation, The Pennsylvania State University, University Park, PA.

Broido, E. M. (2000). The development of social justice allies during college: A phenomenological investigation. *Journal of College Student Development, 41*(1), 3–18.

Broido, E. M., & Reason, R. D. (2005). The development of social justice attitudes and actions: An overview of current understandings. In R. D. Reason, E. M. Broido, T. L. Davis, & N. J. Evans (Eds.), *Developing social justice allies* (pp. 17–28). San Francisco, CA: Jossey-Bass.

Burchell, M. J. (2006). *The construction of whiteness by white anti-racism educators.* Doctoral dissertation, University of Massachusetts, Amherst, MA.

The Carnegie Foundation for the Advancement of Teaching. (2010). *The Carnegie Classifications of Institutions of Higher Education.* Retrieved from http://classifications.carnegiefoundation.org

Cobb, M. D. (2002). *Unobtrusively measuring racial attitudes: The consequences of social desirability effects.* Doctoral dissertation, University of Illinois, Urbana-Champaign, IL.

Cochran, W. G. (1977). *Sampling techniques* (3d ed.). New York, NY: Wiley.

Crowne, D. P., & Marlowe, D. (1960). A new scale of social desirability independent of psychopathology. *Journal of Consulting Psychology, 24*(4), 349–354.

Dovidio, J. F., Gaertner, S. L., Stewart, T. L., Esses, V. M., ten Vergert, M., & Hodson, G. (2004). From intervention to outcome: Processes in the reduction of bias. In W. G. Stephan & W. P. Vogt (Eds.), *Education programs for improving intergroup relations: Theory, research, and practice* (pp. 243–265). New York, NY: Teachers College Press.

Edwards, K. E. (2006). Aspiring social justice ally identity development: A conceptual model. *NASPA Journal, 43*(4), 39–60.

Frankenberg, R. (1993). *White women, race matters: The social construction of whiteness.* Minneapolis, MN: University of Minnesota Press.

Geranios, C. A. (1997). *Cognitive, affective, and behavioral outcomes of multicultural courses and intergroup dialogues in higher education.* Doctoral dissertation. Arizona State University, Tempe, AZ.

Giroux, H. A. (1999). Rewriting the discourse of racial identity: Toward a pedagogy and politics of whiteness. In C. Clark & J. O'Donnell (Eds.), *Becoming and unbecoming white: Owning and disowning a racial identity* (pp. 224–252). Westport, CT: Bergin & Garvey.

Gratz v. Bollinger, 539 U.S. 306 (2003).

Grutter v. Bollinger, 539 U.S. 306 (2003).

Gurin, P. (1999). Expert report of Patricia Gurin: The compelling need for diversity in higher education. Retrieved from http://www.umich.edu/~urel/admissions/legal/expert/gurintoc.html

Gurin, P., Dey, E. L., Hurtado, S., & Gurin, G. (2002). Diversity and higher education: Theory and impact on educational outcomes. *Harvard Educational Review, 72*(3), 330–366.

Gurin, P., Nagda, B. A., & Lopez, G. E. (2004). The benefits of diversity in education for democratic citizenship. *Journal of Social Issues, 60*(1), 17–34.

Halewood, P. (1997). White men can jump: But must try a little harder. In R. Delgado & J. Stefancic (Eds.), *Critical White Studies: Looking behind the mirror* (pp. 627–628). Philadelphia, PA: Temple University Press.

Hardiman, R. (2001). Reflections on white identity development theory. In C. L. Wijeyesinghe & B. W. Jackson, III (Eds.), *New perspectives on racial identity development: A theoretical and practical anthology* (pp. 108–128). New York, NY: New York University Press.

Hardiman, R., & Jackson, B. (1992). Racial identity development: Understanding racial dynamics in college classrooms and on campus. In M. Adams (Ed.), *Promoting diversity in college classrooms: Innovative responses for the curriculum, faculty, and institutions* (pp. 21–37). San Francisco, CA: Jossey-Bass.

Hardiman, R., & Jackson, B. (1994). Oppression: Conceptual and developmental analysis. In M. Adams, P. Brigham, P. Dalpes, & L. Marchesani (Eds.), *Diversity and oppression: Conceptual frameworks* (pp. 1–11). Dubuque, IA: Kendall/Hunt.

Helfand, J., & Lippin, L. B. (2001). *Understanding whiteness, unraveling racism: Tools for the journey.* Cincinnati, OH: Thompson Learning Custom.

Helms, J. E. (1995). An update of Helms' white and people of color racial identity models. In J. G. Ponterotto, J. M. Casas, L. A. Suzuki, & C. M. Alexander (Eds.), *Handbook of multicultural counseling* (pp. 181–198). Thousand Oaks, CA: Sage.

Herbert, J. T. (2000). Simulation as a learning method to facilitate disability awareness. *The Journal of Experiential Education, 23*(1), 5–11.

Hitchcock, J. (2002). *Lifting the white veil: An exploration of white American culture in a multiracial context.* Roselle, NJ: Crandall, Dostie & Douglass Books.

Hogan, D. E., & Mallott, M. (2005). Changing racial prejudice through diversity education. *Journal of College Student Development, 46*(2), 115–125.

Hurtado, S. (2005). The next generation of diversity and intergroup relations research. *Journal of Social Issues, 61*(3), 595–610.

Hurtado, S., Engberg, M. E., Ponjuan, L., & Landreman, L. (2002). Students' precollege preparation for participation in a diverse democracy. *Research in Higher Education, 43*(2), 163–186.

Hurtado, S., Milem, J. F., Clayton-Pedersen, A. R., & Allen, W. R. (1998). Enhancing campus climates for racial/ethnic diversity: Educational policy and practice. *Review of Higher Education, 21*(3), 279–302.

Hurtado, S., Milem, J. F., Clayton-Pedersen, A. R., & Allen, W. R. (1999). Enacting diverse learning environments: Improving the climate for racial/ethnic diversity in higher education. ASHE-ERIC Education Report Volume 26, No. 8. Washington, DC: The George Washington University,Graduate School of Education and Human Development.

Kivel, P. (1996). *Uprooting racism: How White people can work for racial justice.* Philadelphia, PA: New Society.

Kivel, P. (2002). *Uprooting racism: How white people can work for racial justice* (Rev. ed.). Gabriola Island, BC: New Society.

Lincoln, Y. S., & Guba, E. G. (2000). Paradigmatic controversies, contradictions and emerging confluences. In N. K. Denzin & Y. S. Lincoln (Eds.), *Handbook of qualitative research* (2nd ed., pp. 163–188). Thousand Oaks, CA: Sage.

Mahoney, M. R. (1997). Segregation, whiteness and transformation. In R. Delgado & J. Stefancic (Eds.), *Critical White Studies: Looking behind the mirror* (pp. 654–657). Philadelphia, PA: Temple University Press.

Maxwell, K. (1997, February). Dimensions of intergroup consciousness: Preliminary findings. Paper presented at the University of Michigan First Annual Conference on Intergroup Dialogue on the College Campus, Ann Arbor, MI.

Maxwell, K. (2004). Deconstructing whiteness: Discovering the water. In V. Lee & J. Helfand (Eds.), *Identifying race and transforming whiteness in the clasroom* (pp. 153–168). New York, NY: Lang.

Maxwell, S. E., & Delaney, H. D. (1999). *Designing experiments and analyzing data a model comparison perspective.* Mahwah, NJ: Erlbaum.

McLaren, P. (1999). Unthinking whiteness, rethinking democracy: Critical citizenship in gringolandia. In C. Clark & J. O'Donnell (Eds.), *Becoming and unbecoming white: Owning and disowning a racial identity* (pp. 10–55). Westport, CT: Bergin & Garvey.

Mertens, D. M. (2005). *Research and evaluation in education and psychology: Integrating diversity with quantitative, qualitative, and mixed methods* (2nd ed.). Thousand Oaks, CA: Sage.

Mertens, D. M. (2010). *Research and evaluation in education and psychology: Integrating diversity with quantitative, qualitative, and mixed methods* (3rd ed.). Los Angeles, CA: Sage.

Meyers, L. S., Gamst, G., & Guarino, A. J. (2006). *Applied multivariate research: Design and interpretation.* Thousand Oaks, CA: Sage.

Milem, J. F., & Umbach, P. D. (2003). The influence of precollege factors on students' predispositions regarding diversity activities in college. *Journal of College Student Development, 44*(5), 611–624.

Miller, J. B. (1994). Domination-subordination. In M. Adams, P. Brigham, P. Daples, & L. Marchesani (Eds.), *Diversity and oppression: Conceptual frameworks* (pp. 13–17). Dubuque, IA: Kendall/Hunt.

Multi-University Intergroup Dialogue Research Project. (2008). *Guidebook.* Ann Arbor, MI: University of Michigan.

Nagda, B. A. (2006). Breaking barriers, crossing borders, building bridges: Communication processes in intergroup dialogues. *Journal of Social Issues, 62*(3), 553–576.

Nagda, B. A., & Gurin, P. (2007). Intergroup dialogue: A critical-dialogic approach to learning about difference, inequality, and social justice. *New Directions for Teaching & Learning,* (111), 35–45.

Nagda, B. A., Gurin, P., & Lopez, G. E. (2003). Transformative pedagogy for democracy and social justice. *Race Ethnicity and Education, 6*(2), 165–191.

Nagda, B. A., Gurin, P., Sorensen, N., Gurin-Sands, C., & Osuna, S. (2009). From separate corners to dialogue and action. *Race and Social Problems, 1*(1), 45–55.

Nagda, B. A., Gurin, P., Sorensen, N., & Zúñiga, X. (2009). Evaluating intergroup dialogue: Engaging diversity for personal and social responsibility. *Diversity & Democracy, 12*(1), 4–6.

Nagda, B. A., Kim, C.-W., & Truelove, Y. (2004). Learning about difference, learning with others, learning to transgress. *Journal of Social Issues, 60*(1), 195–214.

Nelson Laird, T. F., Engberg, M. E., & Hurtado, S. (2005). Modeling accentuation effects: Enrolling in a diversity course and the importance of social action engagement. *Journal of Higher Education, 76*(4), 448–476.

Pallant, J. (2007). *SPSS survival manual: A step by step guide to data analysis using SPSS for Windows* (3rd ed.). Maidenhead, Il: Open University Press.

Paquette, T. S. (2006). *Ego strength, white racial identity, racial diversity attitudes, and cultural empathy in undergraduate students.* Doctoral dissertation, Purdue University, West Lafayette, IN.

Pascarella, E. T., & Terenzini, P. T. (2005). *How college affects students: A third decade of research.* San Francisco, CA: Jossey-Bass.

Pettigrew, T. F. (1998). Intergroup contact theory. *Annual Review of Psychology, 49,* 65–85.

Reason, R. D., & Broido, E. M. (2005). Issues and strategies for social justice allies (and the student affairs professionals who hope to encourage them). In R. D. Reason, E. M. Broido, T. L. Davis, & N. J. Evans (Eds.), *Developing social justice allies* (pp. 81–89). San Francisco, CA: Jossey-Bass.

Reason, R. D., Broido, E. M., Davis, T. L., & Evans, N. J. (Eds.). (2005). *Developing social justice allies.* San Francisco, CA: Jossey-Bass.

Reason, R. D., & Davis, T. L. (2005). Antecedents, precursors, and concurrent concepts in the development of social justice attitudes and actions. In R. D. Reason, E. M. Broido, T. L. Davis, & N. J. Evans (Eds.), *Developing social justice allies* (pp. 5–15). San Francisco, CA: Jossey-Bass.

Reason, R. D., Roosa Millar, E. A., & Scales, T. C. (2005). Toward a model of racial justice ally development. *Journal of College Student Development, 46*(5), 530–546.

Reason, R. D., Scales, T. C., & Roosa Millar, E. A. (2005). Encouraging the development of racial justice allies. In R. D. Reason, E. M. Broido, T. L. Davis, & N. J. Evans (Eds.), *Developing social justice allies* (pp. 55–66). San Francisco, CA: Jossey-Bass.

Shadish, W. R., & Cook, T. D. (2009). The renaissance of field experimentation in evaluating interventions. *Annual Review of Psychology, 60,* 607–629.

Shadish, W. R., Cook, T. D., & Campbell, D. T. (2002). *Experimental and quasi-experimental designs for generalized causal inference.* Boston, MA: Houghton Mifflin.

Sorensen, N., Nagda, B. A., Gurin, P., & Maxwell, K. E. (2009). Taking a "hands on" approach to diversity in higher education: A critical-dialogic model for effective intergroup interaction. *Analyses of Social Issues & Public Policy, 9*(1), 3–35.

Tabachnick, B. G., & Fidell, L. S. (2007). *Using multivariate statistics* (5th ed.). Boston, MA: Pearson/Allyn & Bacon.

Tacq, J. J. A. (1997). *Multivariate analysis techniques in social science research: From problem to analysis.* Thousand Oaks, CA: Sage.

Tatum, B. D. (1992). Talking about race, learning about racism: The application of racial identity development theory in the classroom. *Harvard Educational Review, 62*(1), 1–24.

Tatum, B. D. (1999). Lighting candles in the dark. In C. Clark & J. O'Donnell (Eds.), *Becoming and unbecoming white: Owning and disowning a racial identity* (pp. 56–63). Westport, CT: Bergin & Garvey.

Vasques Scalera, C. M. (1999). *Democracy, diversity, dialogue: Education for critical multicultural citizenship*. Doctoral Dissertation, University of Michigan, Ann Arbor, MI.

Weinfurt, K. P. (1995). Multivariate analysis of variance. In L. G. Grimm & P. R. Yarnold (Eds.), *Reading and understanding multivariate statistics* (pp. 245–276). Washington, DC: American Psychological Association.

Zúñiga, X. (1998). Fostering intergroup dialogue on campus: Essential ingredients. *Diversity Digest* (1998, Winter), 10–12.

Zúñiga, X., Nagda, B. A., Chesler, M., & Cytron-Walker, A. (Eds.). (2007). *Intergroup dialogue in higher education: Meaningful learning about social justice*. Washington, DC: Association for the Study of Higher Education.

Zúñiga, X., Nagda, B. A., & Sevig, T. D. (2002). Intergroup dialogues: An educational model for cultivating engagement across differences. *Equity & Excellence in Education*, 35(1), 7–17.

Zúñiga, X., Nagda, B. A., Sevig, T. D., Thompson, M., & Dey, E. (1995, November). *Speaking the unspeakable: Student learning outcomes in intergroup dialogues on a college campus*. Paper presented at the Association for the Study of Higher Education Annual Conference, Orlando, Florida.

Zúñiga, X., & Sevig, T. D. (1997). Bridging the "us/them" divide through intergroup dialogue and peer leadership. *The Diversity Factor*, 6(2), 23–28.

Zúñiga, X., Williams, E. A., & Berger, J. B. (2005). Action-oriented democratic outcomes: The impact of student involvement with campus diversity. *Journal of College Student Development*, 46(6), 660–678.

Fostering a Commitment to Social Action: How Talking, Thinking, and Feeling Make a Difference in Intergroup Dialogue

Chloé Gurin-Sands and Patricia Gurin
University of Michigan

Biren (Ratnesh) A. Nagda
University of Washington

Shardae Osuna
University of Michigan

Intergroup dialogue is designed to foster commitment to action. This article analyzes papers written by students in 52 intergroup dialogue courses ($N = 739$) to test a theoretical model of how intergroup dialogue is expected to encourage frequency of acting to educate others and to collaborate with others. The theoretical model posits that dialogue pedagogy fosters distinctive communication processes, which influence psychological processes that, in turn, relate to action (Nagda, 2006; Sorensen, Nagda, Gurin, & Maxwell, 2009). Statistical analyses of the number of references to each of these concepts that were coded in the students' papers provide substantial support for the model. Dialogue pedagogy, communication processes, and psychological processes all influenced how much students wrote about action, and the influence of these concepts conforms to the theoretical model. Results also show that educating others was written about more by students in race/ethnicity dialogues than in gender dialogues, at least partially because students in race/ethnicity dialogues also wrote more about the communication processes and psychological processes that specifically related to educating others.

A commitment to social justice often entails collaboration across the differences of those working toward a common cause. Of course, solidarity-based action of people working within their own group is also important in social change, but, at the very least, many kinds of action require members of different identities to work together. An important question for educators is: How do students become social change agents committed to educating others and collaborating with others to bring about greater social justice?

This article examines how students in an educational program—intergroup dialogue—developed commitments to these kinds of actions. The intergroup dialogue courses bring together an equal number of students from two social identity groups that "share a history of contentious relationships with each other or have lacked opportunities to talk in meaningful ways" (Nagda, Gurin, Sorensen, & Zúñiga, 2009, p. 46). For example, an intergroup dialogue about either gender or race would have equal numbers of white women, white men, women of color, and men of color in the dialogue. Intergroup dialogue focuses on building relationships within and across group differences as well as developing an understanding of group identities and group-based inequalities and fostering commitments to action for social justice. Trained facilitators, representing the identity groups participating in an intergroup dialogue, guide the dialogues by encouraging participants to share their personal perspectives and actively listen to the perspectives of others with the intent to educate and learn from one another about power, inequalities, and actions that are needed to bring about greater social justice (see Zúñiga, Nagda, Chesler, & Cytron-Walker, 2007 for an overview of the practice of intergroup dialogue.)

In this article we present a critical-dialogic theoretical model of how intergroup dialogue is expected to foster action. This model guides our analysis of how dialogue pedagogy (readings and structured learning activities), communication processes that take place within dialogues, and psychological processes that take place within dialogue participants influence the participants' commitments to educate others and to collaborate with others. Qualitative narrative data from 739 final dialogue course papers are analyzed to test this model of action commitments. The model is also used in exploring why students in race and gender dialogue courses may differ in how much they write about action commitments in their final papers.

LITERATURE REVIEW

Two sets of studies, one by scholars studying diversity in higher education and the other by social psychologists studying collective action, are relevant to our study. Turning first to diversity curricular initiatives in higher education, studies have demonstrated that courses can have an impact on increasing students' commitments to social action. A study by Nelson Laird, Engberg, and Hurtado (2005), part of a larger national study looking at how colleges prepare students for a diverse democracy, compared the ratings of the importance of social action engagement by students enrolled in a diversity course and in a business management course. They found that students' enrollment in a diversity course was positively related to students' ratings of the importance of social action engagement. Students' previous enrollment in diversity courses, positive quality of cross-race interactions, and initial valuing of social action engagement were indirectly related to current social action engagement. Another study (Nagda, Gurin, Sorensen, Gurin-Sands, & Osuna, 2009), part of the Multi-University Intergroup Dialogue Research Project (described below), used survey measures to examine the degree of commitment to post-college action by students who had applied to take an intergroup dialogue course who were then randomly assigned either to a dialogue or to a control group. Such action included "influencing the political structure (e.g., voting, education campaigns, get-out-the-vote)," "influencing social policy," "working to correct social and economic inequalities," "helping promote inter-racial/inter-ethnic understanding," and "working to achieve greater gender equality." The dialogue students, compared to the control group students, showed significant increases in post-college commitments over the semester in which the dialogue courses occurred, and moreover this effect of dialogue was still evident a year later. The greater increase in commitments to action among dialogue course students was also found by comparing them to students enrolled in traditional social science courses on race and gender. Students in intergroup dialogue increased in commitments to post-college action significantly more than the social science students. Furthermore, this difference was at least partially explained by the greater presence of communication processes in the dialogue courses than in the social science courses.

Other higher education studies have looked at action orientations in more specific ways or situations. Although not assessing students' own action orientations, Lopez, Gurin, and Nagda (1998) asked students to endorse action options in response to intergroup conflict situations. Using a pretest-posttest design, and comparing students in an introductory course on Intergroup Relations and Conflict and a matched comparison group of students not in the course, Lopez et al. found that students in the course endorsed more structural level actions (such as changing the climate of the university and societal change) as responses to the conflict situation than did their counterparts who were not in the course. Nagda, Kim and Truelove (2004), also using a pretest-posttest design, found that social work students in a Cultural Diversity and Justice course increased in both their motivation for and confidence in engaging in two kinds of action: personal action (self-directed prejudice reduction) and social action (other-directed efforts promoting diversity). Furthermore, the impact of the course components (lecture and intergroup dialogue) was mediated through the students' motivation to bridge identity differences.

In summary, these studies by higher education researchers generally show that courses influence the importance students attach to action, their post-college commitments to action, and their motivation for and confidence in carrying out action. They also show that action is influenced by the course pedagogy and communication processes that take place within the course.

Turning to studies conducted by social psychologists, which focus on collective action, we find evidence that particular cognitions and emotions of individuals are influential in explaining who participates in collective action. In these social psychological studies, collective action generally refers to actions that individuals can take in concert with others that are aimed at improving the status, power, or influence of an entire group—most often a disadvantaged or low-status group (Louis, 2009; van Zomeren & Iyer, 2009). Across a wide range of specific types of collective action and societal groups, three important psychological resources have been stressed: (1) group identity, especially the importance of a politicized group identity that reflects a sense of group-based injustice (Duncan & Stewart, 2007; Gurin, Miller, & Gurin, 1980; Iyer & Ryan, 2009; Stürmer & Simon, 2009), (2) structural attributions for inequality that hold inequality to be both illegitimate and changeable because its origins reside, at least partially, in institutional policies and procedures (Iyer & Ryan, 2009; Stürmer & Simon, 2009; Wright, 2009); and (3) emotions that tend to follow when the existence of inequality and its illegitimacy are recognized (Ellemers & Barreto, 2009; Iyer & Leach, 2010; Iyer & Ryan, 2009; Leach, Iyer, & Pederson, 2006). Collective action is found more frequently among individuals who have developed politicized group identities and who both cognitively and emotionally critique the existence of structurally created and reinforced inequalities. These studies are particularly relevant to the psychological processes that are included in our theoretical model of action discussed below.

A CRITICAL-DIALOGIC MODEL OF INTERGROUP DIALOGUE

The critical-dialogic model of intergroup dialogue that guides this study draws from the literature of communication studies and critical race studies. The term "dialogic" represents a focus on relationships, what communication studies scholar Leslie A. Baxter (2011) defines as a social truth in which people recognize themselves as social selves rather than as sovereign selves. Influenced by theorizing about dialogism in communication studies, the dialogic part of our model includes the two communication processes of engaging self and appreciating difference. Through these two processes, students from two groups, together, reframe and, to some extent, constitute anew what their identities and relationships mean to them (Anderson, Baxter, & Cissna, 2004). The term, "critical," represents what Freire (1970) meant by critical consciousness—a concept that includes both analysis of power and the necessity of action. It also draws from the focus in critical race theory on how structures in the law and other institutions shape race, gender, and class relationships in society (Delgado & Stefancic, 2001). The critical part of our model includes two other communication processes—critical reflection and alliance building. Through these processes, students from the two groups examine the assumptions and biases that they and other students hold because their experiences are shaped by power and privilege. They also learn how to be allies to each other. The critical-dialogical model depicted in Figure 1 posits that pedagogy is expected to influence action both directly and indirectly.

In this model, readings and in-class structured activities are important features of pedagogy, defined as instructional methods by which students learn. A prime example of a structured exercise is a testimonial in which students share how their racial (or gender) identities have formed and how they have dealt with privileges and discrimination they have encountered because of their identities. Testimonials often lead participants to consider action because they can imagine new possibilities for educating others or collaborating with others as they listen to ways that their peers

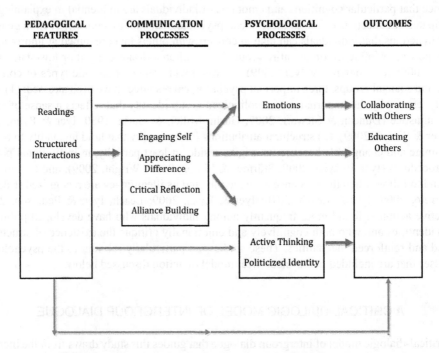

FIGURE 1   Theoretical model of how intergroup dialogue influences action.

have addressed injustices. In a later dialogue session, students connect what they had learned about action from the testimonials to the intergroup collaboration project (ICP). That project requires four students, two from each identity group, to work together to identify an action reflecting a commonly held concern about inequality, to carry out the action project together, and to report back to the dialogue course about what they learned from the dynamics in this cross-group practicum. Through practice in their ICP and hearing what other students learned through their ICP experiences, students think about how they can use their dialogue experience to educate others—friends, family, other students—and to collaborate across differences outside of the dialogue.

In addition to directly influencing action, the pedagogical features are also expected to affect action indirectly through communication processes among participants and psychological processes within participants. The critical-dialogic theoretical framework posits that the pedagogy of intergroup dialogues encourages a new kind of communication among the students, one that is aimed at understanding rather than arguing or attempting to convince each other, and one that connects dialogue to action (see Nagda, 2006; Sorensen et al., 2009). Four communication processes, which were coded from the students' final papers, are crucial in intergroup dialogue (Nagda, 2006). To continue with the example of testimonials, when students are giving or listening to testimonies, they are using these four types of communication. One process, engaging self, occurs when students share their own stories and experiences, are listened to, and take further risks as such sharing often entails. In a second process, appreciating difference, students listen to others, ask questions of each other, try to understand the points of view of other students and why other students believe and think as they do, empathize with others, and create trust across differences. A third process, critical reflection, happens when students examine their own assumptions and sources of bias and stereotypes as well as the assumptions and biases of other students, probing especially how socialization, privilege, power, and inequality together maintain the status quo. Finally, in alliance building, students explore common goals across identity groups and work through intergroup conflicts that inevitably arise during intergroup dialogue.

Both the pedagogy of intergroup dialogue and the communication processes it produces are instrumental in processes that take place within the students. Our theoretical model, following the research described above on collective action, focuses on two sets of psychological processes: cognitive and affective processes. Two cognitive processes were coded from the students' narratives: "thinking actively" about what is going on within the dialogue, what the readings mean in relation to in-class exercises, and how the dialogue experience connects to their own lives, and "developing a politicized identity" by reflecting explicitly on how their identities are connected to systems of power and privilege. One affective process was coded: "expressing emotions" to show how students listen and speak about topics and issues that are often avoided or dealt with superficially in exchanges across race/ethnicity and gender outside of the dialogue course. These psychological processes, in conjunction with the pedagogy and communication processes, are expected to foster commitment to action because students have thought actively about why action is needed. They have understood that the political meaning of their identities has implications for the kind of actions that they can undertake, and they have generated emotions needed to motivate change efforts.

Prior research supports the impact of intergroup dialogue on action as well as the role of psychological and communication processes. Nagda et al. (2004) found that the combination of enlightenment-oriented (didactic information and readings) and encounter-oriented (intergroup dialogue interactions) features of pedagogy significantly predicted students' motivation and confidence for reducing their own prejudices and for educating others. They also found that bridging differences as a psychological process mediated the impact of enlightenment and encounter features on action. In a subsequent investigation, Nagda (2006) found four communication processes—engaging self, appreciating difference, critical reflection, and alliance building—that explained how intergroup dialogue fostered bridging differences.

Hypothesis

Following this theoretical model, the hypothesis tested in this study is that intergroup dialogue pedagogy, communication processes, and psychological processes will have both direct and indirect effects on how much students write about educating others and collaborative action in their final papers.

An Exploratory Question

In addition to testing the hypothesis above, we were interested in whether students wrote about action more in race or in gender dialogue courses and if our theoretical model would help us understand any such differences. We treat this as an exploratory question because relevant research literature on curricular effects on students' action orientations provides little guidance about what to expect in race and gender dialogues. This is largely because most of that research has looked separately at gender-based courses (such as Women's Studies courses) and race/ethnic-based courses (such as courses offered by African American or Latino Studies or diversity courses that focus on race and ethnicity). Denson (2009) conducted a meta-analysis of 22 research investigations of how curriculum related to group-based biases and found that only four studies included both ethnic studies and women's studies courses. Although both sets of courses have an impact on numerous measures of student learning (see Denson, 2009; Henderson-King & Stewart, 1999; Hurtado, 2005; Milem, Chang, & Antonio, 2005), there is little evidence from past research about the relative impact of these two kinds of courses. Thus, it is not clear what to expect about possible differences in the emphasis that students might give to action, as represented by amount of writing in their final papers, in race and gender dialogues.

METHODS

The Multi-University Intergroup Dialogue Research Project

The data analyzed in this study are part of a large multi-university project that investigated if participation in race and gender intergroup dialogues has educational effects not attributable to a predisposition to participate in dialogue (i.e., selectivity). It also investigated what processes take place within dialogues and within the dialogue participants that might account for the demonstrated effects (Gurin, Nagda, & Zúñiga, in press). Conducted across nine universities over a period of four years, the multi-university project carried out 52 parallel intergroup dialogues

(26 race and 26 gender) and 52 control groups (26 race and 26 gender), with each dialogue course lasting 10–14 weeks with weekly meetings lasting 2–3 hours. Students who applied to enroll in an intergroup dialogue course were randomly assigned to either a dialogue or control group. In addition to pre-, post-, and one-year follow-up surveys that were administered to all students in the dialogues and control groups (1,423 students), the final papers—a standardized final assignment across the nine universities—of the students in the dialogue classes (739 students) were content analyzed. In the study presented here these final papers of the dialogue course participants are used to examine how students wrote about their dialogue experiences and commitments to action.

Participants

The participants in both the race and gender dialogue courses were divided as equally as possible across four demographic groups: 27% white women, 24% white men, 26% women of color, and 23% men of color. The participants in the race/ethnicity and gender dialogues were remarkably similar when they enrolled in the two types of dialogues. Of the 31 pretest survey measures, many of which were multiple-item scales, there were statistical differences between participants in the race/ethnicity and gender dialogues on only three measures.

Data

Students in both the race and gender dialogues completed the same final paper assignment at all nine institutions. The final paper asked them to construct a comprehensive ten-page essay that addressed four themes: (1) hopes and fears at the beginning of the dialogue; (2) understanding of their own and other students' identities and of privilege, power, and inequality at the beginning and end of the dialogue course; (3) analysis of how the dialogue group handled a disagreement or conflict and what they learned from those experiences; and (4) the intergroup relations skills they had learned and how they saw themselves applying that learning in society at large.

The students' narratives in their final papers were used to examine the major themes in action and how they connected action to their dialogue experience. These themes were discerned by graduate students who read a sample of papers and conferred with each other to then develop codes that would represent the agreed upon themes. This aspect of the coding process followed generally accepted qualitative analysis procedures delineated by Bryman (2001). The initial codes were tested on another sample of papers and refined in an iterative manner to produce the final codes used by the undergraduate research assistants.

Measures Coded from the Final Papers

The research team of undergraduate and graduate students coded the students' writing for 29 measures, 11 of which we focus on here. Twenty teams of two coders each produced these measures. Training for reliable coding was conducted with each team, and only after each team had achieved agreement of 80% or better for the dimensions for which they were responsible was training considered complete. Thereafter, 10% of the papers coded by each team were checked for reliability. The average percent agreement across the 11 dimensions used in this paper ranged from 67% to 95%. On 9 of the 11 dimensions, average percent agreement was 88%.

Following the coding of the student final papers, the coded data were inputted into the NVIVO qualitative analysis software program. NVIVO provides a count for the number of times a particular dimension/concept was coded across the paper for each individual. Each time a particular concept/dimension appeared in a paper is termed a reference in NVIVO. The measures of each of the concepts in our theoretical model are the number of references a student made to each one in his or her final paper. Descriptions of these measures appear in Appendix A.

Control Variables

The race and gender of the students are used as control variables because previous research has shown these to be related to motivation to reduce one's own prejudices and to promote inclusion and social justice (Zúñiga, Williams, & Berger, 2005), how one experiences intergroup contact (Denson, 2009; Tropp & Pettigrew, 2005), and commitment to an action scale that included making an effort to educate others (Nelson Laird et al., 2005). In the larger project in which the study reported here is embedded, the pretest survey measures also support the significance of race and gender of the students. At pretest, students of color were more involved in social justice activities on campus and had already collaborated across racial differences more than white students had. Both race and gender (favoring students of color and women) were significantly related to higher scores on anticipated post-college action, and frequency of educating others when students were enrolled in the dialogue courses (see Gurin et al., in press). We also use topic (race or gender) of the dialogue courses as an initial measure in our analyses in order to explore whether it mattered in how much students wrote about action.

Data Analysis

Hierarchical regression analyses were conducted to test the theoretical model. The dependent variables were the action outcomes—educating others and collaborating with others. Model 1 included the control variables of race and gender of the students and the dialogue topic (race or gender). Model 2 added the independent variables of measures of pedagogy as represented by readings and structured activities to predict these action outcomes. Model 3 added the four communication processes as predictors. Finally Model 4 added the measures of psychological processes to predict educating others and collaborating with others.

RESULTS

Examining the Theoretical Model

We predicted that intergroup dialogue pedagogy, communication processes, and psychological processes will have both direct and indirect effects on how much students write about educating others and collaborative action. In addition to the direct effects of pedagogy, communication processes and psychological processes on action, the theoretical model specifies two sets of indirect effects: (1) indirect effects of pedagogy on action through communication processes and psychological processes and (2) indirect effects of communication processes on action through psychological processes. Baron and Kenny (1986) specified steps that must be present in testing for mediation or indirect effects. We followed these steps in our analyses. First, one must demonstrate that all independent variables in the theoretical model are significantly related to the dependent variables. Table 1, a summary of intercorrelations among all the measures used in the study, shows that overall this step was met.

Tables 2 and 3 present results from testing our hypothesis, that pedagogy has both direct and indirect effects on educating others and collaborating with others. Table 2 shows results of the hierarchical regression analyses for educating others. Pedagogy only has indirect effects on educating others. (The evidence of indirect effects is seen by attenuation in the size of the beta when communication processes are entered in Model 3 and then by further attenuation in the size of the beta when psychological processes are entered in Model 4). The effect of readings on educating others ($\beta = .101$, $p = .008$ in Model 2) is mediated by communication processes and is no longer statistically significant in Model 3 ($\beta = .044$, $p = .226$ in Model 3). The effect of structured activities ($\beta = .111$, $p = .003$ in Model 2) is mediated by both communication processes ($\beta = .079$, $p = .021$ in Model 3) and by psychological processes and is no longer statistically significant in Model 4 ($\beta = .057$, $p = .125$ in Model 4). Thus, pedagogy's influence on how much students wrote about educating others operates through the processes that pedagogy helps set up. Turning to communication processes, Table 2 shows both direct and indirect effects. For example, critical reflection, which is significantly related to educating others ($\beta = .099$, $p = .010$ in Model 3), is then mediated by psychological processes and is no longer statistically significant in Model 4 ($\beta = .065$, $p = .108$ in Model 4). In contrast, alliance building has a direct effect on educating others ($\beta = .144$, $p < .001$ in Model 3), and its effect is not attenuated when psychological processes are considered ($\beta = .142$, $p < .001$ in Model 4). Finally, Table 2 shows in Model 4 that politicized identity and emotions were significantly related to educating others.

Table 3 shows, as predicted, that the effect of structured activities on collaborating with others ($\beta = .148$, $p < .001$ in Model 2) is direct and then is partially mediated by both communication processes ($\beta = .100$, $p = .005$ in Model 3) and psychological processes ($\beta = .076$, $p = .030$ in Model 4). This is partial mediation because the beta in Model 4, though smaller than in Model 2, is still statistically significant. The significant effect of readings on collaborating with others ($\beta = .169$, $p < .001$ in Model 2) is fully mediated when communication processes and psychological processes are entered and is no longer statistically significant in Model 4 ($\beta = .024$, $p = .226$ in Model 4). These regressions, thus, show that the impact of readings is entirely indirect and that the impact of structured activities is both direct and indirect. Table 3 also supports the role of communication processes in our theoretical model, showing that alliance building is the communication process that is related to collaborating with others ($\beta = .325$, $p < .001$ in both Models 3 and 4). The effect of alliance building is direct and is not attenuated when psychological processes are also considered in Model 4. Table 3 also shows in Model 4 that all three psychological processes—active thinking, emotions, and politicized identity—have direct effects on collaborating with others, with emotions having the strongest relationship.

TABLE 1
Bivariate Inter-Correlations of Kinds of Action and Predictors ($N = 695$)

Number of References	1	2	3	4	5	6	7	8	9	10	11	12
Action												
1. Educating Others	1.00											
2. Collaborating with Others	.312***	1.00										
Pedagogy												
3. Readings	.129***	.203***	1.00									
4. Activities & Exercises	.127***	.173***	.123***	1.00								
Communication Processes												
5. Engaging Self	.123***	.140***	.117**	.177***	1.00							
6. Appreciating Difference	.106**	.086*	.110*	.099**	.325***	1.00						
7. Critical Reflection	.185***	.177***	.263***	.114**	.190***	.310***	1.00					
8. Alliance Building	.222***	.372***	.227***	.147***	.200***	.260***	.319***	1.00				
Psychological Processes												
9. Emotions	.191***	.230***	.115**	.130***	.205***	.125***	.055	.047	1.00			
10. Active Thinking	.177***	.231***	.254***	.109**	.212***	.079*	.259***	.161***	.142***	1.00		
11. Politicized Identity	.241***	.255***	.238***	.131***	.176***	.182***	.263***	.157***	.212***	.269***	1.00	
12. Topic†	.110***	.026	.002	−.019	.099**	.142**	.087*	.164***	.089**	.005	.016	1.00

*$p \leq .05$; **$p \leq .01$; ***$p \leq .001$.
†Topic is coded 1 = gender dialogue, 2 = race/ethnicity dialogue.

TABLE 2
Predictors of Educating Others

	Model 1			Model 2			Model 3			Model 4		
	B	β	SE	B	β	SE	B	β	SE	B	β	SE
Gender	.257	.077*	.125	.191	.058	.125	.175	.053	.123	.154	.046	.122
Race	.363	.109**	.125	.330	.099**	.123	.303	.091**	.121	.174	.052	.121
Topic (Gender or Race)	.359	.108**	.125	.368	.111**	.123	.250	.075*	.124	.236	.071*	.122
Pedagogy												
Readings				.060	.101**	.023	.026	.044	.023	.000	.000	.025
Structured Activities				.063	.111**	.021	.045	.079*	.021	.032	.057	.021
Communication Processes												
Engaging Self							.028	.043	.026	.001	.001	.026
Appreciating Difference							-.003	-.066	.024	-.001	-.018	.024
Critical Reflection							.071	.099**	.029	.047	.065	.029
Alliance Building							.162	.144***	.045	.161	.142***	.044
Psychological Processes												
Active Thinking										.082	.072	.044
Politicized Identity										.096	.142***	.027
Emotions										.021	.116**	.007
R^2		.030			.055			.093			.136	
Change in R^2					.025			.038			.043	

*$p \leq .05$; **$p \leq .01$; ***$p \leq .001$.

TABLE 3
Predictors of Collaborating with Others

	Model 1			Model 2			Model 3			Model 4		
	B	β	SE	B	β	SE	B	β	SE	B	β	SE
Gender	.329	.109**	.116	.234	.077*	.112	.218	.072*	.107	.182	.060	.104
Race	.215	.071	.114	.169	.056	.111	.139	.046	.105	.023	.008	.104
Topic (Gender or Race)	.066	.022	.116	.078	.026	.111	-.088	-.029	.109	-.111	-.037	.104
Pedagogy												
Readings				.091	.169***	.020	.050	.091**	.020	.024	.045	.020
Activities				.076	.148***	.019	.052	.100**	.018	.039	.076*	.018
Communication Processes												
Engaging Self							.029	.048	.023	-.002	-.004	.022
Appreciating Difference							-.027	-.049	.021	-.032	-.058	.021
Critical Reflection							.027	.041	.025	.006	.009	.025
Alliance Building							.333	.325***	.039	.333	.325***	.038
Psychological Processes												
Active Thinking										.114	.111**	.038
Politicized Identity										.058	.095**	.023
Emotions										.027	.164***	.006
R^2		.018			.073			.177			.230	
Change in R^2					.055			.104			.053	

*$p \leq .05$; **$p \leq .01$; ***$p \leq .001$.

Exploring Action Commitments in Race and Gender Dialogues

The intercorrelations in Table 1 show that topic of the dialogue is significantly related to educating others but not to collaborating with others. Students in race/ethnicity dialogues wrote more than students in gender dialogues about educating others. Table 1 also shows that topic of the dialogue is significantly related to how much students wrote about the four communication processes and how many emotion words were used in their final papers. Students in race/ethnicity dialogues wrote significantly more about all four of the communication processes and also used more emotion words. Table 3, thus, helps explain why there was a difference between the two types of dialogues in educating others. The original effect of topic on educating others ($\beta = .108, p = .004$ in Model 1) is reduced when communication processes are considered ($\beta = .075, p = .044$ in Model 3) and slightly reduced again when psychological processes, notably emotions, are considered ($\beta = .071, p = .039$ in Model 4). In summary, topic played only a minor role in these analyses, showing a significant relationship only to educating others and not to collaborating with others. The theoretical model helps explain that its impact on educating others (not sizeable in any case) occurred partly because of the influence of topic on how much students wrote about communication processes and how many emotion words they used in their final papers.

Limitations of the Study

One limitation of the study derives from the necessary assumption in our statistical method that amount of writing in the final papers represents importance or salience to the student of a particular concept. One might argue, however, that amount of writing is apt to be confounded by verbal and writing ability. If that were true, amount of writing about a particular concept might not reflect its importance or salience. Two procedures decreased this possibility. First, the paper assignment controlled overall length of the papers by specifying that the paper was to be ten pages. Nearly all papers conformed to the page specification in the paper assignment. Second, the assignment also required that the students utilize six readings in their papers. We believe that the standardization of paper length and of number of readings both minimize the possible limitation of using amount of writing to represent the importance of a particular concept to the student.

Some might also argue that the focus in this study on the students' reflections about their dialogue experiences involves a limitation from using self-report data. However, these data are not self-report in the usual sense of that term. Self-report data normally come from surveys in which the questions define in an obvious way what is being measured. In contrast, the students who were responding to the final paper assignment had no idea what would be coded from the papers. Thus, we believe that our method of using student writing actually minimizes the possible problem of depending on self-reports.

DISCUSSION

Overall, the results of this study provide substantial support for the theoretical model in Figure 1. They demonstrate that pedagogy, communication processes, and psychological processes all influence how much students wrote about action and that the influence of these variables conforms to the theoretical model. Our results substantiate, as predicted, that pedagogy had both direct and indirect effects in explaining how much students wrote about action in their final papers. Support for the theoretical model is also evident in the results showing that communication processes influenced action both directly and indirectly, and psychological processes had direct effects as the model predicted. Specifically, alliance building, emotions, and politicized identity had the largest direct effects on both educating others and collaborating with others. We speculate that alliance building as a communication process strengthens a relational capacity not only among individuals but also at the group level in the service of social change. It sets a strong foundation for students to grapple with differences that members of the two groups exhibit in their cognitive understandings of politicized identities as well as differences in affective experiences and emotions that arise from connecting individual and personal experiences to social and structural realities. In other education and intergroup relations programs, any of these may be end-goals; however, in intergroup dialogue, as our results show, each of them has a direct consequence for action—both educating others and collaborating with others. In other words, the students' subjective perspectives in writing their final papers highlight tools that they have acquired in intergroup dialogue—tools associated with actions they are taking in their current lives and tools that augur well for continuing to be activists for social justice.

The results from exploring whether or not students wrote about action more in race or in gender dialogues provide a mixed picture: no differences in writing about collaborative action and significantly more writing in race than in gender dialogues about educating others. The results also reveal that part of the reason that students in race/ethnicity dialogues wrote more about educating others was because they also wrote more about communication processes, used more emotion words, and described their identities in politicized ways as affording them more or less privilege. These processes, in turn, were significantly related to educating others in both types of dialogues, although somewhat more highly related in race than in gender dialogues. What the students seem to have taken from the race/ethnicity dialogues, more thoroughly than from gender dialogues, is that educating their friends, families, and acquaintances about social justice demands being able to build alliances, utilize their emotions, and understand their identities in political terms. It is likely that these connections are especially powerful in race/ethnicity dialogues because students often come to race/ethnicity dialogues with little experience of other racial and ethnic groups (Orfield & Lee, 2006). In contrast, students come to the gender dialogues with far more frequent and intimate interaction across groups and accordingly with greater knowledge about the other group. Thus, as students in the two types of dialogues consider what it will take to educate others, those in race/ethnicity dialogues likely sense a larger task, just as they realize that they had come to dialogue with only limited knowledge of the experiences and perspectives of students in the other racial and ethnic group. Realizing the challenge of being able to educate others, students in race/ethnicity dialogues more likely appreciate why alliance building, identity, and emotions may play a role in this form of action.

Implications for Intergroup Dialogue Practice

The findings of the research discussed here have significant implications for both how intergroup dialogue courses are conducted and how facilitators are trained. The importance of communication and psychological processes for action suggests that training of facilitators should put skill development within this process framework. Understanding the overall theoretical framework, and especially what the communication processes and psychological processes are and how they function within the dialogue, can provide facilitators important sense-making tools to use in the dialogue. In turn, this knowledge can be utilized directly in working with participants of a dialogue to help them better understand the communication that takes place within the dialogue and the psychological issues that students tend to face as they dialogue with each other. For example, when facilitators ask students to debrief what has happened in a specific dialogue session, they are involving the students in the communication process of critical reflection. They are asking students to reflect together in a way that names how power and privilege have operated in that dialogue session. They can probe how engaged the students felt during that session and how much listening and appreciating different points of view were evident. Reflection papers also serve the purpose of critical reflection, but at a private level. Since both private and public reflection foster learning (Raelin, 2001), the reflection papers can be brought back into the dialogue for students to make sense of particular moments in the dialogue when politicized identity or expression of emotions have emerged in crucial ways. Such public reflection is an example of a meta-level "dialogue about the dialogue" that can help students internalize the processes, both group and individual, that foster or hinder dialogue.

Knowing that alliance building as a communication process is important in fostering action, intergroup dialogue courses can focus more on alliance building as a process, not just as a product of the dialogue. For example, in the ICP project, students often focus more heavily on the product of their project (a presentation of the action the group takes) than on analyzing and dialoguing about the group dynamics that arose within their ICP group. Intergroup dialogue facilitators can emphasize understanding and talking about group dynamics as crucial learning for building effective alliances throughout the development of the ICP project and in anticipation of alliances the students may try to create after the dialogue course is over. Guidelines for making diverse groups and teams as effective as possible exist (see, for example, Oakley, Brent, Felder, & Elhaji, 2004). Guidelines for effective groups can be used in facilitator training as both a foundation of knowledge and as material for facilitators to examine the dynamics in their co-facilitation pairs and in the facilitator training group as a whole. Then trainers need to provide more substantial readings and activities devoted to what makes groups effective, specifically groups that deal with intercultural communication and team building across identities.

The role of politicized identity proved important for both educating others and collaborating with others. Understanding how positions in the social structure give students more or less privilege is an important part of many social justice education efforts. Our results show that in intergroup dialogue, participants benefit not only from learning about the social positions within which their identities exist but also by connecting this consciousness to their responsibilities to foster social change. Having a politicized identity is not just a goal; it is also a psychological process to motivate action. While the intergroup dialogue curriculum moves from getting acquainted, to understanding identities and social positions, and to action planning, facilitators can integrate the link between politicized identity and action throughout the dialogue. For example, students can be asked to share their learning about socialization and inequalities with their friends or roommates. When students share examples of how they see themselves participating in privileged and less privileged ways, they can be asked to experiment with interrupting that kind of participation. For example, students sometimes talk about how learning about power and privilege changes the ways they watch TV shows or films. They can be encouraged to raise a conversation about power and privilege with the people with whom they watch the shows. Students also can be asked to learn more about campus and community organizations that are geared toward promoting diversity and social justice. These are but a few examples in which facilitators can make the link between politicized identity and action obvious, important, and doable in the everyday environments of the students.

However, understanding one's own and others' positions in society requires sensitivity to possibilities that stereotypes may emerge as students grapple with groups, identities, and cultures. It is one thing to become aware that some behaviors and perspectives are more likely to be expressed by members of one or the other identity group. It is quite another thing to turn such expectancies into stereotypes. For example, when black students express emotions, they may be labeled angry or over-sensitive, while Asian students may be expected to be quiet and reserved. Facilitators' understanding of frequently held stereotypes of particular racial/ethnic groups or of women and men can help them guard against stereotype reinforcement as students struggle to embrace the reality that groups and identities have powerful effects on individuals. Intergroup dialogue must encourage critical analysis of how power and privilege affect various groups while challenging the expression of group-based stereotypes.

Emotions as part of the intergroup dialogue experience also are an important part of becoming action-oriented. Attending to and learning from emotions is not always accepted as a legitimate concern in academic courses, but in intergroup dialogue courses emotions and affective learning complement cognitive learning. Table 1 reveals that emotions are especially related to the dialogic communication processes of engaging self and appreciating difference. Facilitators play a crucial role in normalizing expression of emotions by encouraging students to bring both their own thoughts and feelings to the dialogue as well as listen to the thoughts and feelings of others (Nagda & Maxwell, 2011). For example, facilitators can normalize the role of emotions when the group establishes ground rules, using statements, such as, "Emotions are part of our learning" and "Show respect by validating each other's emotions." They can urge students to reflect back on the emotions they experienced during active listening exercises. In our practice experience, emphasis in active listening is often placed on listening to the content of the speaker's sharing but not always to the meaning and emotions underlying that sharing. By emphasizing emotions in active listening as a foundation for dialogue engagement and then practicing how emotions are involved in active listening in the early sessions of the dialogue, facilitators can help students become more comfortable and effective in expressing, recognizing, and responding to emotions in later sessions. In these later sessions, emotions can be contextualized in systems of power and privilege in two realms. In one realm—locating oneself and one's experiences in systems of inequalities, be it as members of privileged or less privileged groups—a variety of emotions may emerge. Facilitators can urge students to reflect on reasons for their discomfort when focusing on privilege in their lives or why feelings of anger may come up when grappling with marginalization in their own lives. In a second, more relational realm—being aware of the emotions of others—the connection of identities to emotions may become more obvious. In both realms, facilitators need to encourage students to be careful as they attach identity inferences to their emotions and to the emotions of other students.

Lastly, given that students in gender dialogues wrote somewhat less about educating others than did students in race/ethnicity dialogues, facilitators in gender dialogues may need to press communication processes, identities, and emotions even more than in race/ethnicity dialogues. Because interactions across genders are more common and in many ways more intimate than cross-race interactions, special attention needs to be paid to discerning how power and privilege play out in small and large groups in the gender dialogues. Students need to become aware of both similar and different perspectives and emotions that women and men in the dialogue may experience and express. How might facilitators do this? Readings used in dialogue should focus on gender identity and power dynamics that are relevant to current college students. Facilitators can intentionally share their experiences with gender-based privilege, how such privileges and lack of privileges have played a role in their identities and their co-facilitation dynamics, and how politicized identity has helped them to educate others and collaborate with others. Facilitators can help students see that sexism is not "something that happens out there" or "happened during our parents' generation" but is relevant here and now. They can name emotions that are being expressed and normalize the expression of emotion by explaining how emotion can have a positive impact on action.

In conclusion, coding and analysis of students' writings in the final papers that were assigned in intergroup dialogue courses support the critical-dialogic theoretical model of intergroup dialogue. Results show that dialogue pedagogy, communication processes, and psychological processes all influenced how much students wrote about action. Results also show that educating others was written about more by students in race than gender dialogues, at least partially because students in race/ethnicity dialogues also wrote more about the communication processes and psychological processes that specifically related to educating others.

REFERENCES

Anderson, R., Baxter, L. A., & Cissna, K. N. (Eds.). (2004). *Dialogue: Theorizing difference in communication studies.* Thousand Oaks, CA: Sage.

Baron, R. M., & Kenny, D. A. (1986). The moderator-mediator variable distinction in social psychological research: Conceptual, strategic and statistical considerations. *Journal of Personality and Social Psychology, 51*(6), 1173–1182.

Baxter, L. A. (2011). *Voicing relationships: A dialogic perspective.* Thousand Oaks, CA: Sage.

Bryman, A. (2001). *Social research methods.* New York, NY: Oxford University Press.

Cacioppo, J. T., & Petty, R. E. (1982). The need for cognition. *Journal of Personality and Social Psychology, 42*(1), 116–131.

Delgado, R., & Stefancic, J. (2001). *Critical race theory: An introduction.* New York, NY: New York University Press.

Denson, N. (2009). Do curricular and cocurricular diversity activities influence racial bias? A meta-analysis. *Review of Educational Research, 79*(2), 805–838.

Duncan, L. E., & Stewart, A. J. (2007). Personal political salience: The role of personality in collective identity and action. *Political Psychology, 28*(2), 143–164.

Ellemers, N., & Barreto, M. (2009). Collective action in modern times: How modern expressions of prejudice prevent collective action. *Journal of Social Issues, 65*(4), 749–768.

Freire, P. (1970). *Pedagogy of the oppressed.* New York, NY: Seabury.

Gurin, P., Miller, A. H., & Gurin, G. (1980). Stratum identification and consciousness. *Social Psychology Quarterly, 43*(1), 30–47.

Gurin, P., Nagda, B. A., & Zuniga, X. (in press). *Engaging race and gender: Intergroup dialogues in higher education.* New York, NY: Russell Sage Foundation.

Henderson-King, D., & Stewart, A. J. (1999). Educational experiences and shifts in group consciousness: Studying women. *Personality and Social Psychology Bulletin, 25*(3), 390–399.

Hurtado, S. (2005). The next generation of diversity and intergroup relations research. *Journal of Social Issues, 61*(3), 595–610.

Iyer, A., & Leach, C. W. (2010). Helping disadvantaged out-groups challenge unjust inequality: The role of group-based emotions. In S. Sturmer & M. Snyder (Eds.), *New directions in the psychology of helping: Group-level perspectives on motivations, consequences, and interventions* (pp. 337–353). Oxford, England: Blackwell.

Iyer, A., & Ryan, M. K. (2009). Why do men and women challenge gender discrimination in the workplace? The role of group status and in-group identification in predicting pathways to collective action. *Journal of Social Issues, 65*(4), 791–814.

Leach, C. W., Iyer, A., & Pedersen, A. (2006). Anger and guilt about ingroup advantage explain the willingness for political action. *Personality & Social Psychology Bulletin, 32*(9), 1232–1245.

Lopez, G. E., Gurin, P., & Nagda, B. A. (1998). Education and understanding structural causes for group inequalities. *Political Psychology, 19*(2), 305–329.

Louis, W. R. (2009). Collective action—and then what? *Journal of Social Issues, 65*(4), 727–748.

Milem, J. F., Chang, M. J., & Antonio, A. L. (2005). *Making diversity work on campus: A research-based perspective.* Washington, DC: Association of American Colleges and Universities.

Nagda, B. A. (2006). Breaking barriers, crossing boundaries, building bridges: Communication processes in intergroup dialogues. *Journal of Social Issues, 62*, 553–576.

Nagda, B. A., Gurin, P., Sorensen, N., Gurin-Sands, C., & Osuna, S. M. (2009). From separate corners to dialogue and action. *Race and Social Problems, 1*(1), 45–55.

Nagda, B. A., Gurin, P., Sorensen, N., & Zúñiga, X. (2009). Evaluating intergroup dialogues: Engaging diversity for personal and social responsibility. *Diversity & Democracy, 12*(1), 4–6.

Nagda, B. A., Kim, C.-w., & Truelove, Y. (2004). Learning about difference, learning with others, learning to transgress. *Journal of Social Issues, 60*(1), 195–214.

Nagda, B. A., & Maxwell, K. E. (2011). Deepening the layers of understanding and connection: A critical-dialogic approach to facilitating intergroup dialogues. In K. E. Maxwell, B. A. Nagda, & M. C. Thompson (Eds.), *Facilitating intergroup dialogues: Bridging differences, catalyzing change* (pp. 1–22). Sterling, VA: Stylus.

Nelson Laird, T. F., Engberg, M. E., & Hurtado, S. (2005). Modeling accentuation effects: Enrolling in a diversity course and the importance of social action engagement. *Journal of Higher Education, 76*(4), 448–476.

Oakley, B., Brent, R., Felder, R. M., & Elhaji, I. (2004). Turning student groups into effective teams. *Journal of Student Centered Learning, 2*(1), 9–34.

Orfield, G., & Lee, C. (2006). *Racial transformation and the changing nature of segregation.* Cambridge, MA: The Civil Rights Project at Harvard University.

Ortony, K., & Turner, T. J. (1990). What's basic about basic emotions? *Psychological Review, 97*(3), 315–331.

Raelin, J. A. (2001). Public reflection as the basis of learning. *Management Learning, 32*(1), 11–30.

Sorensen, N., Nagda, B. A., Gurin, P., & Maxwell, K. (2009). Taking a "hands on" approach to diversity in higher education: A critical-dialogic model for effective intergroup interaction. *Analyses of Social Issues and Public Policy, 9*(1), 3–35.

Stürmer, S., & Simon, B. (2009). Pathways to collective protest: Calculation identification, or emotion? A critical analysis of the role of group-based anger in social movement participation. *Journal of Social Issues, 65*(4), 681–705.

Tropp, L. R., & Pettigrew, T. F. (2005). Differential relationships between intergroup contact and affective and cognitive indicators of prejudice. *Personality and Social Psychology Bulletin, 31*(8), 1145–1158.

van Zomeren, M., & Iyer, A. (2009). Introduction to the social and psychological dynamics of collective action. *Journal of Social Issues, 65*(4), 645–660.

Wright, S. C. (2009). The next generation of collective action research. *Journal of Social Issues, 65*(4), 859–879.

Zúñiga, X., Nagda, B. A., Chesler, M., & Cytron-Walker, A. (2007). *Intergroup dialogue in higher education: Meaningful learning about social justice.* ASHE Higher Education Report: Volume 32, No. 4. Washington, DC: Association for the Study of Higher Education.

Zúñiga, X., Williams, E. A., & Berger, J. B. (2005). Action-oriented democratic outcomes: The impact of student involvement with campus diversity. *Journal of College Student Development, 46*(6), 660–678.

APPENDIX A

Measures Coded From the Students' Final Papers

Pedagogy

1. Readings. Every instance in which a student referenced an author's name or the title of a publication was coded. The measure used in this study is the number of references to readings across the entire paper.
2. Structured Activities. References to dialogue activities and exercises were coded only if they were associated with the dialogue curriculum. Coders were given the curriculum so that they knew which in-class activities and exercises were explicit aspects of the curriculum. The measure is the number of references to activities and exercises across the entire paper.

Communication Processes

3. Engaging Self was coded when students wrote about sharing their own perspectives, taking risks in dialogue, revising their own opinions, admitting vulnerability, being able to speak openly without feeling judged, and being able to make mistakes. The measure is the number of references to Engaging Self across the paper.
4. Appreciating Difference was coded when students wrote about listening even if hurtful, understanding others' points of view, learning from each other, empathizing with others, showing sympathy for others, and trusting others. The measure is the number of references to Appreciating Difference across the paper.
5. Critical Reflection was coded when students wrote about being challenged to examine sources of biases, stereotypes, or assumptions about how society works, being challenged to consider how socialization operates as an aspect of social systems, being encouraged to think about power and inequality that the students might not have thought about before, and being encouraged to understand how power and privilege affects peoples' lives. The measure is the number of references to Critical Reflection across the paper.
6. Alliance Building was coded when students wrote about bridging across identities to common ground or common goals, talking about possible ways to relate to people from different groups, sticking with dialogue to work through conflict, and overcoming impediments to understanding. The measure is the number of references to Alliance Building across the paper.

Psychological Processes

7. Active Thinking was coded when the writing indicated liking to think, spending time thinking, trying to figure things out, or explicitly mentioning that they spent time reflecting on what they had learned in dialogue. Key words used to determine active thinking included: reflect, ponder, think, wonder, analyze. These terms capture the meaning of the liking to think scale

that has been used in numerous psychological studies (see Cacioppo & Petty, 1982). The measure is the number of references to Active Thinking across the paper.

8. Politicized identity was coded when students showed an understanding that their social identities were connected with subordinate and dominant positions in society. Words used to measure politicized identity included: privilege, power, oppression, advantages, disadvantages, and benefits. The measure is the number of references to Politicized Identity across the paper.

9. Emotion words were circled, although there was no effort to categorize different kinds or valence of emotions in coding of the papers. The measure is the number of emotion words across the entire paper. Coders were given an exhaustive list of emotion words, following a set of clusters of basic emotions (Ortony & Turner, 1990).

Kinds of Action

10. Collaborating with Others was coded when students wrote about working with others to change something, organizing action events on the campus, creating dialogues across different identity groups outside of class, and joining a group or organization aimed at increasing social justice. The measure is the number of references to Collaborating with Others.

11. Educating Others was coded when students wrote about confronting stereotypes and various "isms," sharing knowledge with others, educating about discrimination, and explaining what they had learned in dialogue to others. The measure is the number of references to Educating Others across the paper.

Engaged Listening in Race/Ethnicity and Gender Intergroup Dialogue Courses

Ximena Zúñiga
University of Massachusetts Amherst

Jane Mildred
Westfield State University

Rani Varghese, Keri DeJong, and Molly Keehn
University of Massachusetts Amherst

Although the importance of engaged listening in intergroup dialogue (IGD) is recognized, we know relatively little about when or why participants in IGD actually listen or what they gain from listening. Using qualitative analyses of interviews conducted with undergraduates who had recently completed a race/ethnicity or gender focused IGD course, this study examines what participants said about moments of engaged listening in IGD. We found that engaged listening was associated with specific dialogue activities, reactions to speakers, and dialogue topics. We also found a number of differences in listening between race/ethnicity and gender dialogues that suggest that participants in race/ethnicity IGDs recall more moments of engaged listening and may have gained a more complex understanding of structural inequality from engaged listening than participants in gender IGDs did. The article concludes with a discussion of the findings, possible implications, and some areas for future inquiry.

It is nearly impossible to find words that will do justice to the role of listening in any conversation, and most particularly dialogue ... How we listen, to what and to whom we listen, and the assumptions we listen through all frame our perception of reality ... In group dialogue, the power of listening increases exponentially because of collective listening and creation of shared meaning. (Ellinor & Gerard, 1998, pp. 98–99)

A number of writers have emphasized the importance of listening in various dialogical practices (Chasin et al., 1996; Ellinor & Gerard, 1998; Isaacs, 1999; Zúñiga, Nagda, & Sevig, 2002). These authors distinguish between simply hearing other people's words and the more engaged and active process of taking in and trying to understand the meaning of what is being said. This emphasis on the role of listening in dialogic practice is reflected in the Intergroup Dialogue (IGD) pedagogy and curriculum, which is designed to foster active listening skills and provides opportunities for participants to both speak and listen to one another within and across social identity groups

(Zúñiga, Nagda, Chesler, & Cytron-Walker, 2007). Recent research on learning outcomes in IGD, a critical-dialogic approach to engaging differences (Zúñiga et al., 2007; Zúñiga et al., 2002), suggests that participants do take in, reflect upon, and apply perspectives and information gained from their dialogue group (Nagda, 2006; Sorensen, Nagda, Gurin, & Maxwell, 2009; Zúñiga et al., 2007). While these findings are encouraging, very little is known about what participants in IGD actually listen to, whom they listen to and why, and what, if anything, they gain from listening. This article describes a qualitative analysis of post-dialogue interviews that explores engaged listening in IGD and begins to outline some of its dimensions and correlates. We begin with a brief review of the research literature on intergroup dialogue, with a particular emphasis on IGD process and outcomes to provide a context for the research findings. We also discuss the role and importance of listening in dialogue theory and practice in the literature review section. In the next section, we describe our research methods and discuss some of the limitations of the study. We then present our findings, including information about the aspects of the IGD curriculum most often referred to when participants recalled and described moments of engaged listening in the post-dialogue interviews, whom participants recalled listening to and why, the topics of discussion that appear to be associated with engaged listening, and the ways participants described the consequences of listening for themselves. The article concludes with a brief discussion of the findings and their possible implications and suggests some areas for future research.

RESEARCH ON INTERGROUP DIALOGUE

The practice of IGD has become increasingly common in K-12 and higher education over the course of the last 20 years (Dessel & Rogge, 2008; Diaz, 2009; Schoem & Hurtado, 2001; Zúñiga et al., 2007). IGD offers a critical-dialogic approach to engaging differences that situates intergroup relations within systems of power and privilege in order to promote critical awareness, bridging differences, and personal and collective agency (Zúñiga et al., 2007; Zúñiga et al., 2002). The practice of IGD brings people from diverse social identity groups together over a sustained period of time to engage in a dialogical process of exploring and learning about each others' personal and social identity-based perspectives and experiences, the nature and consequences of privilege and oppression in people's lives, and ways to work together to create a more socially just and inclusive society (Dessel & Rogge, 2008; Diaz, 2009; Schoem & Hurtado, 2001; Sorensen et al., 2009; Zúñiga et al., 2007). An IGD may focus on race/ethnicity, gender, sexuality, social class, religion, or some other identity-based issue and is usually balanced to include equal or fairly equal number of participants from the different social identity groups participating in the dialogue. Two trained facilitators co-facilitate an IGD, each of whom identifies with one of the groups included in the dialogue. IGD courses emphasize both content (e.g., readings, statistics) and process (e.g., experiential activities, structured dialogues, and reflective assignments). The IGD curriculum is designed to encourage participants to consider how relationships between groups have been influenced by historical legacies and how specific power relationships continue to be reinforced and reproduced at the individual, group, community, and institutional levels (Zúñiga et al., 2007).

Parallel to the growth of interest in IGD is a growing body of literature that theorizes about the conceptual and practical foundations of dialogue and IGD from various disciplinary and professional perspectives, including communication studies and cultural studies (Anderson, Baxter,

& Cissna, 2004; Ellinor & Girard, 1998; hooks, 1990), philosophy (Burbules, 1993), social psychology (Stephan & Stephan, 2001), and education (Freire, 1970; Zúñiga et al., 2002). Research within the social sciences and the professions offers empirical evidence of the educational benefits of dialogue for students in higher education (Dessel & Rogge, 2008; Díaz, 2009; Gurin, 1999; Hurtado, 2005; Nagda & Zúñiga, 2003; Sorensen et al., 2009; Zuñiga et al., 2007). Participation in IGD in college has been shown to increase communication and understanding of conflicting issues across lines of difference (Gurin, 1999; Gurin, Nagda, & Lopez, 2004; Gurin, Peng, Lopez, & Nagda, 1999; Nagda & Zúñiga, 2003; Zuñiga et al., 2007), to help bridge differences across groups (Nagda & Zúñiga, 2003) and to inspire action for social justice (Nagda, Kim, & Truelove, 2004). Recent studies conducted as part of a national, multi-institutional longitudinal study on race/ethnicity and gender dialogue courses offer strong evidence of the positive effects of IGD (Gurin, Nagda, & Zúñiga, in press). For instance, Gurin, Nagda, and Sorensen (2011) found significant effects for both race/ethnicity (white/people of color) and gender (men/women) dialogue participation on all but 4 of the 20 measures associated with intergroup understanding, intergroup relations, and intergroup collaboration and action. The results also indicate that these effects applied generally across all four demographic groups (white men, white women, men of color, and women of color). While some scholars have suggested that participants from privileged social identity groups may benefit more from participating in intergroup dialogue groups than participants from less privileged social identity groups (Dessel, Rogge, & Garlington, 2006; Gorski, 2008), findings from recent studies conducted as part of research on IGD in higher education have demonstrated that students from both advantaged and disadvantaged groups change on a range of measures as a result of participating in IGD courses (Gurin et al., in press; Nagda, Gurin, Sorensen, & Zúñiga, 2009).

Perspectives on the Role of Listening in Dialogue Practice

A number of theorists and practitioners have emphasized the importance of listening in dialogic encounters when addressing differences in values, ideology, and social group identities (Chasin et al., 1996; Chesler & Zúñiga, 1991; Isaacs, 1999; McCormick, 1999). According to Ellinor and Gerard (1998), dialogue, which literally refers to speaking, may be a rather misleading term for a practice where both speaking and listening are critical to the sustained communication necessary for developing deeper understanding. Other writers who have also examined the dialogic process have linked meaningful dialogue with how individuals participate in the co-creation of shared meaning, while also developing a sense of trust and mutuality through collective inquiry (Ellinor & Gerard, 1998; Isaacs, 1999; Romney, 2003). Affective responses, such as empathy and respect (Isaacs, 1999; Stephan & Stephan, 2001; Yeakley, 1998) and "voicing," attentive listening, and inquiry behaviors (Brookfield & Preskill, 2005; Ellinor & Gerard, 1998; Isaacs, 1999; Nagda & Zúñiga, 2003) also have been associated with dialogue. While some of these features of dialogue practice focus on a need for thoughtful communicative behaviors (e.g., listening attentively, asking thoughtful questions), others highlight the importance of being emotionally present in the conversation or the ability to think clearly and practice inner reflection before reaching conclusions (Isaacs, 1999; McCormick, 1999). Since all of these practices would require participants to listen and to process incoming information, as well as to speak, these perspectives implicitly link the practice of listening with emotional and cognitive processes that have been said to support successful dialogue (Werkmeister-Rozas, Zúñiga, & Stassen, 2008).

Isaacs (1999) has addressed the role of listening in IGD even more explicitly, writing that "a simple but profound capacity to listen is at the heart of dialogue" (p. 84). According to Isaacs, listening requires that "we not only hear the words, but also embrace, accept, and gradually let go of our inner clamoring" (p. 84). Both Isaacs and others who have written about dialogue are clearly referring to a "deeper" or more fully engaged type of listening, one that involves more than just "hearing" another person's words and, instead, searches for meaning and seeks understanding. According to Teurfs (cited in Weiler, 1994) deeper listening requires holding one's assumptions and judgments loosely and engaging in a process that makes sure people have really heard each other by paying attention, focusing on the moment, and not getting lost in their own thoughts and reactions. Deep listening has been connected to both empathy and perspective taking, meaning that the listener is able to both feel what the speaker is conveying and take in the speaker's perspective while listening (McCormick, 1999). Other writers have also connected deep listening to the processes of learning to value and respect the other; being open to others' perspectives and experiences by suspending judgment of the speaker and of what the speaker is saying; and noticing and reflecting on assumptions and emotions that might interfere with hearing and taking in the intended message (Bohm, 1985, 1990; Ellinor & Gerard, 1998; Isaacs, 1999). Fully attentive listening is believed to mirror some of the intrapersonal and interpersonal processes involved in engaged learning (Fredericks, Blumenfeld, & Paris, 2004). For this reason, rather than using one of the several terms used to describe listening in the dialogue literatures, we refer to the type of listening we are examining here as "engaged listening."

METHODS

Data Source

The findings reported in this study were derived from two separate and sequential analyses of post-dialogue interviews conducted with participants in either a race/ethnicity (white people/people of color) or a gender (men/women) IGD course. These courses were offered at nine public and private institutions of higher education as part of a national study that used a mixed-methods longitudinal design to generalize effects across institutions and assess educational impact over time (Gurin et al., 2011, in press). Institutions with existing IGD programs or faculty with expertise in IGD were included in the study. Interested undergraduates on each campus applied to take an IGD course and were randomly selected to participate in either an IGD course or a control group. Participants were included in an IGD if they identified themselves as either male or female and as either white or a member of a racial/ethnic minority group (e.g., African American, Asian American, Latino/a, Native American). Trained facilitators, using a standardized curriculum, led the IGD courses weekly for 2–3 hours over the course of a 10–14 week term. In addition to completing assigned or individually chosen readings, students wrote weekly reflection logs, participated in an intergroup collaboration action project, and wrote a final reflection paper. Participants were interviewed for 45–60 minutes, 1–2 weeks after completing the course. The main topics covered in the interview were course impact, thoughts and feelings about social identities made salient by the experience, the extent to which students were engaged in the dialogue process, quality of group interaction, their understanding of social inequality and explanations for it, and the acquisition of skills for working with differences, disagreement, and conflicts. All of the 248 post-dialogue interviews were tape-recorded with participants' consent and participants were informed about means for maintaining confidentiality in the gathering, analyzing, and storage of the interview data. The recorded interviews were transcribed and then coded by a team of researchers using a set of a pre-defined codes for a variety of engagement processes, including "listening engagement."

The "engaged listening" research team (the authors of this article), conducted our initial phase of analysis on a dataset that included only those passages from the 248 interviews that had been coded as "listening engagement" by the original coders. Our inductive analysis of this dataset focused on identifying major themes in the data in order to develop a set of grounded or emergent categories and codes to apply to a smaller dataset in our second phase of analysis. This analysis also helped us refine our definition of "engaged listening," which we defined as "times when participants listened to something said in their dialogue that engaged them enough to be able to remember significant details about what had been said and describe them to an interviewer after the IGD course was over." Our purposes for applying the coding paradigm generated by an inductive analysis of the listening passages from the larger dataset to the smaller sample of complete interview transcripts were to examine moments of listening in context and to explore our original findings in greater depth. The categories generated in our initial analysis of the original listening engagement dataset are reflected in the headings and findings presented below. However, the specific findings discussed within each heading reflect the results of our coding and analysis of the 40-interview sample.

The smaller sample of 40 interviews used to examine engaged listening in IGD in greater depth was created by randomly selecting either a gender or a race/ethnicity dialogue group from each of eight institutions participating in the study and one gender and one race/ethnicity dialogue from the ninth institution, which had implemented twice as many dialogues as the other eight institutions. Participants from each of these ten dialogue groups were then sorted into four groups (white women, women of color, white men, and men of color) and one participant was randomly selected from each of these four groups in order to produce equal numbers of participants from each group in the 40 interviews sample. Thus, the sample included a diverse set of participants from different regions of the country, different social and economic class backgrounds, and different types of hosting institutions.

Table 1 describes the areas of findings from our initial analysis of the complete "listening engagement" dataset that we used as major categories and codes in our analysis of the 40-interview sample.

Data Analysis

We used several qualitative approaches and techniques to examine the two datasets in our two-phase analysis of post-dialogue interviews. Most of these approaches have their roots in the tenets of grounded theory, initially proposed as a way to examine qualitative data by Glaser and Strauss (1967) and later elaborated upon, extended, or transformed by writers such as Strauss and Corbin (1990), Miles and Huberman (1994), and Charmaz (2006). In the first phase of analysis, we relied on microscopic methods, such as examining multiple meanings associated with individual words (Strauss, 1987) and line-by-line "in vivo" coding (Strauss & Corbin, 1990), to develop a detailed coding schema to use in our coding of our smaller sample. Throughout

TABLE 1

Emergent Thematic Categories Associated with Engaged Listening (Listed in Order of Frequency Found within Each Category)

When in the dialogues do participants recall listening?	**Curricular activities that were associated with engaged listening** 1. Testimonials 2. Caucus Groups and Fishbowls 3. Open Dialogue/Hot Topics
Whom do people recall listening to and why?	**Social identity group affiliation** 1. Own social identity group 2. Other social identity group
	Reactions to speakers or characteristics of speakers that were associated with engaged listening 1. Identified with the speaker or speakers 2. Did not identify with the speaker or speakers 3. Disagreed with the speaker or speakers 4. Viewed the speakers or the speakers as "different" from themselves

What do people recall listening to?	**Topics of conversation that were associated with engaged listening**
	1. Topics related to race/ethnicity:
	  • Racism and white privilege (structural inequality, power, and privilege are implicitly or explicitly addressed).
	  • Racial/ethnic identities and racial categories (focus is on identity, difference, or similarity, but structural inequality is not addressed)
	2. Topics related to gender:
	  • Gender roles and relationships (focus is on roles, socialization, identity, and cross-gender relationships, but structural inequality is not addressed)
	  • Sexism and male privilege (structural inequality, power, and privilege are implicitly or explicitly addressed)

What are the consequences of listening?	**Information provided by participants about their short- and longer-term responses to what they heard** 1. Immediate responses (emotional, verbal, and reflective responses soon after) 2. Extended reflection, awareness, and learning (new awareness or learning linked to specific moments of engaged listening)

the iterative stages of analysis in both phases, we scheduled frequent team meetings, drafted written memos (Miles & Huberman, 1994), created visual models and diagrams, and used e-mail communication to check with each other about what we were seeing in the data and to examine themes, explore emerging hypotheses, check each other's coding for consistency, and discuss personal and group assumptions and reactions. Using the method of constant comparison to identify patterns, sequences, and variations (Glaser & Strauss, 1967; Strauss & Corbin, 1990) and talking and writing about our emerging findings, the team began to formulate grounded theories and questions that we then returned to the data to re-examine. After our initial paper and pencil codings of both datasets, we used N-Vivo software (QSR International, 2008) for data management and the tools within that program to explore co-occurrences of findings and to correlate findings with information about participants' identities (race/ethnicity and/or gender) and type of dialogue. The integrity and completeness of the findings (Lincoln & Guba, 1996) were examined throughout the data analysis process by looking for negative cases, examining cross-coder consistency, using group discussions to clarify and discuss what we were seeing, and, in our analysis of the 40-interview sample, by examining passages coded for engaged listening within the context of the entire interview.

Strengths and Limitations of this Study

This qualitative study examined interviews with students who had completed their IGD but had not yet received a grade for the course. Although the interviewers informed the participants that the interviewers were not in a position to influence participants' grades, it is possible that anxiety about performance or grades, along with social desirability factors, might have influenced students' responses. Also, the findings are based on participants' responses to interview questions that were designed to solicit detailed information about what participants recalled thinking, feeling, and doing in the dialogue, but we have no way of knowing if their recollections accurately reflect what was actually said in the dialogue. In addition, the types of questions that participants were asked are likely to have influenced what participants recalled and shared during the interview. Therefore, we cannot claim that the moments of engaged listening examined for this research are representative of all engaged listening in IGD.

Finally, the research team that conducted this research consists of five women from diverse racial/ethnic, national, and first language backgrounds, professional roles, and academic disciplines. All of us are actively involved in the practice of IGD in higher education, or have closely studied it, and we have all taught undergraduate or graduate courses that focus on race/racism and gender/sexism. While we made effort to engage in a systematic and rigorous inquiry throughout the research process, we also continually reflected on the partiality of our interpretations and examined our perspectives and frames of reference in relationship to the topics and issues that arose in order to understand how our individual and collective standpoints might influence our findings (Rossman & Rallis, 2003). Among other considerations, we frequently reflected upon and discussed how our mutual involvement with IGD and our shared and different experiences as women living in a racist and sexist society might be both strengths and limitations in relationship to this research. Specifically, we tried to examine whether people who were not familiar with IGD or people with different standpoints or life experiences might draw different meanings and conclusions from the data.

FINDINGS

Almost all of the participants in the 248 interviews were able to describe comments or interactions in their dialogues in sufficient detail to meet our definition of engaged listening. Furthermore, most participants demonstrated multiple instances of engaged listening, although participants in the race/ethnicity dialogues recalled and described many more moments of engaged listening than participants in the gender dialogues did. In this section, we present the results of our coding and analyses of the 40-interview sample and foreground factors that appear to have contributed to or influenced participants' engagement in listening.

When in the Dialogue Do Participants Recall Listening?

Many of the examples of engaged listening found in the interview data are associated with activities or sessions aimed at encouraging speaking and listening in the large group, particularly the Testimonials activity, the Caucus Groups/Fishbowls activity, and the Open Dialogue sessions that focused on "hot topics" (See Zúñiga et al., 2007, for a detailed description of the four stage IGD curriculum and activities). We briefly describe these activities in this section. However, we will not provide specific examples here because the moments of engaged listening described later illustrate well the role and importance of these particular structured activities as contexts for listening. The activity participants most commonly associated with engaged listening is the Testimonial activity used in the third or fourth session of the IGD. In this activity, dialogue participants write about their thoughts, feelings, and experiences as members of two different social identity groups (one advantaged and one disadvantaged) and then share what they wrote with the group. Students often share meaningful and personally challenging experiences and stories in this activity, which may affect other participants and the dialogue process. Another activity that appears to have stimulated engaged listening is the Caucus Group/Fishbowl activity, often used in the fourth or fifth session. The Caucus Group activity involves participating in an intra-group dialogue with group members who share the same social identity, as defined by the type of IGD. The Fishbowl activity follows the Caucus Group activity and involves people from the two social identity groups sitting in concentric circles, with those in the outer circle silently listening to those in the inner circle. The third most frequently mentioned element of the IGD curriculum associated with engaged listening is the Open Dialogue sessions, which are scheduled in the second half of the course. In these sessions, participants explore contested or difficult topics and practice dialogue skills in the large group for most of the session. Open dialogue topics included sexual assault (in the gender dialogue groups) and affirmative action (in the race/ethnicity dialogue groups).

Whom Do People Recall Listening To and Why?

One factor that may be associated with engaged listening is the social identity or identities of the person (or people) speaking. We identified, whenever possible, the social identities (e.g., race and/or gender) of the listener and the speaker(s) during moments of engaged listening. From this, we hoped to learn more about if and when people's social identities influence who listens to whom in a diverse group. We found that most participants recalled and described listening to people in their own social identity group (as defined by the type of dialogue they participated in) as well as to people from the other social identity group. Participants who described something someone in the other social identity group said often noted that this kind of listening helped them to think about things they had not thought about or that what they heard challenged their stereotypes, beliefs, or assumptions about the other group. Participants who described something people in their own social identity group often referred to the discovery of within-group differences between the participant and the speaker.

When participants offered explanations for why they listened, they gave several different reasons. Some said that they listened because they could identify with the speaker, and others said they listened because they disagreed with or were unable to relate to what speaker said. Other participants listened because they were struck by how "different" their own experiences or views were from those of the speaker or speakers. Of these, participants in the sample most often described being engaged by a story, an idea, or an experience that they either strongly identified with or that helped them understand or empathize with someone else's experience or perception.

For example, a woman of color in a gender dialogue described listening to other women in her group who shared their experiences of being molested, an experience she could understand and relate. From a different perspective, a white woman in a gender dialogue became upset about and struggled to understand the experience shared by an Asian woman of mixed heritage who talked at length about not being accepted by her family because she was both a girl and biracial.

Speakers whose views or perspectives were different from the listener's also seemed to stimulate engaged listening. For example, a white man in a race dialogue recalled listening to other white students in the white Caucus Group who said they didn't think they benefited from white priviledge because their parents were poor. While the participant could relate to what his peers were saying on some level because he also grew up poor, he believed he has benefited from white priviledge because he has never experienced negative consequences because of his race.

In some instances, participants were engaged to listen by a conflict or disagreement. For instance, a female participant in a gender dialogue described how she "butted heads" with another female participant because of her traditional views about gender roles. In another gender dialogue, a woman describes a moment when a man talked about his feelings about legalizing gay marriage and whether marriage should be called marriage: "He wasn't just talking about just for gay people. He was talking about it in general, but no one knew that at first. So it became like this big disagreement."

In examining the extent to which the various types of reactions to the speaker was linked to a particular social identity group membership and/or type of dialogue, we noticed some distinct patterns in participants' recollections across race/ethnicity and gender dialogue courses. For example, while participants in both race and gender dialogues mentioned "identifying with the speaker" and "not identifying with the speaker" at similar rates, students of color in race/ethnicity dialogues mentioned identifying with the speaker three times more often than white students did. In addition, participants in race/ethnicity dialogues described listening to a "different" view or experience almost three times more often than participants in gender dialogues. However, "disagreeing with the speaker" was referred to twice as often in gender dialogues as in race/ethnicity dialogues. This pattern suggests that perceived "differences" in experience seem to prompt engaged listening in race/ethnicity dialogues, whereas disagreement appears to influence engaged listening in gender dialogues.

What Do People Recall Listening To?

Both the original listening engagement dataset and the smaller sample of interviews we examined in depth provided a great deal of information about the topics or issues participants recalled being discussed in the dialogue at the time when engaged listening appears to have occurred. This finding suggests that the topic of discussion may be a very important factor to consider when trying to understand what engages students in IGD in listening. In this section, our goal is to explore what these topics are and to provide more detailed and nuanced examples of the kinds of stories and interactions participants recalled and chose to describe in the post-dialogue interviews. It is important to note that these are examples from individual participant's recollections or narratives about what was said in the group and that different members of the group sometimes recalled the same events quite differently. Therefore, we are not providing descriptions of what actually happened in the group, but rather examples of what some participants recalled and described in an interview and how they reflected upon and made meaning of these experiences.

In the 40-interview sample, the specific topic of a recalled story or conversation was mentioned almost 250 times. We created a list of all topics mentioned in the context of engaged listening and found that they quite easily clustered into the three main categories or topical areas we had found during our earlier analysis: "race/ethnicity-related topics," "gender-related topics," and "other" topics. Approximately one-third of these references were to gender-related topics and the remaining two-thirds were mostly references to race-related topics. The number of topics that did not fit into either of these categories ("other" topics) was so small that we were unable to identify any noticeable patterns or themes; therefore, the focus in this section is on topics related to race/ethnicity and gender. For the most part, participants in race/ethnicity (white people/people of color) dialogues described listening to race-related topics and participants in gender (men/women) dialogues described listening to gender-related topics. However, race-related topics were much described more often by participants in gender dialogues than gender-related topics were described by participants in race/ethnicity dialogues. Within these broad categories, we further divided the topics into those instances when the participant's descriptions highlighted some aspect of oppression or privilege (for example, experiences of racism or discussions about male privilege) and those where the participant's description focused more on personal identities or across or within group similarities and differences (for example, gender role socialization or differences between and among racial/ethnic identity groups). Many of the topics associated with engaged listening appear to have engaged participants emotionally or to have been connected to conflict in the group, suggesting that these topics might have been more memorable or important to participants than more neutral topics.

Topics Related to Racism and Racial Privilege

The mostly commonly reported set of topics related to race/ethnicity focused on what we categorized as some aspect of racism. Over half of the topics related to race fit within this category. These included times when participants made reference to or demonstrated engaged listening in response to someone sharing a personal experience of racism, to a discussion about racism as a system of inequality, or to a discussion about white privilege. Of these, there were almost three times as many references to personal experiences of or discussions about racism as there were to topics related to white privilege. Several themes emerged in our analysis of how topics related to race-based oppression and privilege were talked about in the interviews. One important theme that emerged was how firsthand stories about experiences of racism "brought home" for some white participants, and for some of the participants of color, the idea that racism is still very much alive. For example, one white woman in a race/ethnicity dialogue recalled that a black man in her group talking about being stopped on the streets with some friends and being "totally abused" by the police. She said, "And that really upset me because you hear about that, but I haven't heard it from the voice of an individual sitting in front of me. You hear it sort of on the news but it's kind of distant that way." She went on to ask, "Why haven't I heard this before? Perhaps it's something with the group of friends and the environment that I live in that I haven't heard stories like this before. So that also got me thinking." Participants also recalled listening to other participants describe experiences of racism that included being discriminated against and tracked into certain academic majors and courses. While some interviewees presented these primarily as examples of how certain white people still discriminate against people of color (individual acts of racism), other interviewees suggested that these stories helped them to understand what was meant by racism as a system of inequality.

Topics Related to Racial Identities and Racial Categories

The second most commonly mentioned topic area related to race/ethnicity included recalled conversations about how racial categories, racial identities, and racial stereotypes were found by participants, including, at times, the person being interviewed, to be confusing, problematic, or fluid. Most of the recollections in this category focused on conversations about within and across group differences rather than similarities within or across groups. There were several different themes related to within-group differences. According to some participants, there were people of color in their group, particularly immigrant students, who primarily identified with their country of origin, others who said that they saw themselves as primarily "American," and still others who said that they had never thought of themselves as people of color. Though it was clear that the people of color group did develop a strong sense of solidarity in the race/ethnicity dialogues, they continued to be aware of ways in which they might be more or less disadvantaged by within group differences such as gender, socioeconomic class, where they grew up (including the racial/ethnic mix of their schools and neighborhoods), and immigration/citizenship status.

When white people were described as having spoken about within-group differences, a number were said to have highlighted differences among white people based on socioeconomic class. White students also reportedly talked about differences in religion, immigration and citizenship status, first language, gender, and sexual orientation. Reflecting on these conversations, both white participants and participants of color thought that bringing up within group differences among white people might have been used by certain white students to deny that they had white privilege or to present themselves as "good" white people who could understand or relate to the experiences of people of color. On the other hand, both white students and students of color mentioned in their interviews that listening to these conversations had also helped them to understand how difficult it is for white people to talk about race without having people of color present to be the focus of their attention, as well as how difficult it can be for white people to be proud of, or even to acknowledge, their racial identity. For example, one man of color recalled how the people in his group in the Caucus Group activity was talking about how proud they were to be members of their racial/ethnic groups, while white people in his IGD could not say that they are proud of being white "because they were just like, 'That's not right to say.'" This participant's response to this experience was "sad and surprised. It was just an interesting combination of feelings."

Across group differences that participants recalled people of color in the group noting or reflecting on included the idea that people of color speak two cultural languages while white people speak only one and the idea that white people and people of color may have very different understandings of economic disadvantage. Across group (and, at times, within group) differences may have been simply noted in the IGD or used to gain greater insight into each other's experiences, but they also sometimes appear to have led to conflicts as well as engaged listening, in the group. Topics that seemed to generate the most intense conflicts included affirmative action, whether white people who associate mostly or entirely with other white people are racist, how much race affects the choices people have or make, and whether a particular campus is or is not "diverse." These conflicts often appeared to be between several more outspoken members of the groups and sometimes split the group across race/ethnicity or gender lines. In some instances, students in the group attempted to bridge across these conflicts by saying that they agree with points being made by both sides.

The range of topics related to race/ethnicity described by interview participants illustrates the complexity of the issues participants in these dialogues grappled with and the role of listening in helping students to clarify their own viewpoint, understand the experiences and viewpoints of others, and begin to bridge across their differences.

Topics Related to Gender Roles and Relationships

The most commonly reported set of topics related to gender, almost all of which were mentioned by participants in the gender (men/women) dialogues, included personal and interpersonal aspects of gender, such as gender roles and socialization, gender differences, and the complexities of relationships between women and men. More than half of the topics related to gender fell within this category. Specific topics that interview participants recalled listening to included how men and women express or are expected to express emotions differently, how men and women behave differently in same sex and mixed groups, and whether men and women could or should conform to society's traditional gender roles. Participants in gender groups recalled both men and women in their group talking about how men are limited or hurt by their gender roles, how women appear to have more flexibility in their gender roles, and how men experience negative consequences when they fail to conform to traditional ideas of masculinity. For example, one woman recalled hearing a man in the group talking about his failure to meet his grandfather's expectations. She was struck by "how deeply that still affects him and how he still feels that he's trying to live up to these expectations of his grandfather, who's probably dead now."

Another topic related to gender roles had to do with how much group members' families subscribed to or deviated from traditional gender roles. Adherence to more traditional gender roles tended to be attributed to differences in religion, region, and culture. For example, one woman in a gender group reported that another woman in her group, who came from a family with strict religious beliefs, had said that "a women's place is in the home." Other women in the group reportedly had rejected this idea but still talked about how they wanted to be at home with their children. Still other women reportedly talked about wanting to be independent but still hoping to take advantage of some of the benefits of "being a girl."

Topics Related to Sexism and Gender Privilege

The second most frequently mentioned set of topics related to gender focused on issues related to gender-based privilege and oppression, particularly sexism. Of these, there were seven times as many references to sexism as to male privilege. Topics related to sexism that participants recalled being discussed in their groups included gender-based job discrimination, the tracking of women into "feminine" careers, and the mistreatment of women who choose to enter traditionally "masculine" fields. For example, both male and female participants referred to the testimonial of an African American woman dialogue group facilitator who had decided to major in engineering and was told by a guidance counselor that she had only chosen this field in order to "make a point." An Asian American man in a gender group, also an engineering student, reflected on listening to an Asian American woman in his group talk about discrimination and said to the interviewer that he had come to realize that this woman's experience was very different from his because she was a woman in a male-dominated field.

Some female participants expressed appreciation for men's acknowledgment of sexism or of their own privilege. For example, one woman said that she was impressed that a man in her group had been outraged by an article in a school newspaper that focused on women candidates' appearance rather than their ideas. Another woman noted, however, that in her dialogue group women tended to talk about the experience of oppression, while men rarely talked about privilege. She said, "I think one of the best examples was during the Fishbowl activity where the girls . . . all talked about . . . the oppression we felt . . . in different situations . . . (W)hen the guys came in and talked, they never once mentioned the fact that they were a group [with] privilege, and it never came up." Some male participants, however, did describe things that were said in their dialogue that helped them understand sexism. For example, one male participant said he was shocked to hear a friend say in the dialogue that he did not like to take orders from a woman.

The topic of sexual assault was a frequently mentioned topic related to gender, perhaps because it appears to have become a source of disagreement and conflict in some of the gender groups. Several participants recalled and expressed surprise that some of these conflicts did not appear to divide the group along gender lines. For example, a woman of color in a gender group recalled a white male participant claiming that "the rapist is the real victim in sexual assault." She recalled that she and other members of the group, both men and women, responded angrily to this statement. Several female participants also recalled that some of the men in this group spoke defensively or remained silent when issues related to sexual assault came up. These perceptions were supported by recollections shared by a couple of male participants in gender groups. For example, one man of color told the interviewer, "I didn't feel engaged because I didn't connect with that because I wasn't a woman. I just listened." Later, he reflected on what he had heard in the interview and said that he had come to realize that sexual assault "is a serious thing and it's something that I don't normally think about because I'm not at a high risk of being raped." He added, "And that's what I took with me . . . to really listen to a woman describe how she may be fearful in certain situations where she's by herself." Though this participant recalled "just listening" to a difficult conversation in his dialogue, his words illustrate how comments or topics that create conflict in a group may also stimulate engaged listening, reflection, and greater appreciation for the experiences of others.

What are the Consequences of Listening?

The consequences of listening described in this section include both responses and new learning that were explicitly linked by the participants themselves to something they had described listening to in their dialogue. For example, if the participant in the interview said "What she said really made me think" or "What those two students said made me angry," those statements would have been coded for consequences of listening. We found that participants' immediate responses to listening included emotional responses, verbal responses, and reflection. Understandings that developed over time included new and sustained awareness and learning. In some instances, these immediate responses and longer-term understandings occurred independently of each other, and at other times they were interconnected or occurred sequentially. Some participants in the 40-interview sample, for example, simply responded verbally to something they heard and then moved on, while others had an emotional response "in the moment," responded verbally, thought about the exchange afterward, and eventually arrived at a new level of understanding by the time of, or even during, the post-dialogue interview.

Immediate Responses

Immediate responses to engaged listening are emotional, verbal, and reflective responses that participants recalled having immediately after listening to something that was said in their dialogue group. In many cases, these immediate responses were in reaction to stories or exercises that were connected to curricular activities, such as Testimonials, Caucus Groups and/or Fishbowls, and Open Dialogues on "hot topics." Emotional responses included feelings, which were more gut-level reactions, and empathic responses, which involved attempts to understand the feelings of others. Examples of feeling responses included a man of color saying that he felt excited when he heard that another group member understood the experience of being stereotyped; a white man saying he felt upset after hearing group members, and in particular women in his group, making victim-blaming comments in an open gender dialogue about sexual violence; and a white woman's angry response to group members who asked questions about the cause of another participant's gay identity. These emotional responses were often a direct result of hearing something new or experiencing difficult moments. For example, a white man in a gender dialogue said that he was surprised and upset after hearing a black male facilitator say he would consciously act in a certain way so as not be seen as a "typical black male." Though this student was upset by the story, the facilitator's story also brought the impact of racism to the forefront of the participant's consciousness. This was an important moment of insight for him in the dialogue. Examples of empathic responses included a woman of color's recognition that a Jewish woman's reflections about her Jewish cultural and religious identities mirrored some of her own feelings and a recognition, on the part of some white students, that students of color live with nearly constant reminders of their race and status in society.

Verbal responses involved a participant's immediate decision to speak in response to something he or she had listened to. Participants identified several different reasons for responding verbally. These included a desire to move the process of the dialogue forward or in a different direction and the desire to mediate, facilitate, or offer another perspective to a discussion that was stuck or had become polarized. For example, a woman of color in a race/ethnicity dialogue said that she had helped facilitate a conflict between a woman and a man in the group by reminding them of the guidelines for dialogue. One of the most common reasons for choosing to respond verbally was to ask a question to better understand what had been said. For example, a white woman in a gender dialogue told the interviewer that she had used question-posing as a way to understand another participant's feelings about gay marriage. Another reason for responding verbally was disagreeing with or wanting to challenge something that had been heard. Overall, there were more verbal responses reported in race dialogues than in gender dialogues. There were also twice as many verbal responses reported by women as by men and a slightly higher rate of verbal responses reported by people of color than by white people.

Reflective responses were responses that occurred in the immediate aftermath of hearing personal experiences, stories, or testimonials. Participants reported reflecting about what another participant or participants had said about a number of issues. For example, a white woman in a race/ethnicity dialogue recalled reflecting that "part of white privilege is not having to think about it." A white male participant realized that "racist things still go [on]" after hearing a black male student's experiences of racism while participating in a white-dominated sport. A woman of color in a gender dialogue realized, after hearing a white woman share her story of being homeless and not having enough to eat, that she had not thought about the class struggles her classmates faced. A large difference in reported rates of reflection was found when gender and race dialogues were compared. Almost all of the participants in the race dialogues reported reflection, while only half of the participants in the gender dialogues did. However, the issues gender dialogues participants reflected on were more varied than those in race dialogues. Participants addressed a range of topics that intersected with gender (i.e., sexual orientation and race), while in race dialogues, the focus was primarily on race and racism.

Extended Reflection, Awareness, and Learning

New awareness and learning that participants linked to engaged listening involved further reflection over time about something that had been heard in the dialogue. Participants reported reflecting and learning about a range of issues from other participants, such as sexual violence, individual experiences with racism, the costs of institutional racism, and the benefits of privilege. Participants in race/ethnicity dialogues reported having gained new awareness and knowledge about the nature and extent of racism and white privilege, including the effects of racism on people of color, particularly the effects of negative stereotypes and overtly racist behavior. For example, a white man in a race/ethnicity dialogue reported that hearing firsthand accounts of racism from students of color during the testimonials activity made him realize that discrimination really gets in the way of achieving one's full potential, affects job advancement, and results in racial profiling. From these realizations, he learned that "there really IS such a thing as institutional racism in America." This participant also gained awareness of his own white privilege, noting that he could go through his "whole life never having to deal with that." Other white students also gained awareness about the nature of racism. For example, a white woman described an increased awareness of the subtle and covert ways in which racism occurs:

> Before this class, I had thought if someone's racist, you're going to know they're racist, or if someone does something derogatory, you're going to automatically know. But after this class I realized that someone that may not consider themselves racist may be in other ways that [aren't] so visible.

Participants of color also reflected on their own lack of awareness about the extent of racism, how it is experienced by different groups of people of color, and how it is internalized by people of color. For example, a woman of color discussed her increased awareness of power, privilege, and oppression in society after listening to other students of color. Previously, she had held the belief that if someone worked hard, they could "avoid the effects of racism," but the dialogue had made her "more conscious" of the pervasiveness of its effects.

Participants in gender dialogues also reported learning about the negative effects of sexism on women. For example, one white man reported having reflected on the meaning of the word "bitch" after a dialogue session in which group members discussed whether or not gender stereotypes were associated with the word. While he had not been able to determine, at the time of the dialogue, "who was right or wrong," this participant thought and wrote about this issue afterward and concluded that a word that means "female dog," when applied to women, does imply that women are inferior. Participants in gender dialogues also reported insights about gender roles and the inaccuracy of stereotypes about women. For example, another white male participant realized that stereotypes about women are "not true but socially constructed." An older, white, lesbian participant in a gender dialogue also shared that she had stereotyped a group of young heterosexual women in her group as "drama queens," but realized, after hearing their stories in the caucus group, that these women also faced challenges, such as trying to fit into constructions of femininity and dealing with the glass ceiling in the workplace. As a result of reflection over time, this woman came to believe she had more in common with these women than she initially thought she had. A man of color who had participated in a gender dialogue thought about his lack of awareness about sexism and came to recognize his male privilege after really listening to women describe how they may be fearful in certain situations when they are by themselves. Most new learning about gender and sexism focused on the negative effects of sexism on women rather than on how men perpetuate and benefit from gender inequality.

SUMMARY AND DISCUSSION

As cited in our review of the literature, a number of studies have established the positive effects of IGD participation on a variety of outcomes. While several theories and explanations have been offered about how and why these positive outcomes occur, few empirical studies have examined the dialogic processes influencing them (Nagda, 2006; Sorensen et al., 2009; Zúñiga et al., 2007). By opening a window into what participants remember doing, thinking, feeling, and understanding while they were engaged in listening to others in their IGDs, this study's findings shed new light on factors that influence engagement, communication, and learning in IGD.

The importance of listening in IGD has been emphasized by a number of writers and supported by our own work as IGD practitioners, researchers, and theorists. Through this research, however, we have discovered that engaged listening is more multi-layered, rich, and contextual than we had previously understood. We found that participants' motivations to listen closely to other participants in the dialogues appear to be stimulated by specific curricular activities, by characteristics of and reactions to certain speakers, and by particular topics of conversation. These findings may be helpful in ongoing efforts to enhance intergroup dialogue pedagogy and praxis. For example, information that certain dialogue activities (e.g., Testimonials, Caucus Groups, and Fishbowls) appear to be associated with engaged listening may be helpful in designing dialogue courses or scaffolding learning experiences in IGD. Similarly, knowing which topics people in different types of IGDs tend to listen to may be helpful in adapting the IGD design to different sets of cross-group issues. Our findings also challenge some assertions and assumptions that have been made about IGD. For example, Dessel, Rogge, and Garlington (2006) and Gorski (2008) have argued that IGD mainly involves people from disadvantaged groups who educate people from advantaged groups. Our finding that most participants in both race/ethnicity and gender groups listen to people from their own and the other group does not appear to support this assertion. Participants from both advantaged and disadvantaged groups in each type of dialogue appear to have been interested in and to have learned from both groups in their IGD. Finally, our findings in regard to the consequences of listening, in both the short and longer-term, support quantitative findings about the positive effects of IGD and offer insights into the role of listening in fostering some of those outcomes.

In addition to our overall findings about engaged listening in IGD, our analysis of post-dialogue interviews suggests that patterns of listening may be different in race/ethnicity dialogue groups and in gender dialogue groups. We were struck quite early in our analysis of post-dialogue interviews by how many more moments of engaged listening were described by participants from the race/ethnicity dialogues than by participants in the gender dialogues. As we continued our analysis, we also found that reactions to speakers and to different dialogue topics as well as the consequences of listening were different for participants in the two types of IGD. For example, we noticed that participants in race/ethnicity IGDs reflected more on their experiences in their dialogues than participants in gender IGDs did. There also appears to have been a greater focus on the societal and institutional dimensions of race and racism in race/ethnicity dialogues, while gender dialogues focused more on interpersonal aspects of gender, such as intimate relationships between women and men and gender role expectations.

In trying to make sense of the differences between what participants in race/ethnicity dialogues and participants in gender dialogues said in their interviews, we explored a number of possible explanations that might be studied further in future analysis and research. For example, did we find a higher level of interest in and understanding of oppression and privilege in race/ethnicity dialogues than in gender dialogues because participants in race/ethnicity dialogues entered the dialogue with a greater recognition of the realities and consequences of racism or are other factors involved that we have not considered? Similarly, did we find that both women and men in gender IGD appear to be more interested in gender roles and relationships than in sexism or gender privilege because they subscribe to the apparently widespread belief that gender issues are either resolved or trivial in contemporary U.S. society (DeFrancisco & Palczewski, 2007), because they see gender differences as rooted in biology, or because they worry that talking about gender-based inequities is unsafe?

Much of what has been written about IGD, and therefore its pedagogical approaches, draws from the literature that promotes interracial contact as a condition for improving intergroup relations (Sorensen et al., 2009; Stephan & Stephan, 2001), and this literature is largely premised on bringing estranged groups together to develop mutual understanding. Such a premise may not be applicable when members of both groups have close contact with one another for much of their lives, as men and women usually do (Gurin, 1985; Gurin et al., in press; hooks, 1990). Our findings suggest that gender (men/women) dialogue groups may require an approach that addresses the unique historical, social, and emotional/relational contexts of gender relations, particularly in "post-feminist" times (Faludi, 2006). For example, more time may be necessary to examine gender-based social inequities, such as differences in pay for similar jobs, women's responsibility for most care-giving activities, the feminization of poverty, media images of women and men, reproductive rights, and how persistent patterns of male violence at every level of society serve as a form of social control that limits women's independence. Extending the amount of time in same-gender caucus groups and/or offering more training to IGD facilitators about these issues also may be needed to help participants critically examine the impact of sexism on their lives. In addition, while gender dialogues need to attend to a continuum of gender identities and performances that intersect with other identities, they also need to maintain a focus on institutional sexism as a system of social, political, and economic inequality that shapes and limits the life experience of people based on their perceived sex, regardless of how they define or experience their own gender identity.

This study has yielded a number of interesting and provocative findings. However, these findings are largely descriptive. In the future, we plan to explore these findings in greater depth by conducting group level as well as individual level analyses of the interview data. For example, looking at all of the interviews from each of the ten IGD groups represented in this study would help us to identify the effects of different interpersonal, regional, and institutional contexts on listening behavior within each group. Triangulating these findings with findings generated for the same group of students using other data sources (e.g., final reflection papers, survey data) could help to support, negate, or further explain some of the patterns of findings presented in this study.

In conclusion, it is clear from our extensive analysis of post-dialogue interview data that participants in IGD listen attentively to one another and continue to reflect, grapple with, understand, and act upon what they have heard after their dialogue has ended. We hope that future research will build on the strengths of IGD as an innovative pedagogical practice, while also honing that practice in order to enhance the effectiveness of IGD for participants from different social identity groups and for different types of dialogue.

REFERENCES

Anderson, R., Baxter, L. A., & Cissna, K. N. (2004). *Dialogue: Theorizing difference in communication studies*. Thousand Oaks, CA: Sage.

Bohm, D. (1985). *Unfolding meaning: A weekend of dialogue*. New York, NY: Routledge.

Bohm, D. (1990). *On dialogue*. Ojai, CA: David Bohm Seminars.

Brookfield, S. P., & Preskill, S. (2005). *Discussion as a way of teaching* (2nd ed.). San Francisco, CA: Jossey-Bass.

Burbules, N. C. (1993). *Dialogue in teaching: Theory and practice*. New York, NY: Teachers College Press.

Charmaz, K. (2006). *Constructing grounded theory: A practical guide through qualitative analysis*. London, England: Sage.

Chasin, R., Herzig, M., Roth, S., Chasin, L., Becker, C., & Stains, R. (1996). From diatribe to dialogue on divisive public issues: Approaches drawn from family therapy. *Mediation Quarterly, 13*(4), 323–344.

Chesler, M., & Zúñiga, X. (1991). Dealing with prejudice and conflict in the classroom: The pink triangle exercise. *Teaching Sociology, 19*(2), 173–181.

DeFrancisco, V. L., & Palczewski, C. H. (2007). *Communicating gender diversity: A critical approach*. Thousand Oaks, CA: Sage.

Dessel, A., & Rogge, M. E. (2008). Evaluation of intergroup dialogue: A review of the empirical literature. *Conflict Resolution Quarterly, 26*(2), 199–238.

Dessel, A., Rogge, M. E., & Garlington, S. B. (2006). Using intergroup dialogue to promote social justice and change. *Social Work, 51*(4), 303–315.

Díaz, A. (2009). *Composing a civic life: Influences of sustained dialogue on post-graduate civic engagement and civic life*. Unpublished doctoral dissertation, Fielding Graduate University, Santa Barbara, CA.

Ellinor, L., & Gerard, G. (1998). *Dialogue: Rediscover the transforming power of conversation*. New York, NY: Wiley.

Faludi, S. (2006). *Backlash: The undeclared war against American women* (15th anniv. ed.) New York, NY: Doubleday.

Fredericks, J. A., Blumenfeld, P. C., & Paris, A. H. (2004). School engagement: Potential of the concept, and state of the evidence. *Review of Educational Research, 74*(1), 59–109.

Freire, P. (1970). *Pedagogy of the oppressed*. New York, NY: Continuum.

Glaser, B., & Strauss, A. (1967). *The discovery of grounded theory*. Chicago, IL: Aldine.

Gorski, P. C. (2008). Good intentions are not enough: A decolonizing intercultural education. *Intercultural Education, 19*(6), 515–525.

Gurin, P. (1985). Women's gender consciousness. *Public Opinion Quarterly, 49*(2), 143–163.

Gurin, P. (1999). Selections from *The Compelling Need for Diversity in Higher Education*, expert reports in defense of the University of Michigan. *Equity & Excellence in Education, 32*(2), 36–62.

Gurin, P., Nagda, B. A., & Lopez, G. E. (2004). The benefits of diversity in education for democratic citizenship. *Journal of Social Issues, 60*(1), 17–34.

Gurin, P., Nagda, B. A., & Sorensen, N. (2011). Intergroup dialogue: Education for a broad conception of civic engagement. *Liberal Education, 97*(2), 46–51.

Gurin, P. Nagda, B. A. & Zúñiga, X. (in press). *Engaging race and gender: Intergroup dialogues*. New York, NY: Russell Sage.

Gurin, P., Peng, T., Lopez, G., & Nagda, B. A. (1999). Context, identity, and intergroup relations. In D. A. Prentice & D. T. Miller (Eds.), *Cultural divides: Understanding and overcoming group conflict* (pp. 133–170). New York, NY: Sage.

hooks, b. (1990). *Yearning: Race, gender and cultural politics*. Boston, MA: South End.

Hurtado, S. (2005). The next generation of diversity and intergroup relations research. *Journal of Social Issues, 61*(3), 595–610.

Isaacs, W. (1999). *Dialogue and the art of working together*. New York, NY: Doubleday.

Lincoln, Y., & Guba, E. (1996). But is it rigorous? Trustworthiness and authenticity in naturalistic evaluation. *New Directions for Program Evaluation*, (30), 73–84.

McCormick, D. W. (1999). Listening with empathy: Taking the other person's perspective. In A. Cooke, A. Craig, B. Greig, & M. Brazzel (Eds.), *Reading book for human relations training* (pp. 57–60). Arlington, VA: NTL Institute.

Miles, M. B., & Huberman, A. M. (1994). *Qualitative data analysis: An expanded source book* (2nd ed.). Thousands Oaks, CA: Sage.

Nagda, B. A. (2006). Breaking barriers, crossing borders, building bridges: Communication processes in intergroup dialogues. *Journal of Social Issues, 62*(3), 553–576.

Nagda, B. A., Gurin, P., Sorensen, N., & Zúñiga, X. (2009). Evaluating intergroup dialogue: Engaging diversity for personal and social responsibility. *Diversity and Democracy, 12*(1), 4–6.

Nagda, B. A., Kim, C.-w., & Truelove, Y. (2004). Learning about difference, learning with others, learning to transgress. *Journal of Social Issues, 60*(1), 195–214.

Nagda, B. A., & Zúñiga, X. (2003). Fostering meaningful racial engagement through intergroup dialogues. *Group Processes and Intergroup Relations, 6*(1), 111–128.

QSR International. (2008). *NVivo 8 research software for analysis and insight*. Cambridge, MA: Author.

Romney, P. (2003). *The art of dialogue. Animating democracy*. Retrieved from http://www.americansforthearts.org/animatingdemocracy/resource_center/resources_content.asp?id=215

Rossman, G. B., & Rallis, S. F. (2003). *Learning in the field: Introduction to qualitative research* (2nd ed.). Thousand Oaks, CA: Sage.

Schoem, D. L., & Hurtado, S. (2001). *Intergroup dialogue: Deliberative democracy in school, college, community and workplace* (pp. 1–36). Ann Arbor, MI: University of Michigan Press.

Sorenson, N., Nagda, B. A., Gurin, P., & Maxwell, K. E. (2009). Taking a "hands on" approach to diversity in higher education: A critical-dialogic model for effective intergroup interaction. *Analysis of Social Issues & Public Policy, 9*(1), 3–35.

Stephan, W. G., & Stephan, C. W. (2001). *Improving intergroup relations*. Thousand Oaks, CA: Sage.

Strauss, A. L., & Corbin, J. M. (1990). *Basics of qualitative research: Grounded theory, procedures and techniques*. Newbury Park, CA: Sage.

Weiler, J. (1994). Finding a shared meaning: Reflections on dialogue, an interview with Linda Teurfs. Retrieved from http://seedsofunfolding.org/issues/04_06/features_1.htm

Werkmeister-Rozas, L., Zúñiga, X., & Stassen, M. (2008, October). *Psychological, communicative and pedagogical dimensions of student engagement in intergroup dialogues*. Presented at the Northeastern Educational Research Association Conference, Rocky Hill, CT.

Yeakley, A. M. (1998). The nature of prejudice change: Positive and negative change processes arising from intergroup contact experiences. Doctoral dissertation, University of Michigan, Ann Arbor, MI.

Zúñiga, X., Nagda, B., Chesler, M., & Cytron-Walker, A. (2007). Intergroup dialogue in higher education: Meaningful learning about social justice. *ASHE Higher Education Report, 32*(4). San Francisco, CA: Wiley.

Zúñiga, X., Nagda, B., & Sevig, T. D. (2002). Intergroup dialogue: An educational model for cultivating engagement across differences. *Equity & Excellence in Education, 35*(1), 7–17.

White Educators Facilitating Discussions About Racial Realities

Stephen John Quaye
University of Maryland

Facilitating democratic discussions about race among students in classroom environments continues to be a problem facing educators. When these discussions occur, they are facilitated mostly by faculty of color. However, given the underrepresentation of faculty of color within higher education institutions and that white students respond differently to these discussions when facilitated by members of their own race, it is critical for white faculty to learn how to facilitate these exchanges among learners. The present study focused on exploring the role of white faculty facilitating discussions about race in their courses. Findings are presented through case examples from two white participants. Implications for research and practice are also discussed.

Racial/ethnic diversity has become a fashionable and long-lasting buzzword within most institutions of higher learning (Astin, 1998; National Center for Education Statistics [NCES], 1998); yet, students continue to struggle with appreciating peers from different racial/ethnic backgrounds (Hurtado, Engberg, Ponjuan, & Landreman, 2002; Saddlemire, 1996). Racial/ethnic diversity is becoming increasingly synonymous with focusing on the composition of the student body while largely ignoring what transpires when students who have had minimal interaction with peers from different racial/ethnic backgrounds are expected to embrace racial/ethnic diversity upon entering higher education (Chang, Chang, & Ledesma, 2005).

An alternative conception of diversity is sorely needed—one that shifts from simply structural racial/ethnic diversity (a commendable, but insufficient aim) to learning from interracial differences. As Mayhew, Grunwald, and Dey (2005) found: "In terms of formal and public commitment, an institution's ability to achieve a positive climate for diversity is indeed reflected by the faculty's commitment to incorporate diversity-related issues into their academic agenda" (p. 408). Given the critical roles of faculty members in enacting and reinforcing an institution's avowed commitment to diversity through curriculum and pedagogy, focusing on how they attempt to address one strand of diversity—race—by facilitating racial discussions in their courses is a study worth pursuing. I focus on how participants facilitated racial discussions in this article.

Researchers have shown that when these discussions take place, they are most often facilitated by faculty of color (Bergerson, 2003; Sue, Torino, Capodilupo, Rivera, & Lin, 2010; Wahl, Perez, Deegan, Sanchez, & Applegate, 2000). White faculty are uniquely positioned to engage white students, in particular, in these discussions given the predominantly white settings in which they are situated. Yet, if they continue not to facilitate these discussions or lack the preparation to facilitate them, there will continue to be challenges to engaging white students in these discussions (Sue et al., 2010).

The purpose of the present study was to explore how white postsecondary educators[1] facilitated discussions about racial issues in their courses. In order to offer students, educators, and researchers insights into approaches participants used to engage primarily white students in classroom-based discussions on race, I examined the perspectives and experiences of faculty who lead these discussions. This study focuses only on white educators working with mostly white students to demonstrate the unique ways in which this shared racial identity benefits white learners in these discussions. By focusing on white educators, current and future white educators can learn how to structure purposeful engagement activities that enable these exchanges to happen among white students.

LITERATURE REVIEW

The literature presented here is divided into two major sections. First, I concentrate on literature about differences among dialogue, debate, and discussion to highlight the kind of approach (i.e., discussion) utilized by participants and to draw some connections and implications to a specific kind of dialogue: intergroup dialogue. Next, I highlight studies that examine faculty preparedness and readiness to engage racial issues in the classroom and focus, specifically, on white faculty.

Dialogue

Bohm (1996) noted that the goal of dialogue is to come to new understanding through questioning the fundamental assumptions upon which one's opinions rested. Dialogue, Bohm argues, is concerned with examining the whole as opposed to fragmentation: "Dialogue is really aimed at going into the whole thought process and changing the way the thought process occurs collectively" (p. 10). Given the different backgrounds of those engaged in dialogue, there is a tendency to defend one's opinions; however, dialogue focuses instead on suspending one's assumptions in order to free up the empty space that Bohm concludes is necessary where "anything may come in" (p. 19). In this empty space, there is a tendency to come together rather than focus on winning an argument.

Debate

Whereas dialogue is premised on being with others, debate is characterized by divisiveness. Debate is often framed as a situation where one party wins the argument and the other party loses. Hyde and Bineham (2000) clarify the distinction between "debate" and "dialogue." They note that many people are socialized to argue and try to win people over to their side and that this arguing mentality is emblematic of politics within society. Debate is a form of discourse that is characterized by evidence and persuasion to convince others of the rightness of one's opinion.

Whoever sounds the most plausible and persuasive usually wins the debate. In contrast, dialogue is characterized by seeking commonality and common ground (Hyde & Bineham, 2000) or critical reflection and inquiry (Ellinor & Gerard, 1998; Freire, 1970; Nagda & Maxwell, 2011). Debate also presumes that there are two opposing, preexisting ideas, one of which is more right than the other (Hyde & Bineham, 2000). Dialogue is "a way of being with another person" (p. 212) that is premised on relationship-building and the development of mutual understanding. Although Hyde and Bineham distinguish between debate and dialogue, they also note that dialogues can have debates or arguments within them but that these debates look different in that they provide alternative perspectives to consider in the hope that participants come to a stronger understanding. People may support their views with evidence and reasoning, as seen in debates, but the evidence adds further substance to the dialogue.

Discussion

Similar to debate but different from dialogue, Ellinor and Gerard (1998) contend that discussion connotes fragmentation and "breaking the whole down into many parts" (p. 20). Those engaged in discussion strive to justify and defend their opinions by placing emphasis on examining ideas and analyzing the arguments that undergird those ideas. Because the goal of discussion is closure, participants endeavor to develop one meaning on an issue. Brookfield and Preskill's (2005) understanding of discussion is embedded in a dialogic and democratic framework. They assert that democratic discussion is a

> process of giving and taking, speaking and listening, describing and witnessing—all of which help expand horizons and foster mutual understanding . . . [Democratic discussion] is premised on the idea that only through collaboration and cooperation with others can we be exposed to new points of view. (pp. 3–4)

Democratic discussion is a way to work with others to come to newfound understanding about an issue. The discussion is democratic because it involves multiple speakers with varying vantage points and from different backgrounds. Some of the benefits Brookfield and Preskill have found from democratic discussion involve recognizing one's assumptions, appreciating differences, learning collaboratively, and developing a tolerance for ambiguity. Even though Brookfield and Preskill's book is about democratic discussion, they claimed they are "blending or synthesizing the descriptions of discussion, dialogue, and conversation" (p. 6). Therefore, drawing sharp distinctions between these terms is not the purpose of this section; rather, I highlight these terms to clarify how I am situating this article. In the next section, I highlight intergroup dialogue as a further example of the dialogic framework discussed above.

Intergroup Dialogue

Another approach for helping students talk about difficult topics is intergroup dialogue. Nagda and Maxwell (2011) contend that intergroup dialogues have a critical-dialogic framework that focuses on storytelling and sharing one's experiential knowledge (dialogic) and understanding systems of power, privilege, and inequities that marginalize some while advantaging others (critical).

These dialogues bring two groups that have a history of conflict together to explore the sources of conflict and engage across group differences. For example, during a people of color/white people dialogue, participants might speak from their personal experiences as members of various racial groups (dialogic) to explore how race affects people differently based on how they identify (critical) and develop ways to challenge racism in their various communities. The critical-dialogic practice of intergroup dialogues connects with Brookfield and Preskill's (2005) democratic discussion since intergroup dialogue participants have varying social identities and speak from these identities during dialogues. In democratic discussion, participants also work collectively to develop understanding about an issue; this collaboration is consistent with the alliance building communication process of intergroup dialogues that is premised on "collaborat[ing] on action to work against injustices and bring about change" (Nagda & Maxwell, 2011, p. 6). Thus, the framework that guides intergroup dialogue overlaps with democratic discussion in that both are concerned with exploring multiple perspectives in the context of one's membership in various privileged and marginalized groups.

Having laid the groundwork for discussion, debate, and dialogue, in this article, I concentrate on the definition of democratic discussion advanced by Brookfield and Preskill (2005), which describes the discussions facilitated by the participants in my study. However, at times, I also blend democratic discussion with dialogue given that participants used both "discussion" and "dialogue" when speaking with me about their practices. The discussions specified in this article are different from structured intergroup dialogues with two co-facilitators of different social identities in that participants in my study facilitated these discussions without the assistance of a co-facilitator and the discussions were not explicitly organized with the intention of balancing the social identities represented. Despite these differences, I draw implications from intergroup dialogues in the Discussion section since these dialogues inform the participants' facilitation approaches.

Faculty Skills and Preparedness in Facilitating Racial Exchanges

Stassen's (1995) study of white faculty members' responses to integrating racial/ethnic diversity within their courses revealed some paradoxes among faculty. Although those with more formal education tended to hold views consistent with a respect for racial/ethnic differences and a propensity to provide avenues for racial dialogues to occur (Schuman & Bobo, 1988; Schuman, Steeh, & Bobo, 1985), white faculty were the most resistant campus employees to implementing specific measures to improve the climate for students of color (Stassen, 1995). Stassen suggests that part of the reason for this hesitancy and resistance to fostering racially inclusive classroom environments is due to the context for race within postsecondary institutions. When white faculty view addressing racial diversity in the classroom as conflicting with educational quality, they refuse to alter their pedagogy and curricula to be more reflective of racial inclusiveness. This finding is similar to those of Bennett (2001) and Weissman, Bulakowski, and Jumisko (1998) who note that most white faculty fail to revise their courses to address racial diversity and perpetuate the status quo in using readings that do not pertain to the experiences of students of color.

Sue et al. (2010) and Schmidt (2005) provide two particularly illustrative studies of how white faculty engage white students in racial discussions. In a study about white faculty reacting to difficult dialogues about race, Sue et al. found that the participants in their study lacked the training and education to engage race effectively in the classroom. Participants discussed their lack of prior socialization to address race and their lack of knowledge about how to best engage students in these dialogues. They also reported the emotions that were central in these dialogues and how they had underestimated the amount of emotional energy that was needed during these dialogues.

Schmidt (2005) identifies seven concepts that faculty could utilize to respond to racial realities in classrooms. Most relevant to the present study is an examination of white privilege, in which faculty support white students in understanding how white people benefit from racism whether or not they consider themselves racist. A common challenge white educators encounter in addressing race is how to help students examine the structural and systemic factors that influence racism within institutions. White students readily understood that individual people could be racist through the telling of racist jokes or the use of racial epithets; however, they had trouble seeing and understanding the larger system of white supremacy embedded in the practices, norms, and values of postsecondary institutions. Similarly, most white faculty could identify when a student voiced a racist comment during a discussion but were unable to structure meaningful dialogues that moved beyond the individual toward systemic racism (Feagin, 2001).

One means for helping white students examine white privilege is promoting their white racial identity development. Helms (2008) describes the process of white racial identity as white students move from various schemas. In the Contact schema, white students are unaware of their race. The Disintegration schema is marked by disorientation that prompts one to think differently about her or his race. During Reintegration, the person "[mitigates] the anxiety that occurs when one's Disintegration status is dominant" (Helms & Cook, 2005, p. 250). Following this period, the white student embodies the Pseudo-Integration schema when she or he wants to associate with non-racist white people and reject "bad" white people; the Immersion schema is characterized by a desire to reframe one's whiteness and develop alternative images of what being white means. Immersion is followed by the Emersion schema, where the student searches for a community of non-racist white people to figure out how to live a positive white identity. Finally, in the Autonomy schema, white students demonstrate a flexible and critical white identity that is based on an internalized understanding of one's whiteness.

The literature on white racial identity is important because at the center of this literature lies two questions that Helms (2008) does not adequately answer: What does a positive white racial identity look like and how does one promote this identity? Given the literature on white faculty members' lack of preparedness to facilitate racial dialogues, they will conceivably have trouble knowing how to promote this positive white identity among white students and the developmental readiness that is necessary among white learners to engage in these dialogues and reflect on their whiteness (Helms & Cook, 2005).

RESEARCH QUESTIONS AND FOCUS

The following research question guided the present study: How do educators engage students in constructive discussions about racial realities[2] in postsecondary classroom settings? In this article, I focus exclusively on two white participants, Corrine and Dalton (pseudonyms), as case studies. Corrine and Dalton were particularly aware of their white racial identities in their facilitation efforts and represent exemplars that are consistent with the psychological case study design described below. Their stories also represent consistent patterns seen in the other cases. Thus, I present their cases to give readers an understanding of how white educators can facilitate racial discussions through paying attention to the nuances in their strategies. Facilitating discussions about race and racism in classroom settings is a rarity among faculty; however, as noted earlier, these discussions are mostly often facilitated by faculty of color (Bennett, 2001; Stassen, 1995; Weissman et al., 1998). I hope that the insights from these two cases will provide knowledge for other white educators who want to facilitate racial discussions in their own courses.

METHODOLOGY

This article is based on findings from a qualitative study of postsecondary educators who engaged in the exploration of race and racism with students in the classroom. My research was guided by psychological case study, wherein I treated each educator as an individual case (Crotty, 2003; Merriam, 1988, 2002; Stake, 2005). Case studies strive for holistic interpretations of a phenomenon (in the present study, the facilitation of racially-based discussions) through intensive examination and are grounded in the data collected and analyzed (Merriam, 1988). Each case could be seen on its own as one example of how to facilitate discussions about racial realities in a classroom setting, or multiple cases could provide varying insights about the pedagogical process and similar approaches that were noted among different participants (Stake, 1995, 2005).

Site

The primary site for data collection was the 2007 National Conference on Race and Ethnicity in American Higher Education (NCORE) in San Francisco, California. NCORE was created by members of the Southwest Center for Human Relations Studies at the University of Oklahoma. Members wanted to study racism within higher education and create avenues for participants to address the underrepresentation of racial/ethnic minority persons in postsecondary institutions and improve race relations. At NCORE, participants present on a range of topics, including curricular and pedagogical approaches for racial development, policy implications concerning race, theoretical perspectives on race and ethnicity, and the promotion of racial/ethnic inclusion among students, administrators, staff, and faculty. NCORE attracts nearly 2,000 participants annually (National Conference on Race & Ethnicity in American Higher Education, 2007). I selected NCORE as the site for my study due to its comprehensive focus on and examination of race in higher education.

Recruitment of Participants

To select participants, I performed a comprehensive analysis of the Program and Resource Guide (i.e., the program booklet) from the 2004 to 2007 NCORE meetings. In accordance with case study methodology, I purposefully sampled participants who had presented workshops directly related to my study—providing intentional, sustained spaces for racial exchanges to occur within classroom contexts (Creswell, 1998; Merriam, 1988, 1998; Patton, 2002). A direct quotation from a session abstract printed in the 2004 Guide, "Teaching about the Psychology of Race and Racism: Lessons Learned," crystallizes the selection of participants for the study.

> This session should particularly benefit those who teach emotionally-charged classes on race and racism, those who want to learn how to teach such classes and facilitate difficult discussions on race, and those who want to learn how to effectively utilize the racial and ethnic demographics of the classroom to enhance the learning of all students. (Cokley, 2004, p. 74)

The aforementioned abstract details issues with which my study dealt—difficult discussions on race, the role of faculty members in facilitating these discussions, and student responses and resistance to engaging racial realities in postsecondary classrooms.

Based on my comprehensive analysis, I contacted 153 participants via e-mail, described my study, explained that I had chosen them based on a workshop they presented at a previous NCORE, and requested an interview with them should they be attending the 2007 conference. Forty-nine people responded to my request. Of this number, 25 attended NCORE in 2007 and were interested in being interviewed; 24 were unable to attend the conference but were still interested in participating. Because I wanted to conduct the majority of interviews face-to-face, I selected participants to interview from the 25 who attended the conference. Given time constraints at the conference and availability of participants, the total sample for the study included 22 participants, 17 of whom I interviewed face-to-face at the conference and the remaining 5 via telephone.

Given the literature reviewed concerning the lack of involvement in facilitating racial dialogues by white persons and the critical roles of white faculty in engaging learners about racial issues (e.g., Bergerson, 2003; Tatum, 1997; Wahl et al., 2000; Warren & Hytten, 2004), I wanted to ensure that white educators participated in the study. Most of the participants were faculty and worked within predominantly white institutions. All taught courses in the social sciences, education, humanities, or arts.

Data Collection Procedures

I conducted individual semi-structured interviews that lasted between 75 and 120 minutes (Bernard, 1998, 2006; Fontana & Frey, 2000). Since the goal of my research was to understand the facilitation approaches of educators during racial discussions, I asked participants to discuss their teaching philosophies, the meanings they made of racial realities, the organization of their courses around issues of race and racism, how they plan and structure discussions about racial issues, and the advantages and challenges of engaging race in the classroom. The interviews were an opportunity for educators to reflect on their facilitation strategies and detail the distinguishing features of their approaches for helping students personalize and discuss racial issues.

Data Analysis Procedures

Each interview was audio-taped and transcribed verbatim. I then coded and analyzed each transcript using the NVivo® Software Package for Qualitative Research. I explored similarities and differences between participants' philosophies and approaches for organizing these discussions, as well as the meanings they made of their facilitation efforts. As I coded data, I revisited the interviews to clarify my interpretations and make further sense of the data.

I also used convergent and divergent thematic analyses to analyze the collected data. Akin to coding, when researchers use convergent analysis, they look for repeated patterns in the data—ideas or experiences shared by multiple participants. When convergence occurred, it meant this particular experience was important to most participants (Patton, 2002; Yin, 2003). However, exclusively upholding convergence often obscures the different experiences of others. Therefore, conducting divergent analysis also was an important consideration in this study (Patton, 2002). With divergence, I examined data from participants that differed from the common themes. Dissimilar experiences were important because they illuminated issues not cited by others and added depth to and an alternative understanding of the case (Yin, 2003). Finally, I looked across the individual cases through cross-case analysis to explore the patterns and themes from various participants (Stake, 1995).

Trustworthiness Procedures

I provided participants with an opportunity to offer feedback during the study. This important approach—member checks (Guba & Lincoln, 1989; Lincoln & Guba, 1985; Miles & Huberman, 1994; Stake, 1995)—permitted the revision of my interpretations based on participants' reactions. After each interview was transcribed and I developed my initial interpretations, I asked participants to comment on the adequacy of my descriptions. Peer debriefing was another means to acquire feedback on the developing findings. I asked people both familiar and unfamiliar with the study to comment on the data analysis procedures and findings in order to clarify ambiguous descriptions and interpretations (Guba & Lincoln, 1989; Lincoln & Guba, 1985; Merriam, 1988). I also kept a reflective journal to disclose my interpretations, challenges, emotions, revelations, and biases about participants and their narratives. Finally, asking two people to review and offer feedback on the development and execution of the study led to investigator triangulation, where multiple researchers comment on the procedures of a study (Patton, 2002).

Limitations

Despite the steps taken to conduct a trustworthy study, there are several limitations to my methodological decisions. First, selection bias resulted by only selecting participants who attended NCORE. There were likely many other educators who facilitate discussions about racial realities but did not attend or present workshops at NCORE. Next, the non-contextual nature of the study was a shortcoming. Because I interviewed participants via telephone and face-to-face at NCORE, I did not examine how their institutional contexts might have influenced their abilities to facilitate these discussions. Third, I am solely relying on self-reports and participants' understandings of their facilitation. Although the purpose of this study was to understand how educators facilitate the discussion of racial issues in their own words, people sometimes struggle to describe their approaches when they are immersed in their practices. Therefore, an observational component would have offered another perspective to supplement the data from participants. Finally, given my social identity as an African American man and that Corrine is a white woman and Dalton is a white man, I sometimes wondered how these racial and gendered differences might have influenced their willingness to share their stories with me and my ability to analyze the data through my lens. Although I found participants reflective and forthcoming, researchers with other social identities conceivably would have yielded different data.

FINDINGS

I present the findings from two white participants, Corrine and Dalton, to illustrate how they facilitated racial discussions. Although Corrine and Dalton had students of color in their courses, during our interview, they most frequently mentioned how they facilitated racial discussions with white students in their courses, as they believed white students most needed support in discussing and understanding racial issues. After presenting their cases, I connect their experiences to previous research, highlight salient findings, and draw implications for practice.

The Case of Corrine

Corrine, a white woman, has taught for almost 25 years. The courses she teaches in her current position as Professor at a small, private liberal arts institution generally explore issues of conflict between groups, sexism against women, and violence against women of color. She noted that her goal is to engage students in dialogues about these topics. In addition, she stated:

> My idea is to help students who have completed beginning theory courses to spend some time in the community immediately surrounding the university and use people's experiences to challenge the theories they've been taught. So the neighborhood that we're located in is definitely working class, kind of lower middle class, at least as many families of color as white families. I hope that this class will allow students to start to really think about the messages that they've gotten both from the text that they've studied but also from their families and popular culture. The texts will look at questions of race, for sure, questions of class, gender, [and] sexuality.

An important goal of Corrine's classroom facilitation was to find ways to help students concretize the racial issues about which they read and discussed. Therefore, she sought ways to help them make sense of these issues within the community where the University was situated. This helped students make sense of the theoretical concepts in actual, practical, experiences while working within the community.

In order to help students connect classroom discussions to their campus community, Corrine often uses case studies about real incidents that occurred on campus. In her courses, she noted the following:

> I also use case studies a lot in the conflict studies and the women's studies courses. I write versions of things that happen, either on campus or in the community or that are in the newspaper and ask the students to apply the theories that they have learned to these case studies. [I] teach them the theoretical tools are useful in everyday life. There is a case study that I have used a couple of times. It was about the experience of a couple of African American women who were basketball players on our campus. The women's locker room is accessible only to other women on campus, faculty, staff, students, administrators. Everybody came back from practice to their lockers and there were

racial epithets and symbols written on the lockers that the two black women had their stuff in. The case study lays this out. It also lays out the text of a message that, I can't remember if it was the President of the University or the Dean of the College, sent to the whole campus explaining it. Then, that's juxtaposed next to the statement that's on all our literature about what a welcoming and diverse community we are. I sit them [students] at a classroom table, five students sitting at a table. They've never seen the case study before. But they have notes on the different theories that they've used. They pick up the case study and they read it. They have five minutes to read and talk to each other. So this course is also designed to help them develop oral communication skills. So it's not enough to know the theories and to apply them well to the case study, but they also have to do that in a way that involves everyone in the conversation and comes up with the best set of responses. So, they read for five minutes and then they have 15 minutes to use their theories to make sense of what's happening in this case study. In women's studies what they learn is most feminist theory ignores race. That's [using case studies is] maybe one of the better ways for them to learn that [about race]. They get so frustrated, the students, and then they're dying for something more. I use case studies, and I give them a lot of practice in class by also using that method of testing them. It's like a dinner table conversation. I think it feels more authentic.

Several strategies for helping students make sense of discussions are seen in Corrine's example above. She utilized a case study centered on a real racial incident that occurred at her institution to help students concretize the theoretical readings on race with a real-life, practical example. Corrine noted that these case studies helped counter the resistance of white learners in thinking that racism was over; the example from the case enabled them to see that racism still exists despite university language that values a "welcoming and diverse community." Earlier in her interview, Corrine shared that she needed to help students see the impact of race and racism given the mostly white students in her courses, as well as her own white identity. Her quotation above exemplifies her efforts to help white students see racism within their own community.

Recognizing that mostly white learners were in her courses, Corrine assigned relevant readings to engage them in racial dialogues.

There's a book that was published in 1960 called *Black Like Me* [Griffin, 1960]. The guy who wrote it was a white guy who went through a chemical process of changing his skin color because he wanted to document, "Was it [differential treatment by race] really as bad as people said it was?" Students are absolutely horrified at what they read. It's about how this man whose experience as a white man but appears to be dark-skinned, what he sees when he looks in the mirror, how he experiences being treated by others who have no idea that he has experience as a white man. You're so inside his experience. It just turns everything that they have in their heads upside down.

Because Corrine wanted white students to see the influence of racial differences, she asked them to read a book that would help them personalize racial issues. Given Griffin's experiences and racial identity, white students especially related to what he wrote. Corrine stated that white learners often had trouble believing that people of color were treated differently simply because of their racial identities. This book was grounded in white students' experiences and written by an author who was also white; therefore, white students believed the implications of the text.

When Corrine picked readings that were situated in white students' experiences, she saw that they were willing to take more responsibility for their learning by sharing their out-of-class knowledge with other class members. In Corrine's courses, many students, for the first time, had the opportunity to read about and discuss racial issues in ways that mattered to them. Doing so stimulated their interest in seeking out other literature relevant to their circumstances. She also mentioned how videos offered learners different experiences to consider.

> In the [conflict course], documentary footage is incredibly powerful—*Eyes on the Prize* [Hampton, 1987] or any of the others. The text materials, the documentaries, and then the discussions that come out of that are so challenging. They are so immediate and deep. A lot of times they are filled with screaming and crying because white students are sometimes very defensive. "This stuff is history." They can say that until a student of color in the room says, "That's my experience."

As noted above, the combination of media resources made it more difficult for white students to reject the truthfulness of the experiences of students of color. As white students saw, heard, and discussed multiple examples of racism in the past and in contemporary society, they began to appreciate that others had experiences different from their own, and that those experiences provided opportunities for learning. Corrine stated that when students of color addressed how the issues in the documentaries dovetailed with experiences in their own lives, white students lessened their defense mechanisms and started to appreciate the applicability of the videos to their own lives.

Even when Corrine utilized videos, readings, and case studies to engage learners, she was constantly aware of her white identity and how that influenced her ability to facilitate these discussions. When discussing the difficulties of facilitating these discussions, she said:

> One of the things that I worry about constantly is deepening the wounds that students of color have or deepening the conviction that white students have that they don't want to do it. I worry about making it worse instead of better. I worry about the injury that I might do. I also think there's another kind of injury though that is only visible to me because students are willing to talk about it. And that is the kind that happens by default when people don't teach in ways that gives students a chance to do this work. One of the places, at least on our campus, I'm guessing this happens at other places, where students are likely to have these conversations, whether it's about race, gender, class, sexuality, or how all those things intersect, is in co-curricular programs—residential life, multicultural student affairs, leadership programs. It's not in the classroom, which is criminal. I think it's unbelievably problematic for higher education. It's one of the things that makes me most hopeless about the academy and my colleagues.

During this segment of my interview with Corrine, she began to weep when talking about the potential injury to students by white faculty who do not facilitate these discussions in productive ways. As seen in the quotation above, Corrine was quite concerned with doing harm to students of color as a result of these discussions and reinforcing in the minds of white students that they do not have to engage in these discussions. She also alluded to these discussions happening in co-curricular settings but usually not in the classroom. Given her identity as a white woman, she saw the importance of giving students time to do the kind of work necessary to engage in these difficult discussions. She was never sure whether or not she was causing harm, but she endeavored to engage students in these discussions despite her discomfort and worry.

During my interview with Corrine, we talked at length about strategies she employed to facilitate racial discussions in her courses. She repeatedly mentioned the importance of finding a way to include students' emotions during these discussions paired with her own emotions as a white woman facilitating discussions on racial issues.

I have to know who the people are. It matters. I'm not a person for whom it doesn't matter who is in the room. So I guess part of what you would see is my trying to figure out what the students have for assumptions and what their points of ignorance are and what their surprises are. Then, I'm using that to build on their curiosity. I always want to hear connections . . . between what they see in the text that's historical and what's happening now. So, race relations in this country right now, why are they the way they are? It's so easy to talk about when you look at that history. I think you would see, at least in some of the classes that I teach, a lot of first-person narratives, students telling pieces of their own story or reading memoirs and discussing. I try to have a lot of deeply engaging stories so it's not just definitions and theories but always connections so that they can get the personal implications. Colleagues have said to me that this or that was risky. There's a lot of emotion in my classrooms. People want to keep it out. It has to be there. I just don't see how you can do this work without emotion.

Embracing emotion as a necessary aspect of engaging white students in racial discussions, Corrine was convinced that using first-person narratives helped students understand the historical significance of race and also to see how racism still occurred in present day society. Although her colleagues saw her classroom strategies as risky, she continued her facilitation approach because it enabled her to gain a more thorough understanding of the students in her class and use this understanding to find activities that enabled students to concretize the readings.

The Case of Dalton

Dalton, a white man with 13 years of teaching experience, works at a large, research-intensive institution in the Midwest. He teaches Philosophy courses primarily in social theory and race and racism. We started our conversation with a discussion of his students' expectations when they entered his Philosophy course on race and racism.

> On the first day of my class, I'll talk to students about, "Who did you expect to walk in here?" People who didn't know who I was, more often than not, they were assuming that I was going to be a person of color.

Dalton evinced a consciousness of his identity as a white educator, how that influenced his ability to teach about race, and the assumptions students had of who they expected to facilitate the discussion of racial realities. He challenged learners' beliefs by showing that white people, too, could and should be involved in racial dialogues.

He acknowledged the privileges he was granted and how being a white man made it easier to engage students in racial discussions, given the authority and respect that students accorded him.

> I'm at a predominantly white institution, so as a white guy talking about race, I am able to be effective at reaching white students. I'm accorded by the students a certain degree of respect and legitimacy that my white, female colleagues or my black, female colleagues and Latino, male colleagues don't receive. In my class, I talk about what it means for me, as a white guy, to be teaching this, how they perceive that, what their assumptions were coming in, and how they might treat me in the class—what the data show in terms of the reception of faculty who are white or not white.

Given that most of the students who enrolled in Dalton's courses were white, he noticed that he was able to use his race to develop rapport with students in ways that his colleagues of color could not. Students, particularly white students, deemed him legitimate and were able to identify with his racial background. However, rather than simply accepting his privileged race, Dalton asked learners to question the assumptions he held as a white educator and how the course would be different if a person of a different race was the instructor.

Akin to Corrine, Dalton also sought ways to help students make sense of racial concepts and theories beyond the readings and classroom discussions. He recognized the limits of his identity as a white man and wanted students to grapple with racial differences in concrete ways. He utilized service-learning as an effort to achieve this goal. However, he struggled with seeing the outcomes of service-learning in his Philosophy course focused on race and racism.

> They'll [students] have a range of options to go into the community to work with students of color at a local school, helping them with reading or just doing some after-school programming with students of color. And usually the students have really good experiences doing that, and they usually really enjoy it. Not always, but usually. But I still worry that it still has this, even though I try to talk about this in the classroom, get them to reflect on it, give them some reflection assignments, I still worry that the white students go into a community of color, for example, and see themselves as helping these poor kids of color or something, and I don't want them to have that helping attitude. What I want the service-learning to achieve is to give the students a different perspective, to challenge their whiteness, their white viewpoint out in the world. I'm just not sure that the way I've done it effectively does that. I'm sure if I set it up differently, it would work better, but I just don't know how to avoid reinforcing certain stereotypes. And so I think the service-learning, you know, I'm a big fan of it, but on the other hand, I'm just not sure how it can be done well. But I do think it's important to get students out of the classroom and if I could just find the right kind of environment, the right kind of project to get them to work on, it could be much more effective than it has been.

Dalton worried about the white students in his courses developing a "helping attitude" toward those who were different from them (i.e., poor people of color), as they engaged in service-learning. As a white man facilitating dialogues with mostly white students, he knew he needed to find a way to help white students explore differences in a tangible way; however, service learning did not seem to produce the outcomes he wanted. Although Corrine saw students' engagement with case studies about racial incidents that happened on campus as critical to their understanding of racial disparities, Dalton wondered if students' engagement in the community actually worsened race relations and reinforced their stereotypes about different racial groups. He struggled to find a way for students to tangibly make sense of the racial issues discussed in the classroom.

After we discussed the complexities of service-learning, I asked Dalton to return to a previous comment he made about de-centering himself while facilitating racial discussions. Although he observed that white students respected him differently than they did his colleagues of color, Dalton tried to lessen his authority in the classroom to encourage white students to discuss racial issues. He said:

> Even though I de-center myself, I still have a degree of authority, of course, in my classroom that I will use to challenge students, occasionally, to think more deeply about their beliefs. It's very difficult to manage [my authority] in the classroom, and a line that I step over quite often. When you're trying to challenge white students to think a little bit more carefully about what they're saying or to be able to give reasons to justify what they're saying, just asking them for those reasons, they sometimes feel attacked. I use a lot of group work because while I have a degree of control over the discussion when we're all together, which is very useful and important, it's also very important that they participate and that they develop a certain degree of trust with each other and honesty with each other. Small

groups help to promote that. It doesn't necessarily bring it about but it promotes a certain degree of honesty and a level or participation that I can't get with the whole class.

Recognizing the difficult line between using his authority and de-centering himself, Dalton used different approaches to facilitate discussions about race. He noticed that white students in his courses often felt attacked when probed to use evidence to justify their positions; therefore, he tried challenging students to think about their positions and used small group work to invite participation in these discussions. These small groups, he indicated, were a means to help students develop trust with each other. Further, Dalton indicated that he tried to "minimize lecturing as much as possible, though it's still necessary to set the framework for the discussion" and that he facilitated racial discussions through "a Socratic method by just asking probing questions and follow-up questions [but that] it can be challenging, sometimes, when white students are reluctant to participate." The combination of lecturing to frame relevant topics in the discussion and asking many questions enabled Dalton to engage white students in these discussions despite their hesitance to do so at times.

I was intrigued by Dalton's honest reflection on his whiteness and the complexities of his role as an authority figure, so I probed him further to give an example of how his race enables him to better facilitate these discussions with white students. He commented:

I talk about what the data shows, in terms of how they receive or give legitimacy to what I say in the classroom. I think of my role as a white guy in talking about race and racism—I can be especially effective at reaching those white students in the classroom, students who grew up in a white, suburban background the way I did. And I often mention that to them. "I grew up there; I understand exactly what you have experienced. I've been there." So, often, like I said before, I think of those students as my primary audience because I think that's who I can be particularly effective in reaching. Students of color who don't know me might be pretty skeptical about a white guy talking about race or racism, and I understand exactly why. And I understand that hopefully they'll develop a degree of trust in me, or they'll see that I'm serious and that I really know the issues over the course of the 15 weeks. And so, I understand if they're skeptical and are not very participatory early on until they get to know who I am and what I'm really about. But I really do think that my role is to reach out to those white students because I think it's an unfortunate fact they will be more willing to listen to me, at least initially, then they would be if I weren't white.

Recognizing the benefits he is accorded by white students given his race, Dalton endeavored to connect with white students in his courses by sharing his experiences growing up in a similar environment and his early exposure to race. His ability to share data with which white students could connect, coupled with his willingness to be vulnerable in sharing his story, were key strategies he used in facilitating these discussions. His whiteness served as a way to gain trust with white students who were more willing to listen to him given his racial similarity to them.

DISCUSSION

Corrine's and Dalton's stories underscore Brookfield and Preskill's (2005) democratic discussion. Both participants strived to support white students in sharing students' views about race, seeing the historical and systemic implications of race, and engaging with their peers about these issues. Corrine wanted students to engage in discussion using case studies as a method, whereas, Dalton invited white students to engage in discussion by reflecting on his whiteness and asking them to suspend their assumptions about who should facilitate discussions about race. Both participants shared elements of democratic discussion during interviews. Corrine talked about wanting students in her classes to "talk to each other" and to "come up with the best set of responses." This goal was similar to Brookfield and Preskill's point about how democratic discussion is about coming to new understandings based on examining different perspectives. Dalton invited white students to participate in "small groups" in order for them to "participate and develop a certain degree of trust with each other." He also asked questions and lectured to identify important topics for discussion. Corrine and Dalton did not discuss differences between dialogue, debate, and discussion in their interviews, but as seen in the findings, the kinds of discussions about race they facilitated align with Brookfield and Preskill's democratic discussion in that they asked questions, used small group work, and provided space for students to speak to each other with the ultimate goal of coming to an expanded understanding about racial issues. Corrine and Dalton noticed that these discussions served as a way for white students to think about racial realities, hear different perspectives on this topic, and share their own opinions as well.

Bergerson (2003) and Wahl et al. (2000) have shown that there is a lack of white educators facilitating discussions about race; thus, the data from Corrine and Dalton show the value-added benefits from white educators engaging race in their courses and the unique ways they are able to connect with white learners in their courses. Wahl et al. (2000) suggest that white faculty members should participate in teaching race relations courses to demonstrate to learners that it is also the responsibility of white people to address issues of race. Participants understood that facilitating constructive discussions about racial issues began with understanding themselves—their racial identities, assumptions, biases, strengths, and limitations as educators. Reflecting on their racial identities was a means to encourage white students in their courses to do the same.

As a white researcher, Bergerson (2003) notes that those who participated in social justice education were mostly educators of color. Accordingly, she wrote about her journey of developing consciousness of her whiteness and argued for the importance of white people assuming responsibility for facilitating exchanges about racial realities and using their privileges to help white students personalize issues of race. Given that most of the students who enrolled in the courses of participants were white, it was important for Corrine and Dalton to facilitate these interactions. They found that white learners were more likely to believe in the existence of racism and white privilege and more willing to discuss racial issues with their peers when they saw a white person of authority in these discussions. They shared the ways their racial identities afforded them unearned advantages, authority, respect, and legitimacy, and the importance of white people taking an active role in challenging racial injustices and working with students to do the same. The knowledge Dalton and Corrine shared was essential to responding to Bergerson's assertion concerning white faculty. When white faculty treated racial realities seriously, they conveyed to learners the importance of race in students' lives and increased the frequency with which white students discussed racial realities with their peers. When white educators facilitated racial discussions, they removed a portion of the onus from their colleagues of color to be the primary people who cared about and addressed racial realities (hooks, 1994; Tatum, 1997).

Although intergroup dialogue has a specific framework and structure that is different from the kinds of discussions facilitated by Dalton and Corrine, the practical strategies Dalton and Corrine used to facilitate these discussions are supported by research on intergroup dialogue (Zúñiga, 2003; Zúñiga, Nagda, & Sevig, 2002). A critical goal of this process, consciousness raising, was reflected in the willingness of both participants to incorporate various approaches (e.g., readings, reflection, and multimedia) to prompt learners to consider issues of race. As Zúñiga et al. (2007) assert: "Members of both advantaged and disadvantaged groups must gain a deeper understanding of each other's situations and grapple with effects of privilege and subordination on their relationships" (pp. 9–10). When Dalton and Corrine invited white students to reflect on issues of race in their lives through their personal narratives, they demonstrated to learners the importance of placing their own understandings of racial realities at the forefront of their learning. In addition, the use of multiple approaches provided learners with different opportunities to connect with the course content from their own vantage points. An important element of intergroup dialogue is the critical-dialogic framework on which its pedagogy is based (Nagda & Maxwell, 2011). In the literature review, I specified the storytelling and experience-based components of this framework coupled with an attention to systems of power, privilege, and oppression. Corrine and Dalton shared their own stories with students, listened to students' stories and experiences, and worked to help learners understand systemic racism through readings, case studies, and learning beyond the classroom (e.g., service-learning). Consequently, their facilitation strategies are connected, in many ways, to the critical-dialogic framework of intergroup dialogue.

Dalton and Corrine found that in order to engage white students at varying degrees of understanding about racial realities, they had to rely upon multifaceted practices that addressed learners' developmental places and readiness to engage race and racism. For instance, as underscored in the literature review, Helms (2008) and Helms and Cook (2005) discuss different schemas that reflect white students' racial identity development. Corrine and Dalton both examined who the white learners were in their courses and utilized facilitation approaches that aligned with white students' developmental places. Corrine mentioned needing to know who was in the room during these discussions, and Dalton discussed sharing his own experiences engaging race as a white man to connect with white students in his courses. Although neither participant specifically referred to white racial identity development theories, this research is helpful to provide a context for understanding some of the resistance they faced from white learners (e.g., Corrine—"White students are sometimes very defensive. 'This stuff is history.' They can say that until a student of color in the room says, 'That's my experience.'"). Both participants needed to acknowledge the developmental places of white students in their courses and use that knowledge to develop strategies for best facilitating these discussions.

Emotion was also a central theme discussed by Corrine and Dalton. They both sought ways to help white learners emotionally personalize racial issues in their lives, which they believed would prompt them to deem talking about race more seriously. Sue et al. (2010) found that emotions were an important part of difficult dialogues on race. Emotions that they found were common among white students were anxiety, anger, defensiveness, and sadness. For white professors, common emotions were anxiety, disappointment, and uncertainty. Corrine and Dalton also showed anxiety and uncertainty in not knowing sometimes how best to engage students in these discussions, for example, the struggle of using service-learning in Dalton's philosophy courses. Acknowledging these emotions was essential in their abilities to facilitate these discussions.

IMPLICATIONS FOR PRACTICE AND FUTURE RESEARCH

The interviews with Corrine and Dalton yielded helpful information for other white educators hoping to facilitate discussions about race with white students. Both participants illustrated the important role white educators can play in these discussions. Although they both used lectures to help students understand racial concepts and theories, they relied on other facilitation methods as well. Rather than solely lecturing to students about their own perspectives, Corrine and Dalton wanted to enable students to see themselves as knowledgeable. They incorporated materials (e.g., documentaries like *Eyes on the Prize* [Hampton, 1987] and after-school programming) that encouraged white students to place their own experiences at the forefront of the learning process. Thus, a key implication for practice from this study is the importance of white educators partnering with white students during these discussions in ways that enable students to speak from their own vantage points, see themselves as knowers, and situate the dialogues and readings in their own experiences.

Educators interested in engaging white students in these discussions should be cognizant of reflecting on their own white racial identities and examining the developmental places of white learners in order to respond appropriately to resistance among white learners. Using a resource like *Black Like Me* (Griffin, 1960), as Corrine did, or even *White Like Me* (Wise, 2008) might better engage white learners in earlier racial identity schemas of Contact or Disintegration since they can make sense of another white person trying to understand racial issues rather than simply being told that racism is a problem that still exists in society.

Given the strong presence of a range of emotions during these discussions, those interested in facilitating them must normalize emotions and integrate them into the discussion (Sue et al., 2010). Doing so alerts participants, especially those who identify as white, that emotions are an expected and important source to explore during discussions. Engaging in conversations about the source of these emotions can help white learners explore how to work with these emotions and continue discussing racial realities even when doing so is difficult.

An important point to consider is the impact of white educators' approaches on students of color. Notably absent from this paper is how white educators facilitated these dialogues among students of color. The focus of this article is on white educators working with white students for the reasons stated previously. However, with the exception of Dalton's one comment about students of color being "skeptical about a white guy talking about race or racism" and Corrine discussing "deepening the wounds that students of color have," neither participant really addressed how her or his facilitation impacted students of color. An implication from this study is considering how one's white racial identity might impact one's ability to connect with students of color during these discussions. Future researchers should consider the impact of these discussions on students of color, particularly in predominantly white environments where their representation is minimal. White educators should be cognizant of not placing the onus onto students of color for educating their white peers (and educators) about their stories without beneficial outcomes for students of color as well from these discussions. As a means to respond to this challenge of unequal groups, the benefit of intergroup dialogue is the strict attention to balancing representation of social identities in the dialogues.

Although Corrine and Dalton utilized different resources to help students engage race, they had different levels of success with taking students out of the classroom to help them grapple with racial content in more tangible ways. Corrine found that students learned about racial disparities by responding to case studies about incidents that occurred on their campus, while Dalton found no beneficial ways to incorporate service-learning into his courses that did not reinforce white students' stereotypes about people of color. Dalton's struggle was inconsistent with Marullo's (1998) research in which he found that including service-learning on a race relations course increased students' awareness of racial diversity. However, this awareness of racial diversity might not be sufficient enough to counter the presence of stereotypes. Recognizing their white race and that most of the students in their courses were also white, Dalton and Corrine sought ways to incorporate different voices into their racial discussions through asking students to engage others within their communities. Future researchers should further examine the benefits and difficulties of other immersion-type experiences in helping white students concretize racial issues.

White educators are well-situated to model appropriate and meaningful ways to respond to racial issues in classroom environments. Educators of color can no longer be the majority of persons who facilitate these dialogues in their courses. As Corrine and Dalton noted, white students were more likely to participate in these discussions when white educators demonstrated productive ways for them to do so. At present, there is a lack of exposure to white role models who positively engage racial realities. White educators who are committed to these discussions can plan workshops for their colleagues, engage in peer review of colleagues' syllabi to ascertain the level of racial consciousness embedded in course material and their philosophies, suggest readings, and serve as contacts with whom other faculty can discuss the process of facilitating these discussions.

CONCLUSION

I conducted this study to illustrate how white educators can facilitate discussions about race with white students in their courses. For this particular article, I devoted attention to two white participants in my study given the predominantly white contexts in which they taught and their abilities to connect with the white learners in their courses in unique ways. As underscored in the findings, these educators capitalized on the privileges they were afforded given their white racial identities and problematized their whiteness in order to encourage white students to reflect on their own identities.

Readers who are interested in beginning the process of addressing racial issues in the classroom might wonder what steps they can take. First and foremost, participants in the present study stressed the importance of developing knowledge about one's whiteness—privileges, power, and the assumptions one holds. Doing so demonstrates to white learners the significance of their own racial identities and reminds them that educators also struggle with making sense of racial issues. The process of facilitating these discussions is a difficult undertaking, but as the narratives from Corrine and Dalton remind readers, they can participate in these discussions by considering the influence of race on their lives, understanding models of white racial identity development, reflecting on their own white identities, and finding ways to include emotions in the classroom that help students personalize issues of race and racism.

NOTES

1. Throughout this article, when referring to the present study, I use "educators" broadly to refer to tenure-track, tenured, and non-tenure-track faculty members, as well as those who do not hold the title "faculty" but teach college-level courses and work with students out of the classroom (e.g., student affairs educators). However, in discussing previous research, I use the terms used by researchers (most often "faculty").
2. "Racial realities" refers to thinking about how race differentially impacts people.

REFERENCES

Astin, A. W. (1998). The changing American college student: Thirty-year trends, 1966–1996. *The Review of Higher Education, 21*(2), 115–135.

Bennett, C. I. (2001). Research on racial issues in American higher education. In J. A. Banks & C. A. McGee Banks (Eds.), *Handbook of research on multicultural education* (pp. 663–682). San Francisco, CA: Jossey-Bass.

Bergerson, A. A. (2003). Critical race theory and white racism: Is there room for white scholars in fighting racism in education? *International Journal of Qualitative Studies in Education, 16*(1), 15–63.

Bernard, H. R. (1998). Introduction: On method and methods in anthropology. In H. R. Bernard (Ed.), *Handbook of methods in cultural anthropology* (pp. 9–36). Walnut Creek, CA: AltaMira.

Bernard, H. R. (2006). *Research methods in anthropology: Qualitative and quantitative approaches* (4th ed.). Lanham, MD: AltaMira.

Bohm, D. (1996). *On dialogue.* New York, NY: Routledge.

Brookfield, S. D., & Preskill, S. (2005). *Discussion as a way of teaching: Tools and techniques for democratic classrooms* (2nd ed.). San Francisco, CA: Jossey-Bass.

Chang, M. J., Chang, J. C., & Ledesma, M. C. (2005). Beyond magical thinking: Doing the real work of diversifying our institutions. *About Campus, 10*(2), 9–16.

Cokley, K. (2004). Teaching about the psychology of race and racism: Lessons learned. In *National conference on race & ethnicity in American higher education: Program and resource guide* (p. 74). Norman, OK: The University of Oklahoma.

Creswell, J. W. (1998). *Qualitative inquiry and research design: Choosing among five traditions.* Thousand Oaks, CA: Sage.

Crotty, M. (2003). *The foundations of social research: Meaning and perspective in the research process.* Thousand Oaks, CA: Sage.

Ellinor, L., & Gerard, G. (1998). *Dialogue: Rediscovering the transforming power of conversation.* New York, NY: Wiley.

Feagin, J. R. (2001). *Racist America: Roots, current realities, and future reparations.* New York, NY: Routledge.

Fontana, A., & Frey, J. H. (2000). The interview: From structured questions to negotiated text. In N. K. Denzin & Y. S. Lincoln (Eds.), *Handbook of qualitative research* (2nd ed., pp. 645–672). Thousand Oaks, CA: Sage.

Freire, P. (1970). *Pedagogy of the oppressed.* New York, NY: Continuum.

Griffin, J. H. (1960). *Black like me.* New York, NY: Penguin Putnam.

Guba, E. G., & Lincoln, Y. S. (1989). *Fourth generation evaluation.* Newbury Park, CA: Sage.

Hampton, H. (Exec. Producer). (1987). *Eyes on the prize* [Motion picture]. USA: Blackside.

Helms, J. E. (2008). *A race is a nice thing to have: A guide to being a white person or understanding the white persons in your life* (2nd ed.). Hanover, MA: Microtraining Associates.

Helms, J. E., & Cook, D. A. (2005). Models of racial oppression and sociorace. In M. E. Wilson & L. E. Wolf-Wendel (Eds.), *ASHE reader on college student development theory* (pp. 235–258). Boston, MA: Pearson.

hooks, b. (1994). *Teaching to transgress: Education as the practice of freedom.* New York, NY: Routledge.

Hurtado, S., Engberg, M. E., Ponjuan, L., & Landreman, L. (2002). Students' precollege preparation for participation in a diverse democracy. *Research in Higher Education, 43*(2), 163–186.

Hyde, B., & Bineham, J. L. (2000). From debate to dialogue: Toward a pedagogy of nonpolarized public discourse. *Southern Communication Journal, 65*(2 & 3), 208–223.

Lincoln, Y. S., & Guba, E. G. (1985). *Naturalistic inquiry.* Beverly Hills, CA: Sage.

Marullo, S. (1998). Bringing home diversity: A service-learning approach to teaching race and ethnic relations. *Teaching Sociology, 26*(4), 259–275.

Mayhew, M. J., Grunwald, H. E., & Dey, E. L. (2005). Curriculum matters: Creating a positive climate for diversity from the student perspective. *Research in Higher Education, 46*(4), 389–412.

Merriam, S. B. (1988). *Case study research in education: A qualitative approach.* San Francisco, CA: Jossey-Bass.

Merriam, S. B. (1998). *Qualitative research and case study applications in education.* San Francisco, CA: Jossey-Bass.

Merriam, S. B. (2002). Case study. In S. B. Merriam & Associates (Eds.), *Qualitative research in practice: Examples for discussion and analysis* (pp. 178–180). San Francisco, CA: Jossey-Bass.

Miles, M. B., & Huberman, A. M. (1994). *Qualitative data analysis: An expanded sourcebook* (2nd ed.). Thousand Oaks, CA: Sage.

Nagda, B. A., & Maxwell, K. E. (2011). Deepening the layers of understanding and connection: A critical-dialogic approach to facilitating intergroup dialogues. In K. E. Maxwell, B. A. Nagda, & M. C. Thompson (Eds.), *Facilitating intergroup dialogues: Bridging differences, catalyzing change* (pp. 1–22). Sterling, VA: Stylus.

National Center for Education Statistics. (1998). *Digest of education statistics, 1997.* Washington, DC: U.S. Department of Education, Office of Educational Research and Improvement.

National Conference on Race & Ethnicity in American Higher Education. (2007). *About NCORE.* Retrieved from http://www.ncore.ou.edu/about_ncore.html

Patton, M. Q. (2002). *Qualitative research & evaluation methods* (3rd ed.). Thousand Oaks, CA: Sage.

Saddlemire, J. R. (1996). Qualitative study of white second-semester undergraduates' attitudes toward African-American undergraduates at a predominantly white university. *Journal of College Student Development, 37*(6), 684–691.

Schmidt, S. L. (2005). More than men in white sheets: Seven concepts critical to the teaching of racism as systemic inequality. *Equity and Excellence in Education, 38*(2), 110–122.

Schuman, H., & Bobo, L. (1988). Survey-based experiments on White racial attitudes toward residential integration. *American Journal of Sociology, 94*(2), 273–299.

Schuman, H., Steeh, C., & Bobo, L. (1985). *Racial attitudes in America: Trends and interpretations.* Cambridge, MA: Harvard University Press.

Stake, R. (1995). *The art of case study research.* Thousand Oaks, CA: Sage.

Stake, R. E. (2005). Qualitative case studies. In N. K. Denzin & Y. S. Lincoln (Eds.), *The SAGE handbook of qualitative research* (3rd ed., pp. 443–466). Thousand Oaks, CA: Sage.

Stassen, M. L. A. (1995). White faculty members and racial diversity: A theory and its implications. *The Review of Higher Education, 18*(4), 361–391.

Sue, D. W., Torino, G. C., Capodilupo, C. M., Rivera, D. P., & Lin, A. I. (2010). How White faculty perceive and react to difficult dialogues on race: Implications for education and training. *The Counseling Psychologist, 37*(8), 1090–1115.

Tatum, B. D. (1997). *"Why are all the black kids sitting together in the cafeteria?" And other conversations about race.* New York, NY: Basic.

Wahl, A.-M., Perez, E. T., Deegan, M. J., Sanchez, T. W., & Applegate, C. (2000). The controversial classroom: Institutional resources and pedagogical strategies for a race relations course. *Teaching Sociology, 28*(4), 316–332.

Warren, J. T., & Hytten, K. (2004). The faces of whiteness: Pitfalls and the critical democrat. *Communication Education, 53*(4), 321–339.

Weissman, J., Bulakowski, C., & Jumisko, M. (1998). A study of white, black and Hispanic students' transition to a community college. *Community College Review, 26*(2), 19–42.

Wise, T. J. (2008). *White like me: Reflections on race from a privileged son.* Brooklyn, NY: Soft Skull Press.

Yin, R. K. (2003). *Case study research: Design and methods* (3rd ed.). Thousand Oaks, CA: Sage.

Zúñiga, X. (2003). Bridging differences through dialogue. *About Campus, 7*(6), 8–16.

Zúñiga, X., Nagda, B. A., Chesler, M., & Cytron-Walker, A. (2007). *Intergroup dialogue in higher education: Meaningful learning about social justice.* ASHE Higher Education Report Vol. 32, No. 4. San Francisco, CA: Jossey-Bass.

Zúñiga, X., Nagda, B. A., & Sevig, T. D. (2002). Intergroup dialogues: An educational model for cultivating engagement accross differences. *Equity & Excellence in Education, 35*(1), 7–17.

Raising Ethnic-Racial Consciousness: The Relationship Between Intergroup Dialogues and Adolescents' Ethnic-Racial Identity and Racism Awareness

Adriana Aldana, Stephanie J. Rowley, Barry Checkoway, and Katie Richards-Schuster
University of Michigan

Empirical evidence shows that intergroup dialogue programs promote changes in ethnic-racial identity and racism awareness among college students. Expanding on this research, this study examines the effects of intergroup dialogues on adolescents' racial consciousness. Self-reports of 147 adolescents (13–19 years old), of various racial and ethnic backgrounds were used. Repeated-measures ANOVAs, on pre- and post-tests examined changes in racial consciousness (ethnic-racial identity and racism awareness), controlling for parent education. Group differences (ethnic-racial groups, nativity) also were examined. As predicted, ethnic-racial identity and racism awareness increased after completing the program. Although there were statistically significant ethnic-racial group differences in ethnic-racial identity, no group differences in racism awareness were found. The findings demonstrate that intergroup dialogues can promote adolescents' ethnic-racial consciousness.

Developmental psychology suggests that social identity development is an important psychological task during adolescence that provides clarity regarding one's role in society (Erickson, 1968; Marcia, 1980). The development of racial and ethnic identity, in particular, has been found to relate positively to coping, self-esteem, and optimism, and negatively to measures of loneliness and depression (Roberts et al., 1999). In addition, studies suggest that teaching youth about diversity and racism promotes critical thinking and civic agency among youth (Boulden, 2007; Checkoway, 2009; Gurin, Nagda, & Lopez, 2004). Therefore, identifying mechanisms that foster ethnic-racial identity and racism awareness among adolescents may be a worthwhile endeavor for scholars and practitioners.

Empirical studies on intergroup dialogues show that participation in these dialogues leads college students to greater personal awareness, changes in attitudes on issues of identity, and increased motivation for social justice action (Dessel, Rogge, & Garlington, 2006; Nagda & Zúñiga, 2003; Stephan, 2008; Zúñiga, Nagda, Chesler, & Cytron-Walker, 2007). While the institutionalization of intergroup dialogue programs within universities across the U.S. has proliferated evidence on the positive effects of these dialogues on college students, less is known about the impact of intergroup dialogue with adolescents. The purpose of this study is to extend research on intergroup dialogues to the field of adolescent development.

There is a growing body of literature on youth intergroup dialogues that demonstrates that the central aims of intergroup dialogue—to raise consciousness, to build relationships across group difference and conflict, and to strengthen participants' individual and collective capacity to engage in civic activities—can be attained with adolescent populations (Boulden, 2007; Spencer, Brown, Griffin, & Abdullah, 2008; Wayne, 2008). These programs range from community-based leadership training programs to school-based conflict interventions using a variety of dialogic methods. This study focuses on one of the main goals of intergroup dialogues—consciousness raising—to examine in more depth the changes in ethnic-racial identity and racism awareness among adolescents of diverse ethnic and racial backgrounds.

Do adolescents benefit from their involvement in intergroup dialogues on race and ethnicity and, if so, how? More specifically, does race-based dialogue promote adolescents' ethnic-racial identity and racism awareness? This study aims to explore these questions by examining the relationship between a race-based intergroup dialogue programs on adolescents' racial consciousness. These questions are of significance, since social institutions (e.g., community-based programs and schools) serving American adolescents are continuously affected by diversity issues, such as intergroup conflict, lunchroom segregation, and race-based social exclusion in schools (Crystal, Killen, & Ruck, 2008; Tatum, 1997). Therefore, we might expect that American youth would be engaged in conversations about race and ethnicity. However, racial segregation within and across communities and adults' general unwillingness to talk about race provides limited opportunities for youth to discuss race and racism for themselves (Checkoway, 2009).

RAISING ETHNIC-RACIAL CONSCIOUSNESS

Prior to identifying the effects of intergroup dialogue on adolescents' consciousness, we must first determine what constitutes ethnic-racial consciousness. In addition, related concepts of ethnic and racial identity need to be defined. Current theoretical perspectives argue that ethnic- and racial-identity are not separate entities but rather, overlap (Cross & Cross, 2008; Quintana, 2007). Consequently, hereafter we use the term "ethnic-racial identity" to discuss findings on racial and ethnic identity development. Under intergroup dialogue paradigms, consciousness includes participants' development of personal and social identity (e.g., ethnic-racial identity) and knowledge acquisition of social systems (e.g., racism awareness and white privilege). Accordingly, "ethnic-racial consciousness" is a broad construct that we use to refer to: (1) an awareness of one's ethnicity and/or race (i.e., ethnic-racial identity); and (2) knowledge of social systems that create and perpetuate power differentials between groups (i.e., racism awareness). Thus, ethnic-racial consciousness includes an understanding of how people have been historically classified into ethnic and racial groups based on creed, phenotype, and cultural markers, which then serve to maintain social hierarchy that benefits some groups over others.

Youth Intergroup Dialogues and Ethnic-Racial Identity Development

Adolescence marks the developmental phase used in public and academic discourse on identity development and group consciousness (Cross & Cross, 2008; Erikson, 1968; Marcia, 1980; Phinney, 1992, 1996; Quintana, 1994, 1998; Tatum, 1997). Empirical evidence demonstrates that adolescents are actively examining their ethnic and racial identity (Phinney, 1990, 1992; Phinney & Ong, 2007; Tatum, 1997). Phinney and Ong suggest that ethnic identity development consists of two components: (1) learning more (i.e., ethnic identity search) about social roles and cultural norms within one's ethnic-racial group(s); and (2) ethnic identity commitment, which includes self-identification with and the affective connection to one's ethnic-racial group(s). Identity search is not a precursor to ethnic-racial identity commitment. Instead, both dimensions of identity development are interrelated and continuous aspects of ethnic-racial identity.

Developmental perspectives propose that an increasingly mature ethnic-racial identity is associated with positive feelings toward other groups (Phinney, Ferguson, & Tate, 1997). Indeed, empirical evidence demonstrates a positive and predictive relation between ethnic identity and intergroup attitudes (Phinney, Ferguson, & Tate, 1997; Phinney, Jacoby, & Silva, 2007). Literature on ethnic and racial identity development suggests that contextual factors, such as exposure to peers of diverse ethnic-racial identities, may trigger further reflection about one's ethnic-racial identity (Cross & Cross, 2008; Tatum, 1997). Within intergroup dialogues, we might find that sustained contact with others different from oneself affects certain dimensions of one's ethnic-racial identity (i.e., search vs. commitment) differently.

For instance, in race-based dialogues, experiential activities and semi-structured dialogues directly prompt participants to critically examine the socialization messages that have shaped their ethnic-racial identity. Program evaluations of the University of Michigan's Youth Dialogue on Race and Ethnicity program show that after participating in intergroup dialogues, adolescents increase their understanding of their own racial and ethnic group membership, knowledge about others who are different from themselves, and their willingness to take action against racism and segregation (Checkoway, 2009). In a mixed method study with 11th graders who participated in a school-based intergroup dialogue and conflict resolution intervention, Spencer and colleagues (2008) found that after completing the program, students reported increased awareness of their racial identity and consciousness of intergroup relations in their school. It is evident that youth intergroup dialogue programs are effective in promoting adolescents' self- and social-awareness about race.

Youth Intergroup Dialogues and Racism Awareness

There is a growing body of literature that documents adolescents' perceived discrimination in relation to psychological, social, and academic outcomes. Typically, perceived discrimination has been conceptualized as one's reports of and psychological response to past discriminatory experiences (Fisher, Wallace, & Fenton, 2000; Greene, Way, & Pahl, 2006; Landrine & Klonoff, 1996; Pahl & Way, 2006; Seaton et al., 2008). Yet, less is known about adolescents' awareness of racism. Racism awareness is distinct from perceived discrimination in that racism awareness is a conceptual understanding of the social hierarchy that privileges white people and perpetuates racial inequalities that put ethnic-racial minorities at a social disadvantage, regardless of one's experience with discrimination. Thus, awareness of racism requires individuals to think of discrimination and prejudice more abstractly. Neville and colleagues (2000) propose that awareness of racism may range from attitudes that either downplay or deny the presence of racism at the individual, structural, and institutional level to an active awareness of various forms of racism and discrimination.

Intergroup dialogue programs on race and ethnicity have the promise to promote racism awareness among adolescent participants. For instance, to increase participants' knowledge of social systems, intergroup dialogues engage participants in structured discussions about social phenomena (e.g., privilege and oppression) with peers from varying social backgrounds. A mixed-method study of the Anytown program (Matsudaira & Jefferson, 2006), a community-based program for high school-aged youth that uses intergroup dialogues as part of the curriculum to train young community leaders, demonstrates that using dialogic methods in the youth training programs increased participants' understanding and knowledge of various racial and ethnic groups (e.g., white, black, Latino, Asian, and Native American) and increased awareness of how oppression and privilege influence their community (Boulden, 2007; Matsudaira & Jefferson, 2006). In race-based dialogues, semi-structured activities set the stage for intergroup dialogues on the pervasiveness of racism and bigotry in the United States. Thus, we may expect that intergroup dialogues will increase adolescents' awareness of racism.

PRESENT STUDY

As discussed above, empirical evidence suggests that community-based and school-based intergroup dialogues with adolescents are beneficial and effective (Boulden, 2007; Checkoway, 2009; Spencer et al., 2008; Wayne, 2008). To expand on previous research, this study aims to examine the influence of intergroup dialogue programs on adolescents' ethnic-racial consciousness. Our first research objective is to determine if participation in a youth intergroup dialogue increases adolescents' ethnic-racial identity and racism awareness. First, we hypothesize that participants will report higher scores on ethnic-racial identity and racism awareness after participating in the intergroup dialogues program. According to social identity theory, cross-cultural encounters may motivate individuals' exploration of their identity (Kosmitzki, 1996). Participating in intergroup dialogues with individuals different from oneself over an extended period of time may stimulate the exploration of the meaning of one's identity. On the other hand, ethnic-racial identity commitment is an affective component of identity that develops at an early age (French, Seidman, Allen, & Aber, 2006; Rotheram-Borus, Lightfoot, Moraes, Dopkins, & LaCour, 1998) and has not been found to demonstrate growth patterns in later adolescence (Pahl & Way, 2006). Therefore, we also expect to find greater increases in ethnic-racial identity exploration than ethnic-racial commitment after intergroup dialogue participation. No formal hypothesis was generated for differential effects on racism awareness, given the limited research on racism awareness with adolescent samples. However, program effects on specific dimensions of racism awareness (i.e., racial privilege, institutional discrimination, and blatant racial issues) are examined.

Second, this study set out to identify differences in ethnic-racial identity and racism awareness among groups of various ethnic-racial backgrounds and nativity status. We expect that participants of color and foreign born youth will report higher levels of ethnic-racial identity than European American and U.S. born participants. This hypothesis is supported by empirical evidence that suggests that although white adolescents in integrated schools think about race and ethnicity, students of color engage in a more active search for identity (Phinney, 1988, 1992; Phinney & Ong, 2007). Another reason for group differences in ethnic-racial identity development may be related to differences in the salience and centrality of race and ethnicity in the lived experiences of immigrant children (Branch, Tayal, & Triplett, 2000; French et al., 2000; Phinney & Tarver, 1988).

Third, we hypothesize that adolescents with more exposure to discrimination (i.e., ethnic-racial minority and foreign born) will be more aware of racism than European American and U.S. born participants. Empirical evidence demonstrates that youth of color report more perceived discrimination than their white counterparts (Fisher, Wallace, & Fenton, 2000). At a theoretical level, we might expect that adolescents who experience more discrimination (i.e., youth of color) are likely to be more aware of racism. Hughes and colleagues (2006) found that recent immigrant youth in the Unites States attribute experiences with discrimination to their immigration status and not to their ethnic-racial identity. Therefore, we examined ethnic-racial group membership separately from nativity status. With this study we hope to provide more knowledge about the ways in which intergroup dialogues on race and ethnicity contribute to adolescents' ethnic-racial identity development and racism awareness.

METHODS

Participants and Procedures

We used an action research approach in this study, not an experimental-control group design, to examine the influence of intergroup dialogue on adolescents' ethnic-racial identity and racism awareness (Brydon-Miller, Greenwood, & Maguire, 2003; Nolen & Vander Putten, 2007). The present study draws from program evaluation data collected by the University of Michigan's Youth Dialogues on Race and Ethnicity in Metropolitan Detroit. The youth dialogues in Metropolitan Detroit is an eight-week program that enables adolescents of African American, Asian American, European American, Latina/o American, and Middle Eastern American descent to come together in intergroup dialogues to discuss racial and ethnic issues within and across their communities. At the end of the program, the participants attend a weekend retreat that provides training workshops in youth activism and social advocacy skills (for more program details see Checkoway, 2009).

Participants were recruited through 16 community-based agencies located in various neighborhoods within the city of Detroit and six suburbs across the metropolitan area. Parent consent forms were obtained prior to or during the program orientation. During the program orientation participants and their parents were given a description of the evaluation survey. Participation in the program survey evaluation was voluntary. Participants completed two surveys: The pre-test was completed during the program orientation and the post-test was completed at the program retreat. Participant consent forms were obtained prior to completion of both the pre- and post-test surveys.

Sample

Participants ranged from 13 to19 years of age, with a mean age of 16 years. The sample included girls (65%) and boys (35%). The majority (83%) of the participants were U.S. born. Information regarding the citizenship status was not obtained for this study. The use of the term American was used by both domestic and foreign-born participants to indicate their ethnic-racial identity.

Participants' parents or guardians had achieved varying levels of education, ranging from no more than grade school to a graduate/professional degree, with a median parent/guardian educational attainment of an associates degree. The sample included participants from several ethnic-racial groups: black/African American (32%), Asian American (16%), European American (23%), Middle Eastern American (16%), Latina/o American (8%), and multiracial/ethnic (6%).

Data from the 2007 ($N = 81$) and 2008 ($N = 66$) surveys were combined for a total sample of 147. A t-test was used to evaluate the mean difference between cohorts for outcome variables. The two cohorts only differed in their pre-test reports of institutional discrimination, $t(135) = -.41, p < .001$, with the 2008 cohort reporting slightly higher scores ($M = 2.80$) than the 2007 cohort ($M = 2.35$) on the institutional discrimination subscale at pre-test.

Measures

Demographic Variables

Race-ethnicity, nativity, and socioeconomic status (SES) were included in the analyses. Race-ethnicity and nativity were included as independent variables because both have shown an effect on racial-ethnic identity and/or awareness of racism (Phinney & Tarver, 1988; Rumbaut, 1994). Socioeconomic status was used as a covariate, because it is often a confounding factor with race and ethnicity (Spencer & Markstrom-Adams, 1990). We measured SES using a combined score for both caregivers' educational level as a proxy (Hoff, Laursen & Tardif, 2002). Participants reported the level of education, in years, for two primary caregivers on separate items. Nativity was measured by a single, dichotomous (yes or no) item in which the respondent indicated whether he or she was born in the U.S. Participants were also asked to report their ethnic-racial identity on an open-ended item (e.g., "What is your race(s)/ethnicity(ies)?"). Participants created over 40 racial and ethnic labels that were later recoded into five pan-racial/pan-ethnic categories that correspond with the ethnic-racial groups used by the program: Black/African American, White/European American, Arab American, and Latino/Hispanic. Multiracial/Multiethnic youth were not considered a separate ethnic-racial group in the intergroup dialogue program; however, we created a separate category for the analyses.

Ethnic-Racial Identity

An adapted version of the Multigroup Ethnic Identity Measure (MEIM; Phinney, 1992) was used to measure participants' ethnic-racial identity. Subscales assessing identity search and commitment were created using the revised theoretical framework (MEIM-R) suggested by Phinney and Ong (2007), which has demonstrated acceptable psychometric properties with ethnically and racially diverse adolescents (French et al., 2006). Consistent with the MEIM-R, this measure used a 6-item inventory to assess level of ethnic-racial exploration and commitment. However, respondents reported on a 5-point Likert scale, rather than the suggested 4-point scale, ranging from 1 = strongly disagree to 5 = strongly agree. We opted to use a 5-point scale to allow participants to indicate a "neutral" response and be more selective in their response (Adelson & McCoach, 2010; Cronbach, 1950). Moreover, one item in the revised commitment subscale—"I have often done things to understand my ethnic background better"—was replaced with a reverse coded item from the original MEIM scale: "I have really not spent much time trying to learn more about the culture and history of my ethnic group." A sample item for the ethnic identity search subscale is: "I have spent time trying to find out more about my own ethnic group, such as its history, traditions, and customs." Mean scores for each subscale were computed to create continuous scores. Although reliability for the exploration subscale was acceptable at the pre-test ($\alpha = .72$), it was more marginal at the post-test ($\alpha = .63$). Psychometric literature suggest a minimal level of reliability between .60 to .70, therefore, the slight decrease in the reliability coefficient was determined satisfactory (Aiken, 2000; Robinson, Shaver, & Wrightsman, 1999) The ethnic commitment subscale maintained an accepted level of reliability at both time points (pre-test $\alpha = .76$; post-test $\alpha = .70$).

Racism Awareness

A 19-item adapted version of the Color-Blind Racial Attitudes Scale (CoBRAS; Neville, Lilly, Duran, Lee, & Browne, 2000) was used to measure a lack of awareness of racial privilege, institutional discrimination, and blatant racial issues. The scale assesses the continuum of racial attitudes that ranges from a color-blind ideology (the downplaying or denying of the significance and prevalence or racism) to racism awareness. We chose to frame participant responses in terms of racism awareness for this study. Participants reported endorsement of items reflecting racism awareness on a 5-point scale ranging from 1 = strongly disagree to 5 = strongly agree. Neville and colleagues (2000) reported acceptable Cronbach's alpha for each subscale that ranged from .70 (Blatant Racial Issues) to .86 (CoBRAS total).

In the present study, the racial privilege subscale (pre-test $\alpha = .74$; post-test $\alpha = .70$) measured adolescents' awareness of how race and ethnicity relates to social privileges and disadvantages (e.g., "Everyone who works hard, no matter what race they are, has an equal chance to become rich."). A sample item of blindness to institutional discrimination is, "Social policies, such as affirmative action, discriminate against white people." Even after omitting an item that was negatively correlated with other items ("Due to racial discrimination, programs such as affirmative action are necessary to help create equality"), the reliability of the institutional discrimination subscale remained low (pre-test $\alpha = .58$; post-test $\alpha = .63$). Finally, the blatant racial issues (pre-test $\alpha = .70$; post-test $\alpha = .77$) subscale measured awareness of overt forms of ethnic-racial discrimination (e.g., "Racial problems in the U.S. are rare, isolated situations."). A mean score was created for each subscale.

Data Analysis

A pair of repeated measures ANOVAs, using general linear model (Werts & Linn, 1970), were performed on pre- and post-test data where subscales of the ethnic-racial identity (exploration and commitment) and racism awareness (racial privilege, institutional discrimination, and blatant racial issues) variables served as the within-subject dependent variable. The between subjects variables were ethnic-racial groups (African American, Asian American, European American, Latina/o American, Middle Eastern American, multiracial) and Nativity groups (U.S. born vs.

foreign born). To challenge local racial and ethnic segregation and create a diverse group of program participants, the youth dialogue program recruited European American and Asian American participants from affluent suburbs surrounding the metropolitan area, whereas, African America, Middle-Eastern American, and Latina/o American participants were recruited from less affluent neighborhoods throughout the city of Detroit. Thus, we controlled for SES to adjust for the disparities across racial-ethnic groups. Although adolescent girls and young women have been found to report greater levels of ethnic identity (Phinney, 1990; Rotheram-Borus et al., 1998) and racism awareness (Neville et al., 2000), we did not find significant gender differences in mean scores for outcome variables in this study. Thus, we did not include it in our model.

RESULTS

Fourteen participants had missing data on one or more outcome variables (i.e., racial-ethnic identity and racism awareness). Five univariate outliers were identified and removed from the analysis. The existence of multivariate outliers was then examined separately for each analysis. For ethnic-racial identity, Mahalanobis distance was evaluated as χ^2 with degrees of freedom equal to the number of independent and covariate variables, in this case six variables, and at $p < 0.001$. For racism awareness, Mahalanobis distance was evaluated as χ^2 with eight degrees of freedom, and at $p < 0.001$. No multivariate outliers were found for ethnic-racial identity or racism awareness. Listwise-deletion was selected. Method 3 (SSTYPE3) was used to adjust for unequal cell size. After deletion of cases with missing data and multivariate outliers, assumptions regarding normality of sampling distributions, homogeneity of variance-covariance matrices, linearity, and multicollinearity were met.

Ethnic-Racial Identity

A repeated measure ANOVA was used to assess changes in ethnic-racial identity exploration and commitment over the course of the intergroup dialogue program and to identify any group differences in identity search and identity commitment. Ethnic-racial group and nativity status (US born vs. foreign-born) were the between subjects variables, whereas, time (pre-test vs. post-test) and ethnic-racial identity scores (i.e., exploration vs. commitment) were the within subjects variables. Using Wilks' criterion, there was a statistically significant main effect for identity, F $(5, 108) = 10.74$, $p < .001$. This main effect was qualified by a significant Time × Identity interaction, $F (5, 108) = 5.96$, $p < .05$. A post hoc test, using paired sample t-test, indicated a statistically significant increase in ethnic-racial identity exploration from pre- ($M = 3.47$) to post-test ($M = 3.75$). As expected, there was no statistically significant change in ethnic-racial identity commitment. We also found a statistically significant three-way interaction among time, identity, and parent education, F $(5,108) = 4.36$, $p < .05$. A post hoc ANOVA, split by parent education level, demonstrates a change in ethnic-racial identity exploration from pre- ($M = 3.24$) to post-test ($M = 3.76$) for participants from families with lower educational attainment, F $(1,48) = 5.23$, $p < .05$ (Figure 1.). There was no statistically significant change in ethnic-racial exploration or commitment among participants of families with higher educational attainment.

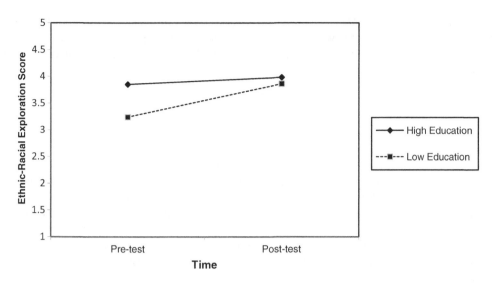

FIGURE 1   Mean group differences in ethnic-racial exploration for participants from families with higher-and lower-educational attainment.

A statistically significant difference between ethnic-racial groups was found, F (5,108) = 2.67, $p < .05$. Marginal means in Table 1 show that, in general, participants of color (African American, Asian American, Middle Eastern American, Latina/o, and multiracial) reported greater levels of overall ethnic-racial identity than European American participants. To test whether minority participants reported significantly higher levels of ethic-racial identity, a post hoc test was conducted. A simple contrast analysis, using European Americans as the comparison group revealed that African American ($M = 3.83$), Asian American ($M = 4.12$), and Middle Eastern American adolescents ($M = 4.00$) reported greater levels of ethnic-racial identity than their

TABLE 1
Mean scores and standard deviations of ethnic-racial identity for adolescents of diverse ethnic-racial groups

| Group | n | Exploration | | | | Commitment | | | | Overall | |
| | | Pre | | Post | | Pre | | Post | | | |
		M	SE	M	SE	M	SE	M	SE	M	SE
African American	38	3.35	0.21	3.8	0.18	4.07	0.19	4.1	0.16	3.83	0.14
Asian American	17	4.06	0.21	4.08	0.17	4.18	0.19	4.16	0.17	4.12	0.14
European American	29	3.03	0.22	3.55	0.19	3.56	0.2	3.71	0.18	3.46	0.15
Latina/o American	7	3.66	0.35	3.66	0.3	3.61	0.31	3.76	0.28	3.67	0.24
Middle Eastern American	11	4.02	0.27	3.75	0.26	4.19	0.24	4.05	0.21	4.0	0.18
Multiracial	6	3.24	0.38	4.02	0.32	3.43	0.35	3.97	0.31	3.67	0.26

Note. Multigroup Ethnic Identity Measure (MEIM; Phinney, 1992; MEIM-R; Phinney & Ong, 2007); All values represent raw, nonstandardized scores.

European American peers ($M = 3.46$). Latina/o American and Multiracial adolescents' ($M = 3.67$) reports of ethnic-racial identity were not significantly different from those of European American ($M = 3.46$) youth. There was no statistically significant difference between participants born in the U.S. and foreign-born participants, $F(1,108) = .45, p = .50$.

Racism Awareness

A second repeated measures ANOVA was used to assess any changes in awareness of racial privilege, institutional discrimination, and blatant racial issues over the course of the intergroup dialogue program, and racial-ethnic group differences in awareness. There was a statistically significant main effect for time, $F(5,108) = 7.83$ $p < .01$. Marginal means in Table 2 suggest that participants reported greater awareness of racial and ethnic discrimination from pretest ($M = 2.51$), to posttest ($M = 2.28$). A main effect for type of awareness was also found, $F(5,108) = 12.28, p < .001$. Participants reported the least awareness to blatant racial issues ($M = 1.77$), followed by white racial privilege ($M = 2.32$), and institutional discrimination ($M = 3.11$). The absence of a time by awareness interaction in this study suggests that the program worked similarly across dimensions of racism awareness. No statistically significant difference in awareness scores was found between ethnic-racial groups $F(1,108) = 1.06, p = .39$ or nativity groups (U.S. born vs. foreign born), $F(1,108) = 1.92, p = .17$.

DISCUSSION

During the transition into adulthood, youth are expected to reframe their childhood perceptions of identity and social roles (Erikson, 1968). Nonetheless, there are few social structures to assist adolescents with this critical developmental task. As expected, after completing the intergroup dialogue, program youth reported greater exploration of their ethnic-racial identity than prior to their participation in the program, while levels of ethnic-racial commitment remained constant. Although the increases that we found may reflect normative development in identity exploration, we believe that the results are more a result of participation in the dialogue program. It is unlikely that change of the magnitude seen in this study would occur over a couple of months. Even though previous research demonstrates a steady increase in identity search among younger adolescence (French et al., 2006) and steady declines in exploring the meaning of their ethnic group in older adolescents (Pahl & Way, 2006), participants reported an increase in the exploration of their ethnic-racial identity, such as talking to others about one's identity or spending time learning more about their racial-ethnic group history. In conjunction with previous literature (French et al., 2006; Pahl & Way, 2006), the current findings provide support that changes in ethnic-racial identity exploration are due to the intergroup dialogues and not simply to maturity.

In the dialogue program studied, adolescents were first asked to critically examine their own ethnic-racial identity with youth of similar backgrounds. Thus, the structure of intra-group dialogue discussions directly prompted students to talk and learn about their identity with others (i.e., identity exploration), which in this case did not influence commitment to one's identity. Moreover, ethnic-racial identity commitment is a more stable dimension of identity and is less likely to change over a short period of time or be influenced by contextual factors such as sustained

TABLE 2

Mean scores and standard deviations of racism awareness for adolescents of diverse ethnic-racial groups

Group	N	Racial Privilege				Institutional Discrimination				Blatant Racial Issues				Overall	
		Pre		Post		Pre		Post		Pre		Post			
		M	SE	M	SE	M	SE	M	SE	M	SE	M	SE	M	SE
African American	38	2.76	0.17	2.82	0.16	2.40	0.13	2.34	0.15	1.94	0.14	1.66	0.15	2.32	0.09
Asian American	17	3.56	0.17	2.96	0.17	2.53	0.12	2.40	0.15	2.08	0.14	1.7	0.15	2.54	0.09
European American	29	3.03	0.18	2.96	0.18	2.56	0.14	2.40	0.16	1.85	0.15	1.64	0.16	2.41	0.09
Latina/o American	7	3.37	0.28	3.01	0.28	1.83	0.21	1.93	0.25	1.77	0.23	1.82	0.25	2.30	0.14
Middle Eastern American	11	3.53	0.23	3.02	0.22	2.52	0.17	2.27	0.20	2.14	0.19	1.79	0.2	2.55	0.12
Multiracial	6	3.26	0.31	2.90	0.31	2.45	0.24	2.20	0.28	1.59	0.26	1.23	0.28	2.27	0.16

Note. Color-Blind Racial Attitudes Scale (CoBRAS; Neville, Lilly, Duran, Lee, & Browne, 2000). All values represent raw, nonstandardized scores.

intergroup contact (Pahl & Way, 2006). The results suggest that intergroup dialogue programs with adolescents have the promise to be a method that facilitates adolescents' exploration of their ethnic-racial identity.

Our hypothesis regarding group differences in ethnic-racial identity was partially supported. In general, and in line with previous research (Branch, Tayal, & Triplett, 2000; French et al., 2000; Phinney & Tarver, 1988), ethnic minority participants had higher scores on our measure of ethnic-racial identity than European American participants. Not all participants of color, however, reported greater levels of ethnic-racial identity than European Americans. Although African American, Asian American, and Middle Eastern Americans reported greater levels of ethnic-racial identity, Latino/a American and multiracial adolescents did not report greater levels of ethnic-racial identity than their European American peers. Moreover, our expectation that youth born in other countries would have higher ethnic-racial identity than native-born youth was not supported.

There are several possible reasons for these unexpected results. First, it may be that we were unable to detect group difference due to the low number of participants within the Latina/o and multiracial categories. Similarly, since 83% of our sample was U.S. born, it reduced our statistical power to identify group differences by nativity. Second, contextual factors outside the scope of this study, regional location (Midwest vs. Southwest), and racial segregation may influence the saliency of ethnic-racial identity for Latina/o American and multiracial youth in Metropolitan Detroit. One's ethnic-racial identity may be more salient in a context in which one is the numerical minority. For instance, Umaña-Taylor (2004) found that Latina/o American adolescents attending a predominately non-Latino school reported significantly higher levels of ethnic identity than adolescents in schools that were predominantly Latino or ethnically balanced. The Latino sample in this study included high school students from a highly segregated neighborhood, which is consistent with empirical evidence that shows that segregation of Latina/o American youth exceeds that of African American youth (Orfield & Lee, 2005; Valencia, 2000). For the Latina/o American youth in this study, ethnic-racial identity may not have been as salient as other social factors (i.e., immigration status, gender, SES), given that they live among people of their own ethnic-racial group. Nevertheless, mean differences in ethnic-racial identity were minimal, suggesting that all youth experience moderate levels of ethnic-racial identity regardless of group membership. It should be noted that these ethnic-racial group differences were main effects and the interaction with time was non-significant. That is, gains in racial-ethnic identity over the course of the program were similar across groups.

In addition, although we did not hypothesize interactions between socioeconomic status and ethnic-racial identity, we found a significant interaction of parents' education level and ethnic-racial identity. Specifically, we found that youth with less well educated parents tended to have greater gains in ethnic-racial exploration over the course of the intergroup dialogue program. This might reflect a social contextual effect in that youth from lower socioeconomic circumstances are also more likely to live in racially segregated neighborhoods and may have less opportunity for cross-racial/ethnic interactions (Orfield, 2001).

For racism awareness, the results were also mixed. The findings support our hypothesis regarding the positive influence of intergroup dialogues on adolescents' awareness of racism. When composite scores for colorblind racial attitudes were considered, participants reported less endorsement of colorblind ideology at post-test, which suggests that the program was effective in increasing awareness of racism. These findings are consistent with research on the effects of multicultural education on racism awareness among college-aged adults. As one example, Probst (2003) reported that awareness of institutional discrimination improved for college students completing a psychology of prejudice and racism course. Similarly, Kernahan and Davis (2007) show that college students taking a prejudice and racism course became more aware of racism, including more subtle forms of racism, such as institutional discrimination and white privilege. The current findings provide evidence that an intergroup dialogue can have an effect on adolescents' awareness of racism.

This study supports previous findings that suggest that knowledge about racism can be promoted through multicultural and anti-racist education (Kernahan & Davis, 2007; Probst, 2003; Rudman, Ashmore, & Gary, 2001). For instance, the program studied supplemented intergroup dialogues with an educational curriculum that included content and experiential activities to help participants scrutinize racism and white privilege. It may be that purposeful use of semi-structured activities and dialogic methods that align with the process and content of the dialogue topic allow participants to consider various forms of privilege and oppression (Dessel, Rogge, & Garlington, 2006; Nagda & Gurin, 2007; Zúñiga, Nagda, Chesler, & Crtron-Walker, 2007).

The findings also suggest that adolescents were more aware of certain forms of racism than others. Participants reported more awareness of blatant racial issues than of racial privilege or institutional discrimination. Perhaps, blatant racial issues are more perceivable than institutional discrimination and white privilege for adolescents because they can recall concrete examples of this type of racism from their day-to-day life. However, institutional discrimination and white privilege may be more cognitively taxing for adolescents, especially in the absence of situational cues and individual experiences that provide information about more subtle forms of racism (Brown & Bigler, 2005). For instance, in a qualitative report of Middle Eastern immigrant youth in Canada, adolescents often reported instances when they were treated unfairly. However, youth did not identify themselves as being victims of racist acts (Khanlou, Koh, & Mill, 2008). Though youth, in that study, were able to describe instances of discrimination, they were unable to attribute these experiences to racism. It seems that adolescents' level of cognitive maturity may limit their ability to link concrete personal experiences (e.g., perceived discrimination) to abstract social constructs (e.g., institutional discrimination, structural racism, and white privilege). More research is needed to inform a developmental theory regarding adolescents' racism awareness.

Surprisingly, the results did not support our hypothesis that ethnic-racial minority and foreign born youth would be more aware of racism than European Americans and U.S. born participants. Moreover, all ethnic-racial groups reported similar gains in awareness of blatant racial issues after completing the program. There are several possible reasons for the lack of group differences. The number of participants within each ethnic-racial category was relatively small, which may have minimized our power to detect statistical differences among groups. Finally, it is possible that differences in racism awareness among racial-ethnic groups do not exist among this sample of adolescents. It may be that differences in racism awareness between ethnic-racial and nativity groups emerge later in life when one has reached adulthood. For instance, as a person of color grows into adulthood—and accumulates life experiences of witnessing or being a target of discrimination—they become more aware of the existence of racism. On the other hand, as a function of white privilege, a white/European American individual may grow up not having to think about race and/or racism (McIntosh, 1989). Indeed, research shows that individuals that are economically and racially privileged are less aware of structural causes of inequality than economically and racially disadvantaged individuals (Cozarell, Wikinson, & Tagler, 2001). Less is known about how youth of color and white youth differ in their knowledge and understanding of racism. We do know, however, that as adolescents of color age they do report more perceived discrimination (Greene, Way, & Pahl, 2006). Future research studies may benefit from using longitudinal research designs that examine changes in racism awareness across racial-ethnic groups across the lifespan.

LIMITATIONS

A number of limitations in this study must be noted. As mentioned previously, the data are from a relatively small sample size, and the number of participants within each ethnic-racial category was even smaller, which may have minimized our power to detect statistical differences among groups. Similarly, the small number of non-native born youth may have masked the effects of immigration on ethnic-racial consciousness. Replication with a larger sample size may yield different results.

Selection bias may have reduced variance within and across groups. Our sample consisted of youth who opted to participate in the program after being nominated by community liaisons. One possibility is that the program attracted adolescents who were already astutely aware of racism and discrimination, as demonstrated by their low endorsement of colorblind racial attitudes.

The study assessed change immediately after the dialogues. The study does not provide evidence that changes lasted over time. On the other hand, it may be possible that some changes were not apparent immediately. Future studies may benefit from gathering follow-up data several weeks or months after the completion of the program.

The measure for awareness of institutional discrimination demonstrated lower than acceptable reliability (Aiken, 2000). A factor that may have affected the coefficient alpha, and consequently reliability, was the small sample size. A larger sample size would have increased variance in construct measurement leading to greater reliability in measurement (Thompson, 1994). The variance for the measure of institutional discrimination was low, given the small sample size, which may explain the lack of significance in change in institutional discrimination. Another potential explanation could be that the CoBRAS scale used to measure (un)awareness of racism has been validated with young adults (Neville et al., 2000) and may not be suitable for use with adolescents.

Finally, the findings are limited to intergroup dialogue participants since we did not randomly assign participants or use a control group for comparison. Although the findings cannot be generalized to adolescents who did not participate in the dialogues, there are lessons to learn from this work as discussed below.

IMPLICATIONS

The racially and ethnically segregated nature of American cities and neighborhoods has theoretical and practical implications for intergroup dialogues with youth in grades K-12. Despite the increase of minority youth in the public school system, students of color are attending schools that are increasingly segregated (Frankenberg, Lee, & Orfield, 2003; Orfield & Lee, 2005). A critical educational element in intergroup dialogues is sustained face-to-face interaction between different ethnic-racial groups. The success of the University of Michigan's Youth Dialogues on Race and Ethnicity in Metropolitan Detroit program may be partially attributed to the engagement of youth from multiple communities. For instance, the structure of the program engaged adolescents from various racial and ethnic enclaves, who otherwise would not have interacted with one another. Implementation of intergroup dialogue with various racial and ethnic groups may be more challenging in highly segregated communities. To be more specific, recruiting students from diverse ethnic-racial backgrounds to participate in intergroup dialogues will be difficult in schools that are not racially or ethnically diverse. Even though empirical evidence of intergroup dialogue in school settings is limited, studies on youth intergroup dialogues underscore the significant contributions of purposeful dialogue to youths' psychological and social development (Boulden, 2007; Checkoway, 2009; Spencer et al., 2008; Wayne, 2008).

Community-based programs, such as youth intergroup dialogues, can be used to challenge school segregation and to provide more opportunities for youth to develop their ethnic-racial consciousness (Rodenborg & Huynh, 2006). Our study shows that intergroup dialogues can successfully engage adolescents in dialogue with one another to critically discuss how to bridge ethnic and racial divides. There are an increasing number of dialogue programs that encourage youth to resolve conflict peacefully and collaborate to promote racial justice (Boulden, 2007; Spencer et al., 2008; Matsudaira & Jefferson, 2006; Wayne, 2008). Intergroup dialogue programs offer opportunities for diverse adolescents to not only interact with one another but also to critically examine their own identity and how they can work toward social justice in their own communities through the analysis of systematic power and understanding issues of equity (Boulden, 2007; Wayne, 2008)

The present program has had effects on its participants, to be sure, but less is known about the effects of participation in dialogues on actual community and civic action. If adolescents in other metropolitan areas, for example, were to participate in intergroup dialogues and to join together in solidarity to address the segregation that divides them, it might make a difference on them as participants, and in so doing, might position them for leadership in a society that is becoming both more segregated and more diverse. Intergroup dialogue perspectives emphasize that both critical awareness regarding cultural distinctiveness and collaboration across differences are necessary to take collective action against social inequalities (Boulden, 2007; DeTurk, 2006; Nagda & Gurin, 2007; Wayne, 2008). Conceivably, and with more research, educators and intergroup dialogue practitioners can find that when the focus of these programs is on youth civic action (in addition to dialogue and intergroup relations) then real community change can begin to occur.

CONCLUSION

Youth are increasingly engaged in informal multicultural situations that highlight issues of race and ethnicity such as intergroup conflict, lunchroom segregation, and race-based social exclusion from peers (Crystal, Killen, & Ruck, 2008; Tatum, 1997). In a diverse democratic society, adolescents can benefit from having a strong ethnic-racial identity and being cognizant of the social and institutional dynamics embedded in American society that perpetuate social inequality. Nonetheless, there are few social structures set in place to assist adolescents with this critical developmental task. Empirical evidence from youth intergroup dialogue programs suggests that, with the help of trained dialogue facilitators, critical discussions about race and ethnicity with peers can facilitate adolescents' development of ethnic-racial consciousness (Boulden, 2007; Checkoway, 2009; Spencer et al., 2008; Wayne, 2008). The emphasis of future research must be on strengthening youths' participation in multicultural efforts that promote positive change at the individual and community level. We urge educators and social work practitioners to explore innovative ways to challenge the negative impact of segregated schools and communities and to provide more opportunities for intergroup contact and multicultural learning within school settings.

REFERENCES

Adelson, J. L., & McCoach, D. B. (2010). Measuring the mathematical attitudes of elementary students: The effects of a 4-point or 5-point Likert-type scale. *Educational & Psychological Measurement, 70*(5), 796–807.

Aiken, L. R. (2000). *Psychological testing and assessment* (10th ed.) Boston, MA: Allyn & Bacon.

Boulden, W. T. (2007). Youth leadership, racism, and intergroup dialogue. *Journal of Ethnic & Cultural Diversity in Social Work, 51*(1–2), 1–26.

Branch, C., Tayal, P., & Triplett, C. (2000). The relationship of ethnic identity and ego identity status among adolescents and young adults. *International Journal of Intercultural Relations, 24*, 777–790.

Brown, C. S., & Bigler, R. S. (2005). Children's perceptions of discrimination: A developmental model. *Child Development, 76*(3), 533–553.

Brydon-Miller, M., Greenwood, D., & Maguire, P. (2003). Why Action Research? *Action Research, 1*(1), 9–28.

Checkoway, B. (2009). Youth civic engagement for dialogue and diversity at the metropolitan level. *The Foundation Review, 1*(2), 41–50.

Cozzarelli, C., Wilkinson, A. V., Tagler, M. J. (2001). Attitudes towards poor and attributions for poverty. *Journal of Social Issues, 57*(2), 207–228.

Cronbach, L. J. (1950). Further evidence on response sets and test design. *Educational and Psychological Measurement, 10*, 3–31.

Cross, W. E., & Cross, T. B. (2008). Theory, research, and models. In S. M. Quintana & C. McKown (Eds.), *Handbook of race, racism, and the developing child* (pp. 154–181). Hoboken, NJ: Wiley.

Crystal, D. S., Killen, M., & Ruck, M. (2008). It is who you know that counts: Intergroup contact and judgments about race-based exclusion. *British Journal of Developmental Psychology, 26*(1), 51–70.

Dessel, A., & Rogge, M. (2008). Evaluation of intergroup dialogue: A review of the empirical literature. *Conflict Resolution Quarterly, 26*(2), 199–238.

DeTurk, S. (2006). The power of dialogue: Consequences of intergroup dialogue and their implications for agency and alliance building. *Communication Quarterly, 54*(1), 33–51.

Erikson, E. H. (1968). *Identity: Youth and crisis.* New York, NY: Norton.

Fisher, C. B., Wallace, S. A., & Fenton, R. E. (2000). Discrimination distress during adolescence. *Journal of Youth and Adolescence, 29*(6), 679–695.

Frankenberg, E., Lee, C., & Orfield, G. (2003). *A multiracial society with segregated schools: Are we losing the dream?* The Civil Rights Project. Retrieved from: http://civilrightsproject.ucla.edu/research/k-12-education/integration-and-diversity/a-multiracial-society-with-segregated-schools-are-we-losing-the-dream/?searchterm=A%20multiracial%20society%20with%20segregated%20schools

French, S. E., Seidman, E., Allen, L., & Aber, J. L. (2000). Racial/ethnic identity, congruence with the social context, and the transition to high school. *Journal of Adolescent Research, 15*, 587–602.

French, S. E., Seidman, E., Allen, L., & Aber, J. L. (2006). The development of ethnic identity during adolescence. *Developmental Psychology, 42*(1), 1–10.

Greene, M. L., Way, N., & Pahl, K. (2006). Trajectories of perceived adult and peer discrimination among black, Latino, and Asian American adolescents: Patterns and psychological correlates. *Developmental Psychology, 42*(2), 218–238.

Gurin, P., Nagda, B. A., & Lopez, G. E. (2004). The benefits of diversity in education for democratic citizenship. *Journal of Social Issues, 60*(1), 17–34.

Hoff, E., Laursen, B., & Tardif, T. (2002). Socioeconomic status and parenting. In M. H. Bornstein (Ed.), *Handbook of parenting* (2nd ed., pp. 231–252). Mahwah, NJ: Erlbaum.

Hughes, D., Rodriguez, J., Smith, E. P., Johnson, D. J., Stevenson, H. C., & Spicer, P. (2006). Parents' ethnic-racial socialization practices: A review of research and directions for future study. *Developmental Psychology, 42*(5), 747–770.

Kernahan, C., & Davis, T. (2007). Changing perspective: How learning about racism influences student awareness and emotion. *Teaching of Psychology, 34*(1), 49–52.

Khanlou, N., Koh, J., & Mill, C. (2008). Cultural identity and experiences of prejudice and discrimination of Afghan and Iranian immigrant youth. *International Journal of Mental Health and Addiction, 6*(4), 494–513.

Kosmitzki, C. (1996). The reaffirmation of cultural identity in cross-cultural encounters. *Personality and Social Psychology Bulletin, 22*(3), 238–248.

Landrine, H., & Klonoff, E. A. (1996). The schedule of racist events: A measure of racial discrimination and a study of its negative physical and mental health consequences. *Journal of Black Psychology, 22*(2), 144–168.

Marcia, J. (1980). Identity in adolescence. In J. Adelson (Ed.), *Handbook of adolescent psychology* (pp. 159–187) New York, NY: Wiley.

Matsudaira, J., & Jefferson, A. (2006). Anytown: NCCJ's youth leadership experience in social justice. *New Directions for Youth Development, 2006*(109), 107–155.

McIntosh, P. (1989, July/August). White privilege: Unpacking the invisible knapsack. *Peace and Freedom*, 10–12.

Nagda, B. A., & Gurin, P. (2007). Intergroup dialogue: A critical dialogic approach to learning about differences, inequality and social justice. *New Directions in Teaching and Learning*, (111), 35–45.

Nagda, B. A., & Zúñiga, X. (2003). Fostering meaningful racial engagement through intergroup dialogues. *Group Processes & Intergroup Relations, 6*(1), 111–128.

Neville, H. A., Lilly, R. L., Duran, G., Lee, R. M., & Browne, L. (2000). Construction and initial validation of the color-blind racial attitudes scale (CoBRAS). *Journal of Counseling Psychology, 47*(1), 59–70.

Nolen, A. L., & Putten, J. V. (2007). Action research in education: Addressing gaps in ethical principles and practices. *Educational Researcher, 36*(7), 401–407.

Orfield, G. (2001). School more separate: Consequences of a decade of resegregation. *Harvard Civil Rights Project*, Cambridge, MA. Retrieved from http://eric.ed.gov/PDFS/ED459217.pdf

Orfield, G., & Lee, C. (2005). Why segregation matters: Poverty and educational inequality. *The Civil Rights Project*, Harvard University, Cambridge, MA. Retrieved from: http://bsdweb.bsdvt.org/district/EquityExcellence/Research/Why_Segreg_Matters.pdf

Pahl, K., & Way, N. (2006). Longitudinal trajectories of ethnic identity among urban Black and Latino adolescents. *Child Development, 77*(5), 1403–1415.

Phinney, J. S. (1990). Ethnic identity in adolescents and adults: Review of research. *Psychological Bulletin, 108*(3), 499–514.

Phinney, J. S. (1992). The multigroup ethnic identity measure: A new scale for use with diverse groups. *Journal of Adolescent Research, 7*(2), 156–176.

Phinney, J. S. (1996). Understanding ethnic diversity. *American Behavioral Scientist, 40*(2), 143–152.

Phinney, J. S., Ferguson, D. L., & Tate, J. D. (1997). Intergroup attitudes among ethnic minority adolescents: A causal model. *Child Development, 68*(5), 955–969.

Phinney, J. S., Jacoby, B., & Silva, C. (2007). Positive intergroup attitudes: The role of ethnic identity. *International Journal of Behavioral Development, 31*(5), 478–490.

Phinney, J. S., Madden, T., & Santos, L. J. (1998). Psychological variables as predictors of perceived ethnic discrimination among minority and immigrant adolescents. *Journal of Applied Social Psychology, 28*(11), 937–953.

Phinney, J. S., & Ong, A. D. (2007). Conceptualization and measurement of ethnic identity: Current status and future directions. *Journal of Counseling Psychology, 54*(3), 271–281.

Phinney, J. S., & Tarver, S. (1988). Ethnic identity search and commitment amongst black and white eighth graders. *The Journal of Early Adolescence, 8*, 265–277.

Probst, T. M. (2003). Changing attitudes over time: Assessing the effectiveness of workplace diversity course. *Teaching of Psychology, 30*(3), 236–239.

Quintana, S. M. (1994). A model of ethnic perspective-taking ability applied to Mexican-American children and youth. *International Journal of Intercultural Relations, 18*(4), 419–448.

Quintana, S. M. (1998). Children's developmental understanding of ethnicity and race. *Applied and Preventive Psychology, 7*(1), 27–45.

Quintana, S. M. (2007). Racial and ethnic identity: Developmental perspectives and research. *Journal of Counseling Psychology, 54*(3), 259–270.

Roberts, R. E., Phinney, J. S., Masse, L. C., Chen, Y. R., Roberts, C. R., & Romero, A. (1999). The structure of ethnic identity in young adolescents from diverse ethnocultural groups. *Journal of Early Adolescence, 19*(3), 301–322.

Robinson, J. P., Shaver, P. R., & Wrightsman, L. S. (1999). Scale selection and evaluation. In J. P. Robinson, P. R. Shaver, & L. S. Wrightsman (Eds.), *Measures of political attitudes* (pp. 1–36). San Diego, CA: Academic.

Rodenborg, N., & Huynh, N. (2006). On overcoming segregation: Social work and intergroup dialogue. *Social Work with Groups, 29*(1), 27–44.

Rotheram-Borus, M. J., Lightfoot, M., Moraes, A., Dopkins, S., & LaCour, J. (1998). Developmental, ethnic, and gender differences in ethnic identity among adolescents. *Journal of Adolescent Research, 13*(4), 487–507.

Rudman, L. A., Ashmore, R. D., & Gary, M. L. (2001). "Unlearning" automatic biases: The malleability of implicit prejudice and stereotypes. *Journal of Personality and Social Psychology, 81*(5), 857–868.

Rumbaut, R. G. (1994). The crucible within: Ethnic identity, self-esteem, and segmented assimilation among children of immigrants. *International Migration Review, 28*(4), 748–794.

Seaton, E. K., Caldwell, C. H., Sellers, R. M., & Jackson, J. S. (2008). The prevalence of perceived discrimination among African American and Caribbean black youth. *Developmental Psychology, 44*(5), 1288–1297.

Spencer, M. S., Brown, M., Griffin, S., & Abdullah, S. (2008). Outcome evaluation of the intergroup project. *Small Group Research, 39*(1), 82–103.

Spencer, M. B., & Markstrom-Adams, C. (1990). Identity processes among racial and ethnic minority children in America. *Child Development, 61*(2), 290–310.

Stephan, W. G. (2008). Psychological and communication processes associated with intergroup conflict resolution. *Small Group Research, 39*(1), 28–41.

Tatum, B. D. (1997). *Why are all the black kids sitting together in the cafeteria? And other conversations about race.* New York, NY: Basic.

Thompson, V. L. (1994). Socialization to race and its relationship to racial identification among African Americans. *Journal of Black Psychology, 20*(2), 175–188.

Umaña-Taylor, A. J. (2004). Ethnic identity and self-esteem: Examining the role of social context. *Journal of Adolescence, 27*(2), 139–146.

Valencia, R. R. (2000). Inequalities and the schooling of minority students in Texas: Historical and contemporary conditions. *Hispanic Journal of Behavioral Sciences, 22*(4), 445–459.

Wayne, E. K. (2008). Is it just talk? Understanding and evaluating intergroup dialogue. *Conflict Resolution Quarterly, 25*(4), 451–478.

Werts, C. E., & Linn, R. L. (1970). A general linear model for studying growth. *Psychology Bulletin, 73*(1), 17–22.

Zúñiga, X., Nagda, B. A., Chesler, M., & Cytron-Walker, A. (2007). Intergroup dialogues in higher education: Meaningful learning about social justice. *ASHE Higher Education Report Series, 32*(4). Hoboken, NJ: Wiley.

Writing the Divide: High School Students Crossing Urban-Suburban Contexts

Gretchen E. Lopez and A. Wendy Nastasi

Syracuse University

Given persisting patterns of racial, ethnic, and class re-segregation, this study considers opportunities that high school-aged youth have to cross these divides. What critical learning might occur? What can educators learn from student reflections toward providing opportunities, experiences, or structures to challenge the status quo? In considering these important questions, we review research literature on youth experience, learning, and reflection through structured opportunities to engage in education and critical thinking across social locations. Program examples, pedagogy, accompanying research, and evaluation are summarized to frame a sustained university-high school collaboration. This collaborative project extends dialogic pedagogy practiced in higher education contexts to engagement with and across urban and suburban schools. We describe a partnership between an Intergroup Dialogue Program at a Northeastern university and two local high schools; one school located in a city school district serving a majority student of color population and the other school located within an outlying suburban district serving a predominantly white student population. This article describes pedagogy and student work from the institute with evaluation focused on students' written responses to open-ended surveys. Three important themes emerged: students' growing awareness of inequalities, reflections on agency, and interest in further engagement. These themes connected with reflections from the high school teachers and university dialogue facilitators who worked with and learned from these youth through the institute. The discussion calls for further research on youth voices and higher education-high school collaboration.

DOCUMENTING THE DIVIDE

Persisting patterns of racial, ethnic, and class re-segregation have been prodigiously documented in social science and education research (Fine, Burns, Payne, & Torre, 2004; Hochschild, 2003; Orfield & Lee, 2006; Tatum, 2007), and legal and policy reports (Brief of 553 Social Scientists, 2006; Linn & Wellner, 2007). Taking a close look at the Northeast U.S., as one regional example, 66% of public schools are majority white in the face of demographics trends indicating that the youth population is comprised of majority students of color (Orfield & Lee, 2006). Orfield and Lee report that white students are learning in increasingly racially isolated environments. At the same time, 78% of Latino/a, 51% of African American, and 50% of Asian American students attend a school that is majority non-white.

149

Socioeconomic class is conterminous to race. The National Center for Educational Statistics summarizes that, as of 2008, "The percentages of children who were living in poverty were higher for Blacks (34 percent), American Indians/Alaska Natives (33 percent), Hispanics (27 percent), and Native Hawaiians or Other Pacific Islanders (26 percent), than for children of two or more races (18 percent), Asians (11 percent) and Whites (10 percent)" (Aud, Fox, & Kewal Ramani, 2010, p. iii). The report reiterates that these socioeconomic disparities exist parallel to geographic and residential segregation. Specifically, more urban fourth graders (62% eligible) qualify for free and reduced-price lunch than suburban fourth graders (39% eligible) (Aud et al., 2010). Consistent with earlier research, the Department of Education (Aud et al., 2010) study further revealed that in each context students of color disproportionately qualify for free and reduced- price lunch.

The economic and racial segregation of youth contributes to a national narrative that urban youth are the (perceived) "problem" to be addressed, with the assumption that these youth have grown up in—and with nothing but—poverty and despair (Henke, 2008; Hosang, 2006; Yosso, 2005). Important research, however, offers a counterstory with the potential to engage, inspire, and bridge youth who are currently divided by the racial, class, residential, and school patterns summarized here (e.g., Aud et al., 2010; Brief of 553 Social Scientists, 2006; Tatum, 2007). This is the story of youth in urban contexts who actively contribute to civic knowledge production, exercise agency, and initiate both personal and social transformation (Ginwright, Noguera, & Cammarota, 2006).

In collaborating with high schools, we center student voices in practice and evaluation. In keeping with this, youth participatory action research and intergroup dialogue evaluation studies are described in detail below. We ask, "How do students view these educational opportunities? What do they take away from these opportunities and apply to their specific school and community locations?" We then describe a partnership between a university-based Intergroup Dialogue Program and two local high schools with diverging demographics reflective of re-segregation school trends in the Northeast U.S. This study describes the structure and content of the annual one-day institute offered at the university for youth from both schools who are taking English courses focused on race, rhetoric, and voice. The results section focuses on program evaluation efforts to listen to and to learn from students through their written responses to open-ended surveys following the institute. We conclude with implications of these results for continuing research on youth dialogues and related programs and the significance of higher education-high school collaboration.

YOUTH PARTICIPATORY ACTION RESEARCH AND EDUCATIONAL IMPLICATIONS

As a critical pedagogy, participatory action research (PAR) not only positions urban youth as the population to be studied but also positions them significantly in the foreground as researchers, constructors of knowledge, meaning, and change. As a methodology, "PAR recognizes that those 'studied' harbor critical social knowledge and must be repositioned as subjects and architects of research" (Torre & Fine, 2006, p. 271). This type of research is collective in its development and impact and includes the perspectives of multiple stakeholders, not just scholars.

In projects described by Morrell (2006) and Torre and Fine (2006), students are taught first to be researchers; they learn method and practice through credit-bearing courses that either meet high school requirements or will garner the students college credit. Second the students work in teams to develop a research question, investigate the problem, and produce knowledge artifacts in the forms of scholarly papers, presentations, and speeches. Students work to gather data and present results to key youth, school, and public audiences. Students in California who work with Morrell and those in New York City's tri-state area who work with Torre and Fine are engaged in academically rigorous coursework that prepares them for the praxis of social investigation that culminates in policy or structural change. Pedagogically, youth action research positions urban adolescents as "critical researchers and transformative intellectuals" (Duncan-Andrade & Morrell, 2008, p. 105).

Participatory action research projects featuring high school youth also produce civic outcomes. Jocson (2006) used poetry as a vehicle for urban youth to express their consciousness. Students used writing to re-present and re-create social narratives. Others use after school programs (Strobel, Osberg, & McLaughlin, 2006), community-based youth organizations (O'Donoghue, 2006), or the urban landscape itself as a setting (Morrell, 2006; Torre & Fine, 2006). In all these settings, including through initiatives that bring urban and suburban students together to learn, investigate, and report research findings, youth develop a sense of connection to their community, an understanding of social issues, a sense of agency, and civic engagement in the form of activism (Checkoway & Richards-Schuster, 2006; Jocson, 2006; O'Donoghue, 2006; Strobel et al., 2006; Torre & Fine, 2006).

YOUTH DIALOGUES, AGENCY, AND CIVIC ENGAGEMENT

In the last ten years, especially around the historic 50-year anniversary of *Brown vs. Board of Education* (1954), a growing body of literature has reported the outcomes of youth action specifically facilitated through intergroup dialogue and cross-school or within-school youth collaboration. Examples include: The Study Circles Resource Center (Nagda, McCoy, & Barrett, 2006), Youth Dialogues on Race and Ethnicity in Detroit (Checkoway, 2009), Echoes of *Brown* in New York City's tri-state area (Fine et al., 2005; Torre & Fine, 2006), and Syracuse's Community Wide Dialogue to End Racism (Pincock, 2008). Each of these projects is summarized below to describe the structure and important outcomes of this work with youth and how these results frame and inform continued, publicly engaged (Ellison & Eatman, 2008) scholarship that directly addresses urban-suburban school divides.

The Study Circles Resource Center's Mix It Up program takes place within individual schools that choose to incorporate its free lesson planning and facilitation materials into either a lunch-time event or into the standard curriculum; there are 29 "model schools" that incorporate Mix It Up's intergroup dialogue curriculum across the entire school (Nagda et al., 2006). Some schools utilize teachers or administrators as facilitators, while at others students co-facilitate. Mix It Up can provide the curriculum and process for youth to reflect, to analyze, and to take collective action with the school to sustain and foster efforts. The Mix it Up program begins with an exploration of identity and continues with discussions across difference that lead to action—in these cases, action mostly centers around school-based concerns.

The Mix It Up curriculum also presents evidence of civic engagement. The program begins with the assertion that "young people are not just our political future; they are a vital part of our political present," which means there is a role for youth in not only addressing problems—but, importantly, in developing the skills and habits that prepare them to be adults engaged in public life (Nagda et al., 2006, p. 48). In surveys, Mix It Up students reported increased understanding of social boundaries within their schools, increased willingness to get to know students outside their social clique, an awareness of how some students are helped or harmed through social grouping, and a new knowledge of their responsibility to break down social borders (Nagda et al., 2006). All students reported increased likelihood to engage in action. Moreover, students of color indicated a greater willingness to share their perspective, to participate in an effort to promote collective action, and they were more likely than white students to "believe that they can make a difference as a result of participation in Mix It Up, and more likely to participate in resulting collective action" (p. 55). It is significant that all student participants indicated that they were more likely to engage with those they consider different and that students of color, who are historically marginalized, also indicated a greater sense of agency.

Youth Dialogue on Race and Ethnicity in metropolitan Detroit is an example of an intergroup dialogue pedagogy deployed through community groups across a city and its neighboring suburbs. This program began when a private foundation uncovered a desire among students to communicate across difference; the students believed they did not have the opportunity to do so. Thus, the foundation approached faculty at the University of Michigan to collaborate on a method that would afford youth the opportunity to address racial segregation and isolation (Checkoway, 2009). With the help of community-based organizations, students were recruited from the city's neighborhoods and from the suburbs; they started by exploring their own identities and then proceeded to discuss differences among groups. Facilitated by trained University of Michigan students, the dialogues helped high school youth to "develop their dialogical skills, explore their similarities and differences, discuss contemporary issues, and organize community projects" (p. 43).

The Youth Dialogue on Race and Ethnicity brings together youth from across the city and its suburbs and students participate in a metropolitan tour and an on-campus retreat at the University of Michigan. At the retreat, students plan their joint action project. These community initiatives include urban-suburban school exchanges, demonstrations, marches, performances, and outreach programs designed and implemented by the youth. Leaders who emerged from among the youth traveled to Lansing, MI, and Washington, DC, to present policy solutions generated by youth to elected representatives (Checkoway, 2009).

Evaluating the Youth Dialogue on Race and Ethnicity dialogue program was not an external process; youth partnered with their adult allies to gather information through journals, interviews, and focus groups to produce reports and recommendations. The evaluation process found similar outcomes to the Mix It Up Program. Youth developed increased knowledge of their own and others' identities, an increased awareness of racism, and an increased understanding of how to take action in their communities. The evaluation shows that a summer program can change students' attitudes and behaviors. Youth will engage in dialogue across difference and take action in their communities if given the opportunity—this action taking is a meaningful form of civic engagement.

Fine et al. (2005) and Torre and Fine (2006) offer findings from a multi-method study, Echoes of *Brown*, that engaged youth from within New York City and its surrounding suburbs and from neighboring urban and suburban communities in New Jersey:

> by intentionally crossing the lines separating suburbs and urban areas, integrated and segregated schools, deeply tracked and detracked schools, we could document the educational consequences

of the co-dependent growth of the suburbs and the defunding of urban America. Revealing the fracture lines of inequity, we could also unearth the pools of possibility that fill the topography of "desegregated" suburbs and urban communities. (Fine et al., 2005, p. 500)

Participatory action research pedagogy was utilized to offer students the vehicle to investigate racial, ethnic, and class injustice while giving them the agency to advocate for social change. Students were taught quantitative and qualitative research design and, calling themselves the Opportunity Gap Project, youth decided on the design, method, focus, and products of investigation (Fine et al., 2005; Torre & Fine, 2006). Having developed sensitivity to inclusion, their survey was printed in three languages and Braille and was provided on an audiotape. High school students from each district took the survey, which totaled 9,174 respondents, and some also participated in focus groups (24 total) or in individual interviews (32 total) that sought to explore the standpoint of students who exist at the margin, the center, and at their intersections (Fine et al., 2005; Torre & Fine, 2006).

The study found that youth appreciate attending desegregated high schools, but they are aware and discontent with the classrooms that continue to be mostly segregated. As in the Study Circle Resource Center study described above, all students indicated high levels of civic commitment or wanting to help others. However, students of color were more likely (nearly twice as much) than their white counterparts to indicate, "We need to create change in the nation" (Fine et al., 2005, p. 506). While a majority of all students indicated that attending a desegregated school was important, they also highlighted inequalities within schools and across districts—urban students were incredulous at the unequal resources of their schools after learning about the science labs, computer centers, and football fields of their suburban counterparts (Fine et al., 2005). Youth researchers participating in the Opportunity Gap Program spoke and shared their data before school administrators and teachers, published articles, were interviewed by local media, and created poetry as a delivery of social consciousness (Jocson, 2006).

Another example of a youth dialogue initiative takes place in central New York, including students from schools in the city of Syracuse and its surrounding area.[1] These youth dialogues organized through Syracuse's InterFaith Works Community Wide Dialogue to End Racism (CWD) bring together high school students from the city school district and several neighboring suburban school districts. Syracuse's Community Wide Dialogue is based in the Study Circles model (Everyday Democracy, 2010). As one of the longest standing community dialogue programs in the country, the curriculum and facilitation has been adapted to the history and local context of central New York communities (Fanselow, 2007). Since 2003, the program has offered youth dialogues across paired urban-suburban located high schools (Pincock, 2008). These dialogue circles are typically offered over a period of 2–3 months (meeting bi-weekly), include approximately 10–14 students, and are co-facilitated by student-peer facilitators with CWD guidance and support. The exchange project covers social identities, racial and school stereotypes, racial and economic barriers, effects of racism for youth and the broader community, white privilege, inequitable resources, and action plans (Fanselow, 2007; Interfaith Works, 2010). Sessions take place at each school alternating locations across meetings.

Pincock (2008) conducted a qualitative study of the program and student outcomes based on interviews with 20 students from two cross-school dialogue offerings. More specifically, this study examined how students understood and articulated the concepts of institutional racism and white privilege after participating in the dialogues. Despite the positive outcomes of youth dialogues and related initiatives described above, this study concluded that students did not develop a structural understanding of racism and inequality; rather, they continued to see racism primarily in relation to individual beliefs and acts. Similarly, students were not able to offer developed definitions of white privilege after the dialogues concluded. There were no significant differentiations in the findings between urban and suburban youth or between white students and students of color. However, while their definitions showed little change, students were able to offer examples of white privilege. Students of color were more likely than white students to talk about white privilege as something present in their own lives instead of something that "exists elsewhere" (p. 40). The researcher posited that racial identity development and the reality that students of color experience social and institutional pressures different from those experienced by white students leads students of color to be more attuned to instances of privilege. Owing to the complexity of structural inequality and white privilege and the different frames of reference that participants bring to dialogue, Pincock concludes that dialogue organizers can only expect modest outcomes from "encounter-based intergroup dialogue programs" (p. 46).

This work raises questions about contact-based youth dialogues that are primarily organized around "encounter" or social/interpersonal relationships with less emphasis on what Dovidio and others (Dovidio, Gaertner, Stewart, Esses, ten Vergert, & Hudson, 2004; Nagda, Kim, & Truelove, 2004) have conceptualized as "enlightenment" or knowledge or content-based education (e.g., elucidating difficult to grasp aspects of structural racism). Critical multicultural pedagogy and social science research often stresses the need for both of these components in order to be effective in educating students about structural causes of group inequalities (e.g., Lopez, Gurin, & Nagda, 1998; Nagda, Gurin, & Lopez, 2003). Specific to intergroup dialogue pedagogy and outcomes, Beale and Schoem (2001) argue that an over-emphasis on process (e.g., relationship building or sharing of personal experience) without covering key content may lead to several problems including giving "disproportionate weight to the idiosyncratic experiences of individual participants" (p. 270). They elaborate, "Clearly, the value of dialogue is to bring to the process the personal experiences of participants, but the absence of any contextualization in existing research and scholarship falsely exaggerates the generalizability of any single individual's experience" (p. 270). This limitation of an encounter-based approach may explain Pincock's (2008) conclusion: "The dialogue appears to raise participants' awareness of relevant examples of these two phenomena [white privilege, institutional racism] in their everyday lives, though it does not equip them to articulate explanations of these examples" (p. 46). This conclusion is qualified, however, through noting the limited sample of student participants interviewed. Moreover, other published research based on interviews with college students supports that the quality of intergroup dialogue processes (e.g., the extent of personal sharing) is important for dialogue outcomes including increased student comfort, connection, friendship, and understanding different perspectives and experiences (Yeakley, 2011). It may be that the balance of content and process is especially important for educating youth about the systemic nature of group inequalities extending beyond their everyday experiences and particular social contexts.

Connections to the Current Study

Some of the most notable results described in this literature review resulted from student engagement in extended contact and academic (knowledge-seeking and knowledge-producing) collaborative projects deliberately focused on community resources and social issues. These initiatives included multiple forms of inquiry, learning, and discovery across difference (e.g., Checkoway & Richards-Schuster, 2006; Morrell, 2006; Torre & Fine, 2006). These projects grew from partnerships with university faculty in education, social science, and social work who are committed and open to diverse youth voices and agency. These qualities of effective university-community collaboration and youth engagement and education were explicitly emphasized in the development of the cross-school institute and youth dialogue practice studied here.

MEETING GROUND: PARTNERSHIP AND PEDAGOGY FOR A CROSS-SCHOOL INSTITUTE

Intergroup dialogue as practiced in higher education settings is described as:

> a face-to-face facilitated learning experience that brings together students from different social identity groups over a sustained period of time to understand their commonalities and differences, examine the nature and impact of societal inequalities, and explore ways of working together toward greater equality and justice. (Zúñiga, Nagda, Chesler, & Cytron-Walker, 2007, p. 2)

Such dialogues focus on "identities—singular or intersecting—and relationships that are embedded in systems of power and privilege" (Zúñiga, Nagda, &, Sevig, 2002, p. 7). Trained or experienced co-facilitators (reflective of the social identities of the groups in dialogue) work to create sustained communication among participants that focuses on listening, sharing, questioning, and developing mutual understandings. More specifically, intergroup dialogue courses for college students are designed to build trust and relationships, explore the lived experiences and implications of socialization and systems of privilege and oppression, identify challenging issues and consciously practice and reflect on dialogue, and address issues and plan action (Schoem, Hurtado, Sevig, Chesler, & Sumida, 2001; Zúñiga et al., 2002; Zúñiga et al., 2007). The sequencing is supported by social psychological research on intergroup contact, as well as educational theory for democratic, multicultural, and social justice education (Adams, 2007; Beale & Schoem, 2001; Chesler, 2001; Dovidio et al., 2004; Pettigrew, 1998).

Early findings from the Multiversity Intergroup Dialogue Research Project, a multi-institution multi-method study, document the shift that takes place for college students in intergroup dialogue academic courses, including increased intergroup understanding (e.g., awareness of inequality), intergroup relations (e.g., willingness to bridge difference and express empathy), and intergroup collaboration (Nagda, Gurin, Sorensen, & Zúñiga, 2009). In keeping with earlier research studies (Hurtado, 2005), students who participated in intergroup dialogue courses expressed a desire to be active in their community after college.

Syracuse University is one of the nine collaborating institutions making up the Multiversity Intergroup Dialogue Research Project.[2] With knowledge of this research-based initiative, two Syracuse-area high school teachers approached the local university's research director seeking a campus educational experience for their students. These teachers, from one of the urban-suburban school pairs that participated in the Community Wide Dialogue to End Racism program, were committed to addressing what they saw as the need for and promise of substantive intellectual as well as cross-school engagement with issues of race and understanding systems of racism, analysis of supporting rhetoric and its effects, and counterstories of empowered cultural voices.

Together, the teachers created an elective English course to offer at their individual high schools (Iodice & Benedetto, 2009).[3] They designed the courses to provide cross-school connections; at least once each semester, students from the urban school would visit their peers at the suburban school and vice versa.

The resulting university-community partnership occurs in a geographic context associated with post-industrial residential racial isolation and community economic decline (Grant, 2009). As with Detroit and the New York/New Jersey locations of projects described above, this location is one of high (re)segregation documented in social science research considering national trends. Since the mid-1970s, residential policies and practices have dislocated most students of color to collectively low-income, urban contexts and schools while many white students reside in parallel racially isolated middle- to upper-income suburbs outside the city area, divided, for example, by interstate highway construction (Grant, 2009; Pincock, 2008). The two high schools are representative of this pattern and the commonly associated school disparities. Central High School (pseudonym) is located in the city school district serving a majority student of color population (67% identifying as Black, Asian American, or Latino/a). East High School (pseudonym) is located within an outlying suburb, less than ten miles away, serving a predominantly white student population (91% identifying as white, 2008–2009, based on New York State educational statistics).

For four years, the university's intergroup dialogue program has hosted high school students taking the courses at both schools focused on race, rhetoric, and voice. The high school teachers look to the university to provide dynamic speakers to spur the exchange of ideas and share a challenging, diverse, academic context for students to experience the significance of deep conversations and critical social analysis of race and linked issues. The most recent institute in 2010, with more than 80 student participants, featured presentations (faculty, staff, graduate student) on writing and youth activism. The institute agenda further included small group work based on writing poetry and drafting letters advocating an issue of shared concern. Organizers, speakers, and facilitators used poetry as a consciousness-raising approach (Jocson, 2006) and used dialogic pedagogy to help students connect their in-class content knowledge with action.

"Raising Our Voices"—Who, What, and How

Institute Theme and Student Participants

The institute theme, "Raising Our Voices," also centered the university program evaluation approach. Initially, this was guided by two related questions. What do students take away from this inter-district, crossing social geography, day-long institute premised on dialogue principles facilitated by local university members? What do teachers and university facilitators see students learning as a result of such an experience? To begin addressing these questions, we present examples of student work from the institute with a focus on small working group activities, together with summaries of youth responses. In total, 88 high school students participated in the institute, with 22 from Central High School and 66 from East High School. The 3:1 ratio of students from the suburban high school relative to students from the urban high school is reflective of course enrollment at each school. At East High the course is offered twice during the school year, often with a waiting list of interested students. At Central High, the course is offered for a smaller number of students and is currently the only remaining English elective at the high school. In some ways, this disparity reflects broader resource disparities and related district-level challenges differentially affecting these two schools and their students.

Small Group Facilitators and Featured Speakers

In addition to the two high school teachers, ten university members participated throughout the day, serving as small group facilitators or individual resources for the working student groups; groups were seated at 13 tables with approximately six to seven students across the two schools at each table. These university members were invited because of their experience with and commitments to high school students or their specific knowledge and experience of intergroup dialogue pedagogy. The high school teachers (tenured) self-identify as white and the university facilitators represented a range of university affiliations and social identities, including academic or student affairs departments and programs (for example, from education, multicultural affairs, LGBT resource center). Between the university program/planning team and the facilitators, faculty, graduate students, and administrators were represented at the institute (including individuals who identify as African American, Latino/a, Asian American, and/or white). The featured speakers included an assistant professor from the School of Education, an administrative staff member from the Office of Multicultural Affairs, and a graduate student from the School of Communications, all of whom identified as African American and described the development and complexity of their social identities as part of their presentation—through poetry, music, call and response, or interactive discussion.

Small Group Work: Examples from Advocacy Letters

During the second part of the institute, small working groups of students discussed, agreed upon, and generated an outline for an advocacy letter—identifying a specific issue of importance to them ("what"), an audience to address the letter to ("who"), and an action proposed to address the issue ("how"). Table 1 summarizes the "who," "what," and "how" from the 13 working groups proposals. Each group shared a summary of the proposed action letter to the full institute group—presenting to peers, their teachers, and university facilitators. Each presentation began with students posting their written outline or proposal on the front wall of the campus room, resulting in pages of visible action advocated by local youth. Groups chose to write to "our generation," local high school and middle school students, teachers, school administrators, editors of local newspapers, New York's Governor Patterson, and Secretary of Education Arne Duncan, among others. One group (Table 1, Group 4) addressed their concerns and hope directly to "the audience in this room," urging them to confront racism. Others addressed stereotyping based on class, gender, and sexual orientation; changing classroom environments and teaching methods; school inequality and college access; and most often, advocacy for more of the courses they articulated have changed their learning and perspective.

157

TABLE 1

Proposed Action Letters Generated by Small Working Groups of High School Students: Who, What, and How

Working Group	Who	What	How
1	Our generation	Stereotyping	Required rhetoric courses starting in elementary school
2	Younger children (before middle school)	Sexism	"We want children to be who they want to be without society influencing them, before they have had a chance to find themselves."
3	Youth in the local community's high schools	Stereotyping based on income level in a community	We need "workshops like today that help us to communicate and to better understand each other's situation's [sic] and point of view's [sic]."
4	The audience in this room (i.e., faculty, staff, and students at the High School Institute)	Ignorance about racism	People in this room have identified as conscious allies; they need to confront racism because "without awareness about ignorance . . . things will never change"
5	Teachers	Classroom environment: • Equal time for each student • Equal opportunities for students to voice opinions/concerns • Interaction with instruction that relates education to life • Empathy and flexibility • Enthusiasm and dedication	Presentations to faculty on: • Variety • Technology • Small group projects • Group discussion • Limited lecture time
6	Administration at elementary schools within respective school districts	Lack of socially diverse interaction among elementary students	Making programs that expose elementary students to members of other school districts more wide-spread
7	Superintendents of both school districts	The course provides a "safe environment for touchy subjects;" "We have learned a lot from one class and want to impact others;" There needs to be involvement from other schools.	Expand (Rhetoric/Cultural Voices)

(Continued on next page.)

TABLE 1

Proposed Action Letters Generated by Small Working Groups of High School Students: Who, What, and How *(Continued)*

8	Superintendents, Boards of Education, Parent-Teacher Association	Lack of cultural awareness	Cultural awareness courses (like Rhetoric of Race) need to be geared toward younger kids and implemented in elementary schools to prevent stereotypes from being "picked up at a very young age."
9	Letters to the editors of local papers	The media influences the values of youth and society	"Challenge the media to use their power to make change and be responsible to teach our youth positive values through entertainment."
10	Governor Patterson/State Board of Education	Where you live should not affect your education opportunities	Resources should be equally distributed across schools.
11	All people in charge of education systems across U.S.	Inequity in education	All schools should have adequate supplies and resources; students in each school should be from a mix of economic backgrounds to ensure equal education for all students and opportunities for the less privileged.
12	Arnie Duncan	Cost of education	"This is important because education is the key to success in America, however not everyone is giving [sic] an equal chance to education due to socioeconomic status."
13	Congress	Marriage equality	There should be "no cost for higher education. Also, more educated citizens means a better society . . . it might be hard at first, but in the end it will come full circle." People should have the right to marry who [sic] they want.

Pedagogical Approach and Integration

Given that the high school institute's activities unfolded over the time span of one school day, the formal structure of this cross-school student engagement is not precisely parallel to the practices of intergroup dialogue in higher education (Nagda et al., 2009; Zúñiga, et al., 2007) or other high school initiatives described earlier (e.g., Checkoway, 2009; Torre & Fine, 2006). That is, these other programs extended over a longer period of time, across a semester or over several weeks or months. Yet, the design and agenda of this day-long institute did build from critical aspects of pedagogies described earlier. As examples, students worked in small groups across schools and multiple social identities, they began with sharing personal narratives expressed through poetry, described varied and linked social contexts, continued to identify key social concerns they collectively felt should be addressed, and moved to charting specific actions to do so. Furthermore, the institute included first defining and engaging the concept of intergroup dialogue and principles of dialogic communication, including across power differences. Activities throughout the day explicitly integrated cognitive, affective, and experiential learning. In addition, while multiple speakers and facilitators guided student exchanges, these exchanges—among students and between lived experiences within their schools—were centered. The institute ended with students presenting their advocacy letters not only to each other but also to teachers and university members present. In this way, the institute captured the basis and significance of PAR: youth have meaningful knowledge, analysis, and voices that should be nurtured and heard.

Evaluation Surveys

Following the institute, open-ended surveys were distributed to better understand students' experiences and responses and the institute's impact. The two high school teachers distributed the open-ended surveys to students approximately one week after the event. Students responded in writing to four (teacher-generated) questions: (1) "Sum up your experience at the institute in one word, and then explain why you chose this word;" (2) "What were the highlights of the day and why?;" (3) "Describe the insight that you gleaned from your experience at the institute, and explain the degree to which this reinforced or altered your previous perspective on the given issue;" and (4) "If you could change one aspect of the institute, what would you change, and why?" Forty-one students (47% of total participants) completed and returned the surveys (12 from Central High School, 55% response rate; 29 from East High School, 44% response rate).

Researchers (university program faculty director and graduate assistant, co-authors) conducted a qualitative analysis of students' open-ended surveys responses. This analysis included reading through the entire set of evaluation data; noting and discussing themes; and co-determining demonstrative, significant responses through an inductive process (Glaser & Strauss, 1967; Strauss & Corbin, 1990). Student responses were discussed with teachers within the context of the individual classes, and the final set of most important themes were similarly reviewed and discussed with teachers to confirm that the saliency of these themes resonated with their understanding of students' experiences and informal as well as formal reflections and feedback.

In addition to these student responses, feedback was directly collected from university facilitators for the institute as well as from the high school teachers. Each researcher also reviewed these evaluation data, noted and discussed prominent themes, and co-determined significant responses through an inductive process similar to that for the student responses. For both student and teacher/facilitator feedback, researchers reviewed the data after first discussing and co-determining central themes to identify any disconfirming responses.

IN STUDENTS' WORDS

Overall, feedback was highly positive across these groups of participants and partners. Student responses are described in the most detail in this article, including examples from student writing. The aim is to center students' reflections of the institute experience, especially in regard to the potential of this dialogic work and what students perceived as a unique educational opportunity. In addition, thoughtfully listening and engaging with these students' perspectives deepens our own (educators') understanding of local students' interests and willingness to engage specific issues.

Students offered positive words to describe their experience at the institute such as "inspiring," "thought-provoking," and "motivating." They also wrote "powerful," "eye opening," "gratifying," "fulfilling," "amazing," "outstanding," and "great." Some named the specific qualities of "hope" or "hopeful" and "pride," while others wrote "unity" or "unifying." These words reflected to us a sense of being positively moved by the day's activities together with other words that communicated a "deep" (another word) level of engagement in the intellectual topics, social issues, and relations analyzed through the day. Students described the institute and their experiences as "interesting," "insightful," "thoughtful," and "intriguing." Still other students offered the words "learning," and "fun and challenging." Some fuller examples of these responses include:

Intriguing. I thought that the institute was really interesting and intriguing and also really thought provoking. It made me look at things through a different light. It opened my eyes to another world.

Inspiring. I chose this word because it really changed my thinking on many things. I never thought I could express myself through words like the way I did. So it inspired me to start writing more. This institute experience also inspired me to really fight to go to college. I never believed I could make it to college because I didn't think I had enough money. However now my view on college is a lot different.

Interesting. I found it to be interesting because it was the first time I've witnessed something so real and powerful. I felt that each poet had an original and unique style telling poetry, and I found that interesting.

Learning. I chose this word because that's what I did. I learned a lot. This experience was great, if I could I would love to do something like this again.

Unique. There were different things discussed and viewed in ways that aren't typically talked about or presented.

Together with more detailed comments regarding the unique social and academic opportunity the institute presented, it was clear that the look and the feel of the room and the day was a novel experience for most students, one not typically encountered in the surrounding community. In total, a full 90% of the words offered by students were positive. In further reading, analyzing, coding, and discussing students' written responses to the open-ended questions, three strong themes emerged: awareness, agency, and a desire for extended engagement with the topics covered and especially with each other (across schools).

Awareness

Students from both schools made note of a new awareness or new realizations about the greater social context in which they live. A Central High School student wrote, "It surprised me how many of the groups' presentations were about the schooling system, shows how much it really has to change." Another student from East High School wrote, "One group talked about education and that it should be available equally to everyone. I already agreed with this, but hearing other kids' perspectives made me realize it is an issue everywhere." This realization that they are not alone and that their observations and experiences have meaning was impactful for students and provided a context from which they could construct new stories of understanding and meaning that were clearly reflected in their action proposals as well as evaluation reflections. A second Central High School student shared, "Something that I got out of being part of this was that racism has always been there, and if we as people don't try and do anything nothing would change." Another East High School student made a similar observation, "I learned how much racism is still in society and how much people are still effected [sic] by it. I knew racism was a big problem throughout the world, and when I left I discovered new ways to stand against racism." These young people from differently resourced schools are learning simultaneously the story of continued racism while coming to understand their role and power as change agents.

Agency

The high school students connected language and the ability to express one's self in terms that described a "coming to voice." A student, from East High School, expressed:

> One insight was to how powerful the voice of these writers were for themselves, and for the people who don't write or speak for themselves. I think writing and speaking for one's self can become an enormous tool for many obstacles in one's life. I learned that our voices can change an entire room and in turn can change the false perception of the racially charged and ignorant words that are used.

This student is connecting the poetry of the campus speakers with the impact of their scholarship activism—advocating or telling the story of constituents who have not yet come to voice. Consequently, this student reflects on her own story or the understanding that she, too, can use her voice to create change in the space that she exists—in both the academic room and the locations where "ignorant" words are used.

Similarly, a student from Central High School expressed: "On education differences, as we discussed other issues after inequality of education it seemed that the difference is definitely more of a resource issue and not a knowledge or problem with quality of education, if the student cares." This student proposes a counter-narrative; the student describes knowledgeable students and quality teachers, who are lacking resources because of inequality in access or resources. This may be read as the student suggesting that outcomes can change when students and teachers dedicate energy to educational pursuits even in the face of such inequality because the quality, the ability, and talent exist across schools.

Alternatively, "if the student cares" may communicate the tension of unlearning individual-based explanations for school and educational outcomes while developing an understanding of the structural roots of these school inequities and student experiences. While student awareness and agency were clearly expressed and evident across student (and school) responses, we recognize that the institute offers an opportunity for students to engage more substantively in an educational experience that began and continues through the courses taken at their respective schools. The institute theme of "Raising Our Voices" is important, too, in how educators communicate raising (or lifting) student voices to further understand lived experience, and an education that is in progress. In this sense too, the institute pedagogy reflects intergroup dialogue. University facilitators begin with the understanding that we are not insisting or expecting all students to adopt a singular position but, instead, invite and demonstrate for students that all of us need to seriously reflect upon and critically examine our current position and positionality within a shared learning environment. Students were not only open to engaging in this simultaneously individual and collective process, they strongly expressed wanting more time to do so.

Engagement

The theme that emerged most frequently and prominently in student survey responses was a keen interest from students, across schools, for more time together. Students from Central High School wrote: "I would change the time. I wish we had more time so we could discuss more." "I would change the time and make the times longer." "I would like to had more time. I feel we should do this again. We all learned a lot and had lots of fun." Students from East High School echoed this: "I think we should go more than once but also have less scheduled. Let our interests drive the time limits." "I wish we could have had more time to discuss some of the issues that were limited because of time."

For us, this synchronicity and strength of the message clearly communicates that not only are these students willing to take on difficult dialogues (across schools/community), they are interested in further opportunities to do so with guided structure and, importantly, also with their input and leadership.

NOTING THE ENERGY: REFLECTIONS FROM TEACHERS AND FACILITATORS

When the researchers asked the two English teachers if this type of feedback (i.e., asking for more time) is commonly shared by the students in their courses or students in general, the teachers responded with a resounding, "No." There appears to be something unique or significant about this type of dialogic experience—bridging students from two socio-geographically distinct school districts—that left youth (students) and adults (professional educators) wanting more. The students' call for additional time emphasized what facilitators' observed—these students were actively engaged and invested in the work of the institute. One facilitator remarked, "The energy and creativity of the participating high school students were the best part for me as a facilitator.

It reaffirms my belief that the tools and practice of dialogue are powerful resources for folks, no matter what their age." When trusted to rise to the occasion and greeted with high expectations, these high school students thought critically and applied broadly.

Feedback from the teachers following the institute echoed the themes from student and university facilitator responses. The teachers observed students as deeply engaged through the day. When asked how to improve the institute, both teachers indicated that students would like more time:

> [I am] very enthusiastic about the institute's format and its results! My only suggestion mirrors our students' concerns that we find ways to build more time.

> The only thing I can think of is they wanted more time. I mean, when you think about the parameters of the time that we could be there, how do you make more time . . . I don't think we could have gotten everything done. They had a working lunch. There was no time to give.

Both teachers shared that it is rare for high school students to ask for additional time to this extent, and that this level of engagement added to the unique richness of the institute experience. In addition to student engagement across schools, the two teachers subsequently identified the power of the presentations by the invited speakers and how well these connected to the content of the institute and the course curriculum, as well as students' interests outside of school:

> [The speakers were] the catalyst for what followed. So, if you asked me what was the most meaningful I would say those two [speakers] because without them what followed wouldn't have happened even though what followed was pretty significant as well.

> You don't always hear teachers and professors talking about hip-hop and music that relates to a big portion of my students, and I think it was very inspiring and profound for them.

Interestingly, the racial/ethnic diversity of the university members participating in the event was noted by students who shared their pride in seeing highly accomplished, engaging, and genuine university representatives with whom they could identify.

The teachers also described students' and their own awareness of a connected community, a sense of the university as a "home" school or shared educational resource. The teachers further explained that the institute and partnering with the Intergroup Dialogue Program provides pedagogical, content rich, and instrumental support.

Summary of Shared Perspectives

The written and follow-up responses of the high school teachers and the university facilitators echoed the themes shared by the student participants in the institute—especially regarding the level of energy, commitment, and engagement that students were willing to give to the cross-school work. Importantly, this work included critical social analysis, creative responses, connection to their home school curriculum/content/discussions, and community building. In addition to the consistency across teachers' and students' evaluations, there also was consistency in the feedback across the two schools.

Also supportive of the themes presented here, during the institute and immediately following, campus members (individuals from administrative and catering staff) who were not involved in the program entered the room to ask "what is/was happening here?" They added that they were hearing a lot of positive energy, and they hear and experience that as rare coming from youth.

LIMITATIONS

Limitations of the current study include a high school student sample that is limited to a particular geographic location (Northeast U.S., central New York, with associated socioeconomic and historical context) and school relations (one urban and one suburban school with existing collaboration/exchanges). Furthermore, given within-school resources and needs, a larger number of suburban school students than urban school students participated in the 2010 university-hosted institute. At the institute meeting ground, however, high school teachers and university facilitators observed that students—who identified as white, as students of color, from immigrant families, with long-standing ties to the city or the suburbs, economically struggling and economically privileged, from both schools—seriously engaged the tasks and challenges of the institute, and they called out for more, offering more of their own input and time. It is the chorus of these youth voices here and across the literature reviewed that requires further listening, research, and "more time." Future research should consider long-term implications of similar initiatives, school-community partnerships, and how best to support the education and action students voice across schools. Clearly evident in earlier studies is both the need for and the significance of this work for diverse students who are currently attending urban and suburban schools, often relatively close in physical proximity yet seemingly distant in school resources and recognition (e.g., Checkoway, 2009; Ferguson, 2007; Linn & Wellner, 2007; Lleras, 2008; Torre & Fine, 2006).

DIRECTIONS: YOUTH DIALOGUES AND DEMOCRATIC ENGAGEMENT

Students learn more than how to explicate Shakespeare or find the derivative in high school. They are subject to the powerful narratives that shape our society: rich versus poor, urban versus suburban. For disenfranchised youth, the practice of schooling is more nefarious; it not only reproduces social inequities, it also forces "youth across social class and race backgrounds" to either "run faster to keep up or run the risk of dropping out entirely" (Weis & Dimitriadis, 2008, p. 5). Ample evidence shows that schooling can be a sorting machine that red-lines students of color, low-income, and first-generation youth out of the schooling system, severely limiting marginalized youth's possibilities for economic success and social access. Yet, when we look to schools as a space of possibility, we can find student voice and agency. At its most basic, student voice is "youth sharing their opinions of problems and potential solutions" (Mitra, 2004, p. 651). Mitra conducted interviews and observations in a school undergoing reform in the San Francisco Bay area. The school included students in school change initiatives. Mitra found that students who participated in one of the school reform committees developed an increased sense of agency, belonging, and competence. As a result of their experience investigating problems and recommending solutions, students reported a belief that they could create change among peers and in their schools. Our students similarly reported increased faith in their ability to be change makers. As the evaluation study presented here documents, these high school students—intersecting school, racial/ethnic, and class social divides—describe in their own words coming to awareness, engaging an opportunity to imagine and practice agency, and feeling a strong interest in further education and commitment to learning about these issues, including how to push for change.

When curriculum and pedagogy help students to understand their own identities, the identities of their peers, and methods for collaboration, students are prepared for democratic participation (Checkoway, 2001). One of the goals of a liberal education is to expand one's perspective (Hurtado, 2007). In engaging diversity, or—as in our case—in engaging students in dialogue about issues of social justice, the university casts itself in the role of democratic agent. As high school students learn to constructively raise their voice and agency, universities must do the same (Boyte & Kari, 2000; Checkoway, 2001; Hurtado, 2007). Cantor (2009) asserts:

> [Institutions of higher education] can and must assume our rightful role today as public goods, merging the work of our disciplines with the work of our communities. In the process, we will authentically and naturally embed our diversity agenda in its rightful role as central to the future of our institutional and our national viability. (p. 3)

In acting for the public good, researchers must work with the community to solve local problems in ways that "regard the community members as research partners and active participants in knowledge development" (Checkoway, 2001, p. 134). As is the case with the high school institute, the university must partner with community stakeholders to define a problem, gather information, and apply that information to action (Checkoway, 2001). In doing so, the university not only teaches about democracy; it also actively engages in the democratic process (Boyte & Kari, 2000; Cantor, 2009; Checkoway, 2001; Hurtado, 2007).

"Writing the divide" in this study not only refers to high school students writing to develop their unique voices, impact, and activism across school divides; it further refers to the role and responsibility of the university to address (to write about, and make right) the divide of (re)segregated schools and disparate educational outcomes for youth and future adults in its neighboring community. Collaborative action research among universities and secondary institutions must continue to explore urban-suburban inequalities, youth dialogue, and agency.

Democracy itself is the leitmotif that unites the research and students' stories we have explored. Youth action and intergroup dialogue are not mere dress rehearsals for the civic responsibilities of adult life. They are genuine interactions with the democratic process that education must take up, not only to prepare our students for their futures, but also to empower our youth to impact the institutions and communities in their present.

"I am from the present, future, and past / So throw away the stereotypes because / I, too, have hopes and dreams" (from a collective poem by an institute cross-school student group)

NOTES

1. This paper identifies the site of this youth dialogue work and research—also the site of the current study—as this location is clearly specified in the research and associated resources cited. The specific location of the Detroit Youth Dialogues, an important preceding model, is also specified in the research and evaluation literature. The current study aims to contribute both to the national and local discussion of the dynamics and outcomes of bringing urban and suburban high school students together through dialogue and related efforts.

2. The other participating institutions include Arizona State University, Occidental College, University of California-San Diego, University of Maryland, University of Massachusetts Amherst, University of Michigan, University of Texas-Austin, and University of Washington (see Nagda et al., 2009).

3. The specific teachers are identified here (with permission) to acknowledge their work in creating this cross-school collaboration and their role as collaborators in the initiative studied.

REFERENCES

Adams, M. (2007). Pedagogical frameworks for social justice education. In M. Adams, L. A. Bell, & P. Griffin (Eds.), *Teaching for diversity and social justice* (2nd ed., pp. 15–33). New York, NY: Routledge.

Aud, S., Fox, M., & Kewal Ramani, A. (2010). *Status and trends in the education of racial and ethnic groups* (NCES 2010-015). U.S. Department of Education, National Center for Education Statistics. Washington, DC: U.S. Government Printing Office.

Beale, R. L., & Schoem, D. (2001). The content/process balance in intergroup dialogue. In D. Schoem & S. Hurtado (Eds.), *Intergroup dialogue: Deliberative democracy in school, college, community, and workplace* (pp. 266–279). Ann Arbor, MI: University of Michigan Press.

Boyte, H. C., & Kari, N. N. (2000). Renewing the democratic spirit in American colleges and universities: Higher education as public works. In T. Ehrlich (Eds), *Civic responsibility & higher education* (pp. 37–61). Phoenix, AZ: Oryx.

Brief of 553 Social Scientists as Amici Curiae in Support of Respondents Parents v. Seattle (2006). Retrieved from http://www.adl.org/civil_rights/ab/parentsinvolved_v_seattle.pdf

Brown v. Board of Education. (1954). 347 US 483, 74 S.Ct.686, 98 L.Ed. 873.

Cantor, N. (2009). *Scholarship in action: Transforming communities and higher education.* Retrieved from http://www.syr.edu/chancellor/speeches/UCDavis.pdf

Checkoway, B. (2001). Renewing the civic mission of the American research university. *The Journal of Higher Education, 72*(2), 125–147.

Checkoway, B. (2009). Youth civic engagement for dialogue and diversity and the metropolitan level. *The Foundation Review, 1*(2), 41–50.

Checkoway, B., & Richards-Schuster, K. (2006). Youth participation for education reform in low-income communities of color. In S. Ginwright, P. Noguera, & J. Cammarota (Eds.), *Beyond resistance! Youth activism and community change* (pp. 319–333). New York, NY: Routledge.

Chesler, M. (2001). Extending intergroup dialogue: From talk to action. In D. Schoem & S. Hurtado (Eds.), *Intergroup dialogue: Deliberative democracy in school, college, community, and workplace* (pp. 294–305). Ann Arbor, MI: University of Michigan Press.

Dovidio, J. F., Gaertner, S. L., Stewart, T. L., Esses, V. M., ten Vergert, M., & Hodson, G. (2004). From intervention to outcome: Processes in the reduction of bias. In W. G. Stephan & W. P. Vogt (Eds.), *Education programs for improving intergroup relations: Theory, research, and practice* (pp. 243–265). New York, NY: Teachers College Press.

Duncan-Andrade, D., & Morrell, E. (2008). *The art of critical pedagogy.* New York, NY: Lang.

Ellison, J., & Eatman, T. K. (2008). *Scholarship in public: Knowledge creation and tenure policy in the engaged university: A resource on promotion and tenure in the arts, humanities, and design.* Retrieved from http://www.imaginingamerica.org/IApdfs/TTI_REPORT%20FINAL%205.2.08.pdf

Everyday Democracy (formerly the Study Circles Resource Center). (2010). About us. Retrieved from http://www.everyday-democracy.org//en/Page.AboutUs.aspx

Fanselow, J. (2007). *Syracuse marks a decade of dialogue to end racism.* Retrieved from http://www.everyday-democracy.org/en/Article.517.aspx

Ferguson, R. F. (2007). *Toward excellence with equity: An emerging vision for closing the achievement gap.* Cambridge, MA: Harvard Education Press.

Fine, M., Bloom, J., Burns, A., Chajet, L., Guishard, M., Payne, Y., Perkins-Munn, T., & Torre, M. E. (2005). Dear Zora: A Letter to Zora Neale Hurston 50 years after *Brown. Teachers College Record, 107*(3), 496–528.

Fine, M., Burns, A., Payne, Y. A., & Torre, M. E. (2004). Civic lessons: The color and class of betrayal. *Teachers College Record, 106*(11), 2193–2223.

Ginwright, S., Noguera, P., & Cammarota, J. (Eds.). (2006). *Beyond resistance! Youth activism and community change* (pp. xiii–xxii). New York, NY: Taylor & Francis.

Glaser, B., & Strauss, A. (1967). *The discovery of grounded theory: Strategies of qualitative research*. London, England: Wledenfeld and Nicholson.

Grant, G. (2009). *Hope and despair in the American city: Why there are no bad schools in Raleigh*. Boston, MA: Harvard University Press.

Henke, S. (2008). Dangerous minds: Constructing urban education between hope and despair. In S. Schramm-Pate & R. B. Jeffries (Eds.), *Grappling with diversity: Readings on civil rights pedagogy and critical multiculturalism* (pp. 97–115). Albany, NY: State University of New York Press.

Hochschild, J. L. (2003). Social class in public schools. *Journal of Social Issues, 59*(4), 821–840.

Hosang, D. (2006). Beyond policy: Ideology, race and the reimagining of youth. In S. Ginwright, P. Noguera, & J. Cammarota (Eds.), *Beyond resistance! Youth activism and community change* (pp. 3–21). New York, NY: Taylor & Francis.

Hurtado, S. (2005). The next generation of diversity and intergroup relations research. *Journal of Social Issues, 61*(3), 595–610.

Hurtado, S. (2007). Linking diversity with the educational and civic missions of higher education. *The Review of Higher Education, 30*(2), 185–196.

Interfaith Works of Central New York. (2010). *Community wide dialogue to end racism*. Retrieved from http: //interfaithworkscny.org/blog/programs/community-wide-dialogue-to-end-racism

Iodice, L., & Benedetto, J. (2009). *Reconstructing racial rhetoric* [New York State Program of Excellence]. Workshop presented to the New York State English Council, Albany, NY.

Jocson, K. M. (2006). "The best of both worlds": Youth poetry as social critique and forms of empowerment. In S. Ginwright, P. Noguera, & J. Cammarota (Eds.), *Beyond resistance! Youth activism and community change* (pp. 129–149). New York, NY: Taylor & Francis.

Linn, R. L., & Welner, K. G. (Eds.). (2007). *Race-conscious policies for assigning students to schools: Social science research and the Supreme Court cases*. National Academy of Education Committee on Social Science Research Evidence on Racial Diversity in Schools. Washington, DC: National Academy of Education.

Lleras, C. (2008). Race, racial concentration, and the dynamics of educational inequality across urban and suburban schools. *American Educational Research Journal, 45*(4), 886–912.

Lopez, G. E., Gurin, P., & Nagda, B. A. (1998). Education and understanding structural causes for group inequalities. *Political Psychology, 19*(2), 305–329.

Mitra, D. L. (2004). The significance of students: Can increasing "student voice" in schools lead to gains in youth development? *Teachers College Record, 106*(4), 651–688.

Morrell, E. (2006). Youth-initiated research as a tool for advocacy and change in urban schools. In S. Ginwright, P. Noguera, & J. Cammarota (Eds.), *Beyond resistance! Youth activism and community change* (pp. 111–129). New York, NY: Taylor & Francis.

Nagda, B. A., Gurin, P., & Lopez, G. E. (2003). Transformative pedagogy for democracy and social justice. *Race, Ethnicity and Education, 6*(2), 165–191.

Nagda, B. A., Gurin, P., Sorensen, N., & Zúñiga, X. (2009). Evaluating intergroup dialogue: Engaging diversity for personal and social responsibility. *Diversity & Democracy, 12*(1), 4–6.

Nagda, B. A., Kim, C.-w., & Truelove, Y. (2004). Learning about difference, learning with others, learning to transgress. *Journal of Social Issues, 60*(1), 195–214.

Nagda, B. A., McCoy, M. L., & Barrett, M. H. (2006). Mix It Up: Crossing social boundaries as a pathway to youth civic engagement. *National Civic Review, 95*(1), 47–56.

O'Donoghue, J. L. (2006). Taking their own power: Urban youth, community-based youth organizations, and public efficacy. In S. Ginwright, P. Noguera, & J. Cammarota (Eds.), *Beyond resistance! Youth activism and community change* (pp. 229–247). New York, NY: Taylor & Francis.

Orfield, G., & Lee, C. (2006). *Racial transformation and the changing nature of segregation*. Cambridge, MA: The Civil Rights Project at Harvard University.

Pettigrew, T. F. (1998). Intergroup contact theory. *Annual Review of Psychology, 49*, 65–85.

Pincock, H. (2008). Teaching through talk? The impact of intergroup dialogue on conceptualizations of racism. *Research in Social Movement Conflicts and Change, 29*, 21–53.

Schoem, D., Hurtado, S., Sevig, T., Chesler, M., & Sumida, S. H. (2001). Intergroup dialogue: Democracy at work in theory and practice. In D. Schoem & S. Hurtado (Eds.), *Intergroup dialogue: Deliberative democracy in school, college, community, and workplace* (pp. 1–21). Ann Arbor, MI: University of Michigan Press.

Strauss, A. L., & Corbin, J. (1990). *Basics of qualitative research: Grounded theory procedures and techniques.* Newbury Park, CA: Sage.

Strobel, K., Osberg, J., & McLaughlin, M. (2006). Participation in social change: Shifting adolescents' developmental pathways. In S. Ginwright, P. Noguera, & J. Cammarota (Eds.), *Beyond resistance! Youth activism and community change* (pp. 197–215). New York, NY: Taylor & Francis.

Tatum, B. D. (2007). *Can we talk about race? And other conversations in an era of school resegregation.* Boston, MA: Beacon.

Torre, M., & Fine, M. (2006). Researching and resisting: Democratic policy research by and for youth. In S. Ginwright, P. Noguera, & J. Cammarota (Eds.). *Beyond resistance! Youth activism and community change* (pp. 129–149). New York, NY: Taylor & Francis.

Weis, L., & Dimitriadis, G. (2008). Dueling banjos: Shifting economic and cultural contexts in the lives of youth. *Teachers College Record, 110*(10), 2290–2316.

Yeakley, A. M. (2011). In the hands of facilitators: Students experiences in dialogue and implications for facilitator training. In K. E. Maxwell, B. A. Nagda, & M. C. Thompson (Eds.), *Facilitating intergroup dialogues: Bridging differences, catalyzing change* (pp. 23–36). Sterling, VA: Stylus.

Yosso, T. J. (2005). Whose culture has capital? A critical race theory discussion of community cultural wealth. *Race, Ethnicity and Education, 8*(1), 69–91.

Zúñiga, X., Nagda, B. A., Chesler, M., & Cytron-Walker, A. (2007). *Intergroup dialogue in higher education: Meaningful learning about social justice.* San Francisco, CA: Jossey-Bass.

Zúñiga, X., Nagda, B. A., & Sevig, T. (2002). Intergroup dialogues: An educational model for cultivating engagement across differences. *Equity & Excellence in Education, 35*(1), 7–17.

Critical Education in High Schools: The Promise and Challenges of Intergroup Dialogue

Shayla R. Griffin, Mikel Brown, and naomi m. warren
University of Michigan

In public high schools across the country young people deal with issues of discrimination and bullying that are often the result of intolerance and misunderstandings across social identities. Progressive educators who advocate for critical multicultural and critical pedagogical approaches have proposed that young people need to have educational experiences in which they learn to think critically and take action toward social justice in order to create schools that are safe and supportive for all students. This study suggests that intergroup dialogue is a promising model of engaging young people in this form of critical education. It describes an intergroup dialogue program currently operating at four high schools and presents some of the successes and challenges of doing dialogue work in public high school settings.

In 2010, anti-gay bullying in schools across the country led to the suicides of at least 13 teenagers in a two-month period. These unfortunate events attracted national media attention and pushed school boards, educators, parents, and even the U.S. Department of Education to confront bullying more seriously. However, many anti-bullying initiatives have been so focused on addressing student behavior that they fail to address the prejudice and intolerance that underlie students' antagonistic interactions (Dessel, 2010; Poteat & DiGiovanni, 2010). This is particularly troubling in light of research that finds that conflict and violence in schools are often linked to discrimination across race (Roberts, Bell, & Murphy, 2008; Rosenbloom & Way, 2004), class (Weis, 2008), gender (Lee, Croninger, Linn, & Chen, 1996), sexual orientation (Brikett, Espelage, & Koenig, 2009), ability status (Flynt & Morton, 2004), and religion (Zine, 2001). Unfortunately, most schools have struggled to address these conflicts in ways that move beyond punitive measures to acknowledge the realities of prejudice.

For example, in January 2010, misunderstandings about the usage of racial slurs at a high school in Southeastern Michigan led to an after school brawl between black, white, and Asian students so large that police had to be called. In the days following the fight, school administrators, the school social worker, and the school psychologist framed the incident as one of bullying, disconnected from race. Even when pressed by one of the authors, these professionals resisted the possibility that the school had a "race problem." Their proposed solution was to monitor hallways more closely, ban students from staying after school if they were not under the supervision of an adult, and enhance zero-tolerance policies.

However, students at the school who participated in an intergroup dialogue program—which engages young people in facilitated, face-to-face conversations across diverse social identities—told a different story. They framed the fight as a climactic event in a series of everyday racial insults that had become acceptable among students but burst into adult consciousness only when physical violence was involved. The disconnect between students' daily experiences of discrimination and adults' reactions to those experiences indicates that schools may lack the tools to effectively prepare young people to live in an increasingly multicultural society (Banks, 2007).

Many progressive scholars have challenged educators to think more broadly about what it means to prepare students for life. These scholars are concerned with not only interrupting problematic behavior, but also with providing opportunities for young people to think reflectively about the world around them in order to become productive, engaged citizens, unwilling to perpetrate or tolerate bullying and discrimination. Progressive scholars advocate for the implementation of pedagogies, policies, and practices that emphasize the importance of building relationships, creating safe spaces, and providing opportunities for students to engage in positive social change. However, these scholars have struggled to identify practice methods that would enable wide implementation of their theories.

This article seeks to address this gap by providing a case study of one promising model of practice that aligns the pedagogical vision of critical educational scholars with the on-the-ground needs of classroom teachers. It explores intergroup dialogue as a form of critical multicultural practice that has the potential to interrupt discrimination and encourage social justice, and presents an analysis of the unique challenges of doing dialogue work in high school settings, with the hope of providing a possible template for other educators.

CRITICAL THEORIES OF EDUCATION AND INTERGROUP DIALOGUE

Critical scholars and educators have long noted the ways in which schools operate in favor of those students who are already most privileged. They have advocated for pedagogical, curricular, and structural reforms that would make schools more equitable (Bourdieu & Passeron, 1990; Morrow & Torres, 1995). Critical multicultural education (Banks & Banks, 2009) and critical pedagogy (Freire, 1970) are two approaches in this tradition that have become particularly prominent. These models seek to create schools and educational systems that value diverse experiences, provide equal access and opportunity to all students, help individuals dismantle their own biases, and prepare young people to be critically engaged citizens (Gay, 1997; Shor, 1992).

Multicultural educators advocate for inclusion in a range of ways. While celebratory multiculturalists may institute cultural awareness weeks, diversity celebrations, or ethnic food festivals—all of which tend to dangerously gloss over conversations about racism—critical multiculturalists are focused not only on recognizing difference, but also on combating structural inequality (Dobbie & Richards-Schuester, 2008).

In their efforts to move toward dismantling unjust systems, many critical multiculturalists have drawn upon critical pedagogy. Rooted in the work of Paulo Freire (1970), critical pedagogy helps students develop a critical consciousness of inequitable distributions of power and learn to situate their own lived experiences in the context of the larger social system. Critical pedagogy is a cyclical process of thinking, reflection, and action (praxis) in which the roles of teacher and learner are blurred, allowing for the co-construction of knowledge. In this model, teachers are intellectuals and cultural workers, rather than technocrats who disseminate information (Freire, 1998; Giroux, 1988). Critical pedagogy creates space for dialogue that questions the dominant norms that privilege, exclude, oppress, and marginalize and has the ultimate goal of empowering oppressed groups to take liberatory action (Giroux, 2006).

In the past 20 years, critical pedagogy has been critiqued and expanded by critical multiculturalists, critical race theorists, and feminist scholars who argue that it has not adequately considered the connection between multiple, intersecting social identities and oppression (Collins, 2000; Ellsworth, 1992; hooks, 1994; Keesing-Styles, 2003; Ladson-Billings, 1995). Other scholars have critiqued these works for being overly theoretical and failing to provide teachers with social justice-oriented models of practice that they can utilize in their classrooms (e.g., Gore, 1993).

Intergroup dialogue for social justice has the potential to bridge this gap between the theory and practice of critical pedagogy. It is a process in which two or more groups of individuals engage in face-to-face conversation in an effort to explore, challenge, and overcome the biases they hold about members of their own and other groups (Adams, Bell, & Griffin, 2007; Schoem & Hurtado, 2001). Unlike discussion or debate, dialogue is not a solely intellectual process. It requires emotional investment and attentive listening (Zuniga, Nagda, & Sevig, 2002). Participants learn to non-violently and collaboratively negotiate intergroup conflict with the goal of increasing social justice and ending oppression (Schoem, Hurtado, Sevig, Chesler, & Sumida, 2001).

Dialogue work draws upon critical pedagogy and theories of multiculturalism as well as intergroup contact theory, which proposes that the tensions among groups can be reduced through systematic contact in a cooperative environment (Allport, 1954; Pettigrew, 1998). Studies find that dialogue participants perceive greater commonality with people from different backgrounds, think in more complex ways about intergroup relations, employ more positive approaches to conflict, and become increasingly confident in their ability to address social justice issues (Gurin, Peng, Lopez, & Nagda, 1999; Nagda, Kim, & Truelove, 2004).

Despite these promising outcomes, intergroup dialogue has occurred largely with college students in university settings. Bringing dialogue to high schools has the potential to transform young people who may never attend a four-year university, join a community organization, participate in a summer program, or take a dialogue course for credit. Unfortunately, the national focus on standards, accountability, and testing leaves little room for schools to provide such opportunities for students to engage in dialogue or for teachers to acquire the knowledge and skills to facilitate these conversations. While federal and state policies have mandated that teachers be "highly qualified" (Darling-Hammond, 2002) in their content area to retain their jobs, policies have not been instituted that would also help them become highly qualified in facilitating difficult conversations about difference or effectively addressing issues of diversity and social justice (Banks, 2001). In addition, current education reform, rooted in market-based solutions to failure, has constrained the work of schools of education in preparing preservice teachers to work with diverse student populations (Smith, 2009). The privatization and corporatization of schooling, which seeks to treat schools more like businesses by focusing on test scores, heightened competition, and punitive sanctions for schools with the most limited resources and the most marginalized students, has made it difficult to enact models of practice in which schools serve as public, democratic istitutions meant to build well-rounded, critically thinking, engaged citizens.

Even in cases in which state boards of education have advocated for more critical models of practice, the political climate has prevented these efforts from being implemented. For example, although the Michigan Board of Education recognized in 2004 that "bullying is often rooted in a rejection of real or perceived differences in race, ethnicity, gender, gender expression, socioeconomic class, sexual orientation, and disabilities," and proposed that "[c]onnectedness should therefore be promoted across differences," education policy in the state does not address, multiculturalism, conflict resolution, diversity, or social justice education (Michigan State Board of Education, 2004, para. 8). In December of 2011, the Michigan Legislature passed an anti-bullying bill known as "Matt's Safe School Law." Although the legislation mandates that all schools adopt policies that "prohibit bullying," it does not mention the specific cause of bullying or identify any of the social identities around which bullying often takes place (The Revised School Code Act 451 of 1976, 2011). As a result, many teachers and administrators simply do not have the knowledge, skills, or incentive to prepare young people from a range of social, economic, and cultural backgrounds to engage the world around them in ways that are critical, deliberative, and dialogic (Gay & Kirkland, 2003; Lahelma, 2004).

Our experience as facilitators and researchers indicates that intergroup dialogue in high schools is possible and effective. Young people from diverse backgrounds are capable of, open to, and excited about participating in dialogue within their schools. When schools provide students with such opportunities, they are taking steps toward the creation of an educational system that many educators have long envisioned. Nonetheless, conducting dialogue outside of universities requires some unique considerations. This article describes an afterschool intergroup dialogue program and presents the outcomes and unique challenges of doing this work within public schools in the current political climate.

INTERGROUP SOCIAL CHANGE AGENTS: SUCCESSES, CHALLENGES, AND LESSONS LEARNED

Program Description

Intergroup Social Change Agents (I-SCA) is a collaborative project between the University of Michigan—Ann Arbor's School of Social Work and four public high schools in three nearby school districts. The four schools differ greatly in size, student population, academic achievement, and per pupil funding. For example, one is a small, majority black, alternative school, while another is a large suburban school with a racially and economically diverse student population. While one school receives $9,490 per pupil in state funding, another receives only $7,316 (Michigan State Senate, 2011). Significant differences among the four schools also can be seen in test scores, graduation rates, and in the number of students who participate in the free/reduced-fee lunch program.

For the past eight years, I-SCA has provided a safe space within high schools for students to explore difference, work through conflict, build relationships, and ultimately work toward social justice (Garvin, 2008). I-SCA runs after school once a week for 20 weeks, starting in early November and ending the first week in June. The program also involves two full-day inter-school exchanges where students from one school spend a day with students at another participating school. At the end of the year, students from all four schools work together to develop a social action project to improve intergroup relations and reduce conflict in their schools and communities.

The program curriculum, written by Charles Garvin, Michael Spencer, and naomi m. warren, draws on methods of conflict resolution and peer mediation (Johnson & Johnson, 1996) as well as the intergroup dialogue model developed by the University's Program on Intergroup Relations. Young people in I-SCA engage in dialogue about privilege and oppression around race, class, gender, sexual orientation, religion, and ability status.

At each school, the program consists of a committed group of 15-35 students who participate for the full year. Our participants generally reflect the diversity of their schools in race, class, and gender. The program is open to all interested 10th and 11th grade students, as well as 12th graders who have participated previously. Although I-SCA is voluntary, students must have consent forms from parents or legal guardians to participate.

Every I-SCA meeting is attended by one program staff member, one to two social work interns, and a school staff person who serves as the program liaison. Meetings are held in a classroom in the school building. During sessions, students and adults sit together in an integrated circle. Each session includes a "lid-opener" activity to help participants build community with one another, an experiential activity that illuminates a particular identity or concept, small group dialogue in which that identity or concept is discussed, and a short closing activity. Each dialogue utilizes LARA, a communication skill in which you Listen with an open mind, Affirm a point of common ground in what the other person has said, Respond, and Add information (Tinker, 2006).

Program Roles and Responsibilities

One crucial component of the I-SCA program structure and facilitation model is the involvement of multiple stakeholders from the schools and the University. Involving people at multiple levels as participants and leaders has encouraged enhanced learning and has helped improve school culture and climate more broadly. Ultimately, our hope is that the involvement of adult stakeholders will create a significant population of people capable of doing dialogue work in high schools. I-SCA has five key program roles: program staff, school administrators, school liaisons, social work interns, and peer facilitators.

Program Staff

We believe that in order to be successful, intergroup dialogues need to be run by trained facilitators with significant knowledge of both social justice content regarding issues of privilege and oppression, and the dialogue process. At each school, I-SCA is led by one of our three lead program staff (the authors) who facilitate and coordinate the program across schools. All three of us hold master's degrees in Social Work, have studied issues of privilege and oppression, and have extensive experience as facilitators with youth and adults. We work in collaboration with two University faculty, Charles Garvin and Michael Spencer, to develop and revise the curriculum, plan sessions, and organize the program at all levels. We are responsible for training and overseeing social work interns, peer facilitators, and school liaisons. In addition, we are the primary program facilitators. None of the three program staff are provided salaries to run I-SCA, although Mikel Brown and naomi m. warren receive small stipends for their work. Shayla R. Griffin volunteers her time but has been granted access to the students and schools for research purposes.

School Administrators

While administrators are not involved in day-to-day program operations, their support sustains the program. School administrators attend advisory meetings every other month, promote I-SCA among colleagues within the school, make funding commitments, and identify a liaison within their school who serves as the link between the University, program staff, and the school.

School Liaisons

School liaisons work closely with program staff. In some cases this person is a teacher; in other instances it is a Community Assistant or other school staff member. The school liaison is, in many ways, the face of the program. They help create and sustain a true partnership between the University and the school. School liaisons assist with program logistics, connect program staff to the school more broadly, advertise the program, help recruit students, and deal with weekly logistical issues and student concerns.

Social Work Interns

Each year, two to four master's students in the School of Social Work serve as interns for the program. We strive to provide interns with both learning and teaching opportunities. Interns have usually either taken a dialogue course or are in the process of doing so at the time of their placement. As a part of their internship, they are required to undergo 32 hours of additional training led by program staff. Interns, like school liaisons, have a significant number of logistical responsibilities, including keeping track of attendance, managing paperwork, writing up notes after every session, and working closely with school liaisons on set up and snack provision. They also assist staff with facilitation and research.

Peer Facilitators

Returning participants are invited to apply to be peer facilitators who assist in planning sessions and leading activities. Our goal is for them to explore topics more deeply and become leaders in I-SCA and their schools more broadly. This requires significantly more commitment than being a participant. Peer facilitators undergo 16 hours of training throughout the year and stay an hour after each dialogue to debrief and help plan for the next session. In addition, they provide adult staff with on-the-ground knowledge of the schools from a student perspective.

Student Outcomes

We have consistently evaluated the I-SCA program using both surveys and semi-structured interviews. Overall the program has demonstrated positive outcomes for students. The quantitative evaluation tools include measures of social identity, critical social awareness, comfort communicating across difference, and confidence in taking action to interrupt oppressive behavior (Garvin, 2008; Spencer, Brown, Griffin, & Abdullah, 2008). In the surveys, participants have reported increased critical social awareness and decreased prejudice. They said they built friendships with people unlike themselves, learned the importance of building relationships before stereotyping, and acquired new knowledge about social issues. In addition, students indicated "an increased desire to solve conflicts peacefully," and "increased capacity to solve conflicts in their school and in their community, as well as in their personal lives" (Spencer et al., 2008, p. 98).

More recent qualitative analysis confirms these findings. The data presented in this article was gathered through post-interviews conducted by Shayla R. Griffin with a representative sample of 12 11th grade participants from two different schools, during the 2006–2007 school year (Weiss, 1994). The sample was chosen to reflect the range of student perspectives and included three black males, two black females, two white males, two white females, one Asian male, one Indian female, and one female student who had recently immigrated from Hungary. The sample also was one of conveniences in that student informants had to be able and willing to participate in interviews outside of the intergroup sessions (Weiss, 1994). Interviews lasted from 30 minutes to 1.5 hours. They took place on the school grounds in a private classroom during students' lunch periods or after school.

Interviews were semi-formal and open-ended (Kvale, 1996). The interview guide included questions about what students felt they learned from the program, what they liked and disliked about participating, and how their perspectives about social identities and inequality had or had not shifted. In addition, the guide asked how they viewed their school as a result of participating in the program. It asked if they noticed any differences in how students got along from different racial, class, and gender backgrounds; how their own relationships with peers from different backgrounds had changed; and if any of their stereotypes had been challenged. Finally, it asked students about their engagement and efficacy in making social change in their schools and communities and working toward social justice. Interviews were tape-recorded, transcribed, and coded for themes that had been identified in previous quantitative analysis. In addition, new and emerging themes related to interpersonal relationships, conflict/resolution, and understandings of social inequity and social justice were identified and analyzed (Saldaña, 2009).

Interviewees reported being more likely to build relationships with those who are different from them and more likely to challenge stereotypes they held about others. They reported noticing and interrupting discriminatory and bullying behavior more frequently and being less likely to engage in discrimination or bullying themselves. In addition, multiple students reported that the skills they learned in I-SCA helped them learn to resolve conflict more peacefully and communicate more effectively and respectfully—particularly with those who held beliefs different from their own. Across the sample, students reported having very positive experiences in intergroup dialogue with regard to improving communication and conflict resolution skills, building relationships across difference, challenging stereotypes, interrupting discriminatory behavior, and developing a commitment to social justice.

Improving Conflict Resolution and Communication Skills

I-SCA gave students the concrete skills to more effectively communicate and resolve conflict. Students reported that they utilized the LARA technique and other skills in their daily lives in ways that proved productive. In describing his communication skills and conflict style after participating in I-SCA, a black male student said:

> If I get into a debate with somebody or I get into an argument with somebody, I try my best to listen to everything they got to say, and I try to take turns with them. I try my best to understand what people

are saying to me and how they feel about something. Because if you don't really know how they feel about something then you can't really understand why they're mad or why they feel a certain way.

The skills he learned enabled him to see the importance of trying to understand where others were coming from and valuing the opinions and perspectives of those he might disagree with. By his second year in the program, this young man had refined his communication skills, along with a number of students at his school who had continued meeting independently after the program officially ended. He talked about the interaction in these additional meetings with pride:

We would just be there and whenever anyone talked everyone else was just quiet. Everybody waited until it was done and like, even if people had conflicting ideas, it was like, "I understand what you're saying, but I feel like this." And we would also work it out. So it was like real cool.

These students were able to incorporate the listening and conflict resolution skills they learned into their lives in ways that facilitated deep sharing, trust, and relationships.

Building Relationships and Increasing Understanding across Difference

Students reported that their relationships with peers improved in two specific ways as a result of participating in I-SCA. First many of them said that they built stronger relationships with students they knew prior to participating in I-SCA. When asked what she got out of the program, one black, female student said:

Stronger relationships definitely. For example, [a black male student and I have] known each other for—we were born on the same day in the same hospital. So we've known each other a really long time. But we've gotten a lot closer this year! And I think Intergroup was a part of it. Partly the time just being there with a person. But, um, I can say, we can see something, and it's like, "Oh, we've got to use those intergroup skills!"

Not only did this young lady's relationship with her friend grow stronger, she also felt that the skills they had learned together in I-SCA provided them with the tools to make better decisions throughout the school day and to hold each other accountable.

In addition, many of the students reported forming new friendships with students who they did not know previously. A white female student said, "I met a lot of people I didn't know and, actually, people I didn't even know were in my grade! So that was cool." The formation of these new relationships grew out of students' overall willingness to be more open to others and their newfound interest in learning more about those who were different from them. One white male student stated, "I guess I'm more conscious and more open to what other people have to say and who I talk to or, I just . . . I'm probably just a better person on a lot of levels. I'm more accepting of other people than I was."

A black, male student described this dual process of improving existing relationships and building new ones in the following way:

I guess I got closer with my friends that did [Intergroup] and tried to make bonds with others. So I guess I was more open to friendships. Whereas before I was kinda close-minded to everyone. Like, even if you were a good person I wouldn't give you a chance to be a good person because, I don't know, you might kind of try to do something grimey to me. . . . I'm open to trusting them more.

In addition to getting to know people from different backgrounds, students also were given the opportunity to work on social action projects with diverse peers. An Indian female student highlighted how rare this was in her school experience:

> Intergroup helped me learn how to work in a group of a lot of people you don't know. Usually when I've worked in groups it's with people I've chosen, people I'd usually interact with. But this group, there's only a couple of people I usually would talk to or spend time with. I hadn't even seen a lot of the people in Intergroup before. So it really taught me that there are other people in the school and how we can all get along. Because everyone is cool in their own way, you just have to get to know them.

Although her school was racially diverse, she had few opportunities to work with peers from different backgrounds in her regular classes. When given the option, she was inclined to work with people she already had relationships with, but was glad to be pushed outside of her comfort zone. Her comments provide evidence of the importance of creating structured spaces within schools in which young people can get to know students beyond their own social circle. Indeed, many of the students reported an interest in continuing to pursue opportunities that would expose them to diverse groups of people.

Moreover, students reported that their expanded acceptance of students who were different form them facilitated more self-acceptance as well. A black female student said:

> It kind of shows you that people can be accepting, and you don't always have to hide everything. [Before] I hid *more* than everything! I hid myself. Ya'll kinda changed my plans up a little bit! I'm supposed to be isolated [laughing]! I'm not isolated no more! My mom's happy about that. She's like, "I'm kinda happy you was in that group cause you were kinda scaring me a little bit for a minute."

These kinds of transformations are particularly rewarding for students as well as program staff.

Challenging Stereotypes

The relationships that I-SCA students formed with each other created opportunities for participants to challenge many of the stereotypes they held about various groups. An Asian male student reflected, "I made a lot of strong relationships and strong friendships through Intergroup, so I think Intergroup has really helped to kind of break the stereotype and break the barrier between different races, different ethnicities, different genders, and brought us all together." As a result, students indicated that they were less likely to make quick assumptions about each other based on perceived differences. The Hungarian, female student remarked, "I think the most important thing I learned is like don't judge people. Cause like a lot of people judge people based on how they look. And just get to know them better before making a judgment about them." By the end of the program, students were quite reflective about the ways in which stereotypes permeate our lives. Many had an increased awareness of the fact that they held stereotypes, but simultaneously acknowledged a newfound ability to challenge their own assumptions. A black, female student described her efforts to challenge stereotypes in the following way:

> Yeah, I think we all hold stereotypes. Obviously, I'm working to get past those. Like, I know this is so cliché, but I do try to look at people as an individual and not see the stereotypes. But there are some that it's easy to fall into, and you kind of have to consciously go against those. Like they say

about "south side kids," that they're all ghetto, and they always get pregnant. So it's like really hard to go against that stereotype when it's true, but it's like "Ahhh!" you just have to tell yourself, "No. It's a stereotype. There are people who are not doing that. You can't say they're all like that."

A white, male student expressed a similar internal conflict regarding his efforts to overcome his own stereotypes:

I think I hold stereotypes. Yeah, I'd say I do. But not, I don't know how to particularly answer this question, but yeah I do. I think I analyze them more when I think of it, and I'll go over it in my head and break it down and see it's not really true. I still have similar thoughts, but I notice that I'm thinking them.

An Asian, male student specifically identified how I-SCA allowed him to put the stereotypes he held in larger social context:

Before Intergroup I had certain stereotypes, and I'm pretty sure everybody does, but through Intergroup I was able to learn why some of these things happen. So like, *why* I have the stereotypes I have. Some of the stereotypes I had have gone away through Intergroup. Through learning more about other people, it's gone away.

All of these students were thinking much more critically about the stereotypes they had and were consciously working to interrupt them. A black, male student discussed how his new interest in building relationships across difference helped him overcome stereotypes:

Like those people, gothics. What they call themselves? Emo? I know this one girl and she is emo. She's really nice and doesn't seem too depressed or anything like that or nothing like negative like that. You see people just walking around with their black on holding their head down and you think, "Oh, they're so depressed and negative about life." But then I got to know her.

For this young man, who had previously talked about his mistrust of people he did not know and his hesitance to reach out across difference, becoming willing to talk to someone who seemed very different allowed him to challenge negative assumptions he held about an entire group of students in his school.

Interrupting Bullying and Discriminatory Behavior

Not surprisingly, students reported being less likely to engage in bullying and discriminatory behavior. Students said they no longer talked about each other negatively or made offensive jokes. Many said that they were more likely to consider how their words and actions might affect others. A black, male student said that the pride of being in I-SCA facilitated this process:

I learned a lot. Like I learned how to be respectful to others and more of a leader now when it comes to walking around the school. Because when I walk around the school I just feel like, you know, "I'm in Intergroup." And I take what I learned from there and put it into school. So now it's like instead of talking about people, I'm helping people.

A white, male student also expressed being more aware of what he says and how it might be interpreted by others:

I watch what I say more, and I think before I speak. Not that I didn't do that before, but I do it more now. Because I just don't want to offend anyone. Because someone could be going through something in the moment and I could say something that would be offensive to them and just make their problems so much worse.

A number of our students who had previously been culprits of bullying behavior said that they were less likely to do so after participating in I-SCA. Moreover, many reported being more likely to interrupt discriminatory and bullying behavior among peers when they witnessed it. An Indian female student discussed her own transformation around issues of bullying and discrimination:

Well, I mean whenever people used to say racist jokes or something, usually I used to laugh along or something, you know I would just go with it. I wouldn't say anything. But now it's like kind of offensive to me. It's sad that it wasn't before, but I couldn't help it. But now, it's like I will say something if it offends me. . . . I feel like [my peers] might value and respect me a little more because I've been standing up.

This student's ability to change her own problematic behavior and interrupt the problematic behavior she witnessed is particularly promising for considering how to create schools that are safe for students from all backgrounds.

Developing Critical Consciousness and a Commitment to Social Justice

In addition to building successful interpersonal relationships across difference and being less likely to engage in bullying behavior, participants also reported an increased critical consciousness of larger social issues, particularly with regard to race and class. A white, male student said:

I think I recognize discrimination more than I did before. . . . I learned that there's a lot of problems that are deeper than just what they appear to be like on the surface. Like even in the school, all the racial problems. I guess I kind of noticed them, but I never realized how deeply integrated into our school they actually are. . . . It's everywhere.

I-SCA brought greater awareness to this young man about how the racial tensions he had casually noticed were a part of a larger school culture in which segregation and racist commentary were commonplace. As a result, he was able to consider ways in which these sorts of behaviors could be interrupted.

A few of our structured activities in particular made students question their assumptions about social mobility in the United States. Early in the year, a middle-class, white, female student strongly expressed her opinion that poor people are poor because they simply are not willing to work hard. However, after participating in a simulation activity in which she was in a low social position she came to a different conclusion:

I learned that you really don't know what you're talking about unless you experience it yourself. It's like, I come from a family with money so that's never been an issue and then, in the game, I had nothing. That really, that really kind of got to me like a big wham because I'm thinking, oh man, I was wrong!

After the activity, in which she became so frustrated she ceased trying to improve her social status, she realized that the nature of the U.S. economic system is much more complex than she had originally assumed. A black, male student from a low-income background had a similarly powerful experience doing this activity. While the white, female student questioned her worldview of how social stratification happens, the black, male student was able to use this experience to make sense of things he had already witnessed in his daily life:

> Well, [the game] really made me think. Because like me living on the [side of town] with a lot of people in the poverty level, it kind of makes me think about the township and how the city revolves. And like, the people on [that side of town], basically they stay [there] most of their lives. It makes me feel bad because like, I think most people should have equal opportunities. I mean I felt [that] before, but it wasn't as bad until I did the activity. I was in it, and I was like, "Man, this is crazy."

By the end of the program, some students were able to analyze their daily observations structurally. One white, female student reflected on her observations of racial segregation in various classes in the school:

> Like if you're in an AP class, there's usually only one or two non-white students. Or, I shouldn't say non-white, [I should say] African American students, because it's predominantly Caucasians and Asians. And I think that ... has to be evidence of some systematic, you know, oppression of some sort, you know. Like why else would it be that way?

While this student did not fully understand why there were racial differences in academic tracks, she was beginning to connect her experience to trends in the larger social system. Rather than assuming that certain students were smarter than others—an assumption many of the participants made early on in the year—she saw systematic oppression as the more likely culprit.

These students not only became more aware of discrimination and inequality, they also grew more committed to doing something about it. A white, male student expressed his new conviction about the importance of social justice, "It's important to want to fight [for social justice] because it's just bad to have stuff like discrimination and stereotypes. It really belittles everybody who ... just everybody." He was able to see that discrimination and stereotypes not only negatively affect those who are targeted, they ultimately demean everyone involved.

As facilitators, we have witnessed youth who struggle to achieve, pay attention, or behave appropriately in traditional classroom settings become attentive and engaged students, thirsty for knowledge in I-SCA. We have seen student participants discuss difficult, politically charged topics in ways that are thoughtful, respectful, and oriented toward social justice. Alumni have told us that what they learn in I-SCA prepares them for life in a way that their traditional classes do not. Others have said that they want to be "intergroup teachers" when they grow up. We hope that by engaging a critical mass of young people in dialogue, we can create more supportive, tolerant, non-violent schools.

Program Challenges

Our work has fostered real successes in affecting students individually and schools more broadly. However, in our many years facilitating dialogues in high schools, we have also experienced the unique challenges of conducting this kind of critical education in public school settings. In the final sections of this paper we present some of these challenges, with the hope of helping other practitioners do dialogue work in high schools.

Creating and Sustaining Partnerships with Schools

I-SCA has been successful for the past eight years because it is truly a partnership between the high schools and the University. We have worked hard to ensure that our project is collaborative in planning, sustainability, and overall facilitation. Since I-SCA staff are outsiders to the schools it is essential that schools have a stake in the program in order to sustain it. In order to achieve this goal, we provide opportunities for I-SCA stakeholders to get to know each other and work together toward program implementation. We hold regular advisory meetings with all adult personnel. We also host a meeting at the end of the year in which students in the program share their experiences with the superintendent of their school district. Beyond these meetings, stakeholders are in constant communication with each other throughout the school year.

We have been very intentional in making sure the collaborative process among adults is in line with our vision of critical education. By creating a space in advisory meetings that feels safe, values the individuals in the room, and provides them with an opportunity to share their own experiences, we are able to give adult stakeholders a clearer picture of ways in which I-SCA can be life-changing for everyone involved. Our own experiences working as facilitators with other programs and organizations has convinced us that it is important to "practice what we preach" with regard to group process in order to build a successful partnership and run an effective program. In turn, we utilize dialogue skills in planning and advisory meetings and spend significant time building personal relationships with administrators and school liaisons. We have found that when the adults have a functioning relationship, our work with students is more effective, rewarding, and sustainable.

Nonetheless, there are limitations to our partnership. One challenge we continually face is the restricted availability of administrators. In our experience, school administrators are excited about the possibilities of more critical approaches to education that proactively address tension and conflict in their schools. However, many public schools function in a state of triage, particularly in light of the demands they face from the state and federal government to raise test scores. Most of the administrators we work with spend their days reacting to emergencies, leaving them little time to think proactively about preventative, innovative approaches to reoccurring problems—particularly regarding student interactions and school culture.

As we add schools to the program it becomes challenging to find times when all of the administrators and liaisons can be available for advisory meetings. One solution has been to meet with two of the four schools at a time or with individual administrators and program staff. This allows us to stay connected while respecting the limitations of everyone's schedule, but presents a challenge to maintaining the group cohesion and process we value so much.

In more recent years, we have had to deal with high rates of administrative turnover in each of the three districts where we work. There have been new principals, new assistant principals, and new superintendents, which has made sustaining supportive relationships even more challenging. In a few instances we have struggled to effectively convince incoming administrators that they should continue to support the program. Other schools have been in such flux that we have not been able to identify to whom we should be talking in order to gain support for the program at a district and school level.

Building a Sustainable Funding Base

We have learned that reliable funding is necessary to facilitate a successful program. Currently, our program staff devote significant time and energy to I-SCA but receive little, if any, compensation. While we have been fortunate to find skilled, competent people willing to do this work, we realize that this is not a sustainable or replicable model and are in constant conversation about ways to create a more reliable funding base.

Our partnership with schools is one essential component of our funding model. The high schools generally cover the school-related expenses of the program, including a small stipend for the school liaison and lead facilitator, snacks for our weekly meetings, and transportation and lunch for the two school exchange field trips. While we have been pleased with the financial contributions the schools have made and view these contributions as an indication of their commitment to the program, funding remains one of our most pressing concerns, particularly since public schools are dealing with significant budget cuts. When our districts' budgets are cut, so is the I-SCA budget. In the past few years the amount that each school contributes has dropped significantly. In the coming years this may be an even greater struggle in Michigan where the current budget includes significant cuts to education (Luke, 2011).

Working through a university has provided us with funding opportunities that would not otherwise be available. We have gotten small research grants to cover expenses and have had success every year applying for community foundation and University grants. Nonetheless, being a university program also has been a challenge. Research grants have sustained our program. However, they cannot do so long term. Although there are researchers on our team, we do this work because we think it is essential to creating a more socially just world and are not interested in continually developing new research questions for grant renewals. Unfortunately, we have not had success with larger foundation grants. In particular, those foundations interested in community work have told us that while they find our program appealing, our affiliation with a wealthy university has hindered their desire to give us funds.

One solution we have considered is moving toward a non-profit model around which we can build a donor base, incorporate fundraising activities, and more successfully apply for grants targeted at community-based organizations. This model might also allow us to more fully involve parent volunteers, teachers, and administrators in funding sustainability efforts. However, being a program of the University carries reputational and tangible advantages. This affiliation initially encouraged some of the schools we work with to partner with us. In sum, we have a number of considerations to wrestle with as we move forward with building a more sustainable funding model.

Recruiting a Diverse Group of Students

High schools are segregated spaces. Athletes hang out together. Students in drama hang out together. Young people in band hang out together. In schools that are racially diverse, friend groups are often racially segregated (Tatum, 1997). As a result of this segregation, there is a sense that certain programs—particularly those that are voluntary—are for particular kinds of students. We have to work hard to ensure that I-SCA is considered a place for everyone. In schools where there is a history of conflict between particular subgroups of students, recruitment can be even more challenging. Specifically, we attempt to recruit a group of students who reflects the demographic make-up of each particular school. This requires using personal relationships to encourage students to join, having former students go to classes in groups that are diverse in race, class, gender, and social group to recruit new students, and asking for teacher nominations of diverse students. Even these efforts are not always enough. Some years the demographic makeup of I-SCA reflects the diversity of each school, while in other years a particular school's I-SCA might be dominated by one race or gender.

In addition, while we are intentional about creating a diverse group, the program is still limited to the students who can stay after school regularly. Unfortunately, working students, students who take care of siblings after school, and students involved in other activities have difficulty participating.

Recruiting a Diverse Group of Adults

Like the student group, we strongly value the importance of creating a group of adult leaders who reflect a range of backgrounds. Many dialogue programs and social justice education trainings are led by people who are white, middle-class, and highly educated. While a number of these programs are successful, we believe that the diversity of the adults is just as significant as that of the students. We think it is particularly important for high school students and personnel to see facilitators model the kinds of cross cultural relationships we are helping them create. For high school students, it can be especially rewarding to see themselves reflected in the faces of the people running the program. We also believe that planning is more effective and innovate when a diversity of experiences and opinions are represented.

Our experience has shown us that the race and gender of the adults involved have a significant impact on who prospective student participants think I-SCA is for. This may be especially true for recruiting in high school settings where many young people are in the process of identity development (Kroger, 2007). Luckily our program staff is quite diverse and includes a white man, a white woman, a black man, a black woman, and a native Hawaiian man. Our ages range from late 20s to 80s. Our diversity has been a real strength in making connections with school administrators, teachers, and students.

Nonetheless, we have had difficulty transferring this diversity to the school level. Although we have always had gender diversity among our school liaisons, we have struggled with racial diversity among school liaisons and social work interns. The school liaison is usually picked by the school administrator, so we have little control over the social identities of that person. We also have fairly limited control over the identities of social work interns, who change every year. While our interns go through an application and interview process, the pool of social work students at the University is primarily white and female. Not surprisingly, in most years, our interns are also white females. Over the past few years, three of our four school liaisons have been African American (although one of these schools has had a long-term, white, female, parent volunteer who attends sessions and planning meetings). In addition, this year (2010–2011) three of our four school administrators were also African American, and for the first time we had two African American interns, one man and one woman, and one white, female intern. This greatly shifted the racial make-up of the adults involved in the program, especially in the faces that student participants regularly see. As a result, at one of our I-SCA schools, which had historically had majority white participants, more than half of the participants are now students of color. We cannot always control the diversity among adults, but it is something we seriously consider when assigning interns and staff to particular schools.

Defining Appropriate Roles for Adult Stakeholders

Involving multiple adults with various levels of knowledge and skill can be complicated. Over the years we have learned to be very clear about each person's role in facilitating the program, both in logistics and the dialogue process. We have also learned that quality dialogue facilitation, particularly with high school students, requires a complex set of skills and experiences. Although we would like for all of the adult stakeholders to facilitate dialogues, we have found that most do not have the training or experience to do so effectively.

In the early years of our program, school liaisons worked in partnership with social work interns to facilitate sessions. Two problems emerged over time. First, the basic orientation and training we provided to school liaisons were not enough to prepare them to effectively deal with all the issues that arose in dialogue. Many teachers had their own struggles with identity that, at times, caused them to undermine the experiences of the students. For example, in a 2007 dialogue session, two black, male students told the group that they had been held at gunpoint by two police officers who accused them of looking like suspects in a robbery. The teacher facilitator said that their experience was not about race; he believed that he was just as likely to have had their experience as a white male. One of the authors was put in the position of having to mediate between the teacher facilitator who had invalidated the students' experience and ignored the realities of racial profiling, and the students who were upset by the teacher's comments.

In addition to lack of knowledge, power dynamics between students and adult staff can also create challenges. We have found that if the school liaison is also the teacher of a participant, he or she may unwittingly transfer the dialogue experience to the classroom in a way that makes the student uncomfortable. Ultimately, we decided that school staff may not be best suited to facilitate the dialogues—particularly if they are not adequately trained.

We face similar challenges with the knowledge and skill of social work interns. Some years we get interns who are very knowledgeable and competent. Other interns have had limited experience with dialogue and program coordination and have struggled to grasp core concepts and complete logistical tasks. In a number of instances, interns have not reflected upon their own social identities enough to facilitate the process effectively with students. Interestingly, many of our most challenging interns have returned in subsequent years and reported that they have grown both as individuals and as facilitators as a result of their work with us. However, while we want to provide interns with opportunities for personal growth, we are also reluctant for them to practice on the high school students. Peer facilitators also range in skill and knowledge greatly. We have had amazingly insightful and responsible peer facilitators who have done a great job of moving the group forward, as well as peer facilitators who have struggled to move beyond the role of participant.

Our solution to the variation in skill and knowledge of our interns and peer facilitators has been two-fold. First, we ensure that one of our program staff is available to serve as the primary facilitator at each school. As our staff has limited capacity, and facilitation and planning require a significant time commitment, we rely on school liaisons, interns, and peers for many logistical tasks, such as, keeping track of program records, updating our data management system, taking notes and typing agendas to document program sessions, disseminating and collecting student consent forms, reserving meeting spaces, and coordinating field trips and snacks. Second, we have created a structure in which adults who are interested in receiving additional training have the option to do so and are able to take on more facilitation responsibility as their capacity and confidence increase. These training sessions happen throughout the year concurrently with the student program. While the trainings are a good first step and provide liaisons and interns with regular dialogic feedback, they still do not engage liaisons and interns in the kind of rigorous, ongoing process that is necessary to truly prepare them to be great facilitators. Moreover, our small staff size limits our capacity to provide as many trainings as we would like.

Fitting into Current School Schedules

Thus far, I-SCA has functioned primarily as an on-site, afterschool program. This model has been successful in many ways. Because the program is on-site, it is viewed as a part of the school. Students and teachers see posters about I-SCA during the school day, hear announcements about it in the morning and afternoon, and often get to participate in the group's final social action project. In turn, many staff and students at the schools consider it to be a co-curricular activity that tackles pressing issues of conflict and discrimination that develop during the day. Hosting the program after school allows for trained, professional dialogue facilitators who do not hold teaching degrees to run the program. Students can participate for multiple years and can come from various academic backgrounds. It also eliminates the need to assign any kind of grade to students' participation or align our program with state curricula.

Running I-SCA as an afterschool program also has limitations. Less privileged students may not be able to stay after school. This is particularly true at our participating schools that do not provide any form of afterschool transportation. In addition, we find ourselves "competing" for participants with sports, credit recovery programs, afterschool tutoring, and other activities. This not only limits the students who can participate in our program, it also means that student participants shift slightly throughout the year as new activities begin and end.

However, our most pressing concern is that as an afterschool program we are limited in how much content we can deliver to students. Unlike university dialogue courses taken for credit, we cannot assign outside readings, give students assignments, or engage in long lectures about specific topics. Moreover, we have found that much of the literature that might be topically appropriate is not written at a level that would be comprehensible to most high school students. In turn, any content students receive is given to them during the dialogues and is garnered from their peers and facilitators.

As a result of the limited content that we are able to provide, we have at times feared that students will think of I-SCA as a "support group" rather than a social justice group. Figuring out how to address students' gaps in knowledge has been a real challenge. Our facilitators have had to take seriously how to help students build social justice knowledge in addition to building relationships—a difficult task when participants do not have a shared body of knowledge upon which to base their conversation. We have addressed this issue by making sure to give mini-content lectures during dialogues. In addition, we have extended the number of sessions from 15 to 20 in order to make time for videos and other educational materials that might increase their knowledge.

In theory, we would like for high school students to be given the opportunity to take a dialogue course for credit that would count toward graduation requirements. Over the past two years, we have even attempted to incorporate dialogue into the school day by facilitating a series of one-time, in-class dialogues in collaboration with English and Social Studies teachers. We believe that if I-SCA were a course, it would have even greater impact on student relationships and overall school climate and safety. In addition, it would address many of the issues we face with regard to accessibility and financial sustainability because I-SCA would simply be another class sustained by each school. However, in reality we have found that the limitations of curriculum, testing, teacher training, and the school-day structure make this very difficult, if not impossible. The major issue is one of facilitation. In order for I-SCA to be a course, teachers would likely have to facilitate the program. While we believe that teachers are capable of becoming great facilitators, our experience, as noted in previous sections, indicates that the majority do not currently have the skills to do so. Unfortunately, preparing teachers to be facilitators will take more training than most public schools and schools of education are willing and able to provide.

Illuminating Structural Inequality

We have found that by the end of the program our participants are able to understand fairly easily that they should treat each other better, that they should not judge each other based on perceived differences, and that they should not bully each other. However, we worry that they do not always understand how interpersonal relationships and experiences are connected to larger institutional structures. This is true for our most privileged students as well as for the students who come from very disadvantaged backgrounds. We have concluded that there are two main reasons for this. First, as noted in the previous section, we are limited in the amount of content we can deliver to students through outside readings and assignments. We have discovered that many of our participants simply lack the historical and social scientific knowledge to build an understanding of structural inequality, privilege, or oppression. For example, participants often say that they know the n-word is "bad" because of "history" but cannot verbalize why it is bad or much about the historical context in which it emerged.

Second, our students often have fairly limited life experiences to draw upon in dialogues, thus, connecting to ideas of structural inequality is difficult for them. We have largely addressed this challenge by being very intentional about the diversity of our program so that students are exposed to peers who have different experience and backgrounds than their own. However, this is not always enough. Many of our students do not have a strong sense of their family's socioeconomic positions or even whether or not their parents went to college. Many students have never worked, paid bills, voted, or paid attention to politics. Few have had exposure to religious beliefs outside of their own or have much awareness of students with disabilities. In addition, parents and teachers often do not provide young people with opportunities to engage in this kind of reflection. In turn, the idea that our country is systematically inequitable is new to most of our participants.

We also have students who have lived very adult lives. Some of our participants are the primary providers for their family. Others have moved multiple times a year their entire lives. Some have children. A few live completely independently. However, they are not necessarily able to connect their individual struggles to larger institutional structures—even at the school level.

Navigating a "Post-Racial" Era of Accountability

Most of the challenges discussed thus far focus on school-level limitations. However, it is important to take note of the political climate in which we are advocating for critical education and intergroup dialogue. In particular, there are two related issues with which we must contend. First, as mentioned previously, the educational reform movement in this country is focused on measuring success through standardized test scores and rewarding and punishing teachers and administrators based on the outcomes of those tests (Ravitch, 2010). Schools are under such strict mandates to focus on achievement, particularly in reading and math, that most simply are not able to devote time, energy, or resources to critical approaches to education. As one administrator told us, if we are not able to show how I-SCA raises test scores, we will have difficulty convincing superintendents and local school boards to value our work. Ironically, the narrowed focus on issues of accountability has occurred at the same time as national awareness of bullying and discrimination has increased.

The push toward more market-based and business models of education is also connected to a conservative trend in education that has made terms, like "social justice," "diversity," and "ethnic studies," politically controversial (Heybach, 2009; Lacy, 2011). In the state of Michigan, this sentiment trickled down to the policy level in the mid-1990s when the state repealed its multicultural education law (The Revised School Code Act 451 of 1976, 1995), further hindering the motivation of schools to engage in critical educational practices. We believe that the work we do is essential to address many pressing issues schools face and to help young people learn to communicate non-violently, build relationships across perceived difference, and combat social injustice. However, we worry the current educational climate will make this work increasingly difficult to implement, particularly in K-12 schools that do not have the same freedoms as universities.

CONCLUSION

Intergroup dialogue in high schools is a promising model of practice that has the potential to engage young people in educational experiences in which they learn to think critically about social inequality and individual discrimination and work collaboratively toward social justice and non-violent conflict resolution. Our quantitative and qualitative evaluations of the I-SCA program have found that participants build successful relationships with peers from diverse backgrounds, learn to resolve conflict and communicate more effectively, gain a better understanding of issues of social inequality, and are more committed to social change.

While these results show the potential of this work, in order to affect sweeping change within schools, broader groups of students, teachers, and administrators will need to be exposed to dialogue and critical education. In turn, we have worked to expand our influence beyond the afterschool program by utilizing dialogue to assist each of the four schools with issues of identity and difference during the school day. At one school, program staff members conducted a series of one-time classroom dialogues with 9th, 10th, and 12th grade students focused on racism and discriminatory language. At another they led the school-wide Martin Luther King Day Celebration two consecutive years. This year, a 5-week teacher dialogue on issues of race and class in the classroom was piloted at one of the schools with the hope of providing teachers with the tools to do this work in their classrooms. We are excited about the potential of these initiatives to touch even more students.

Despite this potential, there are unique challenges and limitations to working within high schools ranging from issues of funding and facilitation to federal and state policies that leave little room for this kind of work. While some of these challenges are unique to the state of Michigan and the schools in which we work, we believe that many of the lessons we have learned are applicable to high schools across the nation. In particular, issues of relationship building, recruiting diverse participants and adults, and figuring out successful ways to incorporate dialogue into existing school structures are challenges that all school dialogue practitioners will have to contend with.

Although the four schools discussed here are located in three school districts and are very different from each other in a range of ways, they do not reflect all schools in the United States. None of the schools are located in very small rural areas. In addition, none of them are in major U.S. cities. Moreover, our program relies on resources made available as the result of a partnership with a major university and depends on staff who volunteer much of their time. While our location and university affiliation make the program unique, we believe that many educators in a number of diverse school settings will find them applicable to their school.

In light of the marginalizing and oppressive experiences of many young people in our public schools, it would behoove administrators, teachers, and dialogue practitioners to think innovatively about the ways in which the practice of dialogue might be utilized to facilitate critical, multicultural, educational experiences for youth that systematically address injustice. Intergroup dialogue is a model of administrators, school staff, and practitioners working together to achieve this goal. We hope that our work will inspire others to consider ways in which they might institute dialogue in high school settings.

REFERENCES

Adams, M., Bell, L. A., & Griffin, P. (2007). *Teaching for diversity and social justice* (2nd ed.). New York, NY: Routledge.

Allport, G. W. (1954). *The nature of prejudice*. Cambridge, MA: Perseus.

Banks, J. A. (2001). Citizenship, education and diversity: Implications for teacher education. *Journal of Teacher Education, 52*(1), 5–16.

Banks, J. A. (2007). *Educating citizens in a multicultural society*. New York, NY: Teachers College Press.

Banks, J., & Banks, C. A. M. (2009). *Multicultural education: Issues and perspectives* (7th ed.). Danvers, MA: Wiley.

Bourdieu, P., & Passeron, J.C. (1990). *Reproduction in education, society and culture*. Thousand Oaks, CA: Sage.

Brikett, M., Espelage, D. L., & Koeing, B. (2009). LGB and questioning students in schools: The moderating effects of homophobic bullying and school climate on negative outcomes. *Journal of Youth and Adolescence, 38*(7), 989–1000.

Collins, P. H. (2000). *Black feminist thought: Knowledge, consciousness, and the politics of empowerment* (2nd ed.). New York, NY: Routledge.

Darling-Hammond, L. (2002). Defining "highly qualified teachers": What does "scientifically-based research" actually tell us? *Educational Researcher, 31*(9), 13–25.

Dessel, A. (2010). Prejudice in schools: Promotion of an inclusive culture and climate. *Education and Urban Society, 42*(4), 407–429.

Dobbie, D., & Richards-Schuester, K. (2008). Building solidarity through difference: A practice model for critical multicultural organizing. *Journal of Community Practice, 16*(3), 317–337.

Ellsworth, E. (1992). Why doesn't this feel empowering? Working through the repressive myth of critical pedagogy. In C. Luke & J. Gore (Eds.), *Feminism and critical pedagogy* (pp. 90–119). New York, NY: Routledge.

Flynt, S. W., & Morton, R. C. (2004). Bullying and children with disabilities. *Journal of Instructional Psychology, 31*(4), 330–333.

Freire, P. (1970). *Pedagogy of the oppressed* (M. B. Ramos, Trans.). New York, NY: Seabury.

Freire, P. (1998). *Teachers as cultural workers: Letters to those who dare teach.* Boulder, CO: Westview.

Garvin, C. (2008). Project program development and implementation. *Small Groups Research, 39*(1), 60–81.

Gay, G. (1997). The relationship between multicultural and democratic education. *Social Studies, 88*(1), 5–11.

Gay, G., & Kirkland, K. (2003). Developing cultural critical consciousness and self-reflection in preservice teacher education. *Theory into Practice, 42*(3), 181–187.

Giroux, H. A. (1988). *Teachers as intellectuals: Toward a critical pedagogy of learning.* Westport, CT: Bergin & Garvey.

Giroux, H. A. (2006). *The Giroux reader: Cultural politics and the promise of democracy.* Boulder, CO: Paradigm.

Gore, J. (1993). *The struggle for pedagogies: Critical and feminist discourses as regimes of truth.* New York, NY: Routledge.

Gurin, P., Peng, T., Lopez, G., & Nagda, B. A. (1999). Context, identity, and intergroup relations. In D. A. Prentice (Ed.), *Cultural divides: Understanding and overcoming group conflict* (pp. 133–170). New York, NY: Russell Sage.

Heybach, J. (2009). Rescuing social justice in education: A critique of the NACTE controversy. *Philosophical Studies in Education, 40*, 234–245.

hooks, b. (1994). *Teaching to transgress.* New York, NY: Routledge.

Johnson, D. W., & Johnson, R. T. (1996). Conflict resolution and peer mediation programs in elementary and secondary schools: A review of the research. *Review of Educational Research, 66*, 459–506.

Keesing-Styles, L. (2003). The relationship between critical pedagogy and assessment in teacher education. *Radical Pedagogy, 5*(1). [On-line]. Retrieved from http://radicalpedagogy.icaap.org/content/issue5_1/03_keesing-styles.html

Kroger, J. (2007). *Identity development: Adolescence through adulthood* (2nd ed). Thousand Oaks, CA: Sage.

Kvale, S. (1996). *InterViews: An introduction to qualitative research interviewing.* Thousand Oaks: Sage.

Lacy, M. (2011, January 7). Rift in Arizona as Latino class is found illegal. *The New York Times*, A1.

Ladson-Billings, G. J. (1995). Toward a theory of culturally relevant pedagogy. *American Education Research Journal, 32*(3), 465–491.

Lahelma, E. (2004). Tolerance and understanding? Students and teachers reflect on differences at school. *Educational Research and Evaluation, 10*(1), 3–19.

Lee, V., Croninger, R., Linn, E., & Chen, X. (1996). The culture of sexual harassment in secondary schools. *American Educational Research Journal, 33*(2), 383–417.

Luke, P. (2011). Michigan House approves massive education funding cut, critics say it "balances the budget on the backs of our children." Retrieved from http://www.mlive.com/politics/index.ssf/2011/05/michigan_house_approves_massiv.html

Michigan State Board of Education. (2004). *Policy on quality character education.* Retrieved from http://www.michigan.gov/documents/Character_policy_final_94134_7.pdf

Michigan State Senate. (2011). *State fiscal agency: Per pupil statutory funding history for schools: FYs 1993–94, 1994–95, and 2000–01 to 2010–11.* Retrieved from http://www.senate.michigan.gov/sfa/Departments/DataCharts/DCk12_FoundationHistorySincePropA.pdf

Morrow, R. A., & Torres, C. A. (1995). *Social theory and education: A critique of theories of social and cultural reproduction.* Albany, NY: State University of New York Press.

Nagda, B. A., Kim, C., & Truelove, Y. (2004). Learning about difference, learning with others, learning to transgress. *Journal of Social Issues, 60*(1), 195–214.

Pettigrew, T. F. (1998). Intergroup contact theory. *Annual Review of Psychology, 49*, 65–85.

Poteat, V. P., & DiGiovanni, C. D. (2010). When biased language use is associated with bullying and dominance behavior: The moderating effects of prejudice. *Journal of Youth and Adolescence, 39*(10), 1123–1133.

Ravitch, D. (2010). *The death and life of the great American school system: How testing and choice are undermining education*. Philadelphia, PA: Basic.

The Revised School Code Act 451 of 1976. (1995). MCL 380.1173-1174a. Repealed by Act 289. Retrieved from http://www.legislature.mi.gov/documents/mcl/pdf/mcl-act-451-of-1976.pdf

Roberts, R. A., Bell, L. A., & Murphy, B. (2008) Flipping the script: Analyzing youth talk about race and racism. *Anthropology and Education Quarterly, 39*(3), 334–354.

Rosenbloom, S. R., & Way, N. (2004). Experiences of discrimination among African American, Asian American, and Latino adolescents in an urban high school. *Youth & Society, 35*(4), 420–451.

Saldaña, J. (2009). *The coding manual for qualitative researchers*. Thousand Oaks, CA: Sage.

Schoem, D. L., & Hurtado, S. (2001). *Intergroup dialogue: Deliberative democracy in school, college, community and workplace*. Ann Arbor, MI: University of Michigan.

Schoem, D., Hurtado, S., Sevig, T., Chesler, M., & Sumida, S. (2001). Intergroup dialogue: Democracy at work in theory and practice. In D. L. Schoem & S. Hurtado (Eds.), *Intergroup dialogue: Deliberative democracy in school, college, community and workplace* (pp. 1–21). Ann Arbor, MI: University of Michigan Press.

Shor, I. (1992). *Empowering education: Critical teaching for social change*. Chicago, IL: University of Chicago Press.

Smith, E. B. (2009). Approaches to multicultural education in preservice teacher education: Philosophical frameworks and models for teaching. *Multicultural Education, 16*(3), 45.

Spencer, M., Brown, M., Griffin, S., & Abdullah, S. (2008). Outcome evaluation of the intergroup project. *Small Groups Research, 39*(1), 82–103.

Tatum, B. D. (1997). *Why are all the black kids sitting together in the cafeteria? And other conversations about race*. New York, NY: Basic.

The Revised School Code Act 451 of 1976. (2011, Dec. 6). *MCL 380.1310b*. Retrieved from http://www.legislature.mi.gov/(C(nm3t3455sret3y3joceu0o45))/mileg.aspx?page=getobject&objectname=mcl-380-1310b&query=on&highlight=bullying.

Tinker, B. (2006). Language to open hearts and minds: The war within. *The Portland Alliance*. Retrieved from http://www.theportlandalliance.org/2006/apr/openhearts.htm

Weis, L. (Ed.). (2008). *The way class works: Readings on school, family, and the economy*. New York, NY: Routledge.

Weiss, R. S. (1994). *Learning from strangers: The art and method of qualitative interview studies*. New York, NY: The Free Press.

Zine, J. (2001). Muslim youth in Canadian schools: Education and the politics of religious identity. *Anthropology and Education Quarterly, 32*(4), 399–423.

Zúniga, X., Nagda, B. A., & Sevig, T. D. (2002). Intergroup dialogues: An educational model for cultivating engagement across differences. *Equity and Excellence in Education, 35*(1), 7–17.

Racial Pedagogy of the Oppressed: Critical Interracial Dialogue for Teachers of Color

Rita Kohli

Santa Clara University

Brazilian education activist Paulo Freire (1970) argues that to create social change, oppressed people must have critical consciousness about their conditions, and that this consciousness is developed through dialogue. He theorizes that dialogue allows for reflection and unity building, tools needed to transform society. When considering racial oppression in K-12 schools, racial minority teachers have an often-untapped insight and power to transform classrooms and schools (Kohli, 2009). Connected through a commonality of racial oppression, it is important for teachers of color to engage in cross-racial dialogues about manifestations of racial injustice in K-12 schools and to develop strategies for change. Utilizing Freire's conceptual lens and a critical race theory (CRT) framework, this article highlights critical race dialogue about the educational experiences and observations of 12 black, Latina, and Asian American women enrolled in a teacher education program. Through cross-racial discussions, the women were able to broaden their multicultural understanding of racial oppression as well as strategize solidarity building among diverse students in urban classrooms. This study demonstrates knowledge and insights of teachers of color and highlights the importance of interracial dialogue in school contexts.

Several years ago, I was invited to attend a professional development session at a middle school in South Los Angeles serving mostly black[1] and Latina/o students. The goal of the workshop was to guide teachers in resolving racial fights between youth on campus. In addition to student tension, dialogue revealed that the staff, made up of mostly teachers of color, also carried tension with their peers of differing racial and ethnic groups. While they were concerned about the student fights, the staff rarely interacted cross-racially and many teachers at the school had deep-rooted stereotypes and misconceptions about other races. They were unable to see commonalities of their oppression and, thus, had limited abilities to support students in solidarity building. All of these factors raised several questions for me: While teachers of color often have insight to racism in schools because of their own racialized realities (Kohli, 2009), how can they facilitate cross-racial understanding and unity among students without having cross-racial understanding themselves? And more importantly, how can teachers of color challenge racial oppression if they do not recognize racism as a systemic problem that impacts all people of color?

Over the past decade, there has been increased recognition of and need for teachers of color (Ladson-Billings, 2001; Villegas & Irvine, 2010). Teachers of color comprise only 10% of the teaching force (National Collaborative on Diversity in the Teaching Force, 2004) and are drastically underrepresented even in districts serving almost entirely students of color (California Department of Education, 2011).

Many researchers have highlighted proven models for increasing the presence of teachers of color, including "homegrown" programs, in which students from urban communities are recruited to teach in the same or similar school district (Hudson, 1998; Irizzary, 2007; Lau, Dandy, & Hoffman, 2007; Sakash & Chou, 2007). This focus on recruitment, however, is complicated by low retention rates for teachers of color. Because teachers of color are placed at higher rates in underserved schools with many structural challenges, they experience faster burnout rates than white teachers (Achinstein, Ogawa, Sexton, & Freitas, 2010). Additionally, having limited networks of support in addressing school challenges can take its toll on the retention of teachers of color (Achinstein et al., 2010; Dingus, 2008; Hernández Sheets, 2001, 2004; Kohli, 2009).

Even with concern around retention, scholars have repeatedly demonstrated the benefits of having teachers of color in classrooms serving students of color, including heightened cultural understanding, connections to the community, and culturally relevant teaching (Kambutu, Rios, & Castaneda, 2009; Martinez, 2000; Quiocho & Rios, 2000; Williams, Graham, McCary-Henderson, & Floyd, 2009). Sleeter (2008) argues that the more students encounter teachers from similar racial and cultural backgrounds, the more culturally relevant and meaningful their education will be. This cultural match has been connected to many benefits, such as increased equity for bilingual students and college access for underrepresented students (Cammarota, 2008).

Although the presence of teachers of color is extremely important for the holistic success of students of color, as demonstrated in the example above, not all teachers of color are culturally equipped to serve multiracial classrooms and promote racial justice. In prior articles, I have argued that critical race reflections of their schooling can support the development of race-conscious practices in teachers of color (Kohli, 2008, 2009). This article broadens this argument to demonstrate how critical interracial dialogue between teachers of color can be instrumental in their growth as educators in multicultural contexts.

To prevent racial climate issues similar to the school I describe above, teachers must have cross-racial understanding. Teachers of color also must have an independent space to dialogue about manifestations of racial injustice and strategies for change. This does not mean that white educators cannot work to challenge racial inequity in schools (Picower, 2009), but rather that, at times, separate spaces are needed to discuss racial privilege and oppression (Kohli, 2009). Utilizing Freire's (1970) concept of critical consciousness and a CRT framework, this article highlights insights gained through the dialogue of 12 black, Latina, and Asian American women enrolled in a teacher education program. The discussions broadened the participants' multicultural understanding of racial oppression and encouraged a pedagogy of cross-racial solidarity building. This model can inform teacher preparation and school professional development practices.

FREIRE'S CRITICAL CONSCIOUSNESS

Brazilian education activist Paulo Freire (1970) argues that to create social change people must have conscientization or critical consciousness. Freire defines critical consciousness as a state in which people are aware of social inequality, understand their place in that inequality, and take action against oppressive elements in society. He theorizes that critical consciousness is developed through a "problem-posing" method, where learners come to their own understanding of injustice through a facilitators' questioning. This study takes a Freirian approach to developing a critical cross-racial understanding about racial oppression with teachers of color from varying racial, ethnic, and cultural groups. Facilitated with a problem-posing framework, participants were given space to reflect on their own experiences, build cross-racial connections, and think through how to respond to racial oppression in school.

CRITICAL RACE THEORY

Critical race theory (CRT) also is used to frame this study. Developed in the 1970s in the field of law, CRT helped to bring racism into central focus through the experiences of people of color. As it extends into other disciplines, including education, it shifts analysis of racism from an individual problem to a structural issue, replicated by institutions within our society. CRT in education is guided by the following five tenets (Solórzano & Delgado Bernal, 2001):

1. Centrality of Race and Racism: All CRT research within education must centralize race and racism, as well as acknowledge the intersection of race with other forms of subordination.
2. Challenging the Dominant Perspective: CRT research works to challenge the dominant narratives, often referred to as majoritarian stories.
3. Commitment to Social Justice: CRT research must be driven by a social justice agenda. Critical race theorists define social justice research as work that (a) responds to the oppression of people of color, which includes intersections between racism, poverty, sexism, and dehumanization; (b) aims to eliminate those oppressive conditions; and, (c) is centered around the empowerment, healing, and liberation of people of color (Solórzano & Delgado Bernal, 2001; Yosso, 2005).
4. Valuing Experiential Knowledge: CRT scholars believe in the power of story. Building on the oral traditions of many indigenous communities of color around the world, CRT research values the experiences and narratives of people of color when attempting to understand social inequality.
5. Being Interdisciplinary: CRT scholars believe that the world is multi-dimensional and research about the world should reflect multiple perspectives.

In this study, these five tenets are used as a framework to engage the voices of women of color educators with a focus on race, racism, and its intersection with gender, culture, and class. All data in this article were collected through qualitative focus-group interviews. Drawing on the fields of Ethnic Studies and education, this project utilizes theory and empirical research to demonstrate how critical race dialogue of diverse teachers of color can improve their understanding and articulation about racial inequity and, in turn, how this critical consciousness can influence their pedagogy. In 2002, Smith-Maddox and Solórzano paired CRT with problem-posing methods and case study to build racial consciousness with, as they described, mostly privileged students. This study uses these two frameworks to strengthen race consciousness in racially oppressed people. As women of color, the participants share struggles and strengths that are often undertheorized within teacher education. This project challenges dominant narratives that lead communities to believe that racial divisions among people of color are normal and acceptable. Instead, this article emphasizes the unifying dialogue between women from multiple racial and ethnic groups as an example of solidarity building against racial injustice in schools.

METHODS

CRT and Freire's theory of critical consciousness also guide the design of the study. These frameworks encourage researchers to not see participants as data sources alone. Rather those who share their stories in interviews are people with voices, complex lives, and struggles (Pizarro, 1998). CRT and Freirian methods demand that research must benefit the participants and their communities (Kohli, 2009; Pizarro, 1998; Smith-Maddox & Solórzano, 2002).

Focus group interviews explored the narratives of women of color enrolled in an urban social justice-based teacher education program in Los Angeles, California. These interviews were designed as dialogues to learn about the impact of racism in schools from a multiracial perspective and provided a safe space for women of color educators to build community and develop as teachers. The women were prompted to reflect on the role of race and racism in their educational experiences with the goal of heightening their consciousness about racial injustice. Additionally, because teachers in multicultural schools need to understand how racism overlaps and diverges for different racial, ethnic, and cultural groups, the focus groups also were structured for participants to improve their cross-racial understanding.

Sample

Focus group interviews were conducted in 2007 with Latina, black, and Asian American female teachers. Human subjects approval was granted before any recruitment or data collection took place. I recruited from teacher education courses and potential participants were asked to fill out a form of interest after a short presentation. The 12 participants were narrowed from a larger pool of 43, based on racial and ethnic diversity and interest in the study. The women taught a range of subjects and grades, were between the ages of 22 and 26 years old, and varied in their comfort discussing race and racism. Each woman was purposefully assigned to a six-person group with two black, two Latina, and two Asian American participants to ensure diversity of race and ethnicity. Participants were engaged in three focus group interviews. All names used in this article are pseudonyms or were kept the same at the request of the participant. (See Appendix A for demographic details.)

Positionality

Although there has been an effort to recruit racial minorities into the teaching profession, the majority of teacher education faculty continues to be white (Ladson-Billings, 2001, 2005). In addition, most education research and teaching strategies are written by and for white teachers (Bennett, Cole, & Thompson, 2000; Ladson-Billings, 2005). As a South Asian American woman and former teacher, I had a unique positionality in facilitating dialogues with women of color preservice teachers. Within the focus group interviews, many of the women articulated that very little of their teacher preparation was taught by faculty of color and felt "relieved" to have a "safe space" to discuss their lived experiences with race and racism. I also hold a Ph.D. in Race and Ethnic Studies in Education and I am well versed in the shared realities with racism that communities of color have and continue to endure; thus, I was able to facilitate connections among the experiences of women from varying racial and ethnic groups.

In constructing interracial dialogue about topics of such a sensitive nature, my identity seemed to bring strengths to the work as articulated above. However, there were also several limitations involving my role as sole investigator. Being the only facilitator of the focus group interviews, the dialogues were shaped both by my perspective about race and racism and my facilitation style. Additionally, beyond member checking practices, the analysis was mine and was limited by the biases of my positionality.

Data Collection and Analysis

While many traditional research paradigms offer a firmly structured interaction between researcher and participant (Berg, 2011), there are emerging design structures that promote intergroup dialogue (Zúñiga, Nagda, Chesler, & Cytron-Walker, 2007; Zúniga, Nagda & Sevig, 2002) and active intervention through models of action-research (Cammarota & Fine, 2008; Pizarro, 1998). Building on these frameworks, I designed and facilitated all focus group interviews as critical interracial dialogues—discussions between diverse participants that analyze inequity and injustice—as it relates to race and schooling. The first focus group was a discussion of race and racism in the preservice teachers' own K-12 educational experiences; the second addressed their observations with race and racism in the schools in which they work; and the third was a space for them to strategize how to address race and racism in their classrooms. Although one goal was to collect data, framed by CRT and Freire's theoretical lens, the questions were also posed as a way for the women to learn from each other's reflections and to gain interracial understanding about racism and schooling. Some sample questions included:

1. What experiences did you have with discrimination in school in your K-12 education?
2. How did these experiences impact your self or worldview?
3. Many of you mentioned that you wanted to hear how others defined race and racism. So, let's discuss this, what is race? What is racism?
4. Do you see race and racism playing out in the school that you currently work in?
5. Does it manifest in similar or different ways from your childhood experiences?

All data were transcribed throughout the study and were reviewed by participants. Grounded theory argues for themes to emerge from data (Flick, 2009); CRT research encourages a co-construction of sense making of data with participants (Pizarro, 1998). Building on these methodologies, participants were asked to reflect on sessions at the end of each focus group to gauge their interpretation of the dialogues. In compiling the findings, I read and re-read all the transcripts, noted reoccurring themes and themes related to the research questions, and sorted the data into categories (Flick, 2009). For this article, I am sharing select findings from the larger study.

In particular, the women articulated that this study proved important for their personal and professional growth, helping them develop a more complex understanding of racism in schools. I highlight two main ways in which participants described critical interracial dialogue as beneficial to their development as educators: (1) enhancing cross-cultural understanding of racial oppression and (2) re-thinking race in the classroom.

ENHANCING CROSS-CULTURAL UNDERSTANDING
OF RACIAL OPPRESSION

Even though many women in the study shared that discussions of racial discrimination with family and friends were commonplace, most revealed that those conversations tended to happen in racially insular settings. Many of the women had parallel experiences with racism within their education, however very few had ever discussed these events in multiracial settings. Without experience talking about race and racism with people who differ racially or ethnically, a majority of the women felt that they had limited understanding of manifestation of racism in communities outside their own.

Because the focus groups were the first time many women had participated in cross-racial sharing of racialized experiences and perspectives, it improved their multicultural understanding of racial inequity. The participants articulated that this was important to their development as critical educators of multiracial or multicultural classrooms. In this section, I share several examples of cross-cultural engagement and understanding that occurred within the interviews, through discussions of: (1) names and ethnic pride, (2) accents, and (3) knowledge of self.

Names and Ethnic Pride

The dialogue often revealed differences or parallels in the racialized experiences of the multicultural group of women of color. While each woman has a unique and complex story, the conversation allowed for black, Latina, and Asian American educators to understand that racism is something that affects all of their lives. Regardless of whether the conversations were specifically tied to the classroom, by learning where their racialized experiences diverge and overlap, participants were able to gain valuable exposure to multicultural perspectives.

One's identity and self-concept are developed through parents' accent, intonation, and pronunciation of their name (Sears & Sears, 2003). Additionally, names can connect children to their ancestors or their country of origin or ethnic group and often have deep meaning or symbolism for parents and families (Kiang, 2003; Kohli & Solórzano, 2011). Elaine shared in a focus group that she witnessed a teacher who was mispronouncing the names of one of her recent immigrant students. She expressed how the teacher's disregard for the student's name and identity reinforced to the student that his culture was not important. Sharing this encounter with the focus group led into a personal discussion about names, in which Elaine and Janet both revealed that they did not have names representative of their ethnic heritage because their parents were afraid of situations similar to what Elaine had seen while student teaching. Even though they understood that their parents were trying to protect them from racism, they both expressed how their names made them feel disconnected from their culture and roots. Janet shared,

> I still complain to this day, "Why didn't I get a more Mexican name?" People always ask me, "Wait, you're Mexican and your and your name's Janet...? Not even Janette...?" and I'm like, "No, Janet."

Don't ask me what my dad was thinking. He's been here since he was seven, so I think for him it was more that he went through a lot growing up, and [he] didn't want [me] to have to go through the same. (Janet)

Empathizing with Janet's longing to have a name reflective of her cultural heritage, Elaine responded, "I don't even have a Korean name . . ., my name is [Elaine] . . . I never really understood why [my mom] didn't go for a Korean name, but it's probably also to make it easier." Like Janet, Elaine shared that her mom had a lot of problems because of her Korean name when she moved to the U.S. and most likely did not want her daughter to experience the same difficulties. Elaine, however, endured a different set of challenges; she felt her "easier," non-Korean name disconnected her from Korean culture and the Korean community. Despite their different backgrounds, an open discussion about these experiences allowed Janet and Elaine to see cross-racial commonalities in their personal struggles with ethnic identity.

Deanna and Alexis, the two black women in the group listened carefully as Janet and Elaine spoke. They then shared that because African Americans were robbed of cultural names due to slavery, the women could not exactly relate to Janet and Elaine's struggles. They felt this was important to consider when understanding the names of many African Americans. Alexis shared, "[For us] it's even more complicated because we were brought here as slaves, and we were given new names, so none of can really be like, 'Oh, I'm from the Zulu tribe.' No [African American] really knows what their ancestors' names are, so there's nothing to reclaim from that." Deanna agreed. She furthered the conversation by explaining that some African American parents try to connect to their heritage by naming their children words from an African language. While she had a name that was commonly used in her community, she wanted others in the group to understand that when African American parents give their children names that may seem "arbitrary," they are often trying to distance themselves from the European names imposed through slavery.

Although Alexis and Deanna had different experiences with the importance and origin of names than Janet and Elaine did, they all felt that names have an important connection to culture. The women agreed that whether names were stripped during slavery or rejected today out of fear of discrimination, names are a subtle way in which the European culture is prioritized over the culture of racial minorities. They expressed that hearing each other's stories helped them to realize that this is not an individual experience but rather plays out in multiple racial and ethnic communities and is tied to racism.

Accents

An accent is a way of speaking, typically tied to a particular geographic location, often intersecting with factors, such as race, class, culture, and language. Speaking like the community in which you are part of has value and capital; it can play a major role in acceptance into that community or context (Perry & Delpit, 1998). In our education system, however, the way a student speaks is often wrongly tied to intelligence, and Standard American English (SAE) is typically valued and deemed superior (LeMoine & Hollie, 2007; Perry & Delpit, 1998). During one of the focus group interviews, several of the women began to engage in a discussion about their "accents." They shared that their manner of speech often played a role in the way they were stereotyped in school.

Unfortunately, many participants felt they had internalized the racist ideology embedded in these stereotypes, and this had affected how they saw themselves both culturally and intellectually.

JoAnn grew up in a working-class Latina/o neighborhood in the South side of East Los Angeles. Although she spoke English, when she got to her predominantly white college, she received many comments about her "accent" from her white peers. These remarks made her very self-conscious, and she felt inferior to her peers.

> Through elementary, junior high, and high school, we all kind of had the same accent. We all sounded the same. When I started college, I would get white guys telling me, "Oh, you sound like a chola, but don't worry, it's cute!" They already start putting you in a box, and you begin [to] internalize that. Like, I don't speak Standard English, I don't have a white accent. I'm never gonna fit in.

Although JoAnn identified as a scholar, she was labeled a chola when she got to college. "Chola" is a Spanish word used to describe a female "gangster." It bothered JoAnn that even though she had worked very hard in school, her peers reduced her identity to a stereotype about her community. This experience made a lasting impact on JoAnn, and began to affect her academic engagement. When one endures racism, the impact does not always end when the incident is over. Racism can seep into the psyche, and affect the way a person sees him- or herself and the world around him or her, a phenomenon defined as internalized racism (Cross, 1995; Kohli, 2008; Perez Huber, Johnson, & Kohli, 2006). JoAnn began to internalize the racist stereotype that her East Los Angeles Chicana/o speech was connected to violence rather than to schooling. She began to feel that she was not as smart or competent as her peers and, thus, stopped participating in class.

After JoAnn shared this emotional story about internalizing racism, Juliana responded by describing her own negative experiences with accents. She explained that growing up as a Latina in a predominantly black neighborhood, she dropped Spanish and practiced speaking English in order to fit in. But as a light skinned woman without a Latin American accent, whenever she said that she was Mexican, no one believed her.

> I don't speak Spanish that well. I always practiced my English because I grew up in a predominantly black neighborhood in Watts. That used to keep me from some communities growing up. [People] would tell me I wasn't Mexican enough because I didn't speak Spanish that well. I remember always feeling, where do I go then? I'm not really accepted anywhere.

Much like the borderlands feeling Anzaldúa (1999) describes for Mexican Americans living near the border, in trying to straddle fitting in within two separate communities, Juliana felt torn between two worlds. She felt pressure to let go of her culture and assimilate to the "accent" of the black majority around her, which left her not feeling "Mexican enough" when she was around her community. This tension between her two realities left her feeling confused and isolated.

Imani grew up in Santa Monica speaking Standard English and similar to Juliana, felt marginalized from the black community based on her accent. Imani attended diverse schools but was never around a significant black population. Whenever she would get around peers of her own racial group, they would label her as "white."

> What you are saying is reminding me of what black people thought about the way that I talked in my own community. They would tell me, "You talk white," and label me the girl from Santa Monica. [It would hurt] when black people would tell me that. I wanted to know that culture so much, 'cause I didn't experience it that much in Santa Monica. But to not really be embraced by them, and just kind

of be pushed into a box—okay, you're not like other black people, so you just can't kick it—that was kind of hard for me.

Like JoAnn, Julianna and Imani were judged and deemed outsiders based on their accents. However, it was their own racial peers that rejected them. As Imani shared, not to be embraced by her racial community because of the way she spoke had a negative effect on her racial identity. Despite her daily reality as a black woman, she saw herself as less black than her peers.

Ashley added to this discussion by sharing another perspective about being a black woman with a "white" accent. Always attending predominantly white schools, Ashley was embraced by her teachers for speaking in a way that was considered "white." She was often pitted against the few black children in her school by being told that she was different and better.

> The way I spoke—because it was considered white—was embraced by my teachers. I was often put up on a pedestal for being the model black student. I was always taught, "Well, Ashley's different." Or "Ashley's very articulate; her vocabulary is extraordinary." They would always push that the way I speak is much different than those other [black] kids. But once in a while I would slip up, and say "ain't" or something, and my classmates would be like, "Ew! Why are you talking like that? YOU don't talk like that."

Unlike the other women who were made to feel bad for their accents, Ashley was made to feel that she was better than other black children because she spoke in a way that was considered white. Teachers affirmed for Ashley an intellectual hierarchy in which black American English was deemed inferior to SAE. Based on her race and the way she spoke, she was told she was "different," "articulate," and "extraordinary" compared to her black peers. These statements are hard to pinpoint as racial insults because they can seem like compliments. In actuality, they are subtle forms of racism that critical race theorists have labeled racial microaggressions (Solórzano, Allen, & Caroll, 2002). Through these comments, Ashley's teachers and classmates reinforced the idea that Standard English is superior and forms of speech that deviate from this are inferior. As a result, Ashley internalized this racism and believed that she was superior to her less "articulate," less "extraordinary," black counterparts.

JoAnn, Juliana, Imani, and Ashley shared that it was useful to reflect on their experiences with racism and accents in a supportive setting. While complex and different from each other, it was important for them to hear that their struggles with speech and accent existed across race, ethnicity, class, and context. They expressed that hearing each other's narratives helped them to heal from their own experiences with racism around the manner in which they speak, and offered them greater understanding to how power and privilege are tied to language and culture.

Knowledge of Self

Continuing the discussion of internalized racism, the women began talking about the lack of cultural representation in the curriculum in their history classes. As a Sikh, South Asian American in a predominantly white school, Sonia believed that much of her lack of esteem about her community was rooted in the absence of curriculum about her culture. She shared,

> Looking back on my childhood, I used to actually wish I was white ... I remember saying that out loud to my sister. "I wish we were white. Why was I born into this family?" I used to blame my

ethnicity for all the problems in my life ... And I think part of it was just not learning about my own community in our history classes. I think having a lack of curriculum about my community kind of made me feel like it wasn't important.

Sonia internalized the bias of Eurocentric history curriculum, which she felt led to feelings of inferiority.

Juliana similarly expressed that she never learned her history. Compounding her experiences with speech outlined above, she also felt that a lack of education about Latina/o history in school led her to feel her identity was insignificant:

Within schools, history was always taught as black and white, and I used to think, then what am I? I used to have a lot of black friends and just wish I was black 'cause it would just put me in a category. I just hated being in between, just not knowing. I mean, I knew I was Mexican American, but no one else perceived me as that, so it's as though I wasn't that at all. And I remember coming to college and not knowing who Cesar Chavez was. I had always heard his name, but it was never even mentioned in school at all.

Juliana shared that in several instances in college she had pretended to know who Cesar Chavez was because she had felt shame and embarrassment over not knowing. She became quite emotional with the realization that she had carried the burden of this shame even though it was not her fault. Overwhelmed, she posed the question to the group, "How can we get students to keep their self-esteem when they don't learn their history in school?"

Kimmy responded that her strategy was adopted from her parents. In the 1940s, both her parents' families were forced into Japanese internment camps, losing all of their property and material wealth. Due to this traumatic encounter, Kimmy's mother and father took painstaking efforts to teach their daughter Japanese and Japanese American history and culture. With a great deal of encouragement and support from her parents, Kimmy dedicated every project in school that she could to the struggles and accomplishments of her ethnic community.

Ashley was struck by Kimmy's perspective and was surprised to hear that Kimmy knew so much about her own history as a child. Like Sonia and Juliana, she was not taught her history in school but expressed that unlike other racial and cultural minorities, African Americans only have so much knowledge they can access about their history and heritage.

I feel like with my Latino students, a lot of them are Salvadorian and Mexican, and they do have a sense of pride 'cause I feel like they do have a connection, somehow. Either from their parents not being born here, or their community ... I don't feel like there's a sense of pride [for African American] students because we don't know where we came from.

In a reflection after the focus group discussion, Kimmy shared that hearing Ashley's perspective helped her to rethink her understanding about her own life and the lives of African Americans.

It was important for me to hear everyone's experiences. I especially liked hearing Ashley talk about not having [an understanding of her] heritage because this was something that I was aware of in the African American community, but I had never really considered. It inspires me to ask her about that, because it is the opposite of what I feel I have undergone during my lifetime, and would love to hear more about.

Hearing a perspective different from her own inspired Kimmy to learn more. Before the discussion, she had not thought about the limited access African Americans have to pre-slavery history. She also never truly appreciated how privileged she was to have access to her own history. Through this exchange, she gained a newfound sensitivity to her own identity, as well as the identities of her future African American students.

Based on Freire's (1970) model of problem-posing dialogue and CRT's focus on challenging dominant narratives about race, the interracial focus groups helped women of color educators contextualize individual experiences with race and racism into a more structural analysis. The women were able to think through manifestations of oppression across race and culture, which offered new ways of seeing and understanding the world. This growth was useful to them personally, as well as in their development as teachers of multicultural classrooms.

RE-THINKING RACE IN THE CLASSROOM

The dialogues in this study provided space for participants to think about how their experiences fit into larger structures of racial oppression. As teachers, these reflections were particularly important because they translated to a more critical approach to their pedagogy and practice. As it relates to names, accents, and knowledge of self, the women felt a heightened awareness around these topics and brainstormed strategies to possibly address or challenge their manifestations in schools. For example, to maintain a respect for all students' names, they discussed having students write out the phonetic spelling for the pronunciation of their names on the first day of school, and playing community building games centered around the meaning behind students' names. To create equity around speech and language, they suggested having students translate phrases from black English to standard English to show how they are both valid forms of speech and brainstormed ways in class for Spanish speakers and English speakers to work together and feel equally valued.

In addition to addressing specific issues from their own experiences within their classroom, the dialogues also created a space where teachers began sharing, deconstructing, and problem-solving other issues of racial injustice in their teaching. For example, Kimmy reflected on a classroom incident when a black student said to a Latino peer, "Speak English! This is America." Kimmy shared that she did not know what to do in the situation so she just glossed over it. She also revealed that she was "ashamed" that she did not have the tools to deal with racial tension in the classroom. Although Kimmy took on the burden of not effectively addressing the racial climate, this poorly facilitated pedagogical moment happened because she was not prepared to discuss race with students proactively, or at all. Kimmy said to her peers, "I need to start thinking of potential situations and ways that I can positively and constructively deal with them so I will be ready when they come up." The women responded by thinking through steps with Kimmy to improve the racial climate of her multiracial math classroom.

Sonia expressed that she could not figure out how to engage her African American students about immigration during history class, so she came to the group wanting help. Collectively, the women agreed that the racial disconnects between black and Latina/o students was a pressing issue that many of them faced. They decided to create lessons to expose students to a Latina/o and African American shared struggle, as it relates to immigration. They developed four themes within the unit: (1) Migration and Integration, (2) Comparing Slave Legislation to Citizenship and Naturalization Legislation, (3) Parallels between Deportation in Immigrant Communities and Incarceration in African American Communities, and (4) Resistance: Marching to Know your

Rights. The women pooled their subject matter knowledge and cultural perspectives to develop interdisciplinary ways of approaching issues of racial injustice and cross-cultural understanding.

Deanna shared with the group that through the dialogues she learned that cross-cultural relationships truly challenge stereotypes. In response, her group decided to plan lessons that cultivated interactions among students through anthologies for their classrooms. The women created both middle- and high school units that involved students interviewing each other, learning about each other's lives, and compiling a book that brought everyone's experiences together. Based on their guided interracial interactions, the participants were inspired to formally apply critical interracial frameworks to their teaching.

While many racial minority teachers have insights into race and racism through personal experience, it cannot be assumed that they are fully equipped to navigate and facilitate race relations within diverse classrooms and schools. In this study, teachers were entering the profession with varying degrees of comfort discussing racial inequity. Carolina was not comfortable talking about race or racism when she started the study. During the dialogues, she had a difficult time articulating issues of race and struggled to characterize her own racial identity. However, recognizing that these topics are important to teaching and that they may come up in her classroom, she was excited by the opportunity to develop a language around racial oppression.

Juliana was comfortable talking about race and racism before the study, but because of limited critical race discussions in her classes, she was disappointed in her teacher education program. She felt that none of her peers really understood or cared about the problems that her students faced. Juliana shared that the interracial dialogues helped her connect with other teachers and commented, "Before meeting up with this group, I felt that no one in [my teacher education] remembered the struggle and the students. This group helped me get re-connected to that." By discussing issues of race and racism among a diverse and committed group of educators, Juliana felt "re-connected" to the passion of educational justice that initially brought her to teaching.

Several women agreed that the discussions re-kindled their enthusiasm for education. Kimmy made the comment that she felt "inspired" after the focus group discussion. Sonia mentioned that she felt "pumped!" JoAnn initially expressed that she felt isolated from other teachers based on her perspective. She commented, "There isn't really a space where people can have these critical conversations about racism that I feel are important in order for people to grow as individuals." However, whenever she met with her group for the interviews she felt "rejuvenated" and motivated to make social change through teaching. She also expressed a sense of relief having the opportunity just for people of color to discuss these issues. She shared,

> People of color—we need to act a certain way in white space—and it's like we're accommodating white people. It's something I deal with, too, because you don't want to sound angry, but I think these are really emotional issues for some of us. Going into schools of color, it's very emotional. It's very personal, so, yes, I'm going to talk about it with emotion. I'm not attacking you. Maybe for her, or for those students, it just seems something very abstract, but for me, it's very personal, it's very emotional.

Seeing youth of color enduring oppression can be an emotional experience, particularly for teachers from similar communities (Kohli, 2008). In her program, JoAnn felt criticized by white peers for discussing issues of racial oppression in an emotional way. For that reason, it was important for her to have an independent space with peers who could relate to these emotions.

Ashley agreed that she could be herself in this separate space. She reiterated the importance of being able to dialogue about race and racism without the presence of white teachers.

> If we included white teachers in the discussion, I feel like a lot of us would feel the need to censor, or maybe bring down what we were saying because we don't want to make them feel uncomfortable. I had actually been approached by a student in our cohort [who said] that the way I spoke made white people feel uncomfortable, and made them withdraw. And so [in class] I'm constantly wondering, is [changing how I speak] something that I need to do?

Several of the participants agreed and expressed that the presence of racial privilege in a discussion about racial oppression would compromise the openness of the dialogue.

IMPLEMENTATION OF THIS CROSS-RACIAL MODEL

The women's voices reiterate the need to include critical interracial dialogues in the education of teachers of color. However, there are several limitations in the application of this study that are important to note. Teacher education programs and schools do not always have balanced racial demographics where all racial minority teachers can feel equally represented in the conversation; thus, dialogues would not be equal between racial and ethnic groups as they were in this study. Additionally, urban school contexts are often plagued with urgent issues and limited resources; thus, there is rarely the personnel to facilitate intimate dialogues with small groups of teachers or the time to explore personal histories and experiences. Even with these limitations, it is important to consider what aspects of the interracial dialogue highlighted in this study can by recreated in both teacher education programs and school-based professional development.

First, creating independent spaces for white teachers and teachers of color to discuss racial privilege and oppression can enhance racial awareness. Similar to the data presented here, Picower (2006) documented dialogues with white teachers about race and racism and suggests that white teachers were perhaps more open and honest about their racial privilege in racially insular settings. Based on these findings, it may be productive for teacher education programs or schools to separate white teachers and teachers of color for dialogues about race and then bring them back together to debrief the discussions. This could be done as a one-time workshop or as an ongoing series.

Second, teacher education programs and schools should be committed to hiring diverse faculty and administrators with a comfort in facilitating conversations on race and racism. Often, teacher education programs and schools operate without a clear definition of social justice (Cochran-Smith, 2004; Kohli, 2009). As revealed through the power of the dialogues, teacher education should include diverse faculty that are equipped to guide critical discussions about racial injustice. Likewise schools must provide professional development opportunities by diverse school leaders with similar expertise.

Third, teachers of color have unique insights about racial inequality in schools that should be acknowledged and built upon within their learning (Kohli, 2008, 2009). Building on Freire's (1970) framework, teachers must reflect on their experiences and those of other oppressed people to develop a critical consciousness. Paired with CRT, critical interracial dialogue about race in schools can support the development of critical consciousness in teachers of color, which can enhance their critical and cross-racial classroom practice.

CONCLUSION

Paulo Freire (1970) theorizes that only through critical dialogue can oppressed people develop a critical consciousness. As CRT emphasizes, because of the reality of race in their lives, there is a need for teachers of color to discuss their racial oppression (Freire, 1970; Martinez, 2000; Kohli, 2009). This study connects these models to provide a space for critical interracial dialogue among teachers of color. The teachers expressed that reflecting in a multiracial setting allowed them to improve their cross-cultural understanding and to understand racism as a larger system of oppression. In addition, these reflections inspired them to apply cross-racial lenses to their curriculum and pedagogy. Because racially representative teachers are important to the academic and emotional well-being of youth of color (Sleeter, 2008; Sleeter & McLaren, 1995; Kohli, 2008), teacher education programs and schools must not only acknowledge and appreciate the wealth of their experiences but must also support their development to navigate the racial climate of schools and successfully teach in diverse classrooms.

NOTE

1. The terms black and African American are used throughout this paper to reference people of African descent. African American refers to people with a historical connection to the United States, while black references a broader diasporic community. In the presentation of data, some participants subscribed to one label or another, while others used the terms interchangably. The use of these terms in reference to participants is guided by their self-designation.

REFERENCES

Achinstein, B., Ogawa, R. T., Sexton, D., & Freitas, C. (2010). Retaining teachers of color: A pressing problem and a potential strategy for "hard-to-staff" schools. *Review of Educational Research, 80*(1), 71–107.

Anzaldúa, G. (1999). *Borderlands/La frontera: The new mestiza.* San Francisco, CA: Aunt Lute Books.

Bennett, C., Cole, D., & Thompson, J. (2000). Preparing teachers of color at a predominantly white university: A case study of project. *Teaching and Teacher Education, 16*(4), 445–464.

Berg, B. (2011). *Qualitative research methods for the social sciences.* San Francisco, CA: Pearson Education.

California Department of Education. (2011). Retrieved from http://www.ed-data.k12.ca.us/App_Resx/EdDataClassic/fsTwoPanel.aspx?#!bottom=/_layouts/EdDataClassic/profile.asp?level=06

Cammarota, J. (2008). *Sueños Americanos: Barrio youth negotiating social and cultural identities.* Tucson, AZ: The University of Arizona Press.

Cammarota, J., & Fine, M. (2008). *Revolutionizing education: Youth participatory action research in motion.* New York, NY: Routledge.

Cochran-Smith, M. (2004). *Walking the road: Race, diversity, and social justice in teacher education.* New York, NY: Teachers College Press.

Cross, W. E. (1995). The psychology of nigrescence: Revising the Cross model. In J. G. Ponterotto, J. M. Casas, L. A. Suzuki, & C. M. Alexander (Eds.), *Handbook of multicultural counseling* (pp. 93–122). Thousand Oaks, CA: Sage.

Dingus, J. (2008). "I'm learning the trade": Mentoring networks of black women teachers. *Urban Education, 43*(3), 361–377.

Flick, U. (2009). *An introduction to qualitative research* (4th ed.). Thousand Oaks, CA: Sage.

Freire, P. (1970). *Pedagogy of the oppressed.* New York, NY: Continuum.

Lau, K. F., Dandy, E. B., & Hoffman, L. (2007). The Pathways Program: A model for increasing the number of teachers of color. *Teacher Education Quarterly, 34*(4), 27–40.

Hernández Sheets, R. (2001). Trends in the scholarship on teachers of color for diverse populations: Implications for multicultural education. *Equity and Excellence in Education, 34*(1), 26–31.

Hernández Sheets, R. (2004). Preparation and development of teachers of color. *International Journal of Qualitative Studies in Education, 17*(2), 163–166.

Hudson, M. J. (1998). Linking school and community to build national recruitment and preparation programs for teachers of color: Emerging leadership qualities. *Education and Urban Society, 31*(1), 62–72.

Irizarry, J. G. (2007). Home growing teachers of color: Lessons learned from a town-gown partnership. *Teacher Education Quarterly, 34*(4), 87–102.

Kambutu, J., Rios, F., & Castaneda, C. (2009). Stories deep within: Narratives of U.S. teachers of color from diasporic settings. *Diaspora, Indigenous, and Minority Education, 3*(2), 96–109.

Kiang, P. N. (2003). Voicing names and naming voices: Pedagogy and persistence in an Asian American Studies classroom. In V. Zamel & R. Speck (Eds.), *Crossing the curriculum: Multilingual learners in college classrooms* (pp. 207–220). Mahwah, NJ: Erlbaum.

Kohli, R. (2008). Breaking the cycle of racism in the classroom: Critical race reflections from future teachers of color. *Teacher Education Quarterly, 35*(4), 177–188.

Kohli, R. (2009). Critical race reflections: Valuing the experiences of teachers of color in teacher education. *Race, Ethnicity and Education, 12*(2), 235–251.

Kohli, R., & Solórzano, D. (2011). Teachers, please learn our names!: Racial microagressions and the K-12 classroom. Unpublished manuscript.

Ladson-Billings, G. (2001). *Crossing over to Canaan: The journey of new teachers in diverse classrooms.* San Francisco, CA: Jossey-Bass.

Ladson-Billings, G. (2005). *Beyond the big house: African American educators on teacher education.* New York, NY: Teachers College.

LeMoine, N., & Hollie, S. (2007). Developing academic English for standard English learners. In H. S. Alim & J. Baugh (Eds.), *Talkin black talk: Language, education, and social change* (pp. 43–55). New York, NY: Teachers College Press.

Martínez, E. (2000). Ideological baggage in the classroom: Resistance and resilience among Latino bilingual students and teachers. In E. T. Trueba & L. I. Bartolomé (Eds.), *Immigrant voices: In search of educational equity* (pp. 93–106). Lanham, MD: Rowman & Littlefield.

National Collaborative on Diversity in the Teaching Force. (2004). *Assessment of diversity in America's teaching force: A call to action.* Washington, DC: Author.

Perez Huber, L., Johnson, R. N., & Kohli, R. (2006). Naming racism: A conceptual look at racism in U.S. schools. *Chicana/o Latina/o Law Review, 26*, 183.

Perry, T., & Delpit, L. (Eds.). (1998). *The real Ebonics debate: Power, language and the education of African American children.* Boston, MA: Beacon.

Picower, B. (2006). The unexamined whiteness of teaching: How white teachers maintain and enact dominant racial ideologies. Unpublished doctoral dissertation. New York University, New York, NY.

Picower, B. (2009). The unexamined whiteness of teaching: How white teachers maintain and enact dominant racial ideologies. *Race and Ethnicity in Education, 12*(2), 197–215

Pizarro, M. (1998). Chicana/o power! Epistemology and methodology for social justice and empowerment in Chicana/o communities. *Qualitative Studies in Education, 11*(1), 57–80.

Quiocho, A., & Rios, F. (2000). The power of their presence: Minority group teachers and schooling. *Review of Educational Research, 70*(4), 485–528.

Sakash, K., & Chou, V. (2007). Increasing the supply of Latino bilingual teachers for the Chicago public schools. *Teacher Education Quarterly, 34*(4), 41–52.

Sears, W., & Sears, M. (2003). *The baby book: Everything you need to know about your baby from birth to age two.* New York, NY: Little Brown.

Sleeter, C. (2008). Preparing white teachers for diverse students. In M. Cochran-Smith, S. Feiman-Nemser, & J. McIntyre (Eds.), *Handbook of research in teacher education: enduring issues in changing contexts* (3rd ed., pp. 559–582). New York, NY: Routledge.

Sleeter, C. E., & McLaren, P. (Eds.). (1995). *Multicultural education, critical pedagogy and the politics of difference.* Albany, NY: State University of New York Press.

Smith-Maddox, R., & Solórzano, D. (2002). Using critical race theory, Paulo Freire's problem-posing method and case study research to confront race and racism in education. *Qualitative Inquiry, 8*(1), 66–84.

Solórzano, D. G., Allen, W. R., & Caroll, G., with Ceja, M., Dinwiddie, G., Guillory, E., González, G., & Yosso, T. (2002). Keeping race in place: Racial microaggressions and campus racial climate at the University of California, Berkeley. *Chicano-Latino Law Review, 23*, 15.

Solórzano, D. G., & Delgado Bernal, D. (2001). Examining transfomational resistance through a critical race and LatCrit Framework: Chicana and Chicano students in an urban context. *Urban Education, 36*(3), 308–342.

Villegas, A. M., & Irvine, J. J. (2010). Diversifying the teaching force: An examination of major arguments. *Urban Review, 42*(3), 175–192.

Williams, E. R., Graham, A., McCary-Henderson, S., & Floyd, L. (2009). "From where I stand": African American teacher candidates on their decision to teach. *Educational Forum, 73*(4), 348–364.

Yosso, T. (2005). Whose culture has capital? A critical race theory discussion of community cultural wealth. *Race, Ethnicity and Education, 8*(1), 69–91.

Zúñiga, X., Nagda, B. A., Chesler, M., & Cytron-Walker, A. (2007). *Intergroup dialogues in higher education: Meaningful learning about social justice. ASHE Higher Education Report Series,* 32(4). Hoboken, NJ: Wiley.

Zúñiga, X., Nagda, B., & Sevig, T. D. (2002). Intergroup dialogue: An educational model for cultivating engagement across differences. *Equity & Excellence in Education, 35*(1), 7–17.

APPENDIX A

Participants' Demographic Data

Name	Group	Ethnicity	K-12 School Demographics	Grade/Subject
Alexis	2	African American	White private middle school/black and Latino HS	Black and Latina/o high school/English
Ashley	1	Black, African American	Predominantly white	Predominantly black middle school/science
Catherine	2	Taiwanese American	Middle-class predominantly Asian	Latina/o high school/math
Carolina	2	Mexican American	Working-class Latino elementary/predominantly white suburban high school	Predominantly Latina/o elementary
Deanna	2	Black, African American	Predominantly Asian American elementary/predominantly black HS	Predominantly black elementary
Elaine	2	Korean American	Predominantly Asian American schools	Latina/o and Asian American elementary
Janet	2	Mexican American	Predominantly white elementary/Latina/o & Filipino middle and high school	Predominantly Latina/o elementary/ESL
JoAnn	1	Chicana	Working-class Latino	Predominantly Latina/o elementary/ESL
Juliana	1	Chicana	Working-class black	Black and Latina/o high school/English (same HS she attended)
Kimmy	1	Japanese American	Predominantly white	Latina/o, black and Asian high school/math
Imani	1	Black, Ugandan/African American	Diverse middle-class	Latina/o and black high school/social studies
Sonia	1	South Asian	Upper-middle-class white	Latina/o and black high school/social studies

Supporting Critical Dialogue Across Educational Contexts

Tasha Tropp Laman and Pamela Jewett
University of South Carolina, Columbia

Louise B. Jennings
Colorado State University, Fort Collins

Jennifer L. Wilson
University of South Carolina, Columbia

Mariana Souto-Manning
Teachers College, Columbia University

We dedicate this article to our good friend and colleague, Jennifer Wilson, a person with whom we loved to think and laugh and write. Through an act of violence, her life was taken away from us on August 28th, 2011.

This article draws upon five different empirical studies to examine how critical dialogue can be fostered across educational settings and with diverse populations: middle-school students discussing immigration picture books, a teacher study group exploring texts on homelessness, a teacher education class studying critical literacy, working class adults in a culture circle in Brazil interrogating systems of poverty, and teens in youth organizations discussing their photo-essays that challenge negative stereotypes of youth. In this paper, we analyze discursive practices that fostered critical dialogue across these settings. In doing so, we seek to describe practices that can support practitioners as they facilitate critical dialogue with learners and one another in order to become more critically engaged participants in their own communities.

As colleagues engaged in critical pedagogy and critical literacy, we have puzzled together about practices that best support learners of all ages in understanding how structures of power, privilege, and oppression are socially constructed and how those structures could be deconstructed and transformed. Examining transcripts from our own classrooms and research sites, we recognized the central role of dialogue in this critical work. We saw, across these transcripts, how participants were engaged in what we came to call "critical dialogue"— identifying, challenging, and reframing status quo discourses that can then be acted upon in new ways that challenge oppression and open opportunities for transformation (Jennings, Jewett, Laman, Souto-Manning,

& Wilson, 2010). Our article draws upon five different empirical studies to examine how critical dialogue can be fostered across educational settings. These five studies examine dialogue in diverse settings and with diverse populations: middle school students discussing immigration picture books, a teacher study group exploring texts on homelessness, a teacher education class studying critical literacy, working class adults in a culture circle in Brazil interrogating systems of poverty, and teens in youth organizations discussing their photo-essays that challenge negative stereotypes of youth.

Critical dialogue relates to intergroup dialogue as a "form of democratic practice, engagement, problem-solving, and education involving face-to-face, focused, facilitated . . . discussions occurring over time" (Schoem, 2003, p. 216). Intergroup dialogues focus on bringing together people from "two or more social identity groups with a history of conflict or potential conflict" (Zúñiga, Nagda, & Sevig, 2002, p. 7) to examine their differences, which are embedded in privilege and power and to work toward shared meanings and actions for social justice (Nagda & Gurin, 2007; Nagda, Gurin, Soresen, & Zúñiga, 2009). "By encouraging open and reflective communication about difficult topics, especially issues of power and privilege, intergroup dialogues help students build skills for developing and maintaining relationships across difference" (Zúñiga et al., 2002, p. 7). Critical dialogues focus not on solving conflicts and developing relationships between different cultural groups but on involving participants of varying and shared social identities in examining issues of power, privilege, and oppression toward a goal of individual and social change. For example, a group of working class adults might meet regularly to critique the oppression of the minimum wage and determine individual and social actions toward a more equitable economic structure These two related forms of dialogue share a common core of bringing people together in a facilitated learning environment to engage in open, deliberative dialogue aimed at critical reflection, consciousness-raising, and collaboration in order to strengthen individual and collective capacities to promote equity and social justice.

Here, we analyze discursive practices that fostered critical dialogue across these five settings. We do so from the perspective that dialogue is often imperfect and unfinished because all human interactions shape and are shaped by issues of power, including but not limited to, gender, identity, race, class, and age (Fairclough, 2003; Habermas, 1987; Wodak, 2001), as is evident in the cases from which we draw. With that in mind, through our analysis across five settings, we seek to inform practices of critical dialogue in a range of contexts. We describe common features and components across settings as we seek to support practitioners to facilitate critical dialogue with learners and one another. In doing so, we believe that educators can become more critically engaged participants in their own communities—in other words, to engage in praxis (Freire, 1970), as we explain in our conceptual framework.

CONCEPTUAL FRAMEWORK

Our concept of critical dialogue draws heavily on the work of Paulo Freire (1970, 2005). We have found that Freire viewed praxis as dialogue that "engages community members in critically unmasking invisible ideologies embedded in institutional structures and processes, thereby laying the groundwork for both new understandings and actions on a personal and social level" (Jennings & Da Matta, 2009, p. 217). We have carefully examined participants' discourse to locate moments and segments of critical dialogue where individuals were naming, reflecting, and questioning status quo discourses, as well as shifting and reshaping them into new, more equitable discourses. This work responds to the call of Comber (2001), who urges those who are committed to critical literacy in education to "build more detailed accounts of such practices as they are negotiated" (p. 280) rather than solely describe critical learning activities or focus on their outcomes.

We use the term "critical dialogue" to describe the discursive work of praxis that involves constructing, deconstructing, and reconstructing knowledge of status quo discourses. When participants engage in critical dialogue, they draw on and share their own narratives—perspectives constructed through and informed by their social, cultural, and lived experiences. Those narratives are shared by other participants and include texts that may lead participants to deconstruct status quo discourses, reconstruct their understandings in more complex ways, and construct new ways of being and understanding the world (Jennings, Jewett et al., 2010). Therefore we see critical dialogue as potentially transformative for individuals and society.

By acknowledging the process of de/re/constructing, we reframe the term "critical" by moving away from the deconstructive agenda of critical analysis and moving toward a reconstructive agenda (Lewis, 2006; Luke, 2000). Our work seeks to integrate a language of critique and possibility (Giroux, 1988) and to recognize how participants use language, space, and time within their dialogue to engage in critical discursive practices. Therefore, we see dialogue as a tool that participants can use to identify critical social practices in order to reflect on, interpret, and change their realities. Each of these studies highlights how, through dialogue, participants came to more complex understandings of particular social issues and developed a more agentive stance toward making some small change with regard to that issue—whether immigration, oppression of youth, minimum wage, or homelessness.

In her study, Souto-Manning (2007) employs critical narrative analysis (CNA), which combines critical discourse and narrative analyses in a way that they each can productively inform the other, blurring artificial boundaries between texts and contexts in a dialogical manner. Through CNA, she engages in critically analyzing narratives in the lifeworld (Habermas, 1987)—the everyday stories people tell—and deconstructing the different discourses present in these narratives. Souto-Manning proposes that doing so allows researchers to deal with real world issues and develop critical meta-awareness (Freire, 1970), demystifying the social construction of reality, challenging commonly accepted definitions of critical, and reframing social interactions as places for norms to be challenged and changed.

Within and across our studies, our understandings of critical dialogue are informed by the work of Paulo Freire. In his early work, Freire (1959) highlighted the role of dialogue in the process of developing critical consciousness (Souto-Manning, 2007, 2010b). Shor and Freire (1987) theorized that dialogue has the potential to support participants to confront differences and to foster reflection. Ultimately, dialogue offers sites of possibility for collective reflection, to "act critically to transform reality" (Shor & Freire, 1987, p. 99).

Language as Social Practice

Our shared foundation of language as social practice grounds our research. In situating language as a social practice, language and language users continually shape and are shaped by contexts (Santa Barbara Classroom Discourse Group, 1993). We believe that people's values, beliefs, and actions are shaped by the construction of "big D" discourses (Gee, 2005). Gee conceptualizes "little d" discourses as strings of language in use, while "big D" discourses relate language to social practices. Big D discourses are inextricably linked to identities and involve "recognition and recognition work" (p. 17). This recognition work involves acting-interacting-thinking-valuing-talking (sometimes writing-reading) in appropriate ways with appropriate props at appropriate times in appropriate places. What is deemed appropriate can often be oppressive for one or more social groups, as appropriateness may value ways of being for some while silencing ways of being for others. Critical dialogue involves unmasking and transforming these often invisible Discourses.

These ways of thinking, acting, interacting, and talking are also tied to cultural models—simplified storylines and theories about how the world works (Gee, 2005). Gee emphasizes that cultural models are our "first thoughts" or taken for granted assumptions about what is "typical" or "normal" (p. 59). Gee also reminds readers that danger lies in these cultural models because ultimately they "can do harm by implanting in thought and action unfair, dismissive, or derogatory assumptions about other people" (p. 59). In interactions, cultural models are powerful because language, when unreflective and unquestioning, can reconstitute status quo practices and ideologies. In a study of critical dialogue, it is essential to analyze how these cultural models and simplified theories of the world are constructed, deconstructed, and reconstructed. This can be slow and painstaking work, not often readily visible in a few sessions of dialogue; however, when we intentionally and critically reflect on oppressive Discourses and cultural models, then our dialogue has the power to create more equitable possibilities (Rymes, Souto-Manning, & Brown, 2005).

Agency

The concept of agency is key to our work in examining critical dialogue across settings because agency is mediated within and through language and culture (Lasky, 2005). Moje and Lewis (2007) argue that agency involves a "strategic making and remaking of selves" (p. 18). When participants question the status quo, including, but not limited to, systems of power and domination, they are asserting agency within these relations of power as they shift their positioning and identities in order to critique what they heretofore assumed as "fact" (Derman-Sparks & Ramsey, 2011; Souto-Manning, 2011) This remaking of selves involves a remaking of identities, activities, relationships, cultural tools and resources, and histories as embedded within relations of power. As Souto-Manning (2010b) describes, taking up agency even in fleeting moments entails a changed perspective or a shift in identity. Agentive language supports participants in asserting their capacity to question, rename, and act (Jennings, Parra-Medina, Messias, & McLoughlin, 2006); a central aspect of critical dialogue is developing critical and agentive language as a resource for developing critical consciousness and taking transformative action (Souto-Manning, 2010b).

METHODOLOGY

Context

We are teacher educators who came together when we discovered a mutual interest in critical discourse analysis. Over the course of two years, we met to discuss our studies, all of which explored the kind of dialogue we thought of as critical, that is, dialogue that questioned oppressive systems and led participants to new understandings and action. The five studies that we examined are all represented in our co-edited volume (Jennings, Jewett et al., 2010). For example, Tasha Laman, drawing on her research with Mitzi Lewison, examined teachers' talk about homelessness, curriculum, and civic action as they examined children's texts about homelessness in a critical literacy teacher study group. Pamela Jewett sought to more fully understand perceived anomalies in one teacher's talk about racial and linguistic diversity in both the teacher's first grade classroom and during her participation in a graduate literature class. Louise Jennings along with Sheri Hardee and De Anne Messias, studied the dialogue of teenagers in after-school service organizations to reveal how they deconstructed and reconstructed stereotyped societal images of teens. Jennifer Wilson studied the language of sixth-grade students engaged in literature group discussions regarding texts on immigration. Mariana Souto-Manning explored how Brazilian adults drew upon their own narratives of work and life to deconstruct social inequities and develop agentive language and actions through their talk within culture circles at an adult education center. (See Table 1 for a more detailed description of the five studies.)

The five of us relied on the work of different scholars in the fields of critical discourse analysis (CDA) and CNA, for example, Gee (2005), Fairclough (2003), Barnes (1992), Ochs and Capps (2001), and Souto-Manning (2007). These approaches are both theoretical and methodological, allowing us to examine how social and power relations and knowledge are constructed as well as mediated through written and spoken texts (Lewis, 2006; Rogers, Malancharuvil-Berkes, Mosley, Hui, & Joseph, 2005). Because CDA and CNA offer researchers a process for analyzing how power works in vernacular texts and exchanges (Lewis, 2006), we believed that analysis of our participants' discursive practices would help us identify individual and socially constructed beliefs as well as participants' efforts to deconstruct and reform their sociopolitical understandings. The question that drove our analysis of data was: What factors and practices supported critical dialogue across the five studies?

Although each study was contextually distinct, we wanted to better understand the kinds of practices that promoted critical dialogue across our studies. While keeping the cases intact illuminated understandings and insights about the processes and character of critical dialogue in each study, we wanted to look across five contexts to locate common practices. Taking an ethnographic stance, we viewed each study as a cultural artifact and noted the particular cultural practices that supported critical dialogue. We focused our analyses on descriptions and interpretations of what people said and did (Glesne, 1999) within these cultural contexts.

Analysis

In our initial analysis, we revisited our own and each other's data and examined the discourse of participants across ages, ethnicities, settings, and languages. We gathered artifacts, such as transcriptions of participants' talk, their writings, and photo essays. We engaged in a focused coding of data (Braun & Clark, 2006; Charmaz, 2003), examining patterns within language that we believed represented critical dialogue, language that initially constructed, deconstructed, and reconstructed issues of power, (in)equity, and humanity.

In a second strand of analysis, we re-coded these instances of critical dialogue to better understand the factors and practices that encouraged critical dialogue across studies through a cross-case analysis (Tuyay, Floriani, Yeager, Dixon, & Green, 1995). We made note of the

TABLE 1

Summary of the Five Studies of Critical Dialogue

Guiding Questions of the Studies Examined in Cross-case Analysis	Setting	Participants	Methods
Laman & Lewison: What were the specific ways that homelessness, curriculum, and civic action were constructed during discussions among study group participants?	Critical Literacy Teacher study group meeting at elementary school	14 elementary school teachers 2 facilitators from nearby university	Examining teachers' constructions of homelessness, curriculum, and civic action
Jewett: How did the participant construct meaning related to reading, difference, and culture?	Graduate children's literature class/Teacher's first grade classroom	Graduate student/First-grade teacher	Locating themes, stories, narratives, and discourse models within teacher's talk and writing
Jennings, Messias, & Hardee: How did dialogue function to support teen participants as they worked to locate, name, deconstruct, and challenge oppressive macroimages and discourses about youth?	Community Service Organization in the context of health promotion and risk reduction around tobacco use.	15 teams of 2–4 youth; Four female adult facilitators	Examining discursive processes of critical dialogue in community service youth group
Wilson: What is the nature of peer-led critical dialogue? What are the dimensions of the students' talk that facilitated critical dialogue as a small group of boys browsed a text set about the collision of two cultures/two worlds during a unit on immigration?	Middle school classroom/literature discussion group	Four European American 6th grade males	Identifying intertextuality and discourse models in literature discussion group
Souto-Manning: How did participants in the culture circles critically analyze their narrative tellings and consider multiple understandings of socially/culturally constructed issues as they co-constructed new narratives over time?	Adult Education Center in Bezerros, Pernambuco, Brazil	Adult members of a culture circle	Identifying discursive turns and agentive possibilities crafted by the circle participants

practices that were employed and the factors that were in place and that recurred across contexts. We found that time, the stance of the facilitator, and the tools that were used played important roles in setting the stage for critical dialogue. We returned to our data and identified telling cases (Mitchell, 1984), cases that effectively demonstrated the theories and ideas we were seeking to explicate across cases.

Limitations of the Study

We believe that research that employs qualitative methods should provide sufficient detail to fully illustrate the events described in the text. We also acknowledge that for our readers to fully and unambiguously understand our arguments about critical dialogue, we need to include large segments of transcribed dialogue. However, the excerpts of transcripts we included, while representative of our findings, were necessarily shortened due to space requirements.

FINDINGS

Across studies, we found that critical dialogue was supported by time, the role of the facilitator, and the use of tools. Table 2 illustrates how our themes of time, facilitator, and tools played out in each of our studies. While all five studies informed our analysis, we highlight each of these findings by choosing a telling case (Mitchell, 1984) for each.

Time

Critical dialogue is complex and rarely accomplished within a single exchange. Time was an essential condition for critical dialogue. Across sites, participants were provided time for talk and for critical reflection as well as time to allow beliefs hovering on the periphery of understanding to come into clearer focus. Not only are long stretches of time necessary for any single meeting, a commitment to multiple meetings over time is important. As seen in Table 2, each context involved time that allowed for the evolution of critical dialogue, time enough to construct knowledge of an oppressive issue, problematize and deconstruct that issue from multiple perspectives, and reconstruct more critical understandings and possible actions. For example, youth organizations rarely allot much, if any, time for youth to critically reflect on their social identities (Jennings, Parra-Medina, Messias, & McLoughlin, 2006), but in Louise Jennings' study, youth participants had over eight weeks to construct their understandings of how youth are positioned in their communities by developing photo-essays; they then had time for critical dialogue about their new understandings through the 90-minute debriefing session. In the critical literacy teacher study group, teachers met monthly over the course of three years to move toward an understanding of the systemic and cultural issues related to homelessness and how it is perceived in schools. Tessa engaged in a full semester of graduate study before enacting her developing critical knowledge in her first grade classroom over the course of another semester. Adults in a Brazilian adult education class met weekly for 11 months to share their stories, to problematize their working class realities, and to take personal and social actions to change those realities.

TABLE 2
Themes across the Five Educational Settings

Themes	Middle School Text Sets Discussion	Critical Literacy Teacher Study Group	Children's Literature Graduate Course	Brazilian Adult Culture Circle	Youth Photo-Voice Project
Time	**Timeframe:** Three 90-minute small group discussions over a 3-day period. Within timeframe, students constructed a common narrative of immigration (day 1), deconstructed the dominant view of immigration (day 2), and reconstructed a new understanding of immigration (day 3).	**Timeframe:** Three years, once a month Within timeframe, teachers moved from view of homelessness as something that is easy to resolve to a more sophisticated understanding of the systemic and cultural issues related to homelessness and how it is perceived in the schools.	**Timeframe:** Two semesters Within timeframe, Tessa spent the first semester learning about issues of critical literacy and then in the second semester took action to include critical materials and social issue books in her first grade classroom.	**Timeframe:** 11 months Within timeframe, participants problematized their realities dialogically and negotiated spaces of possibility. While they took personal responsibility for changing their situations (going to school), they charted a course of action beyond their classroom. They wrote legislators and demanded change.	**Timeframe:** Photo-essay construction process: three 2-hour meetings over 8 weeks; Debriefing sessions: One 1-1$\frac{1}{2}$ hour session per team During debriefing, the students reflected on how the photo-essay process helped them to see societal stereotypes of youth. They moved to deconstructing these hegemonic discourses, complicating dichotomous images of youth, and exploring how to challenge dominant views of youth through possible social actions.
Facilitator Intentionality	Structured the curriculum Protected time for discussions Provided texts that offered alternative viewpoints Posed overarching questions for students to discuss	Leveraged resources to support the group Introduced critical literacy children/young adult books and professional articles Silence from facilitators opened space for teachers to discuss Offered response strategies to facilitate discussions	Offered different reading strategies to critically respond to books Modified transactional approach by looking for openings for critique Introduced social issues in books Used critical questions such as, "Whose voices were heard?"	Documented recurring oppressive issues in participants' lives (generative themes) Codified generative themes into everyday texts—quotidian tools Encouraged participants to ask questions regarding the texts that shaped their lives, use each other as resources, and collectively chart plans of action Asked questions and facilitated the dialogic deconstruction of codifications, thus challenging concepts of (1) Fairness—that the minimum wage was enough to live on; and (2) Meritocracy—that if they worked hard enough they would be able to lead a decent life	Supported youth in photo-essay team project to construct and present their own views of "how youth make a difference in our community" Flexible use of a debriefing interview protocol designed to support youth in critical dialogue regarding their photo essay Offered agentive language Prompted social action/brainstorming ideas for social action Recognized and encouraged critical talk
Tools	**Textual tool:** Text set of picture books that offered alternative perspectives to the dominate view of immigration	**Textual tools:** Picture books and young adult books that focused on issues of homelessness	**Textual tools:** Picture books and young adult books that focused on issues of critical literacy	**Quotidian tools:** Participants' bills & paychecks; information regarding the cost of living expenses (transportation, food, rent, and clothing)	**Visual tools:** Photographs taken by youth & arranged in photo-essays to represent "Youth Making a Difference in the Community"

To further explore the function of time in critical dialogue, we turn to our first telling case, the Middle School Text Sets Discussion depicted in Table 2. In Jennifer Wilson's study, the sixth grade text set discussion occurred over a three-day period in a public middle school in the Midwest. Kathryn, the teacher, assembled sets of texts around the theme of immigration, intentionally selecting books that would provide an alternative perspective to their social studies textbook. On the first day, students were given 90 minutes to browse these text sets and to discuss issues that were brought up from the texts. Kathryn placed the students in groups of four based on who she thought would work well together for this part of their inquiry into immigration. All the students in the class had prior experience with literature discussions. Jennifer's study focused on one group of four European American males as a case of critical dialogue. On the first day of the 3-day literature discussion, the boys began the process of discussing their text set, which included books, such as Levine's (1989) *I Hate English*, Choi's (2003) *The Name Jar*, and Howard's (2005) *Virgie Goes to School with Us Boys*.

Jeff: In lots of books, it's all, like, let's say someone is having a conflict and you're sitting there watching the person go through. You think, "Oh, it's really easy, why are they having such a time?" Like picking a name, people would be like, "Oh, why don't you pick this one? It's my name. It's really cool." It's hard. Lots of times it's harder than you think, than it looks like it is. Let's say you watch someone playing, like, a sport or something and like, "Oh that looks really easy." But then you go out and try it, and it's not at all.

Tim: Especially like, if you have ever tried to catch a ping pong ball, it looks so easy, but it's impossible.

Jeff: Yeah.

Tim: And also I've noticed a common theme among these books. It seems like whenever someone comes to a new country they kinda have to reinvent themselves, and they're like new people when you immigrate. For instance, she had to choose a new name. Like this one is about Native American tribes kinda blending in with the culture and finding their places in it.

In this excerpt, the boys were beginning to make sense and collaboratively build an understanding of immigration drawn from their readings of their shared text set. During this time, the boys were putting forth initial theories of immigration (e.g., "it's harder than you think") and attempting to create a common narrative (e.g., immigrants must "reinvent themselves"). They also recognized that larger sociopolitical forces were limiting choices for immigrants (they *have* to reinvent themselves; she *had* to choose a new name) as well as limited agency on the part of Native Americans to "find" their place in the dominant culture.

On Day 2, the boys began to question this co-constructed view of immigration:

Jeff: What I thought [about] the books that I read—it was more about the culture of the people and not about where they lived. Like I read one, this one right here [pointing to the book *My Name is Jorge* (Medina, 2004)]. It was about a boy and his friend was American and lived in Mexico, but it didn't really talk about how they lived in Mexico. It just talked about how he had a friend that no one else was his friend because he was from another country. So I think that the books talk more [about] culture than where they lived.

Carl: Every time they do one of these books they always do it from a discriminated person's point of view. And you know they talk about how bad the white people were when they came. I was wondering what the white people feel about this? Did they really think they were doing something bad?

Jeff: That's the weird thing. They did it because they thought it was right.

Carl: Yeah, I know. They thought that they were doing the Indians a favor.

Tim: And they thought, like, African Americans were evil at first during slavery.

Jeff: Yeah.

Carl: And also the so-called "great civilization," with more technology and possibly with a greater faith in like Christianity, usually dominated another culture.

In this excerpt we see the boys begin to question the dominant discourse in their text sets. Jeff began this questioning by proposing a new theory of the clashes between people and suggesting that it may not have been the result of where you lived but more the result of two different perspectives or cultures coming together. Thus, as Carl read these alternative views of immigration, he began to question them and wondered "what the white people feel about" the immigration issues brought out in the texts and whether they recognized the injustice of their actions. His question prompted the boys to name racist myths of white supremacy, Jeff pointing to the "weird thing"—the contradiction—that white people thought that these injustices were justified and "right." Carl questioned the narrative of the so called "great civilization" pointing to the tendency of the dominant culture to use these myths to justify their domination over targeted groups. Carl and his peers were beginning to see multiple narratives within immigration and to recognize how systems of power were constructed and maintained. For the three days, the boys had spent time reading alternative views of immigration. The intentional textual choices of the facilitator and the growing ability of these sixth graders to question and consider alternative storylines allowed the boys to first interrogate the dominant view of immigration (i.e., "the Land of the Free"); they also brought into the discussion previously studied material (i.e., slavery) and attempted to make sense of oppression and discrimination as much bigger issues that encompass immigration.

The following excerpt from Day 3 shows briefly how the boys began to reconstruct new views of immigration:

Tim: I think kind of the perseverance is what keeps prejudice from being really, really bad. Because when you think about it, there will probably always be at least one person that's prejudice against someone in the way that Jeff said but as long as there are people that aren't prejudice and actively trying to be not prejudice, there won't be like, people won't be put back into slavery and everything.

Jeff: Like, and it's all about believing that you can still do it. Like Dr. Martin Luther King got arrested like 50 times, but he always got back out of jail and did the same thing over again. That's why people heard him.

Carl: Like you said before, people who come to the country they don't get favored. I don't understand back in the 1800s through the Civil War and slavery, when they were coming over they said that America was to be the land of tolerance and to honor all people's rights, but what I don't get is that only white men got rights, nobody else got anything. They were considered inferior, and they still kept saying that we are in the right, we get all the equal rights.

Jeff: It's like all about, it's about them just trying to get people to come over because they had so many jobs they needed to have people who [could work], it's basically a lie. They say we're the land of tolerance, so if you come over here, you'll have rights and lots of money, and they come over, and they have no choice to go back. So they have to stay, and they get taken advantage of.

Whereas dominant discourses were not always critiqued in the boys' talk on Day 2, this excerpt illustrates how the boys reconstructed a view of immigration that questioned the myth of "the land of opportunity," recognizing that for most newcomers, immigration often means discrimination and oppression. The boys used critical language in explicitly pointing to a discourse of white supremacy as well as agentive language in recognizing the importance of individual "perseverance" in standing up against injustice, even if they have not yet recognized the need for collective social action.

For the middle school students, immigration was not the only theme that appeared continually in the students' dialogue. Instead, the students' cyclical talk was laden with multiple perspectives. The middle school boys first used the idea of taking on multiple perspectives as a tool (e.g., in the hypothetical narrative of picking an English name). In a later discussion, multiple perspectives were brought up again, this time by their interrogating the idea of multiple perspectives as a concept. The students listed books highlighting differing views and questioned what others' were thinking (i.e., "How did the white people feel about this?"). The next day, the students used the knowledge gained from the previous two discussions of multiple perspectives to take a stand and recognize the injustice that occurred (i.e., "and they come over, and they have no choice to go back. So they have to stay, and they get taken advantage of"). This talk did not move chronologically, nor did Kathryn force it. Instead, it was as Gilles (1993) states, "dynamic, circular discursive movement that unconsciously occurred when the students were given large quantities of time over several days to engage with books and talk" (p. 206). The students drew on their discussion from the previous day, in which they engaged in hypothetical talk to see multiple perspectives and extend their discourse, to later using multiple perspectives as a tool to further construct, deconstruct, and reconstruct their views of immigration. In the end, it was this nonlinear growth of the ideas of the complexity of immigration that enabled the students to construct new possibilities by drawing on others' views as demonstrated when participants referred back to one another's previous dialogue. Spending time inside a themed text set, revisiting ideas, and exploring issues revealed how time permitted students to examine the complexity of the topic, pick up discussion threads, revise previous thinking, and move from hesitant questioning to more confident interrogation of dominant discourses. Kathryn had also supported students in effectively using their time by demonstrating and encouraging them to deconstruct issues by rephrasing their comments as questions and by posing critical questions herself. She would also redirect their talk by helping students tie their connections back to an abstract idea. Importantly, Kathryn protected ample class time for learners to effectively problematize and reconstruct their understandings of critical issues through talk (Jennings, Jewett et al., 2010).

The Role of the Facilitator

In many educational settings, even if there is space and time created for dialogue, participants may not be oriented to critical dialogue and reflection. Gilles and Pierce (2004) referred to the importance of creating a culture of talk in classrooms that is often missing when activities become controlled and contrived. As we discuss next, the facilitators in each study played an important role in creating a culture of critical dialogue, one of intentionality—thoughtful, knowledgeable action that is oriented to critical inquiry. Disrupting dominant discourses often entails becoming comfortable with being uncomfortable. In all five settings, the role of the facilitator was important for supporting a culture of critique. Beyond hoping that, eventually, participants in dialogue will engage in critique, facilitators need to cultivate a deliberate, intentional stance toward supporting critical dialogue without overtaking it.

As illustrated in Table 2, intentionality was prominent across all five study settings, where the facilitators were cognizant about their role in constructing an environment to support critical dialogue, their choice of tools, and their use of language. The intentional acts available varied depending upon the context. For example, Kathryn structured the curriculum to protect time for peer discussions (environment), provided texts that offered alternative points of view (tools), and posed overarching critical questions for students to discuss (language). The facilitators of the critical literacy teacher study group leveraged resources to create the opportunity for the study group, introduced the teachers to critical literacy children's books and professional articles, and intentionally refrained from overtaking conversation by remaining silent on many occasions when they were otherwise tempted to speak. In the Children's Literature course, the facilitator used a variety of critical literacy tools, including offering graduate students strategies for critically responding to books. Such strategies include the use of "whose voices?" in which the class discussed whose voices were heard in the book and whose were missing and what they might have said. Another strategy is "hot seat," in which students ask questions of other students who role-played parts in the book. The facilitator also built on transactional theory (Rosenblatt, 1978), which honors people's responses to texts based on their personal, social, and cultural histories, to help students look for natural openings to critique in their own and others responses. The facilitator of the youth project constructed an environment conducive to critical dialogue by organizing teams of teenagers in after-school youth programs to construct photo-essays that focused their attention on the social positioning of youth in their communities. She extended this environment by creating a space for critically reflecting upon their photo-essays through a debriefing protocol designed to help youth deconstruct and reconstruct the messages of their photo-essays. During the debriefing, she offered agentive language to the youth (e.g., "Are you telling me that having information on a topic helps empower you?"), prompting youth to think about social actions they could take, and recognizing and encouraging their critical talk.

The importance of the facilitator's use of language is underscored in the following telling case. Mariana Souto-Manning's study features a Brazilian culture circle, a setting in which the participants and the facilitator understood that the purpose of the circle was to develop literacy skills and critical insight through dialogue. In this excerpt (translated by Mariana) the facilitator, Sandra, intentionally, yet infrequently, questioned the group to help them construct and then deconstruct their idea of a minimum wage (please note that double pamntheses indicate nonverbal interactions):

Solange: But don't you make a minimum [wage] salary?

Sandra: What does that mean?

Solange: That means she [Josie] should have enough to live.

Josi: I work hard, but the salary is not enough. I don't know what I am doing
wrong—

José: —Wrong?

Josi: Yes, because I work, earn a minimum [wage] salary, but it's never enough to pay the bills and
put food on the table.

Solange: But the minimum [wage] salary is enough. Isn't it? ((looks around seeking approval))

Miriam: I don't have enough money for all my bills either. Do you have—

Solange: —What? Enough money?

Josefa: Yes—

Solange: —No. I am not the owner of my own house. I pay rent every month. I can't buy everything
that my family needs. Some days all we eat is manioc flour—a handful of manioc flour to fill
the belly. We don't have meat on the table. ((Many nod, showing agreement and empathy))

In this excerpt, Sandra asked a single significant question. This question was posed to enhance
the discussion, to encourage participants' deconstruction of minimum wage, and to reconstruct
their own understandings of this important issue in light of their lived experiences. In this
exchange, Sandra posed a timely question that encouraged the participants to construct a common
definition/understanding of the minimum wage—a topic raised by the group, not the facilitator.
However, Sandra did more than pose well-timed questions that provided the group a chance to co-
construct knowledge. In the following excerpt the culture circle participants began to interrogate
the system that created and fosters minimum wage:

José: So who decided how much is enough?

Marina: I don't know. It wasn't me.

((laughter))

Solange: Who was it?

((side talk as they try to figure out who sets the minimum wage salary))

Sandra: The government is who approves the minimum [wage] salary—

Josi: —That's not fair. They don't earn a minimum salary. I just saw Lula [the Brazilian president] in
a big car on a store's television. I can't buy a car like that. I can't even pay to go to work by bus.
I go walking.

Miriam: Me too.

Solange: Who earns a minimum [wage] salary?

((most raise their hands))

Solange: Who earns less than a minimum [wage] salary?

((four women raise their hands))

José: Do you work the entire day?

Laurinda: I work—

Neto: —the entire week?

((women who earn less than the minimum wage nod))

Laurinda: Who earns more than the minimum [wage] salary?

((five of the eight men in the room raise their hands))

Sandra: What do you perceive?

Luís: That we earn more than they [do].

Solange: Men earn more money—

Neto: —but it's not enough to live.

In this excerpt, the facilitator helped the group question who decided on the minimum wage by offering the answer to José's question ("So who decides it is enough?"). Sandra's response identified the institutional power structure, offering participants a chance to reflect on the power dynamics inherent in the current system of wage determination. The facilitator also encouraged the group to identify gender inequities within the power structure by asking, "What do you perceive?" after participants indicated gender inequities in salaries by a show of hands. This follow-up question encouraged the participants to theorize from their discussion, recognizing their own lives and experiences as situated representations of a larger phenomenon—socioeconomic disparity and wage inequities.

Across all five contexts, the facilitator played different roles to support dialogue that is critical. In addition to providing time and space for discussion, they used critically facilitative language by, for example, posing overarching questions and questions that challenged hegemonic concepts or pointed to structural power dynamics, as illustrated in the telling case. Facilitators also encouraged participants to pose their own questions, offered agentive language, and prompted participants to consider social actions. Importantly the facilitators' intentionality must include an intention for critical dialogue to be participant-driven and participant-focused, which often means guiding from the periphery rather than from the center.

Textual, Visual, and Quotidian Tools

In all five settings, talk and interaction were often organized around one or more textual tools, key to supporting critical dialogue. As illustrated in Table 2, the tools included picture books and young adult literature, photo-essays, printed bills and paychecks, and verbal texts reflecting Brazilian adults' living expenses. These tools brought participants into critical dialogue with each other and with the larger communities in which they lived and worked and encouraged many to ask, "Why is it like this?" a question that Edelsky (1999) asserts is central to critically examining the systems of domination that shape our experiences.

In the Youth Photovoice project, young people created a visual tool that helped them to construct visions of youth in the local community (Jennings, Messias, & Hardee, 2010; Wang &

Burris, 1997). Teams of teens from four youth organizations developed photo-essays on the theme "Youth Making a Difference in the Community." Through their photo-essays, participants called attention to oppressive societal images of youth as troubled, troublemakers, or unproductive. Tawanda, one of the participants, explained, "I have never heard so many not positive things in my life about people ... The most ridiculed group is probably teenagers just because everybody thinks they're slack and don't do anything."

In the following excerpt, Joyce, Emma, and Robert, three teenaged youth from diverse ethnic and social class backgrounds, teamed together to develop their photo-essays. They talked about the photo-essay and what they learned from creating it with an adult facilitator, Ms. Mot. When Ms. Mot asked the youth what it was like to construct the photo-essay, they reflected together on what they came to learn through this project—that an oppressive societal discourse of youth negates a more realistic, comprehensive characterization of young people:

Joyce: Well, when you took the pictures ... you had a good feeling ... when you really realized that youth did a lot more than you thought, it was really good.

Ms. M: Do you think other people realize that youth do more than they do?

Emma: Ah, some somewhat.

Ms. M: What about adults?

Joyce: They think youth are bad for some reason. They look at us and say, "Oh, they're teenagers. Teenagers are the worse children. When they come to that age, they're the worse or whatever." But, if you look at it, some teenagers are better ... well, I won't say they're better. They just more mature than others and all teenagers aren't the same.

Ms. M: Umm hmmm

Joyce: So, they just tie you with the same.

Emma: Some are bad.

Robert: And another thing I realized as I was going through the photo book like throughout this whole project ... a lot of adults kind of look down on us ... Because, I mean, there are a lots of things like teen pregnancies, things like in-school violence. Things like that that would actually kinda show them, you know, where they give them a false view of what the youth actually represent.

Ms. Mot: Umm hmm

Robert: When, actually, there are a lot of people that don't really get seen, all the positive things that they do, maybe by helping each other out with school, with different activities in the community. Things like that that a lot of adults really don't take the time to look at.

Joyce and Emma identified and challenged a dominant discourse of teenagers being positioned as "the worse" children. They pointed out some teenagers might fit this characterization, but that they aren't all the same, suggesting that creating their photo-essay helped them to "realize that youth did a lot more" for their communities than many think. Robert deconstructed the process of societal stereotyping and ageism that can lead people to overlook "the positive things that they do."

Throughout their hour-long discussion with Ms. Mot, Emma, Joyce, and Robert continued to deconstruct and reconstruct this hegemonic discourse to reflect a more realistic, comprehensive, agentive identity of youth. For example, they challenged a dichotomous view of youth as either "good" or "bad," offering a more complex perspective of young people as individuals and as a group. They also discussed specific photographs that illustrated positive contributions of teens to their communities. Emma pointed to the photo, labeled "Hand Me the Hammer," that depicts her sister and father involved in a construction project and pointed out that young people help elders through building projects and other projects, such as yard cleaning.

Ms. M: Is that something more young people need to do or you would like to see?

Robert: As a matter of fact, that is something that we should all consider doing if we, as young people, are gonna be anchors—because older people have a misconsumption (sic) that we are bad people.

Ms. M: Umm hmm

Robert: We don't have good morals. That type thing. We should take the time to do something like this helping older people out. And that'll show them directly that we aren't as bad as they may think that we are.

Ms. M: And that's the whole issue. You need to change that stereotyped attitude that adults have about youth.

The process of actively seeking out and then displaying examples of stereotyped images of teens as well as agentive examples helped these young people to, in the words of many participants, "see" both the hegemonic discourse as well as the more comprehensive, agentive reality of youth experiences. With support from the facilitator, who, in the last line, offered agentive language that captured their growing critical consciousness, the teenage participants had an opportunity to construct societal visions of youth in their communities and hold them up to their personally-constructed images of youth that drew on their own lived experiences as represented in their photo-essay. They concluded the session by brainstorming social actions they could take to transform the hegemonic discourses they had identified.

DISCUSSION

Across studies, time, space, and authentic texts (textual, visual, and quotidian tools) were essential components for critical dialogue—dialogue that nurtured the development of critical consciousness among participants. Dialogue about homelessness, immigration, racism, gender inequities, and stereotyping are not topics that come with ready-made diagrams for solutions. They are uneasy subjects for many and complex for all. Participants needed physical, curricular, and temporal spaces for a careful and measured entry into the risky territory they encountered when they discursively examined their lived realities in relation to these significant social issues.

Rethinking time is a key element for critical dialogue. It may not be a surprise that time was significant; however, most educational settings seem to have a shortage of it. Yet the work of critical dialogue and social action cannot happen without time (Stires & Genishi, 2008). Through time, participants develop their thinking, cycling through their thinking in new ways (Genishi & Dyson, 2009). This cycling was present in all of our studies and prominent in the middle school study, in which the teacher intentionally created space for students to revisit the same texts. In our other studies, time was essential in moving beyond the tyranny of politeness (Judith L. Green, personal communication, no date) that oppresses honest dialogue about difficult topics as speakers fear offending others by their critique. These settings challenged traditional definitions of time that rule educational institutions. Lesko (2001) characterizes traditional "panoptical time" as emphasizing "the endings toward which youth are to progress and places individual[s] . . . into a sociocultural narrative that demands 'mastery' without movement or effect" (p. 35). Ample time—and a reconceptualization of the very construct of time—were essential for studying the historical roots and current iterations of issues, for building relational foundations, and for considering possible action.

Time as a condition for critical dialogue reinforces the need to engage in long-term discussion in order to cultivate learning and critical insight over time (Jennings & Smith, 2002; Mills, 2001). In two cases, the texts were constructed from the lives of the participants (visual and quotidian tools), such as the photo-essays created by youth or personal utility bills discussed by Brazilian laborers during their culture circle discussions. Challenging the panoptical time that has come to define contemporary education, teachers developed temporal compasses focused on the processes guided by students, as opposed to orienting to fixed curricular guides. "We suggest that in the current educational movement, we live in panoptical time, which captures learning and experience in a highly compressed way" (Stires & Genishi, 2008, p. 64). This conceptualization of time fails to capture the caring, authentically relational aspects of each of the five settings described here.

Teachers and facilitators in these studies created room to move (Siegel & Lukas, 2008) within their own settings, approaching curriculum and teaching as dynamic and co-constructed. In each setting, it was important to make room for students' interests and knowledge—not as peripheral but as central to the curriculum. Each group explored issues of power and privilege, and authority was dialectically negotiated (Freire, 1970). In some cases, the facilitator/instructor brought texts to the group (textual tools), and those texts served as the springboard for discussion. For example, in the critical perspectives on literature course, the teacher study group, and the middle school text set discussions used children's and young adult literature that focused on critical social issues. In other cases, the text selection and construction was negotiated by teacher-students and student-teachers (visual and quotidian tools). These texts served as tools that brought into clearer focus—through stories of injustice, typecast photographs of youth, invoices and statements for everyday items—cultural and racialized inequities children faced, stereotyped representations of youth in our local community, and the gendered and cultural inequities in homes and workplaces of women in Brazil. These texts became situated representations of prevalent phenomena affecting the lives of each community of learners. Texts—whether conceptualized as textual, visual, or quotidian tools—in turn, provided access to the knowledge and processes needed to question realities and to revision (a hybrid of revise and re-envision) (Souto-Manning, 2010a) texts and contexts. For example, the participants in the Brazilian culture circle came to rethink the minimum wage text they had constructed as "enough to live on;" they revisioned this text as "not enough to live on" as they critically reflected on their own realities, textual, and quotidian tools. As they moved ahead, they sought to revise the minimum wage itself by writing to representatives. They also sought to revision their own contexts by contesting power injustices with regard to gender and salary in their workplaces.

These spaces also allowed participants to challenge the fixed boundaries of teacher and student roles, problematizing what it meant to teach in critical and transformative ways. In each setting, teacher-students and student-teachers problematized their own pedagogies and challenged their own assumptions. The teachers/facilitators also used sparse but facilitative language to nurture dialogue that was critical, rather than using language that centered around and imposed their own views.

In each case, the orchestration and (re)conceptualization of time, space, and texts were essential for critical dialogue to take place, for learners to cultivate critical and agentive language that supports critical consciousness and action. Practitioners—across grades and space—problematized curricular and temporal compasses. Together, each community of learners developed collective moral compasses that guided their talk and action. As proponents of critical dialogue as a tool for transformation, we invite practitioners to reconsider time, space, and texts in the classroom and "look at things as if they could be otherwise" (Greene, 1988, p. 3).

NOTE

All authors contributed equally to this manuscript, which is not reflected in the order of authorship.

REFERENCES

Barnes, D. R. (1992). *From communication to curriculum* (2nd ed.). Portsmouth, NH: Boynton/Cook.

Braun, V. & Clarke, V. (2006). Using thematic analysis in psychology. *Qualitative Research in Psychology, 3*, 77–101.

Charmaz, K. (2003). Qualitative interviewing and grounded theory analysis. Qualitative interviewing and grounded theory analysis. In J. A. Holstein & J. F. Gubrium (Eds.), *Inside interviewing: New lenses, new concerns* (pp. 311–330). London, UK: Sage.

Choi, Y. (2003). *The name jar.* New York, NY: Dragonfly.

Comber, B. (2001). Critical literacies and local action: Teacher knowledge and a "new" research agenda. In B. Comber & A. Simpson (Eds.), *Negotiating critical literacies in classrooms* (pp. 271–282). Mahwah, NJ: Erlbaum.

Derman-Sparks, L., & Ramsey, P. (2011). *What if all the kids are white? Anti-bias multicultural education with young children and families* (2nd ed.). New York, NY: Teachers College Press.

Edelsky, C. (1999). On critical whole language practice: Why, what, and a bit of how. In C. Edelsky (Ed.), *Making justice our project: Teachers working toward critical whole language practice* (pp. 7–36). Urbana, IL: National Council of Teachers of English.

Fairclough, N. (2003) *Analysing discourse: Textual analysis for social research.* New York, NY: Routledge.

Freire, P. (1959). *Educação e atualidade brasileira.* Unpublished doctoral dissertation. Universidade de Recife, Recife, Brazil.

Freire, P. (1970). *Pedagogy of the oppressed* (M. B. Ramos, Trans.). New York, NY: Continuum.

Freire, P. (2005). *Education for critical consciousness.* New York, NY: Continuum.

Gee, J. P. (2005). *An introduction to discourse analysis: Theory and method* (2nd ed.). New York, NY: Routledge.

Genishi, C., & Dyson, A. H. (2009). *Children, language, and literacy: Diverse learners in diverse times.* New York, NY: Teachers College Press.

Gilles, C. (1993). We made an idea: Cycles of meaning in literature discussion groups. In K. M. Pierce & C. Gilles (Eds.), *Cycles of meaning: Exploring the potential of talk in learning communities* (pp. 199–218). Portsmouth, NH: Heinemann.

Gilles, C., & Pierce, K. M. (2004, March). *Creating spaces for talk in the classroom.* Presented at the Hofstra International Scholars Forum, Long Island, NY.

Giroux, H. (1988). *Teachers as intellectuals: Toward a critical pedagogy of learning.* Granby, MA: Bergin & Garvey.

Glesne, C. (1999). *Becoming qualitative researchers: An introduction.* New York, NY: Longman.

Greene, M. (1988). *The dialectic of freedom.* New York, NY: Teachers College Press.

Habermas, J. (1987). *The theory of communicative action, Vol. 2, Lifeworld and system: A critique of functionalist reason.* London, UK: Heinemann.

Howard, E. F. (2005). *Virgie goes to school with us boys.* North Richland Hills, TX: Aladdin.

Jennings, L. B., & Da Matta, G. B. (2009). Rooted in resistance: Women teachers constructing counter-pedagogies in post-authoritarian Brazil. *Teaching Education, 20*(3), 215–228

Jennings, L. B., Jewett, P., Laman, T. T., Souto-Manning, M. V., & Wilson, J. L. (Eds.). (2010). *Sites of possibility: Critical dialogue across educational settings.* Cresskill, NJ: Hampton.

Jennings, L. B., Messias, D. K. H., & Hardee, S. (2010). Addressing oppressive discourses and images of youth: Sites of possibility. In L. B. Jennings, P. Jewett, T. Laman, M. Souto-Manning, & J. Wilson (Eds.), *Sites of possibility: Critical dialogue across educational settings* (pp. 39–67). Cresskill, NJ: Hampton.

Jennings, L. B., Parra-Medina, D. M., Messias, D. K. H., & McLoughlin, K. (2006). Toward a theory of critical social youth empowerment: An examination of youth empowerment models. *Journal of Community Practice, 14*(1/2), 31–55.

Jennings, L. B., & Smith, C. P. (2002). Examining the role of critical inquiry for transformative practices: Two joint case studies of multicultural teacher education. *Teachers College Record, 104*(3), 456–481.

Laman, T. T., & Lewison, M. (2010). The discursive production of homelessness: Teachers' discursive constructions, deconstructions, and reconstructions. In L.B. Jennings, P.C. Jewett, T.T. Laman, M.V. Souto-Manning, and J.L. Wilson (Eds.). *Sites of possibility: Critical dialogue across educational settings.* New York, NY: Hampton Press.

Lasky, S. (2005). A sociocultural approach to understanding teacher identity, agency and professional vulnerability in a context of secondary school reform. *Teaching and Teacher Education, 21*(8), 899–916.

Lesko, N. (2001). Time matters in adolescence. In K. Hultqvist & G. Dahlberg (Eds.), *Governing the child in the new millennium* (pp. 35–67). New York, NY: RoutledgeFalmer.

Levine, E. (1989). *I hate English!* New York, NY: Scholastic.

Lewis, C. (2006). "What's discourse got to do with it?" A meditation on critical discourse analysis in literacy research. *Research in the Teaching of English, 40*(3), 373–379.

Luke, A. (2000). Critical literacy in Australia: A matter of context and standpoint. *Journal of Adolescent & Adult Literacy, 43*(5), 448–461.

Medina, J. (2004). *My name is Jorge: On both sides of the river.* Honesdale, PA: Boyds Mill Press.

Mills, H., with Jennings, L. B., Donnelly, A., & Mueller, L. (2001). When teachers have time to talk: The value of curricular conversations. *Language Arts, 79*(1), 20–28.

Mitchell, C. (1984). Case studies. In R. Ellen (Ed.), *Ethnography: A guide to general conduct* (pp. 151–153). London, UK: Academic.

Moje, E., & Lewis, C. (2007). Examining opportunities to learn literacy: The role of critical sociocultural literacy research. In C. Lewis, P. Enciso, & E. Moje (Eds.), *Reframing sociocultural research on literacy: Identity, agency, and power* (pp. 15–49). Mahwah, NJ: Erlbaum.

Nagda, B. A., & Gurin, P. (2007). Intergroup dialogue: A critical-dialogic approach to learning about difference, inequality, and social justice. *New Directions for Teaching and Learning, 2007*(111), 35–45.

Nagda, B. A., Gurin, P., Sorensen, N., & Zúñiga, X. (2009). Evaluating intergroup dialogue: Engaging diversity for personal and social responsibility. *Diversity & Democracy, 12*(1), 4–6.

Ochs, E., & Capps, L. (2001). *Living narrative: Creating lives in everyday storytelling.* Cambridge, MA: Harvard University Press.

Rogers, R., Malancharuvil-Berkes, E., Mosley, M., Hui, D., & Joseph, G. O. (2005). Critical discourse analysis in education: A review of the literature. *Review of Educational Research, 75*(3), 365–416.

Rosenblatt, L. M. (1978). *The reader, the text, the poem: The transactional theory of the literary work.* Carbondale, IL: Southern Illinois University Press.

Rymes, B., Souto-Manning, M., & Brown, C. (2005). Being "critical" as taking a stand: One of the central dilemmas of CDA. *Journal of Critical Discourse Studies, 2*(2), 195–198.

Santa Barbara Classroom Discourse Group. (1993). *Linguistics in Education: An International Research Journal* [Special Issue], 4(3–4).

Schoem, D. (2003). Intergroup dialogue for a just and diverse democracy. *Sociological Inquiry, 73*(2), 212–227.

Shor, I., & Freire, P. (1987). *A pedagogy for liberation: Dialogues on transforming education.* Westport, CT: Bergin & Garvey.

Siegel, M., & Lukas, S. (2008). Room to move: How kindergartners negotiate literacies and identities in a mandated balanced literacy curriculum. In C. Genishi & A. L. Goodwin (Eds.), *Diversities in early childhood: Rethinking and doing* (pp. 29–47). New York, NY: Routledge.

Souto-Manning, M. (2007). Education for democracy: The text and context of Freirean culture circles in Brazil. In D. Stevick & B. Levinson (Eds.), *Reimagining civic education: How diverse nations and cultures form democratic citizens* (pp. 121–146). Lanham, MD: Rowman-Littlefield.

Souto-Manning, M. (2010a). Challenging ethnocentric literacy practices: (Re)Positioning home literacies in a Head Start classroom. *Research in the Teaching of English, 45*(2), 150–178.

Souto-Manning, M. (2010b). *Freire, teaching, and learning: Culture circles across contexts.* New York, NY: Lang.

Souto-Manning, M. (2011). Playing with power and privilege: Theatre games in teacher education. *Teaching and Teacher Education, 27*(6), 997–1007.

Stires, S., & Genishi, C. (2008). Learning English in school: Rethinking curriculum, relationships, and time. In C. Genishi & A. L. Goodwin (Eds.), *Diversities in early childhood: Rethinking and doing* (pp. 49–66). New York, NY: Routledge.

Tuyay, S., Floriani, A., Yeager, B., Dixon, C. N., & Green, J. L. (1995) Constructing an integrated, inquiry-oriented approach in classrooms: A cross-case analysis of social, literate, and academic practice. *Journal of Classroom Interaction, 30*(2), 1–15

Wang, C., & Burris, M. A. (1997). Photovoice: Concept, methodology, and use for participatory needs assessment. *Health Education and Behavior, 24*(3), 369–387.

Wodak, R. (2001). What CDA is about—a summary of its history, important concepts and its developments. In R. Wodak & M. Meyer (Eds.), *Methods of critical discourse analysis* (pp. 1–13). London, UK: Sage.

Zúñiga, X., Nagda, B. A., & Sevig, T. D. (2002). Intergroup dialogues: An educational model for cultivating engagement across differences. *Equity & Excellence in Education, 35*(1), 7–17.

Speaking Across Difference in Community Dialogues on Affirmative Action Policy

Kristen L. Davidson and Michele S. Moses

University of Colorado Boulder

This study investigated the relevance of participants' social group differences with regard to the processes and outcomes of community dialogues on affirmative action. We found that participants' professional status was most salient to both the quantity of participants' contributions as well as their persuasiveness within the dialogues, with participants' race and gender also being potential factors. Participants across all social groups used the communicative strategy of argument as well as other forms of discourse that Young (2000) identified: greeting, rhetoric, and narrative. Our findings counter the assumption that communicative styles vary systematically by social group and suggest the need for research into the ways in which political equality can be fostered in deliberative dialogues in addition to the inclusion of multiple forms of discourse.

In 2008, Colorado voters halted the aim of Amendment 46, a ballot initiative to ban affirmative action in the state. Despite the narrow margin of the outcome—50.8% against and 49.2% in favor—a subsequent study estimated that two-thirds of voters would have voted against the initiative had the ballot language and campaign messages been clearer (Moses et al., 2010). This disparity between the election outcome and the public will highlights the need for an informed citizenry, especially given the disproportionate impact of ballot initiatives, such as Amendment 46, on ethnic minorities and women. Sustained, intergroup dialogue is an important means to promote understanding among citizens across differences. Closely related to the intentions and characteristics of intergroup dialogue, our study offers insights into the group dynamics of one-time community dialogues on affirmative action that were informed by deliberative democratic theory. As Niemeyer (2011) shows, community-based deliberation can have an "emancipatory effect" on participants and counter the political symbols that (intentionally or not) serve to distort citizens' understandings and result in expressed preferences that do not align with their interests and desires.

In the months preceding the 2008 election, the second author led a team of researchers in facilitating community dialogues that were initially conceived to engage voters around the issues relevant to Amendment 46. Because Colorado's Fair Campaign Practices Act (Colorado Fair Campaign Practices Act, 2004) constrains the election activities of state employees, however, the research team was unable to structure the dialogues around the ballot initiative specifically, and instead focused them on affirmative action policies generally. Each of the one-time, 90-minute dialogues aimed to expand participants' understandings of a public policy of contemporary significance without the end goal of group agreement. Yet as participants would subsequently have the opportunity to vote on a related ballot initiative, the dialogues reflected a unique niche along a deliberative spectrum that is often characterized as spanning from decision-making forums to open-ended dialogues (Bächtiger, Niemeyer, Neblo, Steenbergen, & Steiner, 2010; Chambers, 2003; Delli Carpini, Cook, & Jacobs, 2004; Walsh, 2007). The "community dialogues" in our study offer an informative example of deliberative practices that reflect both the ideals of deliberative democracy and the local political practices of citizens.

Largely because the interrelated principles of reciprocity (Gutmann & Thompson, 2004) and political equality (Young, 2000)—that is, respect for and inclusion of all relevant perspectives—are fundamental to all deliberative democratic theories, many models of civically-oriented dialogues are now recognized as constitutive of a democratic system (Chambers, 2003; Niemeyer, 2011; Thompson, 2008; Walsh, 2007). While deliberative dialogues differ as to whether they aim for group agreement, most have recognized emotional expression and various forms of discourse in an aim to foster inclusion, under an assumption that communicative styles vary by social groups (Bächtiger et al., 2010; Burkhalter, Gastil, & Kelshaw, 2002; Chambers, 2003; Young, 2000). Nonetheless, deliberative settings have continually reflected unequal participation and influence by professional status, race or ethnicity, and gender (Delli Carpini et al., 2004; Kaplan & Martin, 1999; Sanders, 1997; Strodtbeck, James, & Hawkins, 1957). While these findings are perhaps not surprising (Ryfe, 2007; Thompson, 2008), it is important to retain the concern for power and difference that initiated the expansion of deliberative democratic theory as a means to counter the marginalization of minority viewpoints (Mansbridge, 1999; Sanders, 1997; Young, 2000).

Attention to political equality was especially important to our study, as we made efforts to include voters that often are marginalized in political processes and that would be most affected by changes in affirmative action policies. Perhaps because of the goals and effects of affirmative action policies, the 80 participants in our 12 dialogues reflected disproportionately high numbers of ethnic minorities and women in relation to local demographics. Nine dialogues were ethnically diverse, and ten dialogues included both female and male participants. Given the differences in social group status among participants within our dialogues, we sought to examine whether and how power was manifested. To do so, we considered Young's (2000) attention to the inclusion of participants from all relevant social groups, as well as communicative strategies that would promote participatory parity.

The study was guided by the following questions:

- Were participants' social group differences, such as professional status, race, and gender, related to dialogue processes and outcomes? If so, how?
- What communicative strategies did participants use?

We examined the extent to which participants both contributed to the dialogues and had their views considered and taken up by others. We found that participants' professional status was paramount to whose ideas were persuasive, while participants' race and gender also were salient. Furthermore, participants across all social groups used the communicative strategy of argument, as well as the forms of discourse that Young (2000) identified: greeting, rhetoric, and narrative. This research therefore offers a counter-example to the assumption that communicative styles differ systematically across social groups, while underscoring the need for continued attention to the ways in which unequal social power is manifested.

In what follows, we review the theoretical and empirical literature on deliberative democracy that served to conceptualize the format of our dialogues as well as our study of group dynamics. We then describe the qualitative methods of our exploration of communicative processes within the dialogues, followed by our findings on the relevance of status, race, and gender with regard to both participation and persuasiveness. Next, we note the limitations of our study due to the one-time nature of the dialogues as well as the sample of participants that, overall, was highly educated and disproportionately represented by ethnic minorities and women. We conclude by considering the preliminary insights from our findings that suggest how political equality can be advanced in deliberative settings.

CONCEPTUAL FRAMEWORK AND REVIEW OF THE LITERATURE

The conceptualization of our study was informed by current understandings of deliberative democratic theory in which the principles of decision-oriented deliberations often overlap with those of open-ended community dialogues. Theorists have depicted a spectrum of "deliberative dialogue" as ranging from Habermas's (1984) and Cohen's (2003) foundational ideals of rational discourse among equals aimed at consensus to Mansbridge's (1999) and Sanders's (1997) feminist arguments for the democratic value of everyday talk and personal testimony.

As our dialogues reflected a unique position in the spectrum from consensus-oriented deliberation to open-ended dialogue, our study was informed by both Gutmann and Thompson's (1996, 2004) theory of deliberative democracy and Young's (1996, 2000) arguments for inclusion in a communicative democracy. While drawing from Habermas (1984) and Cohen (2003), Gutmann and Thompson argue that deliberation must not only reflect procedural principles of reciprocity, accountability, and publicity, but also comprise substantive principles of basic liberty, equal access to primary goods, and nondiscrimination in the distribution of non-primary goods. Echoing Mansbridge (1999) and Sanders (1997) in critiquing deliberation for privileging rational argument, Young further advocates the recognition of three forms of discourse that she claims will foster inclusion: (1) Greeting, which can establish trust and respect through the use of "mild forms of flattery, stroking of egos, deference, and politeness" (p. 58); (2) Rhetoric, which can aid in persuasion through humor, wordplay, images, figures of speech, and emotion; and (3) Narrative, which can validate the authority of each person over his or her own story, evoke empathy, and reflect the values of others who overlap with the speaker's social position. Because the participation of citizens as equals is fundamental to all deliberative democratic theories, calls for more inclusive conceptions have contributed to modern understandings in which reason-giving can take many forms and the goal of consensus has been relaxed (Chambers, 2003; Thompson, 2008).

Nonetheless, it is useful to recognize the differences in the intentions and character of deliberation that aims for legitimate group-based decision-making from those of group dialogue that aims for improved and shared understandings (Bächtiger et al., 2010; Chambers, 2003; Thompson, 2008; Walsh, 2007). Mansbridge (1999) suggests that the commonly recognized deliberative principles outlined by Cohen (2003) and Gutmann and Thompson (1996) have counterparts in dialogue that differ in character. Most centrally, the principle of reciprocity (i.e., mutual

230

respect among equals) applies to both decision-oriented deliberation and open-ended dialogue. Accountability (i.e., fair representation of constituents' interests) does not apply directly to dialogues, but can be understood as the increased awareness of others' perspectives as well as the search for common ground. Similarly, the principle of publicity is relaxed in dialogues that may protect the confidentiality of participants. Mansbridge argues that the deliberative conception of reasoned debate should shift to one of considered debate that includes emotion and multiple forms of discourse. In all forms of deliberative dialogue, inclusion requires that participants not only have equal access to the venues for debate, but also have equally effective voices in terms of opportunities to make verbal contributions and have their ideas considered (Burkhalter et al., 2002; Cohen, 2003; Young, 2000).

As models of community dialogues have proliferated since the "deliberative turn" in democratic theory over two decades ago (Chambers, 2003; Conover & Searing, 2005; Niemeyer, 2011), deliberative democracy has become a "working theory" that is now being tested empirically (Bächtiger et al., 2010, p. 32). While Fishkin's (1995) national deliberative polling has shown some promise, face-to-face dialogues in local settings have had mixed results (Delli Carpini et al., 2004; Ryfe, 2005; Thompson, 2008). Despite the highly contextual nature of dialogues, however, empirical studies have found that participants broaden their understandings of other perspectives and are subsequently more likely to become civically engaged (Conover & Searing; Hartz-Karp, 2005). Authors of empirical studies often give guidelines for effective dialogues that reflect a comfortable but focused atmosphere that allows for authentic sharing among equals such that participants can find common ground within diverse perspectives (Burkhalter et al., 2002; Hartz-Karp, 2005; Mansbridge, Hartz-Karp, Amengual, & Gastil, 2006; McCoy & Scully, 2002; Ryfe, 2005).

On the other hand, some studies suggest that deliberative dialogue is not the most effective means to increase understanding of public issues. In a review of the empirical research, Delli Carpini (2004) noted that in some studies, groups quickly adopted the majority perspective. In another Colorado study, Schkade, Sunstein, and Hastie (2007) found that participants' views became more extreme after deliberations on global warming, affirmative action, and civil unions.[1] In an Australian study that involved two days of information-giving followed by one day of dialogue, Goodin and Niemeyer (2003) found that participants learned more from information and internal reflection than they did from the dialogue segment. Kohn (2000) maintains that other forms of political resistance may be more important than democratic dialogue because "linguistic competence is hierarchically distributed" (pp. 408–409) and "deliberative democracy privileges the communicative strategies of elites" (p. 426). Although Ryfe (2007) clearly supports deliberation, he points to long-standing findings that participants in deliberative settings are often middle class and highly educated, as the habits and skills that are taught in educational settings reflect the common deliberative principles of open-mindedness and reciprocity. In the initiation of local dialogues in Kempala, India, Fischer (2006) found that to promote widespread participation, "the participatory process had to be organized and cultivated" (p. 35) through various pedagogical means and well-trained facilitators.

Due to mixed findings, deliberative scholars are calling for empirical research that specifically aims to address theoretic principles, including the distribution of power within deliberative settings and the qualities of discourse that promote equality among participants. (Delli Carpini et al., 2004; Rosenberg, 2005; Thompson, 2008). The few studies that have examined political equality have found that participants who are of higher professional status, white, and/or male tend to take on leadership positions in deliberations, speak more, and have more influence on the outcome (Delli Carpini et al., 2004; Kaplan & Martin, 1999; Sanders, 1997; Strodtbeck et al., 1957). Walsh (2007) examined the use of both power and narrative within interracial community dialogues in the Midwest, and found that white people and men overall took more speaking turns, on average, at each dialogue. Although a wide range of participants in Walsh's study used narrative, the stories of ethnic minorities held more import in impacting others' views. Similarly, Ryfe's (2006) study of five National Issues Forums found that narrative played an essential role in deliberation, and that facilitator styles were key to the amount and effectiveness of stories shared. He maintains that facilitators should be trained to occupy a middle ground between "strong" (interjecting frequently) to "weak" (minimal involvement) moderation of the group, such that facilitators are "willing to call attention to emerging narrative themes, to intervene with contradictory information when a conversation threatens to devolve into self-congratulation, and generally to prod the group to remain open to alternative accounts" (p. 89).[2]

Our study focused on the central democratic principle of political equality by examining the influence of power in our dialogues along the lines of professional status, race, and gender, as well as the forms of discourse that are claimed to foster inclusion. As noted above, our analysis of the community dialogues in our study is most centrally informed by Gutmann and Thompson's (2004) recognition of the central role of reciprocity, as well as Young's (2000) argument for the "political inclusion" (p. 12) of participants through open-ended dialogues that value communicative strategies of greeting, rhetoric, and narrative in addition to traditionally recognized forms of argument.

METHODS

After describing the format, setting, and sample of our study, we describe our methods for coding the dialogues, identifying patterns, and triangulating our data with pre- and post-questionnaires. In our data analysis, we aimed to assess the quantity of participants' contributions to the dialogue, the extent to which participants' ideas were taken up by others, and the uses of the communicative strategies of argument, greeting, rhetoric, and narrative. Once we assessed these measures of individual participation, we connected findings to participants' professional status, race, and gender.

Format, Setting, and Participants

Due to the FCPA regulations noted in the introduction, we modeled our dialogue format on the Public Conversations Project protocol (Herzig & Chasin, 2006), in which the researchers acted as neutral facilitators rather than occupying the "middle ground" or "critical" role that Ryfe (2006) and House and Howe (1999) suggest. Facilitators held their participation in the conversation to a short list of facts that only included the 1965 Executive Order and court rulings relevant to affirmative action. In this way, facilitator values would not be construed as influencing the outcomes of the dialogues (and possibly, the election), but participants could still express, exchange, and consider their own views.

Each dialogue was typically 90 minutes long. Upon arrival, participants completed a short pre-questionnaire that asked for demographic information as well as knowledge and perspectives on affirmative action. The questionnaire seemed to spark an interest in specific knowledge about affirmative action policies, as many participants brought related questions to the conversation. At the beginning of the dialogue, we attempted to establish an atmosphere of mutual respect and equal participation by providing a handout on the expectations for respectful communication, and by asking each participant to state what brought them to the dialogue. Participants then watched two five-minute video clips of a debate on affirmative action, which provided a common base of knowledge on the topic. We encouraged narrative as an acceptable means of communication by asking each participant to respond to the question, "What personal experiences of being treated fairly or unfairly influence your perspective of affirmative action?" Facilitators then invited open dialogue, and gave a final five-minute warning to share any concluding thoughts. At some dialogues, all participants gave a concluding statement at this time, while at others, some of the quieter participants used the opportunity to speak. Upon concluding, participants completed a short questionnaire, which again surveyed their knowledge and perspectives of affirmative action, and queried their experiences in the dialogue.

Varying pairs of researchers facilitated 12 dialogues in universities, libraries, churches, the YWCA, and neighborhood association meetings in Boulder and Denver, Colorado.[3] Three to eleven participants attended each dialogue for a total of 80 participants. Although we made concerted efforts to seek venues that would attract diverse viewpoints, the voluntary nature of participation and the research team's inability to provide transportation, child care, and multiple language formats precluded a proportionally representative sample with regard to social class, race or ethnicity, and gender. Although participants tended to have low incomes, they were highly educated across venues, with 98% having at least some college education and 62% having at least some graduate school education.[4] Although there were strong representations of ethnic minorities (42%) and women (63%) as a whole, three dialogues consisted entirely of white participants, and two consisted entirely of women. Participants ranged from 18 to over 65 years old, with 70% of participants ranging between the ages of 18 and 44 years. Save one retirement community venue, each dialogue had some age diversity.

Data Analysis

Eleven of the twelve dialogues were audio-recorded successfully, with nine dialogues also video-taped. We transcribed and analyzed the 11 recorded dialogues, for a total of 71 participants included in this analysis. We assessed the quantity of each individual's participation[5] as well as the extent to which individual contributions were taken up by others within the dialogues. We consciously attended to validity through searches for disconfirming evidence, blind participant labels during the analyses,[6] and data analysis grounded in rigorous methods (Barbour, 2007; Erickson, 1986; Maxwell, 2005; Miles & Huberman, 1994).

Quantity of Participant Contributions

Similar to the technique used by Strodtbeck et al. (1957), we estimated the quantity of participation by the number of speaking turns that each participant took as a proportion of the total number of turns that were taken in a given dialogue. We then noted which participants took a disproportionately high number of turns. For example, if there were five participants, anyone who took substantially more than 20% of the total turns at speaking was considered to have been a highly active participant.

Participants' Influence and Communicative Strategies

Through systematic analysis of the dialogue transcripts, including two levels of coding followed by pattern analysis (Miles & Huberman, 1994), we simultaneously examined the ways in which participants' ideas were taken up by others and the communicative strategies that participants used. In the first level of coding, the authors and one additional researcher used low-inference codes to separate segments of dialogue by topic of conversation. For the first two dialogues, pairs of researchers conducted this level of coding separately, which was then discussed and reconciled among all three researchers with over 90% inter-rater reliability. We divided the remaining nine dialogues such that each was coded at this low-inference level by one researcher.

In the second level of coding, the authors coded each segment using "organizational categories" derived from our conceptual framework, including participants' uses of Argument,[7] Greeting, Rhetoric, and Narrative, as well as "substantive categories" that became apparent during the process of reading and coding transcripts, including References to Expertise or Professional Status (Maxwell, 2005, p. 97).[8]

The following example highlights how References to Expertise or Professional Status sometimes occurred [Dialogue 1]:[9]

> I've done some work with the university in anticipation of Amendment 46, looking at class-based admissions policy and have found . . . that your probability of getting into a 4-year college, part of that is aptitude and part of that is SES [socioeconomic status]. The class-based admissions policy argument says well, if we account for the SES part and we account for the aptitude part, then that takes care of it, then race is really no longer a factor. What I'm finding is that that's not true. (Joseph)

In a similar manner to the above quote, some participants indicated their own professional status, while others referred to an outside source of authority, including the debaters featured in the video clips, government officials, and significant others with expertise. We, therefore, coded the above segment and comparable indications of status as "References to Expertise or Professional Status." Interestingly, those with professional status—whether or not it reflected expertise related to affirmative action policies—typically revealed their position to others in the dialogue.

During the two levels of coding, we noticed that participants appeared to question and persuade each other in some dialogue segments, while they simply seemed to share their own views in other segments. On the whole, seven of the community dialogues included segments in which persuasion occurred, while four dialogues did not. Because instances of persuasion provided concrete examples of participants' ideas being taken up by others, we used these segments as a means to assess participants' influence within the dialogues.

The first author proceeded to identify patterns with regard to whose ideas were persuasive in these segments, as well as whose ideas received the most airtime in dialogues in which no persuasion occurred.[10] The following gives an example of how we identified which ideas were taken up by participants. In this segment, a multi-racial female college student (Kaylin) introduces a theme of "trust," which an older white male student (David) attempts to consider, but the Latino male director of the venue's organization (Diego) changes the focus to one of "resources" [Dialogue 4]:

Kaylin: . . .if you were to totally do away with affirmative action, the way in which society seems to be so shocked by intelligent people of color like, oh, wow, you're so articulate . . . And then you're like ok, am I going to trust this person to really let me into college and really give me a fair shake if they're shocked that I speak so well . . . I don't think that there's this level of trust there. [TRUST]

David: There's no space for equality in the system that we've got. [EQUALITY]

Kaylin: Yeah, exactly. And so you have to stir stuff up. Because it's . . .

David: How can we mandate diversity? . . . we're dealing with a basic . . . reality of, we gotta get along.

Diego: That's interesting how things change in systems when there's resource issues. . . . I don't think we speak in those terms of what humanity is. I think we speak in terms of very immediate results. . . . And you [David] talk about the young man coming from the community and having all the bling, and you look back at the community that that individual comes from and the house is not owned, the property is not owned, and there's not . . . a base that's been built upon. . . . So I think that's what we're trying to correct with affirmative action. [RESOURCES]

The remainder of the dialogue focused on the theme of resources, such that Kaylin and other participants characterized their own experiences in this way:

Kaylin: I had a discussion [with] three women of color, and we were all pretty much very low income. And we . . . never heard anything about affirmative action. . . . and yet . . . my friend's boyfriend, . . . he's Caucasian, and he had heard . . . about how you could get all of this financial aid and . . . there's unfair advantages and . . . we were like, well how come we didn't hear about this? And so . . . it's a resources thing again, like even the resources to hear about the resources, like . . . who's hearing about affirmative action? [RESOURCES-INFORMATION]

Courtney (white female student): . . . I had a high school counselor who told me about scholarships, and perhaps . . . another school couldn't afford a . . . counselor to tell their students about scholarships. [RESOURCES-INFORMATION]

Diego: In my high school, the Latinos basically weren't counseled about college. . . . I was one of the top students . . . and nobody talked to me about college. [RESOURCES-INFORMATION]

David: . . . when it came to [seeing] the different reps from the colleges, . . . all these kids that were considered prep . . . they were the ones at these things, but people who didn't have a certain level of income . . . [weren't] invited . . . I mean, *is* our society just based on resources? Is that really what it's all about? It seems like it. [RESOURCES-INFORMATION/FINANCIAL]

Ethan (white male student): Caucasian males especially will feel very threatened by distributing financial resources . . . [and] they are not acknowledging that they have the resources to go to school and do these things. [RESOURCES-FINANCIAL]

The theme of resources was thus taken up by all of the other participants. In the same way, we tracked patterns of themes that were introduced and subsequently reflected among participants across all 11 dialogues. In segments in which persuasion seemed to occur, we labeled participants whose ideas were taken up by others as "persuasive" and those who dropped their own views and took up others' views as "persuaded." In this case, Diego was identified as persuasive, and Kaylin and David were labeled as persuaded.

At the same time, we coded segments of dialogues that indicated participants' use of communicative strategies. In the above segment, for example, Diego's reference to David was coded as Greeting, Kaylin's mention of a "fair shake" was coded as Rhetoric, and Kaylin's reference to her discussion with three women of color was coded as Narrative. When the pattern analysis was complete, we connected both participants' persuasiveness within the dialogues and their uses of communicative strategies with participants' professional status, race, and gender.

Triangulation of Data

We triangulated our findings by matching the participants that we had identified as being either persuasive or persuaded with their pre- and post-questionnaire responses. We assessed how often participants that we had identified as being persuasive or persuaded had claimed to have changed their views about affirmative action, as well as the extent to which participants gained factual knowledge about the policies. We also examined changes in views and factual knowledge for the four dialogues that did not include instances of persuasion.

FINDINGS

We present findings on the extent to which participants' professional status, race, and gender were related to the quantity of their participation, their influence within the dialogues, and their uses of argument, greeting, rhetoric, and narrative. Both quantity of participation and uses of communicative strategies were assessed for all 11 dialogues. In addition, we present separate findings for the eight mixed-race dialogues (all but Dialogues 6, 10, and 11) and nine mixed-gender dialogues (all but Dialogues 7 and 8) where relevant. As noted above, our findings regarding participants' influence are focused on the dialogues in which persuasion occurred (Dialogues 1, 2, 4, 5, 6, 8, and 9). For these seven dialogues, we also present separate findings for the six dialogues that were mixed-race (Dialogues 1, 2, 4, 5, 8, and 9) and a slightly different group of six dialogues that were mixed-gender (Dialogues 1, 2, 4, 5, 6, and 9). We begin with participants' quantity of participation, followed by participants' influence, and conclude with participants' uses of communicative strategies. We tied all findings to participants' status, race, and gender. As noted above, participants with professional status almost always revealed their expertise within the dialogues, even if it was unrelated to affirmative action policies.

Quantity of Participation

As described in the Methods section, we considered participants who took a disproportionately high number of turns to be highly active participants. Most notably, the participants who had indicated their professional status during the dialogue took more than their fair share of speaking

TABLE 1
Highly Active Participants by Race and Gender

	Mixed-Race Dialogues ($n = 53$)					Mixed-Gender Dialogues ($n = 61$)
	White	Latino/a	Multi-Racial	Black	Asian	
No. of Participants	28	13	6	5	1	61
Percent of Total Participants	53%	25%	11%	9%	2%	—
Female	57%	69%	67%	20%	100%	56%
Male	43%	31%	33%	80%	0%	44%
No. Highly Active	13	4	2	1	0	23
Percent of All Highly Active	65%	20%	10%	5%	0%	—
Female	69%	0%	50%	0%	—	48%
Male	31%	100%	50%	100%	—	52%

turns in all but one dialogue. In fact, the great majority (82%) of participants who had revealed a position of status were highly active, while the majority (68%) of participants who had not indicated professional status took less than their fair share of the floor (the remainder took an approximately proportionate number of speaking turns).

Table 1 summarizes highly active participation by race and gender in heterogeneous settings. In the eight mixed-race dialogues ($n = 53$), white participants were disproportionately highly active. Although 53% of participants were white, they made up 65% of highly active participants. Interestingly, of the 13 white highly active participants, 69% were female, although only 57% of the white participants in these eight dialogues were female. On the other hand, only one (14%) of the highly active participants of all other races was female, even though 60% of the participants of color in these dialogues were female.

In the nine mixed-gender dialogues ($n = 61$), men disproportionately took more than their fair share of the floor. Although men made up 44% of participants in these dialogues, they accounted for 52% of those who were highly active. On the other hand, although women made up 56% of participants at these dialogues, they accounted for 48% of those who were highly active. In sum, white participants overall, men of all races, and white women in particular comprised a higher proportion of the highly active participants.[11]

Participants' Influence within the Dialogues

As noted above, instances of persuasion provided evidence of participants' influence within the dialogues, such that we identified which participants were persuasive (by having their ideas reflected in others' subsequent contributions) and which participants were persuaded (by changing their prior perspectives and taking up themes suggested by others). Again, professional status was most salient, while race and gender also indicated some important differences.

First, almost all of the participants whose ideas were persuasive had revealed a position of professional status. Participants sometimes mentioned their credentials when introducing themselves, and other times referenced their own expertise when making a point. In four of the dialogues (4, 5, 6, and 8), the participants who had revealed their professional status were the most persuasive, including a director of the venue's organization, an attorney, a dentist, and a scientist. In dialogue 1, some expertise was mentioned by other participants, but the most persuasive participant referenced his university expertise multiple times. In dialogue 9, while three undergraduate students participated in persuading a graduate student that racism still exists, the most persuasive participant was a retired professor and veteran. In dialogue 2, a business owner and a professional were the most persuasive, but there was very little information shared overall about professions.

On the other hand, participants who were persuaded did not reveal a position of status or expertise, with the exception of one participant who had mentioned working as a secretary in the University Admissions Office. At another dialogue, a naturopathic doctor (identified in her pre-questionnaire) was persuaded by a scientist and the director of the venue's organization, but she had not revealed her credentials to other participants. In this way, perceived professional status was related to who was persuasive and who was persuaded.

With the intersections of status, race, and gender among all participants, it is impossible to accurately identify the significance of each characteristic separately. However, we found it important to consider race and gender separately in order to examine related patterns across all dialogues. Considering only the dialogues in which persuasion occurred, Table 2 summarizes participant effectiveness for the six dialogues with mixed-race participants ($n = 40$), and a slightly different set of six dialogues with mixed-gender participants ($n = 41$). We identified a total of eight participants in the mixed-race dialogues and seven participants in the mixed-gender dialogues as being persuasive. While it is hard to draw conclusions with these small numbers, it is interesting to note that in the mixed-race dialogues, Latino and black participants were disproportionately persuasive, while white and multi-racial participants were not. In the mixed-gender dialogues, men overall were disproportionately persuasive.

We likewise identified 12 participants in the mixed-race dialogues and 13 participants in the mixed-gender dialogues as having been persuaded. The mixed-race dialogues mirrored the findings for the racial characteristics of persuasive participants, as a disproportionately large number

TABLE 2
Persuasiveness by Race and Gender

	Mixed-Race Dialogues ($n = 40$)				Mixed-Gender Dialogues ($n = 41$)	
	White	Latino/a	Multi-Racial	Black	Female	Male
No. of Participants	21	9	5	5	22	19
Percent of Total Participants	53%	23%	13%	13%	54%	46%
No. Persuasive	2	4	0	2	1	6
Percent of All Persuasive	25%	50%	0%	25%	14%	86%
Female	0%	50%	0%	0%	—	—
Male	100%	50%	0%	100%	—	—
No. Persuaded	8	0	3	1	7	6
Percent of All Persuaded	67%	0%	25%	8%	54%	46%
Female	50%	0%	67%	0%	—	—
Male	50%	0%	33%	100%	—	—

of white and multi-racial participants were persuaded, while Latino and black participants were not. However, in the mixed-gender dialogues, men and women were proportionately persuaded.

Overall, then, Latino and black men disproportionately persuaded white and multi-racial men and women. This finding is likely related to the significance of racial experiences in the topic of affirmative action, and echoes Walsh's (2007) findings that the narratives of ethnic minorities held more import. Yet despite the significance of ethnicity, men on the whole were much more persuasive than women. In fact, there was only one mixed-gender dialogue in which a female participant appeared to be persuasive. Interestingly, she seemed to influence the perspectives of the other two white women, but not the white male participant. This persuasive white female also had the highest status profession in the group as a dentist. Therefore, the three persuasive women only persuaded other women. While racial inequality was a central topic of every dialogue, gender inequality was only discussed (beyond slight mention) in one dialogue.

Of course, it was not always the case that status, race, and gender tied neatly to participants who were either persuasive or persuaded. As a disconfirming example, two Latina females (Ann and Julie) persuade a white female (Molly) to reconsider her assumption that beneficiaries of affirmative action in the workplace are less qualified [Dialogue 8]:

Molly: [My friend argues] that in education, it's one thing, but that in the workplace it should be a different standard. And so . . . I'm a little muddled on the workplace issue because don't we want the best qualified person overall to do that job? . . . And then, . . . that same person . . . is a doctor now, and he used to . . . joke . . . how it didn't matter that he finished last in his class because he's still gonna practice medicine. [ASSUMPTION OF LESS QUALIFIED; QUESTIONING AFFIRMATIVE ACTION]

Julie: I always think that it's not about a lesser qualified person getting something . . . it's an attribute that might be more positive in certain situations or might balance something else in a resume, or might balance out something in someone else's resume. . . . it's more often used when people are fairly equal, too, as something that just kinda gives them an extra advantage . . . [BROADER DEFINITION OF QUALIFIED]

Molly: When the [anti-affirmative action debater in the video] started talking, there was something in there that made me second guess some of my thoughts on it, when it came to the workplace, . . . that you would have a less qualified person in that position. [ASSUMPTION OF LESS QUALIFIED; QUESTIONING AFFIRMATIVE ACTION]

Julie: And maybe it's how you define qualified, too, you know. [BROADER DEFINITION OF QUALIFIED]

Ann: The president [of our company] . . . would always end his presentation with "we need to continue . . . to hire our minorities." And I always felt like that was a slap in the face. And so we were in a meeting with a lot of women and . . . I asked everyone in the room to raise their hand that didn't have a college education and everybody had some kind of degree behind them. So I said, "So here, with the mixture of all of us people here, some from other countries, you know some of different colors, a lot of women, I said, we're here because we're educated and qualified to be here." [ALL ARE QUALIFIED]

Molly: It seems to me that that's the big problem with affirmative action in the workplace is, like your experience, that you talked about so well, that other people's assumptions about someone, some minority and that in a way it kinda highlights the need for it even more, because I think that's just the symptom of the inherent racist-ness in our society, that would be someone's conclusion in the first place. [AFFIRMATIVE ACTION NEEDED TO COUNTER ASSUMPTIONS]

Although Molly was a naturopathic doctor, she did not reveal this to others. However, Ann referenced her work at an esteemed company and as a board member for the venue's organization, and Julie noted her affiliation with the venue's organization.

Thus, in the dialogues that included instances of persuasion, professional status was clearly related to whose ideas were most persuasive, while race and gender were also noteworthy. Interestingly, in three of the four dialogues without instances of persuasion, the ideas and interests of white females with professional status were most fully considered, as these participants did most of the talking while others asked them to expand upon their views.

Communicative Strategies

In examining participants' uses of argument, greeting, rhetoric, and narrative, we did not include the segments in which participants introduced themselves and shared their personal experiences, but rather looked at how these types of speech were used during the "open dialogue" portion of the protocol. Because four participants did not speak during this portion of the dialogues, we excluded them from this part of the analysis (resulting in a total of 67 active participants). We first summarize the extent to which participants used each form of discourse, and then consider to what effect each communicative strategy was used.

Participants' Uses of Communicative Strategies

Across the 11 dialogues, all participants used the communicative strategy of argument. The majority of participants used greeting at all but two dialogues, rhetoric at all but one dialogue, and narrative at all but three dialogues. Uses of greeting and rhetoric were widespread, with narrative less prevalent but still, on average, used by a majority of participants. Table 3 summarizes the percentage of participants using greeting, rhetoric, and narrative.

We then examined whether uses of greeting, rhetoric, and narrative varied by race and gender (summarized in Table 4). The first column shows the proportion of all active participants comprising the corresponding race and gender. (For example, white females made up 40% of all participants who verbally contributed during the "open dialogue" portion of the dialogues.) Each column then shows the proportion of participants that used that particular form of speech by the corresponding race and gender. For instance, a total of 45 participants used greeting in the dialogues. Of these 45 participants, 36% (16 participants) were white females, 24% (11 participants) were white males, and so on. If the uses of each type of speech were evenly distributed across participants of various races and genders, we would expect each of the proportions to be close to the overall percentages of the sample. In this way, white females made up over one-third (40%) of the sample, and also made up over one-third (36%) of the participants that used greeting, roughly reflecting what we would expect.[12]

What is striking from this table is the balance of use of each type of speech across participants of various races and genders. The only notable exception is in narrative, where white females

TABLE 3
Percentage of Participants Using Each Mode of Communication

Dialogue	No. of Participants ($n = 71$)	No. of Active Participants ($n = 67$)	Greeting	Rhetoric	Narrative
1	7	7	100%	86%	71%
2	11	9	44%	78%	44%
3	7	6	67%	33%	67%
4	5	5	100%	100%	80%
5	7	7	71%	86%	86%
6	4	4	100%	75%	25%
7	6	6	83%	83%	50%
8	3	3	67%	100%	67%
9	7	7	57%	57%	43%
10	3	3	100%	100%	100%
11	11	10	40%	80%	100%
Average	7	6	75%	80%	67%

were overrepresented and Latina females were underrepresented. Therefore, it was not the case that different means of communication were more often reflected by participants of different races and genders. Instead, all of these types of speech were used by participants across social groups, and for a variety of purposes.

Purposes Served through Communicative Strategies

Young (2000) notes that greeting can be used to develop trust and respect, rhetoric can be used to get attention, and narrative can evoke empathy and establish authority. We found that these types of communication sometimes served these purposes in our dialogues, but other times did not. We refer to instances that appear in the examples of dialogue given above to illustrate these points.

TABLE 4
Proportion of Total Participants Using Each Type of Speech by Race and Gender

	Percent of All Active Participants	Greeting	Rhetoric	Narrative
White Female	40%	36%	35%	48%
White Male	22%	24%	25%	20%
Latina Female	13%	13%	15%	7%
Latino Male	6%	7%	6%	7%
Multi-Racial Female	6%	9%	6%	7%
Multi-Racial Male	3%	4%	2%	2%
Black Female	3%	2%	4%	2%
Black Male	4%	2%	6%	5%

Greeting was sometimes used as a form of flattery or deference, as in Molly's final statement in dialogue 8, where she states, "like your experiences, that you talked about so well." Yet greeting was also used in silencing, such as in dialogue 4, when Diego references David's earlier story while in effect silencing David's view that we need to consider "humanity" in favor of his own view of access to "resources."

Some participants used rhetoric extensively in efforts to persuade. However, rhetoric also appeared throughout the dialogues as a natural part of speech. For example, in dialogue 4, Kaylin questioned getting "a fair shake" and David described a man with "bling" when recounting a personal experience. Likewise, in dialogue 8, Ann felt that her boss's statement was "a slap in the face."

Finally, narrative can be seen as a means of persuasion when Ann describes her experiences at work in dialogue 8, which evokes the empathy of Molly. In effect, Ann used this experience to argue that all affirmative action beneficiaries are qualified, although she only makes this point through the lens of her story. In the same segment, Molly had initially reflected on conversations with a friend to express confusion about her view.

In this way, greeting, rhetoric, and narrative were often used, but did not always reflect the purposes that Young (2000) proposed. Indeed, these communicative strategies were at times also used in the same competitive spirit that Young critiques, suggesting the need for deliberative theorists and researchers to consider the ways in which inclusion can be fostered within dialogues beyond including various forms of discourse.

Questionnaire Data

In comparing our findings to participants' pre- and post-questionnaire responses, we found that 60% of the participants that we had identified as persuasive indicated that they had not changed their views on affirmative action, while 64% of those that we labeled as persuaded had changed their views to becoming either "slightly more" or "much more positive" toward the policy. Surprisingly, however, participants who we identified as persuasive showed the greatest gain in factual knowledge about affirmative action policies, on average, while those who we labeled as persuaded showed the largest decrease. Within the dialogues in which persuasion occurred, participants who we did not identify as either actively persuasive or persuaded reported the highest percentage (13%) of becoming more negative about affirmative action and the lowest percentage (31%) of feeling more positive towards the policy, with the remaining 56% reporting no change in their views.

On the other hand, in the four dialogues with no instances of persuasion, 44% of the participants became more positive towards affirmative action. In fact, this was the group with the highest percentage of participants feeling "much more positive," and on average, this group reported having "learned" more, being "more knowledgeable," being "better prepared to discuss affirmative action," feeling more "comfortable" in the dialogues, and more likely to "engage in more deliberation about policy issues in the future." Moreover, these participants demonstrated increased knowledge of factual information.

Comparing our findings with questionnaire data in this way not only provides some confirmation of our identification of the participants who we identified as persuasive and persuaded, but also offers insights into ways in which the types of communication that occur in deliberative dialogues may influence outcomes. That is, while participants who were persuaded reflected the highest proportion of those that changed their views, the dialogues without instances of persuasion also evidenced changed views, increased factual knowledge, and high levels of participant satisfaction with dialogue processes.

LIMITATIONS

Although our findings offer insights into the dynamics of social group status within one-time community dialogues, we emphasize that our study was exploratory in nature and can only suggest considerations for future work in both deliberative and intergroup dialogue settings. In particular, it is important to note two key limitations. First, because participants were highly educated, our results cannot speak to the literature on power reproduction through education and class (e.g., Mansbridge, cited in Kohn, 2000). Despite our attempts to host the dialogues in venues that would attract diverse viewpoints and that would not be confined to the university, it is common for all types of deliberative dialogues to attract participants from more traditionally educated backgrounds (Ryfe, 2007). This consideration is essential to the format and accessibility of community dialogues that aim to include a wide variety of life experiences.

Second, while ethnic minorities and women were overrepresented compared to the local population, comparisons that attended to both race and gender resulted in very few participants of color, particularly multi-racial, black, and Asian participants. We found it important to include this information, however, as our findings confirmed those of Walsh's (2007) larger study. Our findings regarding race should be used only as a consideration in the design and facilitation of dialogues that aim for thick inclusion and the mitigation of social inequalities.

DISCUSSION

With regard to our research questions, first, professional status was most salient to both quantity of participation and influence within the one-time, community dialogues. That is, participants who had revealed professional status disproportionately took more than their share of speaking turns and were also more persuasive. Whether or not participants' expertise was related to affirmative action policies, participants who had indicated a position of status tended to guide the direction of the dialogue. We, therefore, suggest that facilitators be cognizant of these communicative moves and tendencies in order to encourage participatory parity.

Due to the small number of participants of each race or ethnicity, we were unable to adequately examine racial dynamics, so we hesitate to generalize across our findings with regard to race. However, the finding that Latino and black males were persuasive is informative in that it contradicts the literature that suggests that interracial dialogues are ineffective venues for minority viewpoints (e.g., Kohn, 2000; Levinson, 2003; Sanders, 1997), and instead supports Walsh's (2007) view that "people do listen to difference" (p. 235). Although white women were disproportionately highly active (along with men of all races), it is important to acknowledge that only three (white) women were persuasive, and only to other women.

Second, the communicative strategy of argument was used by virtually all participants, while greeting, rhetoric, and narrative were also widely used across all dialogues. Our findings with regard to communicative strategies, however, raise interesting questions with regard to Young's (2000) arguments regarding legitimate forms of communication in deliberation. Although our findings suggest that she is indeed correct to stress the need to foster inclusion through the recognition of various forms of discourse in deliberative dialogues, such as greeting, rhetoric, and narrative, these forms of communication were not tied to race, ethnicity, or gender among the participants in our study. In addition, while these communicative strategies were necessary to effective dialogue, they were not sufficient to mitigate power imbalances among participants. These forms of discourse were used throughout the dialogues by a majority of participants across social groups, and for a variety of purposes.

Finally, by comparing our findings to pre- and post-questionnaire data, we found that the atmosphere of each dialogue may have been a factor in participants' satisfaction with dialogue processes and their subsequently reported attitudes and knowledge about affirmative action. In the dialogues in which persuasion occurred, changes in participants' views about the policy did not necessarily align with increased understanding of the meaning, history, and legality of affirmative action policies. On the other hand, in dialogues without outright persuasion, participants reported higher levels of satisfaction with dialogue processes as well as both more favorable views and increased knowledge about the policy. Although the dialogues were designed to expand participants' understandings of affirmative action through an open sharing of perspectives, it is possible that some participants simply "did what they know" and attempted to convince others of their own views (Ryfe, 2007). Moreover, our neutral facilitator role limited our ability to intervene in instances in which participants appeared to ignore or silence others.

While our exploratory study was not designed to be generalizable, this research can contribute to deliberative theory and inform intergroup dialogue theory and practice (Eisenhart, 2009). Overall, our findings suggest the need for deliberative theorists and researchers to consider the ways in which inclusion can be fostered within dialogues in addition to including various forms of discourse. To this end, McCoy and Scully (2002) suggest that participation in a series of dialogues (rather than one-time meetings such as ours) is essential to building trust and fostering shared understandings characteristic of deep communication. They and other authors likewise underscore the importance of a comfortable atmosphere and the "opportunity to sort out" (p. 123) differing views. Furthermore, Ryfe (2006), House and Howe (1999), and Fischer (2006) all emphasize the role of trained, engaged facilitators in moderating the flow of ideas such that all relevant views are considered and participatory parity is fostered. Just as a teacher moderates participation in a classroom dialogue in efforts at inclusion, an active facilitator can attempt to ensure that participants have a fair opportunity to speak, and that reasonable views are not silenced.[13]

Policies, such as affirmative action, that promote racial, ethnic, and gender diversity in educational and professional institutions can promote equitable access and participation. As more diverse students attain college and graduate degrees, more will engage in democratic participation and deliberation (Anderson, 2002). The opportunity for more frequent dialogue among diverse participants can foster mutual respect and advance political equality. While our findings suggest the ways in which power imbalances may be manifested within one-time dialogue settings, our research highlights the potential for community dialogues to contribute to an informed citizenry in the face of increasing numbers of ballot initiatives related to education policy and civil rights (Moses & Farley, 2011). As such, we hope our work informs theory and practice related both to deliberative democracy and to intergroup dialogue, as well as education policies that importantly offer opportunities to build understanding across differences.

NOTES

1. It is important to note that in the Schkade et al. (2007) study, politically homogeneous groups were asked to come to consensus in just 15 minutes with one participant assigned as moderator. The authors gave no information on the relevant participant characteristics of class, race, gender, or sexual orientation.
2. House and Howe (1999) make an argument for "critical" facilitation that fosters participatory parity.
3. Twenty-one dialogues were scheduled originally; 12 dialogues had enough participants to proceed.
4. The relatively high level of education is evidenced by its comparison to the 24% rate of graduate degrees among county residents, which itself is one of the highest proportions in the country (U.S. Census Bureau, 2004).
5. It has been argued that "listening" is equally as participatory as talking (Barber, cited in Young, 2000, p. 130). However, our intent was to examine whose views were offered, considered, and taken up, and, as such, we conceive participation here to be spoken contributions to the dialogue.
6. Since the researchers were facilitators at some dialogues, there was some familiarity with participants.
7. We followed Young's (2000) definition of argument as "the construction of an orderly chain of reasoning from premises to conclusion" (p. 37).
8. Both authors conducted and reconciled second-level coding of the first two dialogues, and the remaining nine were divided such that each was coded by one researcher and reviewed by both authors.
9. All names are pseudonyms.
10. The second author agreed upon and verified the pattern analysis for the first 2 dialogues, and reviewed findings once the pattern analysis for all 11 dialogues was complete.
11. Of course, it is not necessary that every participant have an equal number of turns at speaking. However, Sanders (1997) points to research that suggests that participants who speak more than others during deliberations tend to have a greater influence on the outcomes.
12. A different way to analyze types of speech by race and gender would be to look at the percentage of all white females that used greeting, etc. Since this would be based on less than ten participants for each race/gender combination save white participants, we did not consider this to be worthy of inclusion here.
13. See Beale, Thompson, and Chesler (2001) for a facilitator training guide for intergroup dialogue.

REFERENCES

Anderson, E. (2002). Integration, affirmative action, and strict scrutiny. 77 New York University Law Review 1195.

Bächtiger, A., Niemeyer, S., Neblo, M., Steenbergen, M. R., & Steiner, J. (2010). Disentangling diversity in deliberative democracy: Competing theories, their blind spots and complementarities. *The Journal of Political Philosophy, 18*(1), 32–63.

Barbour, R. (2007). Doing focus groups (Vol. 7). In U. Flick (Ed.), *The Sage Qualitative Research Kit*. Los Angeles, CA: Sage.

Beale, R. L., Thompson, M. C., & Chesler, M. (2001). Training peer facilitators for intergroup dialogue leadership. In D. Schoem & S. Hurtado (Eds.), *Intergroup dialogue: Deliberative democracy in school, college, community, and workplace* (pp. 227–246). Ann Arbor, MI: The University of Michigan Press.

Burkhalter, S., Gastil, J., & Kelshaw, T. (2002). A conceptual definition and theoretical model of public deliberation in small face-to-face groups. *Communication Theory, 12*(4), 398–422.

Chambers, S. (2003). Deliberative democratic theory. *Annual Review of Political Science, 6*, 307–326.

Cohen, J. (2003). Deliberation and democratic legitimacy. In D. Matravers & J. Pike (Eds.), *Debates in contemporary political philosophy: An anthology* (pp. 342–360). London, England: Routledge.

Colorado Fair Campaign Practices Act. (2004). Retrieved from http://www.elpasoelections.com/fcpa/2008/Dis_Req_Docs/Article_2045_20FCPA.pdf

Conover, P. J., & Searing, D. D. (2005). Studying "everyday political talk" in the deliberative system. *Acta Politica, 40*, 269–283.

Delli Carpini, M. X., Cook, F. L., & Jacobs, L. R. (2004). Public deliberation, discursive participation, and citizen engagement: A review of the empirical literature. *Annual Review of Political Science, 7*, 315–344.

Eisenhart, M. (2009). Generalization from qualitative inquiry. In K. Ercikan, & W.-M. Roth (Eds.), *Generalizing from educational research: Beyond quantitative and qualitative polarization* (pp. 51–66). New York, NY: Routledge.

Erickson, F. (1986). Qualitative methods in research on teaching. In M. C. Wittrock (Ed.), *Handbook of research on teaching* (pp. 119–161). New York, NY: MacMillan.

Fischer, F. (2006). Participatory governance as deliberative empowerment: The cultural politics of discursive space. *The American Review of Public Administration, 36*(1), 19–40.

Fishkin, J. S. (1995). *The voice of the people: Public opinion and democracy.* New Haven, CT: Yale University Press.

Goodin, R. E., & Niemeyer, S. J. (2003). When does deliberation begin?: Internal reflection versus public discussion in deliberative democracy. *Political Studies, 51*(4), 627–649.

Gutmann, A., & Thompson, D. F. (1996). *Democracy and disagreement.* Cambridge, MA: Belknap Press of Harvard University Press.

Gutmann, A., & Thompson, D. F. (2004). *Why deliberative democracy?* Princeton, NJ: Princeton University Press.

Habermas, J. (1984). *The theory of communicative action, vol. 1: Reason and the rationalization of society.* Boston, MA: Beacon.

Hartz-Karp, J. (2005). A case study in deliberative democracy: Dialogue with the city. *Journal of Public Deliberation, 1*(1), 1–15.

Herzig, M., & Chasin, L. (2006). *Fostering dialogue across divides: A nuts and bolts guide from the Public Conversations Project.* Watertown, MA: Public Conversations Project.

House, E. R., & Howe, K. R. (1999). *Values in evaluation and social research.* Thousand Oaks, CA: Sage.

Kaplan, M. F., & Martin, A. M. (1999). Effects of differential status of group members on process and outcome of deliberation. *Group Processes and Intergroup Relations, 2*(4), 347–364.

Kohn, M. (2000). Language, power, and persuasion: Toward a critique of deliberative democracy. *Constellations, 7*(3), 408–429.

Levinson, M. (2003). Challenging deliberation. *Theory and Research in Education, 1*(1), 23–49.

Mansbridge, J. (1999). Everyday talk in the deliberative system. In S. Macedo (Ed.), *Deliberative politics: Essays on democracy and disagreement.* (pp. 211–239). New York, NY: Oxford.

Mansbridge, J., Hartz-Karp, J., Amengual, M., & Gastil, J. (2006). Norms of deliberation: An inductive study. *Journal of Public Deliberation, 2*(1), 1–47.

Maxwell, J. A. (2005). *Qualitative research design: An interactive approach* (2nd ed.). Thousand Oaks, CA: Sage.

McCoy, M. L., & Scully, P. L. (2002). Deliberative dialogue to expand civic engagement: What kind of talk does democracy need? *National Civic Review, 91*(2), 117–135.

Miles, M. B., & Huberman, A. M. (1994). *Qualitative data analysis: An expanded sourcebook* (2nd ed.). Thousand Oaks, CA: Sage.

Moses, M. S., & Farley, A. N. (2011). Are ballot initiatives a good way to make education policy?: The case of affirmative action. *Educational Studies, 47*(3), 260–279.

Moses, M. S., Farley, A. N., Gaertner, M., Paguyo, C., Jackson, D., & Howe, K. R. (2010). *Investigating the defeat of Colorado's Amendment 46: An analysis of the trends and principal factors influencing voter behaviors.* Technical Report. Publisher: Author. http://www.colorado.edu/education/faculty/michelemoses/docs/finalmosesamendment46.pdf

Niemeyer, S. (2011). The emancipatory effect of deliberation: Empirical lessons from mini-publics. *Politics & Society, 39*(1), 103–140.

Rosenberg, S. W. (2005). The empirical study of deliberative democracy: Setting a research agenda. *Acta Politica, 40*(Part 2), 212–224.

Ryfe, D. M. (2005). Does deliberative democracy work? *Annual Review of Political Science, 8*, 49–71.

Ryfe, D. M. (2006). Narrative and deliberation in small group forums. *Journal of Applied Communication Research, 34*(1), 72–93.

Ryfe, D. M. (2007). Toward a sociology of deliberation. *Journal of Public Deliberation, 3*(1), 1–27.

Sanders, L. M. (1997). Against deliberation. *Political Theory, 25*(3), 347–376.

Schkade, D., Sunstein, C. R., & Hastie, R. (2007). What happened on deliberation day? 95 California Law Review 915.

Strodtbeck, F. L., James, R. M, & Hawkins, C. (1957). Social status in jury deliberations. *American Sociological Review, 22*(6), 713–719.

Thompson, D. F. (2008). Deliberative democratic theory and empirical political science. *Annual Review of Political Science, 11*, 497–520.

U.S. Census Bureau. (2004). *American Community Survey 5-Year Estimates for Boulder County, Colorado*. American FactFinder. Retreived January 7, 2012 from http://factfinder.census.gov/servlet/STTable?_bm=y&-state=st&-context=st&-qr_name=ACS_2009_5YR_G00_S1501&-ds_name=ACS_2009_5YR_G00_&-tree_id=5309&-redoLog=true&-_caller=geoselect&-geo_id=05000US08013&-format=&-_lang=en.

Walsh, K. C. (2007). *Talking about race: Community dialogues and the politics of difference*. Chicago, IL: University of Chicago Press.

Young, I. M. (1996). Communication and the other: Beyond deliberative democracy. In S. Benhabib (Ed.), *Democracy and difference: Contesting the boundaries of the political* (pp. 120–135). Princeton, NJ: Princeton University Press.

Young, I. M. (2000). *Inclusion and democracy*. Oxford, England: Oxford University Press.

Index